Father–Daughter Succession in Family Business

Father–Daughter Succession in Family Business

A Cross-Cultural Perspective

Edited by

DAPHNE HALKIAS,
PAUL W. THURMAN,
CELINA SMITH and
ROBERT S. NASON

Routledge
Taylor & Francis Group
LONDON AND NEW YORK

First published 2011 by Gower Publishing

2 Park Square, Milton Park, Abingdon, Oxfordshire OX14 4RN
52 Vanderbilt Avenue, New York, NY 10017

Routledge is an imprint of the Taylor & Francis Group, an informa business

First issued in paperback 2020

Gower Applied Business Research
Our programme provides leaders, practitioners, scholars and researchers with thought provoking, cutting edge books that combine conceptual insights, interdisciplinary rigour and practical relevance in key areas of business and management.

British Library Cataloguing in Publication Data
Father–daughter succession in family business : a cross-cultural perspective.
1. Family-owned business enterprises—Succession. 2. Family-owned business enterprises—Succession—Cross-cultural studies.
I. Halkias, Daphne.
658.1'6-dc22

Library of Congress Cataloging-in-Publication Data
Father–daughter succession in family business : a cross-cultural perspective/ by Daphne Halkias ... [et al.].
p. cm.
Includes bibliographical references and index.
ISBN 978-0-566-09220-6 (hbk. : alk. paper)
1. Family-owned business enterprises—Succession—Cross-cultural studies. 2. Women chief executive officers—Cross-cultural studies. I. Halkias, Daphne.

HD62.25.F39 2011
658.4'02—dc23

2011024954

ISBN 978-0-566-09220-6 (hbk)
ISBN 978-0-367-60549-0 (pbk)

Contents

List of Figures ix
List of Tables xi
About the Editors xiii
Notes on Contributors xv
Acknowledgments xxi

PART I PROLOGUE

Preface: Where Culture, Family and Business Meet: Developing Cross-National Research on the Father–Daughter Succession Process in Family Firms 3
Daphne Halkias

Introduction: "How Did All This Get Started?" A Pioneer of Father–Daughter Family Business Succession Research Remembers and Looks Ahead 9
Colette Dumas

A Historical Perspective: From Hidden Giants to Visible Leaders? The Evolution of Women's Roles in Family Business 15
Christine Blondel

PART II ASIA

Chapter 1 China: A Case Study of Father–Daughter Succession in China 25
Xin Deng

Chapter 2 India: A Socio-Cultural Perspective on Father–Daughter Succession in Family Business in India 35
Geetika Goel, Shefali Nandan and Piyali Ghosh

Chapter 3 Lebanon: Father–Daughter Succession in Family Business within a Middle Eastern Culture 45
Janine Saba Zakka and Josiane Fahed-Sreih

Chapter 4 Malaysia: The Challenge of Father–Daughter Succession in Malaysian Family Business 55
Norashfah H. Yaakop Yahaya Al-Haj and Ahmad Hj. Zainuddin

Chapter 5	Pakistan: Father–Daughter Family Business Succession in Pakistan: A Case Study *Shehla Riza Arifeen*	63
Chapter 6	Philippines: Father–Daughter Succession in Family Business: A Philippine Case Study *Andrea L. Santiago*	73
Chapter 7	United Arab Emirates: The Al Jaber Group: Traditions and Transitions in a United Arab Emirates Family Business *Katty Marmenout, Elizabeth Florent-Treacy and Manfred Kets de Vries*	81
PART III	**AFRICA**	
Chapter 8	Egypt: Lessons from a Father's Culture and Life Values: A Female Entrepreneur Builds her own Family Firm in Egypt *Sam Abadir, Daphne Halkias, Despina Prinia, Mirka Fragoudakis and Patrick D. Akrivos*	93
Chapter 9	Nigeria: Sociological Issues in Father–Daughter Business Succession in Nigeria *Chinedum U. Nwajiuba and Chinyere A. Nwajiuba*	101
PART IV	**EUROPE**	
Chapter 10	France: Father–Daughter Succession in France: The ONET Group Case Study *Katia Richomme-Huet and Julien de Freyman*	109
Chapter 11	Germany: Family Business Paradox and Gender Role Strain: An Example of Father–Daughter Succession from Germany *Christina Erdmann*	117
Chapter 12	Greece: Dreams of My Father: A Father–Daughter Succession Story in a Greek Family Firm *Daphne Halkias, Eleanna Galanaki, Norma A. Juma and Patrick D. Akrivos*	129
Chapter 13	Italy: The Challenges of Father–Daughter Succession in an Italian Family Business *Lucio Cassia, Alfredo de Massis and Federica Giudici*	141
Chapter 14	Russia: Father–Daughter Succession in a Russian Family Business: A Case Study *Evgeny Polyakov and Natalia Vinokurova*	157

Chapter 15 Spain: Father–Daughter Succession in Spain: Success Factors in a Male-Dominated Sector 167
María Cristina Díaz García and Ángela González Moreno

Chapter 16 Scotland/United Kingdom: Driving a Scottish Family Business Forward: From Faither to Wee Lassie 175
Stuart Graham and Claire Seaman

Chapter 17 Sweden: Two-Fold Succession in a Family Business Matriarchy: A Swedish Case 183
Cecilia Bjursell and Leif Melin

Chapter 18 Switzerland: Encouraging Success: A Father–Daughter Succession Story in a Swiss Family Firm 193
Claudia Binz, Simone Schweikert and Jens O. Meissner

PART V NORTH AMERICA

Chapter 19 Canada: Gender and Culture in Father–Daughter Succession in the Family Business: A Canadian Case Study 205
Lucie Bégin, Christina Constantinidis, Daphne Halkias and D.-Claude Laroche

Chapter 20 South Carolina, USA: The Challenge of Father–Daughter Succession in Family Business: A Case Study in South Carolina 217
Teresa L. Smith and Jean-Luc E. Grosso

Chapter 21 Washington, USA: It's a Sweet Life: A Daughter Successfully Manages an Immigrant Family Business 227
Meenakshi Rishi and Daphne Halkias

Chapter 22 West Virginia, USA: Father–Daughter Succession in a West Virginia Family Business 235
Leann Mischel and Cindy Iannarelli

PART VI SOUTH AMERICA

Chapter 23 Brazil: The Course of Father–Daughter Succession in a Brazilian Family Business 245
Celina Smith and Rosamond Tompkins

Chapter 24 Brazil: The Challenge of Female Successors in a Brazilian Family Business: A Case Study 255
Hilka Vier Machado

Chapter 25 Colombia: Father–Daughter Succession Issues in the Colombian Family Business Context 263
Melquicedec Lozano, Kathy Kessler Overbeke and Keanon J. Alderson

Chapter 26 Peru: From Father to Daughter: A Case Study of Family Business Succession in Peru 273
Marina Niforos and Penelope Robotis

PART VII OCEANIA

Chapter 27 Australia: The Challenge of Father–Daughter Succession in Family Business: A Case Study from the Land Down Under 285
Mary Barrett and Ken Moores

Chapter 28 New Zealand: The Daughter Takes Over a Residential Home Building Family Business: A Case Study from Aotearoa New Zealand 295
Franco Vaccarino

Epilogue: Future Considerations for Cross-Cultural Research in Father–Daughter Succession 303
Daphne Halkias

Index *305*

List of Figures

Figure P.1	A multidimensional model of succession in family businesses	5
Figure H.1	Hidden giants	17
Figure H.2	Marguerite d'Hausen	20
Figure 11.1	Main arguments against women as successors	118
Figure 13.1	Manzoni family tree and successions	145
Figure 13.2	Organizational chart of Nuova Termostampi Spa	146
Figure 17.1	The Atteviks family chart	186
Figure 18.1	Comparison of GLOBE German-speaking Switzerland *As Is* and *To Be* scores	195
Figure 27.1	Australia's ratings on Hofstede's cultural dimensions	286

List of Tables

Table 2.1	Multidimensional analysis of father–daughter succession	41
Table 2.2	Impact of socio-cultural dimensions on father–daughter succession in India	42
Table 9.1	Unemployment rate by sex in Nigeria (1999–2000)	103
Table 11.1	Family system and enterprise system	119
Table 13.1	Key events in the history of the family business	145

About the Editors

Daphne Halkias, PhD, is a distinguished psychologist, international business consultant and academic. Publications carry her name in research on entrepreneurship, women's issues, family business, organizational behavior, education and clinical psychology. She is currently a Senior Research Fellow at The Center for Young and Family Entrepreneurship (CYFE) at University of Bergamo, Italy, Research Affiliate at the Institute for Social Sciences at Cornell University and Research Associate at Center for Comparative Immigration Studies (CCIS) at University of California, San Diego , and Affiliate at Institute of Coaching at McLean Hospital, Harvard Medical School. She is an online entrepreneur and CEO of Executive Coaching Consultants, specializing in international academic and business projects and with associates in Athens, New York, Paris and Cairo. Her forthcoming applied research books in the areas of international management, immigrant entrepreneurship and sustainability, corporate governance in immigrant family enterprises and cross-cultural e-negotiation will be published by Gower Publishing in 2011 and 2012. She is Editor of *International Journal of Social Entrepreneurship and Innovation.*

Paul W. Thurman, MBA, DrPH (Doctor of Public Health) Candidate, is a Clinical Professor at the Columbia University graduate schools of Public Health, International and Public Affairs, and Business. In addition to winning several prestigious teaching awards and having 20 years of senior management consulting, Professor Thurman has been a Visiting Professor, Research Fellow and Research Affiliate at London Business School, the Haas School of Business at University of California, Berkeley, Hellenic American University (Athens, Greece), Reykjavík University (Iceland), Guanghua School of Management in Beijing, Moscow School of Management SKOLKOVO (Russia) and National Cancer Institute's Center for Cancer Research. His texts, *MBA Fundamentals of Statistics* (2008) and *MBA Fundamentals of Strategy* (2009), were published by Kaplan Publishing (USA). His forthcoming research compendia, *Female Immigrant Entrepreneurship* (2011), *Father–Daughter Succession in Family Businesses* (2011), and a text in International Management (2012) will all be published by Gower Publishing.

Celina Smith, PhD, is Assistant Professor in Entrepreneurship at EMLYON Business School, and a Visiting Fellow at Imperial College, UK. Her research focuses on new ventures and social networks. She holds a PhD in Entrepreneurship and MBA from Imperial College. Dr Smith has spent many years working as a successful entrepreneur launching and running two companies in the television industry in the UK. She has worked in an advisory capacity on a number of media industry forums and chaired various policy groups on media-related issues.

Robert S. Nason, MBA, is Global Program Manager of the STEP Project for Family Enterprising at Babson College, Massachusetts, USA. STEP, with over 40 partners globally, is the largest cross-cultural collaborative research project on family business taking place today. As an active researcher in the field of family business, he has published in *The Family Business Review* and has presented at leading conferences, including The Academy of Management and the Babson Entrepreneurship Research Conference. Mr Nason's current research interests include stakeholder theory, family-based entrepreneurship and systems theory in family firms. He currently serves on the Board of the New England Chapter of the Family Firm Institute.

Notes on Contributors

Dr Sam Abadir is a Visiting Professor at INSEAD (France) and Fellow of the Judge Business School, University of Cambridge (UK).

Ms Shehla Riza Arifeen is Associate Professor of Marketing and Management at the Business School of Lahore School of Economics, Pakistan.

Dr Mary Barrett is Professor of Management in the School of Management and Marketing at University of Wollongong, New South Wales, Australia.

Dr Lucie Bégin is Senior Lecturer in Strategy at Normandy Business School, Researcher at the Métis Laboratory and Responsible for the Pedagogical Hotbed at Normandy Business School, Le Havre (France). She is also Affiliated Researcher at NIMEC Laboratory – University of Caen (France).

Ms Claudia Binz is a Research Assistant at Lucerne School of Business and a Doctoral student at the University of Berne, Switzerland.

Dr Christine Blondel is Adjunct Professor of Family Business at INSEAD, France.

Dr Cecilia Bjursell is Research Fellow at CeFEO, Jonkoping International Business School, and Lecturer at Jonkoping University in Sweden.

Dr Lucio Cassia is Professor of Strategic Management and Entrepreneurship at the Department of Economics and Technology Management of the University of Bergamo, Italy, and Director of the Center for Young and Family Enterprise (CYFE) of the same University.

Dr D.-Claude Laroche is Associate Professor in the Department of Accounting Studies at HEC Montreal, Canada.

Ms Christina Constantinidis is Researcher and pursues Doctoral work in the centre EGiD for Studies on Gender and Diversity in Management, at HEC Management School – University of Liege, Belgium, and Invited Entrepreneurship Scholar at SOM Simmons School of Management in Boston, USA.

Dr Julien de Freyman is Associate Professor in the Department of Innovation and Entrepreneurship at Groupe ESC Troyes, France.

Dr Alfredo de Massis is Assistant Professor of Family Business and Entrepreneurship at the Department of Economics and Technology Management of the University of Bergamo, Italy, and Member of the Executive Board of the Center for Young and Family Enterprise (CYFE) of the same University.

Dr Xin Deng is Lecturer in Economics at School of Commerce, and Associate Member of Centre of Regulation and Market Analysis, University of South Australia.

Dr María Cristina Díaz García is Assistant Professor at the University of Castilla La Mancha in Spain.

Dr Colette Dumas is Professor of Management and Entrepreneurship and Director of the Center for Innovation and Change Leadership at Suffolk University's Sawyer Business School, Boston, USA.

Dr Christina Erdmann is Assistant Professor at Witten Institute for Family Business at the Witten/Herdecke University, Germany, and a freelance Coach and Trainer in Essen, Germany.

Dr Josiane Fahed-Sreih is Associate Professor of Management at the Department of Business Studies, and Director, Institute of Family and Entrepreneurial Business at American University of Lebanon.

Dr Elizabeth Florent-Treacy is Research Project Manager at INSEAD, Fontainebleau, France, and Singapore.

Dr Eleanna Galanaki is Lecturer in the Department of Marketing and Communication at the Athens University of Economics and Business and Tutor at the Hellenic Open University in Greece.

Dr Piyali Ghosh is Assistant Professor at Motilal Nehru National Institute of Technology, Allahabad, India.

Dr Geetika Goel is Head and Professor of Strategy and Entrepreneurship at the School of Management Studies, Motilal Nehru National Institute of Technology, Allahabad, India.

Dr Ángela González Moreno is Associate Professor at the University of Castilla La Mancha in Spain.

Mr Stuart Graham is Senior Lecturer in Marketing and Strategic Management at Queen Margaret University, Edinburgh.

Dr Jean-Luc E. Grosso is McDavid Professor of Business Administration at the University of South Carolina, USA.

Dr Daphne Halkias is Research Affiliate, Institute for the Social Sciences, Cornell University, USA; Senior Research Fellow, Center for Young and Family Enterprise, University of Bergamo, Italy; Affiliate, Institute of Coaching at McLean Hospital, Harvard Medical School, USA; and Editor, *International Journal of Social Entrepreneurship and Innovation.*

Dr Cindy Iannarelli (1958–2010) was President at Bernelli University in West Virginia, USA and Italy.

Dr Manfred Kets de Vries is Clinical Professor of Leadership Development, The Raoul de Vitry d'Avaucourt Chaired Professor of Leadership Development and Director, INSEAD Global Leadership Centre (IGLC) at INSEAD, France.

Dr Melquicedec Lozano is Director of Research and Special Projects at Center for Entrepreneurship Development, Universidad Icesi in Cali, Colombia.

Dr Hilka Vier Machado is Professor of Management at Universidade Estadual de Maringá, Parana State, Brazil, and Researcher of Brazil National Council of Research – CNPq.

Dr Katty Marmenout is Assistant Professor in Management at EMLYON Business School in Lyon, France.

Dr Jens O. Meissner is Professor of Management at Lucerne School of Business, Lucerne University of Applied Sciences and Arts, Switzerland.

Dr Leif Melin is Professor of Strategy and Organization and Founding Director of CeFEO, Centre for Family Enterprise and Ownership, at Jönköping International Business School in Sweden.

Dr Leann Mischel is Associate Professor of Management and Entrepreneurship at Susquehanna University in Pennsylvania, USA.

Dr Ken Moores, AM is Founding Director and Professor, Australian Centre for Family Business, School of Business, Bond University in Australia.

Dr Shefali Nandan is Faculty Member at the School of Management Studies, Motilal Nehru National Institute of Technology in Allahabad, India.

Dr Marina Niforos is Managing Director of the American Chamber of France and former Director of the INSEAD Diversity and Leadership Center of Excellence, France.

Dr Chinedum U. Nwajiuba is Professor at Imo State University Owerri, Nigeria, and Executive Director at the Nigeria Environment Action Team in Ibadan, Nigeria.

Dr Chinyere A. Nwajiuba is Member of the Sociology of Education Unit, Department of Education Foundation and Administration, Imo State University in Owerri, Nigeria.

Dr Evgeny Polyakov is Head of the Russian–British Business Centre and Senior Lecturer in Business Strategy at the University of Huddersfield Business School.

Dr Katia Richomme-Huet is Associate Professor of Management at Euromed Ecole de Management in Marseilles, France.

Dr Meenakshi Rishi is Associate Professor of Economics at the Albers School of Business and Economics at Seattle University in Seattle, USA.

Dr Andrea L. Santiago is Associate Professor at the Business Management Department, College of Business, at De La Salle University in the Philippines.

Dr Claire Seaman is Academic Director, Management and Enterprise, at Queen Margaret University in Edinburgh and a Director of the Scottish Family Business Association.

Prof. Dr oec. Simone Schweikert (1967–2011) was Head Interdisciplinary Focus Creative Living Lab at the Lucerne University of Applied Sciences and Arts, and Professor of Strategy and Innovation at the Institute of Management and Regional Economics of the Universities School of Business in Switzerland.

Dr Celina Smith is an Assistant Professor of Entrepreneurship at EMLYON Business School in Lyon, France.

Dr Teresa L. Smith is the Julian T. Buxton Professor of Business Administration at the University of South Carolina, USA.

Prof. Paul W. Thurman is Clinical Professor, School of International and Public Affairs, Mailman School of Public Health, Columbia University in New York, USA.

Dr Franco Vaccarino is a Senior Lecturer in Cross-Cultural Communication in the School of Communication, Journalism and Marketing at Massey University in Palmerston North, New Zealand.

Dr Natalia Vinokurova is a Senior Lecturer and Assistant Dean for International Relations, School of Global Economics and International Affairs, State University Higher School of Economics In Moscow, Russia.

Dr Norashfah H. Yaakop Yahaya Al-Haj is Associate Professor of Finance at Faculty of Business Management, University Technology of MARA Malaysia and Associate Director of World Institute of Action Learning, Malaysia.

Dato' Prof Ahmad Hj. Zainuddin is Director of Academy Leadership Training at The Ministry of Higher Education in Malaysia.

Ms Janine Saba Zakka is a Faculty Member at the Lebanese American University in Lebanon.

Chapter Co-Authors

Mr Patrick D. Akrivos is a Psychotherapist in private practice and Research Associate at Executive Coaching Consultants in Athens, Greece.

Dr Keanon J. Alderson is Assistant Professor in the Robert K. Jabs School of Business at California Baptist University, Riverside, USA.

Ms Mirka Fragoudakis is Research Assstant at Center for Young and Family Enterprise (CYFE) at University of Bergamo, Italy.

Ms Federica Giudici is Research Assistant at the Center for Young and Family Enterprise (CYFE) of University of Bergamo, Italy.

Dr Norma A. Juma is Assistant Professor of Strategic Management at Washburn University, USA.

Dr Kathy Kessler Overbeke is an Executive Coach and CEO of Generation Planning Strategies for Family Business Renewal in Ohio, USA.

Dr Despina Prinia is a Professor of Strategic Communication at Hellenic American University in Athens, Greece.

Ms Penelope Robotis is a Licensed Psychotherapist and Associate Member of The Adlerian Institute, Athens, Greece.

Dr Rosamond Tompkins is a Principal of Family Business Strategies, LLC, and an affiliate of The George Washington University Executive Leadership Program.

Acknowledgments

This book began back in 2005 as a small preliminary study I conducted while a Visiting Professor in the International MBA Program of the American College of Greece and teaching Organizational Behavior. Half the student enrollment in that course was female and many of these young women's concerns centered on the relationships with their fathers while working within the family business. So, it was then that I administered to my female students a survey, developed by Dr Eleni Stavrou who is now at the University of Cyprus, on their intentions to succeed their fathers in the family business. I thank Eleni for giving me permission to use her survey and the study she conducted during her doctoral studies at George Washington University. The research question of that study focused on the factors compelling son and daughter successors to remain in or leave the family business. From that original study grew papers, conference presentations, and published research. Having a personal and professional interest in cross-cultural business and family relationship issues, it was my goal to someday bring together scholars from around the world to compare cultural variables of the father–daughter succession process.

With all that said, my first thanks must go to my great friend and valued colleague, Dr Sam Abadir, faculty at CEDEP and INSEAD and Fellow at Judge Business School at University of Cambridge, who helped me bring the preliminary results of the father–daughter succession study to a presentation at the Wendel International Centre for Family Enterprise at INSEAD in 2006. This effort was also supported by the Centre's Director at that time, Mrs Christine Blondel, who has contributed a wonderful chapter to this book on the historical evolution of women's roles in family business. Once the first results of the study were presented at INSEAD, the presentations and further research took off to culminate in this compendium of unique case studies of daughter successors from around the world and told from over 30 unique cultural vantage points.

The realization of that goal is this book, which is neither an edited book nor a single-authored book. Instead, it is a team book. At various stages of its preparation, as many as 35 people have been involved in its creation. The Research Associates who represent their countries or regions in this cross-cultural study of father–daughter succession issues in family business gathered the data in the cultural settings of what would become the basis of each chapter case study. The contributing authors are researchers, scholars, and entrepreneurs from around the globe collaborating through the Internet to write each country/regional case study. From Brazil to Egypt to the United Arab Emirates to Greece to New Zealand and the United States, this applied research book is in the reader's hands today thanks to the collaborative efforts of an international network of scholars dedicated to telling the cultural story of daughters who are already building a niche for themselves as female entrepreneurs in their countries and regions.

A special thanks goes to Dr Colette Dumas, the pioneer researcher of father–daughter succession in family business. Dr Dumas graciously accepted my invitation to participate in this book project. I am honored to include her introductory chapter in this book on the past, present, and future of this research field.

I owe a great debt of gratitude to the book's Managing Editor, Sylva Caracatsanis. Sylva is unfailing in her work ethic, loyalty, and amazing ability to single-handedly perform damage control in a moment's notice. Sylva has been integral in managing all the editing details of the final manuscript and in coordinating this global team of 35 professionals that made this book possible. Sylva knows that I could have never completed this manuscript without her professional strength, devotion, and impeccable professionalism. Every book author/lead editor should be so lucky as to have a Sylva on their team.

Finally, I wish to thank the fine team at Gower Publishing starting with my Commissioning Editor, Martin West. It is a dream for a scholar to work on putting together a book with an editor like Martin. He is professional, supportive, humane, and a great stress manager with his wry sense of humor. My thanks also to the other team members at Gower I have worked with on this project: Donna Shanks, Emily Ruskell, Sue White and their staff—particularly for their professionalism and patience. The team at Gower believed in this project from the very beginning and supported it in every way possible. I look forward to working with Martin West and the good people of Gower Publishing in my future book projects.

Daphne Halkias
Athens, Greece
September 1, 2011

PART I Prologue

Preface: Where Culture, Family and Business Meet: Developing Cross-National Research on the Father–Daughter Succession Process in Family Firms

DAPHNE HALKIAS

Why Focus on Culture in the Succession Process of Family Business?

The family firm is an increasingly vital player in the global economy. One of the events that may disrupt the smooth evolution of a family business is a generation transition and succession. An important issue that is evolving in the family business literature is the increasing involvement of women in leadership/management roles in businesses and, more specifically, the family firm. In the developing economies of Asia and Africa as well as the developed ones in North America, Europe, Australia, and New Zealand there is sparse case study research in the extant literature on cross-cultural gender issues in the family firm ownership and succession (Halkias et al., 2008; 2010).

If entrepreneurship can be considered as an event induced by socio-cultural factors (Shapero and Sokol, 1982), the cultural variable gains greater significance when applied to the quality of the relationship between family members involved in the succession process and specifically, in this book, for the case of father to daughter. National culture generates behavioral changes through family, training, education, traditions, lifestyles, politics, religion and degrees of masculinity–femininity, individualism–collectivism (Hofstede, 1997; Trompenaars and Hampden-Turner, 2003). Within family firms, the cultural context can affect behaviors and, in the same way, management styles, be they an individual's, the family's or the firm's (Barbot, 2004). In line with this, other recent research has addressed the issue of national cultural attitudes influencing the entrepreneurial behavior and outcomes of an ethnic or regional population (Ibid.).

With respect to the lack of research integrating culture on one hand and the specificity of females taking over family businesses, the research presented in this book by an eminent group of scholars aims at exploring the influence of culture—ethnic, regional, religious—on the process of father–daughter succession in family firms. We were particularly interested in exploring the cultural variables influencing father–daughter succession in family businesses across 14 cultural settings never before considered in the extant literature.

> *Entrepreneurship is truly a phenomenon which is above all cultural. With this in mind, the successful transmission of a firm involves respecting the national culture in which it is found.*
>
> *(Barbot et al., 2004:4)*

The research model used as a foundation for developing a methodology for these case studies was presented in a landmark cross-national study conducted by Barbot et al., (2004) exploring the influence of culture among father–daughter succession in France and Tunisia. This study identified factors which influence the succession process according to two different cultural contexts. Its hypotheses highlighted that beyond sexual diversity (female/male), the stages of the succession process could change within the same gender of successors (females) due to cultural factors. Within the succession frame of the daughter taking over, differences can be stated and explained through the predominance of national culture in family and managerial relationships. On the basis of these observations and adopting a comparative approach, Barbot et al. (2004) investigated differences and/or similarities between how father to daughter successions occur in Tunisian and French family businesses.

In their conclusions, Barbot et al. (2004) stated that with respect to entrepreneurship in general and family business succession in particular, their investigation illuminated that researchers must take into account the cultural context.

> *The recognition of the importance of tradition leads us, by no means, to consider societies as motionless, mere reflections of folkloric caricatures. Finally, we may conclude that best practice research cannot be undertaken as an end to itself. Indeed, instead of imitating other countries, it is necessary to identify the value of one's own traditions. Each country is characterized by "fundamental traits which pass the test of time."*
>
> *(D'Iribarne, 1989)*

A Defining Model to Research the Cultural Variable in Family Business Succession

In order to address the question of the specificity of father–daughter transfer, while considering the impact of the cultural variable, Barbot et al. (2004) adopted a dialectic model (see Figure P.1) stressing the character of the two types of transmission (managerial and patrimonial) and the psychological characteristics of the key actors. By depicting the succession process as based on two principal actors (in this case father and daughter), the retained model integrates both the psychology of the actors and their intertwining (which constitutes one of the essential characteristics of family business). Equally demonstrated is the impact of culture on relationships between the primary subjects of the process.

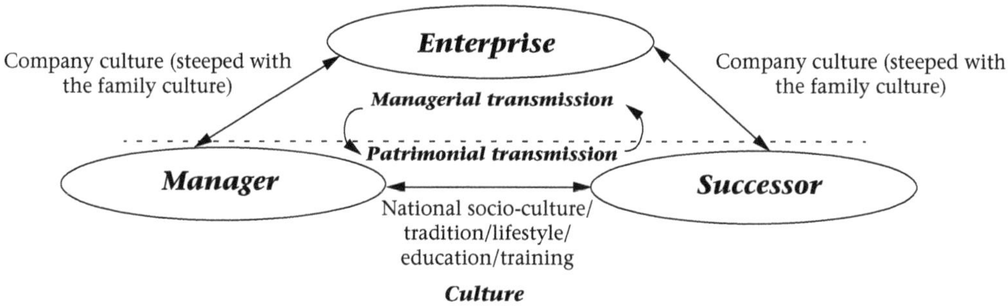

Figure P.1 A multidimensional model of succession in family businesses
Source: Barbot, Bayad and Bourguiba, 2004

Family relationships change and vary across cultures. This difference will eventually give way to modifications in father–daughter succession across culture. On the basis of this model and in line with a comparative framework, our study aimed to be cross-cultural in nature. The main interest of this book's contribution lies in illustrating the importance of the cultural dimension in the process of handing over family businesses from father to daughter. The cultural approach chosen seeks to better understand the systems of representation, the internal reasoning of each firm (the ways of being together) so as to adapt management practices to national/cultural particularities. The case studies presented differences and/or similarities between how 14 family businesses, representing different ethnic cultural value systems, are passed on from father to daughter.

Biographical Narration: Giving Voice to the Daughter Chief Executive Officer and Father's Legacy

Biographical data for the case studies of the father–daughter succession process across cultures as personated in this book were collected through the qualitative method of *biographical narration*. This method follows a swiftly increasing interest on the part of social sciences in the study of lives. Among others, methods of oral history, ethnography, narrative, and autobiography are relaying how individuals give meaning to their life experiences. Methodological and theoretical developments in this kind of research within the social sciences have given rise to an increase in literature addressing issues regarding the collection of materials, the use and interpretation of oral and written biographical accounts, audience, and reflexivity. Biographical narrations draw out common themes and emerging concerns between the subject and the researcher on his/her environment, past history, present moment, and future life path (Halkias and Caracatsanis, 2011; Lund Thomsen, 2006). The biographical narrative method presents a viable research method for understanding how the past lives of family firm leaders allow us to make sense of the reasoning behind certain actions in the father–daughter succession process, as well as highlight cultural elements of this succession process.

If one is to understand how daughter–successors navigate in diverse national and cultural settings, it is methodologically sound to gather data on their personal history. By this approach, a researcher can assign pertinence to the daughter's recounting of experiences and interactions. Such modes of investigation further allow for similarities and differences among the daughter–successors being studied cross-nationally to emerge and, through this undertaking, cultural influence, entrepreneurial dynamics, and common practices can be identified. Researchers can then also link personal value systems and exogenous factors relating to cultural, political and/or social movements and how interplay in these areas influences identity construction of the individual daughter–successor in the family business.

Epilogue

The told story of the father–daughter succession must first be presented from the individual daughter–successor's biographical account. This takes us to an innovative research approach for holistically studying the father–daughter succession process in family businesses across cultures. In this book, we combine the two variables of enduring cultural values and the daughter's biographical narration into a single story presented in each of these case studies. The methodological significance of bringing these two variables together lies in giving researchers the means to explore the personal evolution of these women and thus give meaning to the family and managerial imperatives inherent in enabling a smooth father–daughter succession for family businesses across cultures.

Bibliography

Barbot, M.C., Bayad, M. and Bourguiba, M. 2004. *Transmission, des PME Familiales: Étude Exploratoire de la Relève Père-Fille en Tunisie*. Paper presented at the Actes du Séminaire, l'Entrepreneuriat en Tunisie, Quelles Recherches? Quelles Formations ?. ENIT, Tunis, 29–30 April 2004.

D'Iribarne, P. 1989. *La Logique de l'Honneur - Gestion des Entreprises et Traditions nationals*. Paris: Seuil. p. 280

Halkias, D. and Caracatsanis, S. 2011. The Evolution of Researching Female Immigrant Entrepreneurship: A Commentary, in *Female Immigrant Entrepreneurs: An Economic and Social Phenomena* (pp. 3–7), edited by D. Halkias, P. Thurman, N. Harkiolakis, and S. Caracatsanis. Farnham: Gower Publishing.

Halkias, D., Thurman, P., Harkiolakis, N., Katsioloudes, M., Stavrou, E., Swiercz, P.W. and Fragoudakis, M. 2010. Father–Daughter Succession Issues in Family Business among Regional Economies of Asia. *International Journal of Entrepreneurship Venturing*, 2(3/4), 320–346.

Halkias, D., Thurman, P., Abadir, S., Katsioloudes, M. and Harkiolakes, N. 2008. *Daughters' Intentions to Succeed Fathers in the Family Business: Securing the Future of the Family Enterprise in the Local Economies of Asia*. Paper presented at the 2emes Journees Georges Doriot, HEC, Paris, 15–16 May 2008.

Hofstede, G. 1997. *Cultures and Organizations*. New York: McGraw-Hill.

Lund Thomsen, T. 2006. *Self-employment Activities Concerning Women and Minorities: Their Success and Failure in Relation to Social Citizenship Policies*, PhD Defence, March 3. Available at: http://www.amid.dk/assets/pdf/Phd-TLT-abstract.pdf [last accessed December 2009].

Shapero, A. and Sokol, L. 1982. The Social Dimensions of Entrepreneurship, in *The Encyclopaedia of Entrepreneurship* (pp. 72–90), edited by C. Kent, D. Sexton and K. Vesper. Englewood Cliffs: Prentice-Hall.
Trompenaars, F. and Hampden-Turner, C. 2003. *L'Entreprise Multiculturelle*. New York: McGraw-Hill.

Introduction: "How Did All This Get Started?" A Pioneer of Father–Daughter Family Business Succession Research Remembers and Looks Ahead

COLETTE DUMAS

Over 20 years ago, when I researched, wrote, and published my doctoral dissertation on the topic of father–daughter succession in family-owned firms, daughters faced an uphill battle if they wanted to be seriously considered as their fathers' successors. Despite their myriad of accomplishments and breakthroughs, despite having proved their capabilities in the organizational, political, and leadership arenas, to be considered as viable successors to their fathers in the family firm was rare. At the time, daughters represented what Lyman et al. (1985) called an "untapped resource" for the estimated 98 percent of the 1 million registered corporations in the USA that were believed to be family-owned (Alcorn, 1982:1) and for 175 of the Fortune 500 companies that were considered family-owned (Beckhard and Dyer, 1981:1), as well as for 90 percent of America's 15 million businesses that were thought to be family-owned at the time (Pine and Mundale, 1983).

Women were overlooked as potential leaders for the family business as a result of the stereotypes that business families and society held about women and work. Such attitudes were woven into the fabric of generations and shaped not only the family but also the culture of the business. Daughters were often viewed as temporary employees in the business—until they married or had children—and thus were not given the same encouragement and developmental opportunities in the business as their brothers. There was no assumption that daughters would work in the business during the summer and holiday breaks; in addition, daughters were not included in any discussions about the business around the dinner table; daughters were not encouraged to get a business education. Because of these limiting stereotypes, 50 percent of potential heirs to the family business—the daughters—were excluded from crucial early training. While the reason often given for advancing a son over a daughter is that he possessed experience and had a certain readiness, in many cases, it was, in fact, often the result of gender bias.

The absence of daughters as successors despite the prevalence of family firms in the United States of America (USA) and despite the increasing numbers of women in the workforce, offered an excellent research opportunity. It was within this context that I turned my attention to the topic of father–daughter succession in family-owned firms. At the time, there was no empirical research that had been conducted on the topic.

I had the opportunity to break new ground. I didn't do it alone, of course. I built on the work of dear colleagues such as Barbara Hollander and Dr Mathilde Salganicoff. I was guided by my brilliant and insightful dissertation advisor, Dr Will McWhinney, who saw the need for this research. I benefitted from the critique and rigorous questioning of my dissertation committee including Dr Salganicoff, Dr Jody Veroff, and Dr Ana DiStefano.

In my long career as a professor, researcher, trainer, and consultant, working with families in business, I have seen successful transitions between generations, and some failures as well. I have seen strong women succeed against great odds, and I have seen some equally strong women succumb to the pressures of prevailing attitudes and leave their family business. In my current role as Professor of Management and Entrepreneurship and Director of the Center for Innovation and Change Leadership at Suffolk University's Sawyer Business School in Boston, I lead seminars and consult with executives in every kind of business, from small shops to large global corporations. From the family businesses I have worked with, I have learned much about the perseverance and dedication it takes to turn a dream into a business reality, and I've met many wonderful families who sustain the dream and keep their business thriving, despite the challenges.

I grew up in a business family and have worked with business families throughout my career. I know what it's like to be a woman in a family business. I have worked with daughters who wish to take over their father's construction business, and with daughters who must compete with their brothers for the CEO position of a multinational corporation.

The role of daughters in family enterprise is heavily influenced by the societal context that relates to the role and expectations of women in business, and in the family. Over the past 20 years, there has been a growing cultural acceptance of women in top leadership roles, developed concomitantly with the rise in the percentage of organizations expecting women to succeed as leaders of family firms. Notable companies with daughters in top management roles included, for example: (USA) S.C. Johnson, Carlson Companies, Mars, LA Lakers, Marriott, Fidelity Investments, L.L. Bean, The Schaeffler Group, Playboy Enterprises, Jockey International and (Europe) Monodor S.A., The Ronveaux group, L'Oréal, The A. Lagrou Companies, Detry S.A., Bister Mustard factories, Tri Thy Needlecraft Centre, and Brian McMahon & Daughters.

Today, daughters are more likely to decide to join their family's businesses and to pursue their professional careers there. They are more actively involved in the business; they hold ownership positions, and positions of responsibility, including being president, CEO, or director. Over the past 20 years, many excellent researchers have added their theoretical contributions, enhancing our understanding of women's increasing presence, participation, and advancement in family businesses. These studies have examined women's changing roles and the advantages that the family business can offer women, the pathways these women take to positions of respect and responsibility, and their achievements.

Unfortunately, gender issues will persist in some form or another for women in business as long as gender differences exist. Even in today's business world, where by some estimates 90–95 percent of US-run businesses are family controlled, most women, especially the daughters of family business owners, are not headed for the CEO's office. Primogeniture continues to dominate the value system of many family businesses; sons are more likely to join the business while daughters are given a choice—or not invited.

When a son doesn't succeed his father in the family enterprise, and when a daughter does, this is still a newsworthy event in local and national press.

However, while many of the obstacles facing women in family businesses are the same today as 20 years ago, we know more today about what is needed to overcome them. We also know more about the opportunities and challenges that positively influence women's entry into the business and contribute to their success.

The Road Ahead

This book is timely due to the key role of family enterprise in the global economy and the increasing role of women in business leadership, including family enterprise. As Pyromalis et al. note, "There will be an upsurge in female inheritance, ownership, and management of companies founded immediately post-war, over the period 2000–2020" (2006:422). This book makes such an important contribution to the literature because it is still relatively rare that research on succession takes cultural variables into account.

And yet, the family firm is an increasingly vital player in the global economy. In the developing economies of Asia, such as China, the Gulf Region, India, Malaysia, and Singapore, there is little research in the literature on gender issues in the family firm ownership and management (Sonfield and Lussier, 2003). Worldwide, family-owned and run businesses contribute significantly to national as well as local economies (de Jordy, 1991; Dunlop, 1993; Lank et al., 1994). It is estimated that these types of firms provide the majority of employment throughout the world, while generating some 40 percent of the US gross national product. Other estimates show that in Canada family-owned firms constitute approximately 80 percent of all the country's businesses and generate USD 150 billion in sales (Dunlop, 1993; de Jordy, 1991). In Europe and Australia, over 70 percent of businesses are family-owned or controlled (Lank et al., 1994).

Halkias et al. (2008) make an important contribution to the literature in their investigation of the trend for daughters in Asian family-owned businesses to take over leadership roles from their fathers in the family firm. Family enterprise is a crucial source of private wealth in Asia. From the ABN AMRO 2006, Report on *Asian families: Emotional aspects of wealth transfer and inheritance*:

> *As a result, the long-term success and well-being of the region's high-net-worth families increasingly depend on how they master the following issues:*
>
> - *Finding new ways of involving the next generation in the responsibilities of managing the family business and wealth.*
> - *Understanding the complex emotional aspects of succession between generations.*
> - *Minimizing the potentially destructive effects of emotions on the continuity of the family business and the family itself by carefully and professionally planning for succession as a long-term process.*

Due to cultural changes, increased chances of higher education, and a younger generation of fathers accepting women in the workforce, daughters have been gaining influence in more family businesses (ABN-AMRO, 2006). An important finding of their study is that male respondents found the family business more of a secure and a certain job, whereas females did not mind working outside the family business, thus, taking more risks in an uncertain, dynamic, business environment. It seems that the women were willing to take the risk to pursue a career outside the family business, whereas male respondents gain societal recognition and prestige if they are in control of the family business rather than working for someone else. The results of their study also revealed more male respondents seek to maintain family relationships through the family business compared to females who do not. The authors saw in this a tendency for the women to detach themselves from the family business since they see it being an oppressive situation and they want to "run away" and gain their independence. Clearly the authors' research offers great potential for understanding and facilitating important issues of father–daughter succession in Asian family businesses.

Among the many promising contributions in the literature for what it can offer the field going forward is the research that uses gender theory to explore the entrepreneurial process of business succession, as proposed by Ahl (2006) and de Bruin et al. (2007), for example. The GLOBE framework (House et al., 2004), and specifically its cultural dimension of gender egalitarianism, provides a frame of reference to consider the issue of women's participation in family enterprise (Moore and Gupta, 2007). The gender egalitarianism measure in the framework evaluates the level of gender-dependent divisions of roles, expectations, evaluations, and power within cultural groupings including Nordic Europe, Latin America, Germanic Europe, Confucian Asian, and Anglo, among others. In gender egalitarian cultures, men and women have more freedom to participate in the workplace and in the family, and this translates into an enhanced role for women in earned income and business leadership positions.

While there is a very strong belief in gender egalitarianism in principle in the USA and the EU, it is not fully realized in practice. Work by Ahl (2004; 2006), de Bruin et al. (2007), Ely and Padavic (2007), Fletcher (2001, 2004), Kolb et al. (1998), and others, help to explain this gap between theory and practice by portraying gender as a socially constructed phenomenon structured around separation (what is considered to be masculine or feminine) and hierarchy (the valorization of the masculine, considered as the norm). This theoretical perspective is based on the idea that men's and women's realities are shaped differently by society, through embedded systems, structures, rituals, and power dynamics resulting in an environment that can be ineffective and inequitable. This perspective concerns daughters' self-perceptions and cognitions (Ahl, 2006:611)—as well as societal values and norms that create those perceptions and cognitions (Ibid.). Thus we can shift responsibility for failure to reach gender egalitarian goals beyond the individual, and, in so doing, better conceptualize and consider the conflict within business families regarding the simultaneous role of daughters as family members, and as potential and actual family enterprise leaders.

When we consider this research in light of the succession process, we see links with family dynamics and power relations influence consideration of the daughter as a successor and her ease and success in assuming the leadership role. Daughters may also face particular challenges in management, especially in terms of leader legitimacy, that may be explained by the gendered relations within the family, the family business system, and society, including interactions and perceptions of parents, employees, suppliers, and customers.

Another promising perspective going forward is research on gender dynamics in the family firm when applying Gatewood et al.'s (2003) "pull" and "push" motivations for engagement with the family enterprise. Daughters who have grown up to perceive the family business as their own, with a desire to play an active role, to contribute to the necessary changes and to ensure the continuity of the family firm, exhibit "pull motivations" to the family firm. Other daughters faced with more difficult contexts may form a "reactive vision" of the family business, not considering themselves "true" potential successors (Dumas, 1998); these woman experience "push motivations" in regard to the family firm. The motivations of daughters of entrepreneurs are thus built in relation to their environmental cues and positioning, their own perceptions and aspirations, and their family's attitudes and predilections. This confluence of input, perhaps aligned or perhaps unaligned, bypasses women not occupying the daughters' familial role. The potential conflicts of acting on the ambition of embracing entrepreneurship within the family, given a socially constructed environment that challenges female participation at the highest level, may lead daughters to question their role in the family business regardless of their interest in entrepreneurship, or their support of the family, per se. For the daughters of family firms then, at the individual level, these major social shifts in the role of women in society and in the conceptualization and actualization of career offers more opportunities and a greater ability to define and choose among alternate constructions of professional life.

In Closing: An Invitation

I would like to close by extending an invitation to you our readers: take an enlightening voyage of discovery, tap into the knowledge generated by the dedicated authors in this volume and the families in business who collaborated with them, as they open the doors of these cross-cultural case studies to you. And, congratulations to the editors and the authors for the excellent job they have done bringing this important topic to life through these cases.

References

ABN-AMRO. 2006. *Asian Families: Emotional Aspects of Wealth Transfer and Inheritance*. ABN-AMRO Private Banking, published in partnership with INSEAD, Fontainebleau, France.

Ahl, H. 2004. *The Scientific Reproduction of Gender Inequality: A Discourse Analysis of Research Texts on Women's Entrepreneurship*. Malmö: Liber.

Ahl, H. 2006. Why Research on Women Entrepreneurs Needs New Directions. *Entrepreneurship Theory and Practice*, 30(5), 595–623.

Alcorn, P. 1982. *Success and Survival in the Family-Owned Business*. New York: McGraw-Hill.

Beckhard, R. and Dyer, W.G. Jr. 1981. *Challenges and Issues in Managing Family Firms*. Cambridge: Alfred P. Sloan School of Management, Massachusetts Institute of Technology.

de Bruin, A., Brush, C. and Welter, F. 2007. Advancing a Framework for Coherent Research on Women's Entrepreneurship. *Entrepreneurship Theory and Practice*, 31(3), 323–340.

De Jordy, H. 1991. Go-it-Alone Owner can Stymie Success of Family Business. *The Toronto Star*, September 2. D3.

Dumas, C. 1998. Women's Pathways to Participation and Leadership in the Family-Owned Firm. *Family Business Review*, 11(3), 219–228.

Dunlop, M. 1993. Parents' Beliefs can Cause Trouble in Family Firm. *The Toronto Star*, 20 November. k2.

Ely, R. and Padavic, I. 2007. A Feminist Analysis of Organizational Research on Sex Differences. *Academy of Management Review*, 32(4), 1121–1143.

Fletcher, J. 2001. *Disappearing Acts: Gender, Power, and Relational Practice at Work*. Cambridge: The MIT Press.

Fletcher, J. 2004. The Paradox of Post heroic Leadership: An Essay on Gender, Power, and Transformational Change. *Leadership Quarterly*, 15(5), 647–661.

Gatewood, E., Carter, N., Brush, C., Greene, P. and Hart, M. 2003. *Women Entrepreneurs, Their Ventures, and the Venture Capital Industry: An Annotated Bibliography*. Stockholm: Entrepreneurship and Small Business Research Institute (ESBRI).

Halkias, D., Thurman, P., Abadir, S., Katsioloudes, M. and Harkiolakes, N. 2008. *Daughters' Intentions to Succeed Fathers in the Family Business: Securing the Future of the Family Enterprise in the Local Economies of Asia*. Paper presented at the 2emes Journees Georges Doriot, HEC, Paris, 15–16 Mai.

House, R., Hanges, P., Javidan, M., Dorfman, P. and Gupta, V. 2004. *Culture, Leadership and Organizations: The GLOBE Study of 62 Cultures*. Thousand Oaks: Sage Publications.

Kolb, D., Fletcher, J., Meyerson, D., Merrill-Sands, D. and Ely, R. 1998. *Making Change: A Framework For Promoting Gender Equity In Organizations: CGO Insights No. 1*. Boston: Center for Gender in Organizations, Simmons School of Management.

Lank, A., Owens R., Martinez, J.I., and Riedel, H. 1994. The State of Family Businesses in Various Countries Around the World. *The Family Business Network Newsletter*, (9), 3–7.

Lyman, A., Salganicoff, M. and Hollander, B. 1985. Women in Family Business: An Untapped Resource. *Sam Advanced Management Journal*, 50(1), 46–49.

Moore, L. and Gupta, V. 2007. Overview of Gender in Family Business in *Culturally Sensitive Models of Gender in Family Business: A Compendium Using the GLOBE Paradigm*, edited by V. Gupta, N. Levenburg, L. Moore, J. Motwani and T. Schwarz. Hyderabad: ICFAI University Press.

Pine, C. and Mundale, S. 1983. Til Death Do Us Part. *Corporate Reports*, 14(9), 77–83.

Pyromalis, V., Vozikis, G., Kalkanteras, T., Rogdaki, M. and Sigalas, G. 2006. An Integrated Framework for Testing the Success of the Family Business Succession Process According to Gender Specificity in *Handbook of Research on Family Business* (pp. 422–441), edited by P. Poutziouris, K. Smyrnios and S. Klein. Cheltenham: Edward Elgar Press.

Sonfield, M.C. and Lussier, R.N. 2004. First-, Second-, and Third-Generation Family Firms: A Comparison. *Family Business Review*, 17(3), 189–202.

A Historical Perspective: From Hidden Giants to Visible Leaders? The Evolution of Women's Roles in Family Business

CHRISTINE BLONDEL

Marguerite d'Hausen showed tremendous tenacity, energy, and courage on all fronts: in the forge to supervise production and in Paris to demand payment from the government in order to provide for her workers and their families (Blondel and Van der Heyden, 1999).

This energetic and courageous woman was not a twenty-first century "super-woman", but lived in the eighteenth century in Revolutionary France. She had married Charles de Wendel, the second generation owner/manager of the Wendel family iron business. Toward the end of Charles' life, she had started to manage the forges with the help of her two sons-in-law, her son being occupied by the development of forges initiated by the King in another part of France. The French Revolution, which erupted in 1789, started an era of turbulence for France and for the Wendel family. A death sentence was pronounced for one of the children. Most members of the family then chose exile. But Marguerite d'Hausen, despite her age (she was 69 in 1789), stayed in France to run the family forge. She was alone, her son and sons-in-law having emigrated. Unfortunately, she was arrested in 1794, and the forges sold.

But the story was not to end there. Marguerite's grandson, François de Wendel, repurchased the then-bankrupted forges in 1803, upon his return from exile. To do so, he sold all his belongings and substantially indebted himself. But thanks to the need for iron created by Napoleonic wars, he quickly reimbursed his debts and expanded the activities. Marguerite was not there anymore to see the renewal of the business to which she had given so much energy, but another woman was to play a very important role in its survival and continuity. When François died in 1825, he left the ownership of the forges to his wife, Josephine de Fischer de Dicourt. Becoming a widow at age 41, she lived for another 47 years. She managed the forges with her son and her son-in-law over a period that saw significant development of the business with the construction of railways and iron ships. New coal collieries were open, new forges built as well as schools, housing, and churches for employees—the forges employment figures exceeded 10,000.

At her son's death in 1870, Josephine still owned the forges and had no surviving children. It was clear that her grandchildren would take over the destiny of the forges. To ensure family cohesion and the future of the business, she created a partnership company in 1871, called "Les Petits-Fils de François de Wendel" ("François de Wendel's grandsons"—which actually included granddaughters).The company owned 100 percent of the Wendel mines and forges. The first shareholders of this partnership company were François de Wendel's nine surviving grandsons and granddaughters. The articles of association stipulated that shares could only be owned by François de Wendel's descendants. The principles set out by Josephine survived the numerous crises that the business and family overcame over time—and are still the basis for the family functioning nowadays.

The case of the Wendel family, though extreme in its longevity, is not unique. Many women played important roles in family businesses in past centuries, sometimes in visible business leadership roles—as has been the case for widows in several dynasties, such as the Haniels and Krupps in Germany (James. 2006), de Dietrich in France (Blondel and Dumas, 2008), or the famous Veuve Clicquot in Champaign—and often in less visible but still vital roles. These roles were mostly assumed by the leaders' wives and mothers of the next generation. Daughters do not appear much in the history of dynasties, or in an indirect way, when their husbands contributed to the business. We will review some of the roles historically played by women in family businesses—and the challenges and opportunities created by the evolution of women's roles in society and business.

Women's Traditional Roles in Family Businesses: The Hidden Giants[1]

The role played by women in family-owned businesses—a category that accounts for about half of the traded companies in France and Germany, and at least 75 percent of all medium-sized businesses in the world—is both important and rarely visible. Women contribute directly and indirectly to building family businesses, maintaining them, and preparing their futures, but in many cases they do not appear in boards or executive offices. This situation has deep and documented roots, and to understand how it is changing—quickly in some firms, slowly in others, and sometimes not at all, despite pain for the families involved—we must first look into them.

The traditional roles of women in family enterprises, principally as wives and mothers (and wives and mothers to be), have been largely overlooked. Yet as the Swedish researcher Annelie Karlsson Stider (2001) observed, "To disregard the home and the wives in the management process is to present an incomplete picture of management." In many family firms, the home was also a workplace. Frequently, women kept the books. Just as often, they handled supplier and client relations, too. Their opinions about subjects like recruitment and appropriate associates were heard. Everywhere, women represented the family firm in society, images of its success and talent, and vectors of its influence.

Their key external strategic function was to develop the firm's social capital—its network of relations, allies, and sources. As Karlsson Stider reported:

> *The daughters of Albert Bonnier, founder of the Bonnier empire, and the wives of the following generations ... gave dinners for company associates [including artists and writers] in their homes. In later generations, now that the company had become a cultural as well as a financial institution in Swedish society, most of these associates were also friends, as business relations*

1 Blondel, C. 2005. The Hidden Giants of Family Business. INSEAD Quarterly. Issue 10 (March–May). Available at: http://www.insead.edu/discover_insead/publications/docs/IQ10.pdf [last accessed August 2011].

> *were now closely intertwined with social relations. The wife's role was to give business meetings a personal—even a private—air, and to strengthen the family's personal ties with potential customers and business associates.*[2]

Another hugely important role was played within the family itself. Grandmothers, mothers, and aunts in particular linked family members to each other, and to the next generation. That made them responsible, among other things, for transmitting essential family values. Women also had the power, if they used it, to transmit a positive or negative image of the family enterprise to the children. In so doing they taught family members how to get along together, in and out of the business (in family enterprises, the boundary between the two domains is hardly watertight). Women who meet these needs have sometimes been called, only half-jokingly, "Chief Emotional Officers". Beyond the nuclear family, someone besides the mother can play this role. What matters in family businesses is that *someone* must be there to play it. In families where no one is filling this role, its absence can be palpable: family members are unused and sometimes unable to work together, let alone happily.

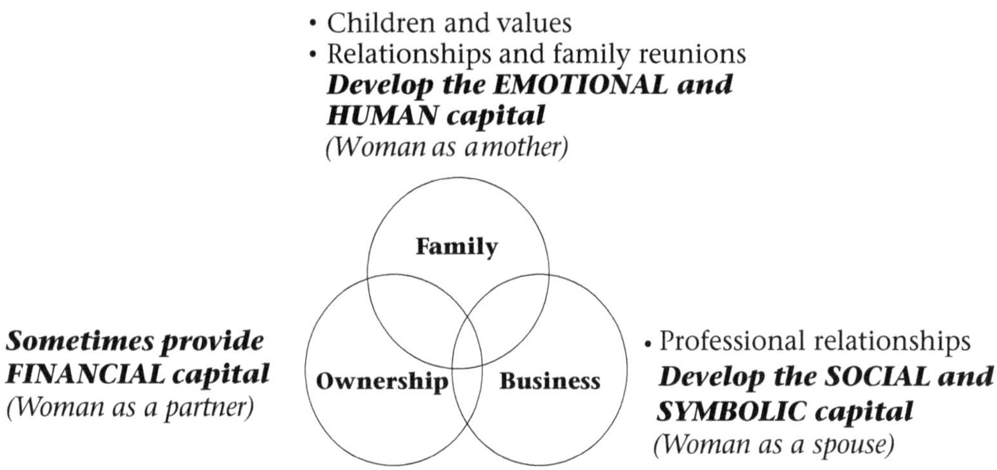

Figure H.1 Hidden giants

Source: Blondel, C. 2005. Les Femmes et l'Entreprise Familiale: Rôles et Evolution. INSEAD Working Paper, 2005/64/WICFE (translated as Blondel, C. Women and Family Firms: Roles and Evolution. Unpublished Working Paper)

There was always one prominent exception to the rule that women could not be visible leaders of a family business—when the death of their husbands left them in an ostensibly transitional role, managing affairs until their children grew up, that became more or less permanent. We have seen the examples of Marguerite d'Hausen and Josephine de Fischer de Dicourt, two widows from the Wendel family. More recently, Katherine Graham, the late, great publisher who led the *Washington Post* from the

2 Ibid.

Pentagon Papers to the twenty-first century, acceded to her job by the same route. The daughter of the newspaper's owner, like many women in family-owned businesses she was never considered a potential chief executive. Her husband, Philip Graham, took over the business with the majority of ownership. Only his premature disappearance thrust her into a position for which she was admittedly ill-trained, but where she established a literally historic presence (Graham, 1997).

Graham's story reminds us that in family businesses, one of the traditional roles of daughters was to ensure the renewal of management—by marrying if necessary. France's famous Galeries Lafayette stores offer a remarkably telling illustration of this mechanism, because for three successive generations, the absence of male heirs led the family women to "recruit" executives through marriage (though probably not with such explicit planning ...). More typically, daughters in family businesses married into other families that owned enterprises—a milieu and function for which they have been expertly trained and where they could become one of the invisible giants—but they were seldom expected to take any visible role in their family business. In fact, quite often and until recently—sometimes still now—they were not included in the business succession process.

The Dangers of "Forgetting" Daughters

In many enterprising families, women were given buildings and cash as their heritage, while men were given shares. This was normal practice until one generation ago, and linked ownership to management and risk – indeed protecting daughters from the business downturns. However, in some instances—where the business had been successful—this led to a double dose of pain and resentment for the women: they felt excluded from the business and the shares had appreciated far more rapidly than the real estate.

Ravages can also occur when young women are deprived of opportunities within their families, on the grounds that "they are not interested" or that they can't understand or assume executive responsibilities. It is not that all women *must* become executives. That would be just as much a denial of their choice, and of "Fair Process" (Van der Heyden et al., 2005), as confining them eternally in a traditional role. But fairness requires to at least check what their aspirations are. An instant survey done with voting devices at the Family Business Network Summit in Berlin (2007) showed an interesting twist in perception: when asked the likeliness of a woman becoming the next family business leader, 30 percent of the men in the room replied positively, compared to 50 percent of the women![3] Families in which these issues remain buried, rather than being exposed, weighed, discussed, and translated into decisions that can be accepted by all, are running increasing risks of fracture.

They are also running up against a particular form of the diversity business case, the argument that talent pools for winning enterprises must recruit as widely as possible. In family firms where development, especially in new businesses or subsidiaries, is entrusted to family members, rapid growth can quickly exhaust the possibilities of executive staffing through male offspring only. Instead of widening its resources and influence, the family ends by restricting them—almost imperceptibly at first, but progressively.

---

3 Survey conducted by the author, with voting devices, in an audience of about 500 members of business families, Family Business Network Summit, Berlin 2007.

The traditional distribution of wealth—shares for the boys, other assets for the girls—likewise appears increasingly dangerous for many family firms, because it entails taking capital out of the business to compensate women. Moreover, the concentration of shares in branches of the family with male offspring means that the exclusion of women within the firm will then be inflicted on their children. This was the case, for instance, for a talented male MBA with a successful background in multinational firms, who knew that he would never play a significant role in his family's company, because his mother owned no shares. He ultimately witnessed the sale of the company by his uncle. In extreme cases the family may create formidable enemies or competitors, as excluded offspring can bring their knowledge of the business to other firms, or harm the family and the business through other means.

The Evolution of Society and Roles

Traditions evolve, and daughters are filling an increasing number of roles in their family's enterprises. In the continuation of historical roles, contemporary women family members can work in family councils or contribute to the family philanthropic endeavors. Closer to the business, they can serve as board members. Last but not least, we see an increasing number of daughters succeeding their fathers or uncles as CEOs of family businesses, including in very large businesses: a highly visible example in the USA (United States of America) is Marilyn Carlson Nelson, who headed the Carlson Companies founded by her father—now employing about 150,000 persons in the world, directly or indirectly. She was instrumental in changing the company culture to a more family-friendly culture and in developing women's empowerment to management responsibilities (increasing their presence from 5–40 percent of executive jobs during her tenure) (Stern, 2011).

The evolution differs according to each family's culture. Overwhelmingly, it is women who still manage the role of "family glue", this is changing too. In large families in the third generation of ownership or beyond, men sometimes play this role. In some nuclear executive families, the men stay home with the children, or put their wives' careers first. It's a difficult role in a changing society: there is barely any traditional role or related training for men in the home, in society at large as in family enterprises—some men in such situations start creating their own support groups. The situation can also be rough on the women, because they often remain chief emotional officers to some extent along with their other responsibilities. In other words, the wives, too, need wives (a Catalyst survey of executives showed that while 75 percent of male executives had non-employed wives, 74 percent of female executives had husbands employed full time).[4] It is worth noting that enterprises, and not just family enterprises, which value productivity more than presence, make it far easier for women to play these two roles.

Why do women choose to confront these challenges? The first reason is that some of them love their jobs—they thrive on being leaders. But there can be a stronger motivation to lead the family firm: what is unique in a family firm is that if one chooses the executive path, one is still choosing to spend time with and serve the family, contrary to the executive path in non-family firms. Certainly, it is time with the family at large, and not just the nuclear family. But it still involves dealing with emotional issues, and with future generations.

4 *Leaders in a Global Economy, A Study of Executive Women and Men*. Families and Work Institute, Catalyst, Boston College Center for Work and Family, January 2003.

We should see more significant changes in future generations with a very strong proportion of women starting their own businesses. And the fact that men are increasingly aware of these questions in family firms presages continuing transformations.

Figure H.2 Marguerite d'Hausen

Source: Marguerite d'Hausen, anonymous portrait, private collection (reproduced in Blondel and Van der Heyden, 1999, The Wendel Family: "Affectio Societatis" (A), INSEAD case

Additional Abridged Bibliography

Blondel, C. and Dumas, A. 2008. *L'Entreprise Familiale sauvera-t-elle le capitalisme? Portraits (Will the Family Firm Save Capitalism?)*. Paris: Editions Autrement.

Blondel, C. and Van der Heyden, L. 1999. The Wendel Family: 'Affectio Societatis' (A) The Story of an Industrial Dynasty. INSEAD case, Fontainebleau, 1999.

Brown, D.A.H., Brown, D.L. and Anastasopoulos, V. 2002. *Women on Boards, Not Just the Right Thing but the Bright Thing,* Conference Board of Canada. Available at: http://www.europeanpwn.net/files/women_on_boards_canada.pdf [last accessed August 2011].

Brown, L.M. and Gilligan, C. 1992. *Meeting at the Crossroad.* Cambridge: Harvard University Press.

Carlock, R.S. and Florent, E. 2002. *Love and Work, Finding One's Place in the Family Firm.* INSEAD case study.

Catalyst. 2003. *Leaders in a Global Economy, a Study of Executive Women and Men, Families and Work Institute*, Chestnut Hill, The Center for Work and Family at Boston College.

Catalyst. 2004. *The Bottom Line: Connecting Corporate Performance and Gender Diversity*. Available at: http://www.catalyst.org/file/44/the%20bottom%20line%20connecting%20corporate%20performance%20and%20gender%20diversity.pdf [last accessed August 2011].

Dumas, C. 1998. Women's Pathways to Participation and Leadership in the Family-Owned Firm, *Family Business Review*, 11(3), 219–228.

Fletcher, J.K. 2001. *Invisible Work: The Disappearing of Relational Practice at Work*. CGO Insights. Available at: http://www.simmons.edu/som/docs/centers/insights8.pdf [last accessed August 2011].

Gilligan C. 1982. *In a Different Voice*. Cambridge: Harvard University Press.

Graham, K. 1997. *Personal History*. New York: Knopf.

Hollander, B.S. and Bukowitz, W.S. 1990. Women, Family Culture, and Family Business. *Family Business Review*, 3(2), 139–151.

James, H. 2006. *Family Capitalism: Wendels, Haniels, Falcks, and the Continental European Model*. Cambridge: Harvard University Press.

Lansberg, I. 1999. *Succeeding Generations: Realizing the Dream of Families in Business*. Boston: Harvard Business School Press.

Nelton, S. 1988. When Widows Take Charge. *Nation's Business*, December. Available at: http://findarticles.com/p/articles/mi_m1154/is_n12_v76/ai_6875486/ [last accessed August 2011].

Ruderman, M.N. and Ohlott, P.J. 2000. *Learning from Life: Turning Life's Lessons into Leadership Experience*. Greensboro: Center for Creative Leadership (CCL).

Ruderman, M.N. and Ohlott, P.J. 2002. *Standing at the Crossroads: Next Steps for High Achieving Women*. Hoboken: Jossey-Bass/CCL.

Stider, A.K. 2001. The Home – A Disregarded Managerial Arena, in *Invisible Management, The Social Construction of Leadership* (pp. 98–99), edited by S.-E. Sjöstrand, J. Sandberg and M. Tyrstrup. London: Thomson Learning.

Stern, M. 2005. *The Collegial CEO*, Families in Business, Campden FB, n°20, May/June, 27–30. Available at: http://www.campdenfb.com/article/collegial-ceo [last accessed August 2011].

Van der Heyden, L., Blondel, C. and Carlock, R. 2005. Fair Process, Striving for Justice in the Family Business. *Family Business Review*, March 2005.

Wittenberg-Cox, A. and Milan, M. 2004. *Women@work: Women, Careers and Competitive Advantage in the New Millenium*. Paris: Paris Professional Women's Network, Paris.

PART II Asia

CHAPTER 1

China: A Case Study of Father–Daughter Succession in China

XIN DENG

This chapter investigates succession between father and daughter using a case study of a family firm in China. This is the first empirical research on this issue in China. The study is based on an in-depth interview with a female CEO who has assumed management of the family business established by her father. It considers four issues in father–daughter succession: the impact of Confucian ideology, gender conflict, the role of other family members, and succession planning and training for successors. Drawing on the information gathered in this case study, the author discusses the managerial implications of succession planning, the importance of training, strategies to manage the second generation's reluctance to take over, and managing gender conflicts during succession.

Introduction

Family firms returned to the stage in China in the late 1970s after 20 years of absence. They are the dominant form of private firms and contribute more than 65 percent of gross domestic product (GDP) in China (Wang et al., 2009). As the founders of many family firms approach retirement age, how these firms manage succession presents an interesting area of research. Prior research suggests that only 30 percent of family businesses survive the second generation, while only 10 percent survive the third generation (Beckhard and Gibb Dyer, 1983). Successful succession is, therefore, vital for the survival of the family business. While it is possible to learn from existing experience and research based on the developed economy, it is worth noting that "the Chinese business enterprise family differs in fundamental ways from the usual Western business firm" (Weidenbaum, 1996:141).

When considering succession, family members will always be the preferred choice (Weidenbaum, 1996). Empirical studies in China confirm that nearly half of surveyed owners consider family members as the first preference for successors (Yu, 2009; Zhu, 2006). Because there has been limited research on succession in mainland China, in-depth analysis of succession is not available, and succession between father and daughter in particular has not been analyzed in the existing literature.

Aiming to fill this gap in research, this study investigates father–daughter succession in China by drawing on an in-depth interview with a female successor. This chapter is organized as follows: the next section is a review of the literature on succession in Chinese family firms; a description of the data and major results are then presented; following that, the managerial implications of succession planning, training, and strategies for the second generation's reluctance to take over and gender conflicts are discussed in depth. The chapter concludes with a summary of findings and a discussion of the limitations of this study.

Literature Review

There has been little research on succession in family businesses in mainland China. While succession has been raised as a major concern faced by the first generation of private entrepreneurs (Lawrence, 2003), the author is not aware of any empirical research published in English related to succession in family businesses in mainland China. A study based on a survey of 24 family businesses in Hong Kong explored challenges faced by second generation owners (Chung and Yuen, 2003). This study focused on authority and management style, and did not cover the social and cultural factors. Other scholars have studied the effect of Confucian values on succession in family business and presented a theoretical model. However, they did not conduct empirical research to test the hypotheses proposed (Yan and Sorenson, 2006). Weidenbaum (1996) noted a strong preference toward family members as successors as one of the outstanding differences between Chinese and western firms, and supported his argument with two examples, but, again, the author did not explore this issue in great depth.

Research on succession in family businesses has recently emerged with publications in Chinese journals from 2002 (Zhang and Wei, 2006). However, most of these papers are general introductions of theory and research findings in English publications. Among the limited empirical research, the survey is the dominant research methodology. One study investigated the determinants of satisfaction level of the succession process based on a survey of 198 family business owners, and identified factors that included consistency in goals, the attitude of relevant parties, following procedures, organization, and the talents and experience of successors (He and Jiang, 2009). The reasons family businesses may opt for family members as successors were explored with a survey of 123 family firms in the South Fujian area (Dong and Wang, 2008). There are two survey-based studies in Zhejiang: one surveyed 128 family firms across the province and presented characteristics of successors and founders as well as documenting organizational change after succession (Zhu, 2006). The other focused on one city, Wenzhou, and investigated the owners' preference for potential successor, their criteria for selecting successor, the factors influencing succession, and succession planning (Yu, 2009). While these studies considered succession, none of them looked specifically at the issue of father–daughter succession, or used interviews as part of their method. In summary, father–daughter succession in China remains an unexplored research area, and in-depth analysis is needed to understand this issue.

Data

The data is drawn from an in-depth interview with a female CEO who has taken over the family business from her father. The interview was conducted in mid-May 2010 at the office of the interviewee in Jiangsu Province. The company at the centre of this case produces, installs, and maintains street lamps and local government departments in charge of infrastructure and facilities are its major clients. It was registered in 1995 by the father–owner, who had been involved in the luminaries industry since 1989. Annual sales revenue in the last three years has ranged from 90 to 100 million RMB, and the total number of employees is between 160 and 180. It is a small firm according to the official standard (State Council, 2003).[1]

The founder–owner's daughter joined the company in 2000. After rotating through various departments within the company, she formally took over as the CEO in 2006. At the time of interview, the father was 60 years old, and the daughter was 35 years old. The daughter was in charge of everyday operations, but the father was still consulted on major decisions and remained in charge of the sales department. The daughter still refers the firm "my father's company" even if the father made it clear many years ago that "it will eventually be yours."

Results

IMPACT OF CONFUCIANISM

Confucianism is deeply embedded in Chinese society for both mainland and overseas Chinese (Greenhalgh, 1994). According to Yan and Sorenson (2006), there are five aspects of Confucian ideology related to succession in Chinese family businesses: the family is the basic unit of society, there are certain obligations of the parent and child to one another, there are rules that govern relationships with other family members, and there are rules that govern other social relationships and inheritance of family property. In this case study, all except the last one can play an important role in succession.

Confucianism regards the family as a whole to be more important than any individual members, and that harmony is the most important value for all family members (Hofstede, 1991). It was clear from the interview that responsibility for family played an important role in the interviewee's decision to join the company. The interviewee cited "family interest" and her "father's push" as the main reasons for her to join the company. Her work in the business gave her aged father the support he desperately needed as the business grew and also removed pressure from her younger sister (who is 12 years younger) so that she could pursue her own interests. A strong support of her younger sister suggests that this is something she herself has missed; as she says, "I would like to do the same if I had the opportunity."

The parent–child relationship in Confucianism is a reciprocal relationship in which children serve their parents with filial piety and submission (*xiao*), and parents treat their children with kindness and care (*ci*) (Hsu, 1998; Tu, 1998). Filial piety (*xiao*) is

1 A firm is classified as medium sized when all of the following three criteria are met: number of employees is more than 300, annual sales revenue is above 30 million RMB, and total assets are more than 40 million RMB.

displayed by high levels of devotion, including affection, respect, duty, and obedience. In this case, a father–daughter relationship consistent with the Confucian ideology helps with succession, as the daughter in this case points out she had only considered a career running a lighting company for the sake of her father, and describes the job as "demanding" and "not suitable for a female" even though she has been running the company successfully for more than four years. On the other hand, she was fully aware of and appreciated her father's support and care: "Sometimes [if] I did something wrong, he would not point it out straightforwardly. Instead, he would mention it when I was more ready to hear different opinions."

Other family relationships are less important in this case. In a Chinese family, a child is taught to be respectful and obedient to all the other senior family members. In terms of succession, the oldest son assumes the family leadership position when the father passes away (Tu, 1998). In this case, the elder sister was chosen as the successor, which provides an interesting contrast to many overseas Chinese family firms' practice of choosing a son-in-law to be the successor (Weidenbaum, 1996). There are several possible reasons: first, the daughter was not married at the time she joined the company, so a son-in-law was not an option, second, daughters have acquired a more equal status in families in mainland China after the propaganda of "women holding up half the sky" and implementation of the one-child policy. Third, the son-in-law in this case is not interested in running the business according to the interviewee, and finally, it may be easier to organize final ownership division if a direct family member such as a daughter rather than a son-in-law is in charge.

Social norms that deal with the relationship between superiors and subordinates appear to contribute to a smooth succession. Since the firm is owned by the family, daughters are accepted as the rightful inheritor. As a result, the interviewee was accepted by both senior management and employees (subordinates) at lower levels with few problems.

GENDER ISSUES

The street lighting industry is male-dominated; the interviewee herself noted: "Most people I work with are male." Just as importantly, more than 90 percent of the company's clients are male. Being a female leader in a male-dominated sector nevertheless poses some challenges; the "biggest challenge" according to the interviewee is to "deal with clients" who are government officials. In China, *guanxi*, or "good relationship," is extremely important in winning contracts from the government (Xin and Pearce, 1996). Cultivating and maintaining good *guanxi* involves social interactions between two parties (Park and Luo, 2001), since almost all of their clients are male who are similar in age to the father, it is relatively easy for the father to maintain and develop the *guanxi* network for the firm. However, the daughter, being from a younger generation and of a different gender, found it quite difficult to socialize with those clients. Consequently, the father–owner is still in charge of sales.

The story is different inside the company. The daughter has developed a close, almost family-like relationship with members of senior management, and the role of gender has diminished. However, the interviewee did find that she was more likely to be challenged in her decisions compared with her father. In a situation where there are two sides with different opinions, her father usually acts as arbitrator, however, her stand does not have much impact on the direction of the argument. Nevertheless, this could also be due to authority instead of gender as she remains relatively new and young compared with others in management.

The line between father and daughter throws little light on the issue as each has a good relationship with the other in this study. The interviewee pointed out that she and her father were "in a good relationship" despite the occasional disagreement, and suggested that the fact that daughters are "less interested in power" may contribute to a good relationship. This is consistent with other studies suggesting that the father–daughter relationship can be seen as complimentary (Dumas, 1992).

ROLE OF OTHER FAMILY MEMBERS

The interviewee and her father are the only two people from the core family working in the family business. There were relatives in the father's generation who had worked with him from the start of the business, but as the company grew they became unfit due to their limited education and capacity according to the interviewee. Given their contribution to the company, they were either offered a part of the business and became a supplier of the company, or were placed in a position that did not have much impact on decision making. The interviewee's father has long been the leader of the extended family, and his decision to pass the business to his daughter was not challenged by other relatives because "this is a business within our family." Nevertheless, the decision to remove relatives from key positions has helped to establish his daughter's authority.

PLANNING AND TRAINING

In this case, the daughter was rushed into the family business. This is not uncommon, given the Chinese entrepreneurs' strong preference for integrating their children into their business (Weidenbaum, 1996) and the limited options for successors due to the one-child policy. However, it does suggest that that the succession may not have been well planned. In this case, the daughter was aware of her father's intention to have her and her sister run the family business, but was not well-prepared to take over the business. She obtained an unrelated degree in education and worked as a teacher after finishing university; her involvement in the business was minimal prior to joining the company consisting of occasional company visits during vacations and brief chats with managers that she knew. The training she had received was limited. Nevertheless, she had been rotated through all sections of the company had received mentoring support from different department heads, and was increasingly assigned more responsibilities, until finally she was able to take over the role of CEO. However, her father–owner has never talked about training and planning, she has never received a formal management education; instead any relevant knowledge was attained on the job, supplemented by reading business magazines and books.

Discussion

Research shows that succession is more likely to be successful with planning (Sharma et al., 2003; Stavrou, 1999). Despite a desire by first generation entrepreneurs to have their offspring inherit their business, our case study suggests that often little in the way of formal planning takes place and this confirms findings from other researchers (Yu, 2009). The lack of planning may be explained by the educational background and experience of first generation founders themselves, since most attain only a low level of education by the time they start their business, succession planning may call on skills they may not have developed. Furthermore, based on their own experience of starting a business from scratch they may believe that that there is little need for a formal plan.

A lack of formal training is another issue that needs consideration. Indeed, training needs to be provided for both generations as reconciling the expectations of both generations regarding succession can facilitate succession (Cabrera-Suárez et al., 2001). The training of founders should focus on understanding the needs and interests of successors, and finding alternative ways of introducing them into the family business rather than using the fathers' authority to influence children's decisions. Training of successors should cover a much longer time span, and involve more planning. Potential successors need to have reasonable exposure to the family business at an early stage, and be encouraged to learn relevant knowledge and acquire relevant experience related to the family business. A formal training program needs to be organized and clearly communicated to the successor once they have formally joined the business (Barach and Ganitsky, 1995; Venter et al., 2005).

However, founders of family businesses need to be aware that the firm they are passing on to the next generation is likely to be quite different from the small business started by them some time ago, and the second generation may not be as committed to the business (Handler, 1994). A separate approach needs to be adopted, and external consultation may be necessary to avoid some common pitfalls, such as rushing under-prepared children into the family business, over-reliance on learning by doing and ignoring children's own needs and interests.

China's one-child policy has led to small family sizes; many families have just one child. Given Chinese entrepreneurs' strong preference for succession among their children, many of these children can find themselves earmarked to take over at a very young age. However, potential successors may not necessarily be interested in joining or taking over the family business as planned by their parents (Stavrou, 1999); a lack of motivation has been cited as one of the major factors preventing intra-family succession (De Massis et al., 2008). Indeed, the successor in this case observed that it was not uncommon for the second generation to openly challenge their parents and to decline to become involved in the family business.

Rushing potential successors into family businesses as soon as they have completed tertiary education may not be a positive arrangement for either the business or successor (Stavrou, 1999). This is because there may be little opportunity to obtain external experience or build human capital, so they may have less to contribute to the business or take longer to learn and understand the business. It may even be more difficult for daughters as they may also be expected to have children (Salganicoff, 1990, Mathewsa and Moser, 1995).

Father–daughter succession implies a transfer of management (and eventually ownership), but this can be problematic in male-dominated industries, where male dominance may act as an advantage for the father, but impose extra challenges for the daughter. In this case, the daughter decided that she was less able to work with the company's male clients, so she developed an alternative strategy in which she delegated key tasks to other male employees. She developed and appointed regional sales agents who could also deal directly with government officials; this meant that she could avoid dealing with male clients directly yet still retain control over sales. Other tactics may simply involve developing and delivering better customer services more innovative goods and services. The father–owner in this study had become adept at courting his male clients, some of whom eventually became friends; his daughter has shown however that there may be other ways of developing good relationships with clients notwithstanding her gender.

While conflicts with employees and senior management due to gender difference are not evident in this case, they cannot be completely ruled out in father–daughter succession. This case suggests that a good personal relationship between senior management and the family may be extremely helpful in supporting the successor and solving potential conflicts between father and daughter.

Conclusion

The second generation of the first group of entrepreneurs in China following reform provide a valuable resource for family businesses; they are largely well-educated, and have been exposed to the family business at a younger age. Given proper planning and training, many of them should be able to carry on the family business successfully, although this research indicates that this is an area that is need of more attention by family businesses. The study confirms that the Confucian ideology of family focus helps to define roles and encourages the second generation to join the family business. The father–daughter relationship and other social relationships defined by Confucian ideology can facilitate a smooth succession. Gender difference appeared to have a relatively low impact on succession itself; however, special difficulties may arise for daughters taking over in male-dominated industries. From the data presented in this case it would seem that women are able to adopt strategies that can mitigate these difficulties.

Limitations

The limitation of this study is also evident. It only presents a single case. Findings need to be interpreted in the light of this, and more research is needed before any general conclusions can be drawn. Nevertheless, it has yielded some fresh insights, it is also the first empirical research to investigate the father–daughter succession issue in the Chinese context, and insights drawn from this study may be helpful for both researchers and family businesses who are considering passing over the management of their firms to daughters.

References

Barach, J.A. and Ganitsky, J.B. 1995. Successful Succession in Family Business. *Family Business Review*, 8(2), 131–155.

Beckhard, R. and Gibb Dyer, W. 1983. Managing Continuity in the Family-Owned Business. *Organizational Dynamics*, 12(1), 5–12.

Cabrera-Suárez, K., Saá-Pérez, P.D. and García-Almeida, D. 2001. The Succession Process from a Resource- and Knowledge-Based View of the Family Firm. *Family Business Review*, 14(1), 37–48.

Chung, W.W.C. and Yuen, K.P.K. 2003. Management Succession: A Case for Chinese family-Owned Business. *Management Decision*, 41(7), 643–655.

De Massis, A., Chua, J.H. and Chrisman, J.J. 2008. Factors Preventing Intra-Family Succession. *Family Business Review*, 21(2), 183–199.

Dong, W. and Wang, W. 2008. Motivation and Obstacles of Family Firms' Power Succession: A Survey on Family Firms in South Fujian in China. *Productivity Research*, 8, 54–55.

Dumas, C. 1992. Integrating the Daughter into Family Business Management. *Entrepreneurship: Theory and Practice*, 16, 41–55.

Greenhalgh, S. 1994. De-Orientalizing the Chinese Family Firm. *American Ethnologist*, 21(4), 746–775.

Handler, W.C. 1994. Succession in Family Business: A Review of the Research. *Family Business Review*, 7(2), 133–157.

He, X. and Jiang, T. 2009. Satisfaction on Succession among Family Firms in China: A Survey Outcome (*in Chinese*). *Productivity Research*, 1, 142–143.

Hofstede, G. 1991. *Cultures and Organizations*. New York: McGraw-Hill.

Hsu, F.L.K. 1998. Confucianism in Comparative Context, in *Confucianism and the Family* (pp. 53–71) edited by G.D.V. WH Slote. Albany: State University of New York Press.

Lawrence, S.V. 2003. The Son Also Rises. *Far Eastern Economic Review*, 166(33), 24–27.

Mathews, C.H. and Moser, S.B. 1995. Family Background and Gender: Implications for Interest in Small Firm Ownership. *Entrepreneurship & Regional Development*, 7(4), 365–378.

Park, S.H. and Luo, Y. 2001. Guanxi and Organizational Dynamics: Organizational Networking in Chinese Firms. *Strategic Management Journal*, 22(5), 455.

Salganicoff, M. 1990. Women in Family Businesses: Challenges and Opportunities. *Family Business Review*, 3(2), 125–137.

Sharma, P., Chrisman, J.J. and Chua, J.H. 2003. Succession Planning as Planned Behavior: Some Empirical Results. *Family Business Review*, 16(1), 1–15.

State Council. 2003. *Temporary Standards of Small and Medium Firms*.

Stavrou, E.T. 1999. Succession in Family Businesses: Exploring the Effects of Demographic Factors on Offspring Intentions to Join and Take Over the Business. *Journal of Small Business Management*, 37(3), 43–61.

Tu, W-M. 1998. Probing the 'Three Bonds' and 'Five Relationships' in Confucian Humanism, in *Confucianism and the family* (pp. 121–136), edited by G.D.V. WH Slote. Albany: State University of New York Press.

Venter, E., Boshoff, C. and Maas, G. 2005. The Influence of Successor-Related Factors on the Succession Process in Small and Medium-Sized Family Businesses. *Family Business Review*, 18(4), 283–303.

Wang, H., Liu, J., Zhang, L., Wei, Z. and Li, Y. 2009. Thirty Years' Development of Private Enterprises in China Since Reform and Openness, in *Report on Development of Private Economy in China (no. 5) (2007–2008)* (pp. 292–313), edited by M. Huang. Beijing: Social Science Academic Press.

Weidenbaum, M. 1996. The Chinese Family Business Enterprise. *California Management Review*, 38(4), 141–156.

Xin, K.K. and Pearce, J.L. 1996. Guanxi: Connections as Substitutes for Formal Institutional Support. *Academy of Management Journal*, 39(6), 1641–1658.

Yan, J. and Sorenson, R. 2006. The Effect of Confucian Values on Succession in Family Business. *Family Business Review*, 19(3), 235–250.

Yu, X. 2009. Successful Inheritance and Successor Selection in Family Enterprises: An Empirical Analysis in Wenzhou. *East China Economic Management*, 23(6), 13–18.
Zhang, W. and Wei, H. 2006. A Study on the Succession of China's Family Owned Businesses. *Management Review*, 18(2), 31–36.
Zhu, S. 2006. A Survey on Family Firms in Zhejiang. *Collected Essays On Finance and Economics*, 4, 96–100.

CHAPTER 2

India: A Socio-Cultural Perspective on Father–Daughter Succession in Family Business in India

GEETIKA GOEL, SHEFALI NANDAN AND PIYALI GHOSH

Introduction

India is the seventh largest country of the world with a population of 1027 million (2001 Census), spread over an area of 3,287,240 sq.km. The unique quality of Indian culture is that it is an assimilation of various cultures in its own traditional cultural set up. Twenty-two national languages have been recognized by the Constitution of India which together create 844 dialects. India is home to several thousand ethnic groups, tribes, castes, and religions. Diverse Indian culture has impacted all aspects of its people including economic activities.

The family businesses in India initially started in the 1890s as a means to promote import substitution and attain economic freedom from the British. As per an estimate by Confederation of Indian Industries (CII), 95 percent of the registered firms are family businesses and together contribute 60–70 percent of Gross Domestic product (GDP) in India. According to *Business Today* (1997), family-run businesses account for 25 percent of India Inc.'s sales, 32 percent of profits after tax (pat), almost 18 percent of assets and over 37 percent of reserves. Some of the prominent business families include the Tatas, Ambanis, Bajajs, Modis, Birlas, Wadias, Godrej, Thapars, Shrirams, and Singhanias (Business Today, 1997).

The objective of this chapter is to understand the succession process in family business and to understand the influence of cultural variables on the succession process. Succession in family business has typically been governed by the overriding Indian ethos and culture. India has been found to have family culture, long power distance, and high masculinity index (Hofstede, 1991). Naskar (1996) concurs that the traditional Indian family may be described as *patriarchal* and it applies to gender relations within the family; this is true in all family systems except the defunct matrilineal system of the Nayar castes in Kerala. A study by Ramchandran (2005) shows that there exists an unwritten rule that daughters-in-law do not get involved in business while daughters, anyway, go to their in-law's house. The current generation shows signs of this rule changing slowly.

Literature Review

Most discussions in the area of succession in family business are based on research in advanced countries. Studies show that in the American context families choose their most competent member(s) to manage the business, disregarding age, gender, or bloodline (Chrisman et al., 1998). This is a reflection of the family's willingness to separate family hierarchy from organizational hierarchy. Given the level of socio-economic and cultural contexts prevailing, it is difficult for this to be true in the Indian context (Ramchandran, 2005).

FEMALE ENTREPRENEURSHIP IN INDIA

According to the Global Entrepreneurship Monitor (GEM) Report on India for 2002 (Manimala, 2002) on India, males are twice as likely as females to engage in entrepreneurial activities. Indian women generally have less access to formal education; consequently, they have less participation in the formal sector and hence many of them take up self-employment. However, in the state of Kerala, (where female literacy is at 87.86 percent) women entrepreneurs are a relatively well-educated group (D'Cruz, 2003). It has been found that women entrepreneurs in the service sector are more educated than those in the trading sector (Lalitha Rani, 1996).

The needs and contributions of female entrepreneurs vary widely from state to state in the country. In the south, female entrepreneurs are found to be engaged in coir manufacturing, readymade garment manufacturing, food processing, pickle making, bakery, handicrafts, printing, and book binding, in electronics and assembling units and others (D'Cruz, 2003). In the northern part of India, a majority of women entrepreneurs are concentrated in the light-manufacturing sector (leather, garments, engineering goods, and beauty products), services (interior designing, management and placement, consultancies, and nursery schools), and the retail trade sector (boutiques, home furnishing, automobile dealing, and so on) (Lalitha Rani, 1996; Sharma and Dhameja, 2002; Ganesan, 2003).

Gujarat, Maharashtra, and Karnataka have more women entrepreneurs than other states; they are either from families that are already in business, or have highly educated fathers or husbands (Lalitha Rani, 1996; Sharma and Dhameja, 2002; Walokar, 2001; Ganesan, 2003; Das, 2000). Only about one-fifth of women have been found to become entrepreneurs by "pull" factors, such as the need for a challenge, urge to try something on their own, to be independent, and to show others that they are capable of doing well in business (Das, 2000).

Organizations and associations have and are being formed to support female entrepreneurship in India. One such representative example is Consortium for Women Entrepreneurs in India (CWEI). CWEI is a voluntary organization that has the mission "to motivate the new generation and women to opt for entrepreneurship as a challenging career—the only answer to unemployment." The Ministry of Human Resource has declared CWEI as the Nodal Agency to guide and assist NGOS, SHGs, institutions, and entrepreneurs and organize various economic activities in the country.[1]

1 See http://www.cwei.org online.

SUCCESSION PLANNING IN FAMILY BUSINESS

Studies (Watts and Tucker, 2004) have reported that families hesitate to address the issue of ownership and management succession in spite of the fact that these are the key concerns of a large number of business families and India is no exception. The unclear succession planning has seen the split and downfall or demise of many previously successful businesses, including the Modis, the Walchands, the Raunaq Singhs, the Bhai Mohan Singhs, and a dozen other joint family firms. The most recent, unexpected, and hostile split in India's largest private sector company, Reliance Industries, after the death of the patriarch was due to unclear succession planning. The conflict resulted in a loss to the investors' wealth.

THE INDIAN CULTURE AND ITS INFLUENCE ON FAMILY BUSINESS

According to Kluckhohn and Strodtbeck (1961), Indian culture is characterized by orientation for subjugation and belief that destiny and God control everything; status in life is derived from birth, age, sex, family, and social connections—more so than individual achievements; also, people have an orientation toward the "past." Some of the prominent dimensions of Indian culture which impact business and succession decisions are mentioned below:

Joint family system

The Hindu joint family is a patriarchal organization in which the senior-most male ascendant is revered as the elder of the family or karta or manager. The karta occupies a fiduciary position; when the karta dies, his eldest son becomes the manager. The close-knit structure of families, which fosters teamwork combined with respect to family values and family elders, has been the key to success of many family businesses in India (Pawar, 2009).

As per Hofstede's dimension concept of a culture, India has Masculinity as the third highest, ranking at 56. The higher a country ranks in this dimension, the greater the gap between value of men and women. However, the situation is changing in favor of women, with the Hindu Succession (Amendment) Act 2005. Under Section 6 of the Amendment Act, a daughter has got the same rights in the coparcenary property as a son.

Male preference

Studies concur that there is a generalized tendency to give preferential treatment to boys over girls in South Asian socicties (Das Gupta, 2007). In India, couples have a strong preference for sons over daughters (Arnold 1996; 1997). Mutharayappa et al. (1997) observe that studies in India have identified three major factors for son preference. First, the economic utility of sons; sons are more likely than daughters to provide support on the farm or in the family business and support their parents during old age. Second, the socio-cultural utility of the son; after marriage, he brings a daughter-in-law into the family, while a daughter goes away to another family. Finally, only sons can carry out important religious functions, such as perform the last rites of their deceased parents and carry the family name through generations.

Bhattacharyya (2007) posits that sons and male family members are more likely to hold higher positions and succeed the CEO in the family business while the role of women is that of facilitator to the male members and as the mother figure to the family and employees.

Caste system

Among Hindus there are castes and sub-castes who inherit the set of values, beliefs, and behavior patterns through a process of socialization. Indian firms, by and large, continue to be family-run by the traditional trading castes. It is predominantly the Agarwals and Guptas in the north, the Chettiars in the south, the Parsees, Gujarati Jains and Banias, Muslim Khojas and Memons in the west, and Marwaris in the east and, in fact, across the country. Fifteen out of the 20 largest industrial houses in 1997 were derived from the Vaishya or Bania trading castes (Business Today, 1997).

FATHER–DAUGHTER SUCCESSION IN THE INDIAN CONTEXT

Jaffe and Brown (2003) have reported that the concept of father–daughter succession is gaining ground in India, like other parts of the world. Daughters have not just inherited businesses, they have been deeply involved in running them (Khaleej Times, 2009). Vera and Dean (2005) surveyed daughter–successors of family businesses and found them enjoying a number of advantages, such as a flexible work schedule, a comfortable place to work, and shared family and business goals. However, they still expressed difficulties and challenges with maintaining boundaries between business and family.

The popular press and company websites report that promoters of some of the large family business houses have involved their daughters in the management and governance of key units. To mention a few, Preetha Reddy has succeeded her father's business of health service provider Apollo Hospitals. Sulajja Firodia Motwani is the joint managing director of two-wheeler firm Kinetic Motor Company, a position she inherited from her father. Roshni Nadar, at the age of 27, has taken over from her father as executive director and CEO of HCL Corporation. Her role is in the development of business in the investment company HCL Corp, while her father and founder of HCL, Shiv Nadar, has full discretion to take key decisions. Schauna Chauhan, eldest of the three daughters of Prakash Chauhan, joined as the CEO of Parle Agro after a split in the family business between her father and his brother. Pia Singh, daughter of KP Singh, Chairman DLF Group, manages her father's entertainment venture as well as handling the group's retail business as its managing director. KP Singh has recently announced that his son's two daughters would be his successors in the DLF Realty (The Economic Times, 2010). Priya Paul took the reins of Apeejay Surrendra Park Hotels after the untimely death of her father, Surrendra Paul.

These instances show that change is taking place, albeit slowly, in the transmission process of family business. It is noteworthy, however, that in most of these cases, either there are daughters only, or the son is very young to take charge of the business.

The Case Study

In view of the research objectives, the present case study concerns a daughter who is already engaged in the succession process through active management responsibilities within the firm and participation in the patrimony. The semi-guided interview was carried out with the daughter of the business founder using an interview guide provided by this book's editor and inspired by the literature review. The case is typical of a family business in India, status of women in the family, and the impact of parents' education and background on various aspects of family matters including patrimonial transfer.

BRIEF HISTORY OF THE FIRM

After graduating in business administration with specialization in international business from Germany, Raveena returned to India in 1996 and started assisting her father, Prakash, in the family business at the tender age of 22 years. The family business was jointly owned by Raveena's grandfather, his three brothers and their sons. Prakash, after getting his mechanical engineering degree from the UK went to Germany to work in a firm. In 1970 he returned to India to join his family business. While in Germany, Prakash had developed good contacts with a few firms and, utilizing these, he started his own company manufacturing machine tools in 1971, as a joint venture with a German firm, under the umbrella of the family business. The technology component was totally managed by the German counterpart. In 1985 the firm went public to bring in professionalization and to ensure expansion. The firm is now a leading public limited company in the region producing and marketing high-quality machine tools. Gradually, ownership disputes emerged in the family and finally the family business split in 1995. Just before the split, Prakash, in his early fifties, decided to expand his business and established a new firm as a private limited concern in 1994, manufacturing machine consumables in collaboration with the German firm. Studies (for example, Ramchandran, 2005) show that very few business firms in India have survived beyond the third generation and most face a split.

THE SUCCESSION PROCESS

After the split Prakash got full control over both the companies founded by him. Almost at the same time he had developed some health problems and needed someone who was trustworthy, competent, and technically qualified to assist him. Raveena, the younger of his two daughters, had been helping him unofficially in the management of the business since 1994 as a non-working director. Prakash inducted Raveena as a working director at the beginning of 1996 and the managing director of the new firm by the end of the year "on the basis of her competence and performance, and on recommendation of the German partner."

The succession was not a planned step-by-step process in the literal sense, though it was the transmission of part of the family business to the daughter with full autonomy. The succession turned out to be very smooth: (a) there were no other claimants, the elder daughter was married and settled abroad and had no interest in the family business, (b) the German partner had experience of her caliber and was convinced of her capabilities.

As Raveena puts it:

> *I just entered the family business by chance, initially I wanted to go back to Germany to complete my master's degree and then come back to join the family business but father had a major heart surgery and the business was being restructured after the split, so I decided to join my family business.*

With the end of the joint venture coming about in 2005, the business is now managed and controlled by Prakash with the help of an independent board of directors; however, Raveena and her mother are fully involved in the running of their business. Father and daughter own cross holdings in each other's companies. The two firms together employ about 150 people and supply machine tools and consumables to industries in India, Thailand, the United States of America (USA), Germany, and Iran.

The year 2006 ushered in another important process which could be seen as the *planning stage of patrimonial succession*. In 2006, Raveena was inducted to the board of directors of her father's company as a Director. During the interview she accepted that this was a step toward transmission of her father's business to her as his heir. Her induction to the board was to create an acceptance in the company for her. She showed confidence that there were no probabilities of any dispute with her sister as she was "married, settled abroad, and not interested in the family business."

THE PREDECESSOR–SUCCESSOR RELATIONSHIP

Raveena was educated and trained abroad and brought up in a very modern environment. She states that both her parents are educated and open-minded. Her ancestral family has been in business for the last three generations and therefore it can be said that she has inherited business traits in her blood. However, Raveena "would not have joined the family business if there was no split." She did not like the manner in which the business was managed by the family.

Raveena has an excellent relationship with her father. She assists her father in his business and takes his advice whenever she needs it. Prakash, as a concerned father, keeps a constant eye on her business and continuously advises her on technical and other aspects of the business. She quipped, "people have a strong bias against my education, they think I am not qualified enough because I am not an engineer." However, she believes that her training in business administration and international business overcomes the lack of technical knowledge.

The generational differences are visible in the father–daughter duo personalities. In Raveena's words: "My father is an excellent engineer and is a pioneer of a brand of machine tools. He is passionate about how to make the machine perfectly." Raveena is dynamic, modern, and looks at the business in a more commercial way; her first priority is profit. In managerial style, her father is compassionate and employee-oriented, whereas Raveena is more concerned about the work and productivity.

Raveena and her parents believe that daughters have different bonding experiences with fathers than the sons. "Daughters are less aggressive, more understanding, and empathetic than the sons." However, she is an exception in the extended family as being the only daughter to succeed her father.

Discussions and Conclusions

The case study has been analyzed using the multidimensional model of succession in family businesses proposed by Barbot et al. (2004). Table 2.1 presents a discussion on father–daughter succession in the context of the variables in a multidimensional model framework. Table 2.2 summarizes the cultural context of India and its impact on succession process in the present case study.

Table 2.1 Multidimensional analysis of father–daughter succession

Links	
Manager–firm link	• Strong autonomy
Father–daughter link	• Very strong closeness • Owner–manager relationship favored
Successor–firm link and motivations	• Attachment with father • Interest for the firm • Capacities, formation, experience within the firm • Willingness to ensure the continuity of the firm
Stages	
Planning	• Managerial transfer with planning of patrimonial transfer
Choice of successor	• Natural successor as sibling disinterested in family business
Education of successor	• Bachelor in management • Work experience in the family firm
Strategy to guarantee the passing on of the firm	• Commitment to a strategy of high visibility • Proactive: initiated by the father–founder
Entry of successor	• Progressive
Disengagement of founder	• Progressive
Managerial transfer	• Progressive
Patrimonial transfer	• Underway

Source: Adapted from Multidimensional Model (Barbot et al., 2004)

THE SOCIO-CULTURAL CONTEXT

At the onset, the case is no exception to the findings of other researchers that family businesses normally avoid succession planning. Raveena too happened to enter the business "by default".

The case study manifests the Indian culture of deep family bonding. Raveena joined her father's business to provide him with support during his sudden illness. Although she maintained that her father never showed any bias toward her being a daughter, it cannot be pre-empted that the situation would have been the same if she had a brother. Also, the married daughter is not engaged in the family business and is not expected to show interest, since as per Indian culture after marriage, the daughter goes to another family.

Another very important finding of the case study is the impact of *parents' education* on decision making. Her parents have never made her believe that she is any less than a son. Blotnick (1984) has come up with several cases of daughters who have successfully managed to take over from their fathers; he attributes this success to good family communication and mentoring by their fathers.

Summarizing her experience in the business world, Raveena emphatically says:

> *There is a strong gender bias all over the world and it is not peculiar to India. In the beginning people (clients, vendor, employees) did not accept that a young woman could run a machine business.*

They expected her to run a "softer" business. She shared an incident: "When I accompanied father for the first time for a business deal abroad, the client told his assistant to give some chocolates to the baby." But she proved herself during the deal and later developed very good relations with that client. Over the last 14 years she has created a niche for herself and has earned the confidence of his clients, vendors, and employees. However, at 36, Raveena is single because she feels "most men are intimidated" by a successful woman.

Table 2.2 Impact of socio-cultural dimensions on father–daughter succession in India

Socio-cultural Dimensions	Impact on Succession
Joint family culture	Discontinued studies to join business due to father's illness
Patriarchal society	Initially father did not look at her as the potential successor
Married daughter belongs to a different family	Married daughter not seen as successor and not expected to lay claim
Gender discrimination	Clients thought she was in wrong type of business Employees thought she was working "till she got married"
Education	Well-educated parent, therefore no discrimination in the family
Social hierarchy	Respects her father's opinions and advice as he is more experienced, which in other cultures may be taken as interference

Source: Authors' analysis of case study entrepreneur on basis of macro social variables

To conclude, it can be said that a new wave of healthy approaches toward female descendents in the family has begun which is likely to change the face of family business in the future. Hollander (1990) points out that family businesses have the potential to be especially productive environments for women. However, as carriers of family culture and processes that may contain gender bias, they can also be the last bastion of resistance to cultural change.

References

Arnold, F. 1996. *Son Preference in South Asia*. Paper presented at the International Union for the Scientific Study of Population (IUSSP) Seminar on Comparative Perspectives on Fertility Transition in South Asia, Islamabad, 17–20 December.

Arnold, F. 1997. *Gender Preferences for Children: Findings from the Demographic and Health Surveys*. Paper prepared for the 23rd General Population Conference of the International Union for the Scientific Study of Population (IUSSP), Beijing, 11–17 October.

Barbot, M.C., Bayad, M. and Bourguiba, M. 2004. *Transmission, des PME Familiales: Etude Exploratoire de la Relève Père-Fille en Tunisie*. Actes du Séminaire 'l'Entrepreneuriat en Tunisie, Quelles Recherches? Quelles Formations?', ENIT, Tunis, 29–30 April.

Bhattacharyya, R. 2007. *Road Blocks in Enhancing Competitiveness in Family-Owned Business*. Paper presented at Conference on Global Competition & Competitiveness of Indian Corporate. Available at: http://dspace.iimk.ac.in/bitstream/2259/518/1/623-629+.pdf [accessed: 7 July 2010].

Blotnick, S. 1984. The Case of the Reluctant Heirs. *Forbes*, 134, 180.

Business Today. 1997. *India's Fifty Business Families*. BusinessToday.com, August 22, p. 218.

Chrisman, J., Chua, J. and Sharma, P. 1998. Important Attributes of Duccessors in Family Businesses: An Exploratory Study. *Family Business Review*, 11(1), 19–34.

Das, G. 2000. *India Unbound: The Social and Economic Revolution from Independence to the Global Information Age*. New York: Anchor.

Das Gupta, M. 1987. Selective Discrimination against Female Children in Rural Punjab, India. *Population and Development Review*, 13(1), 77–100.

D'Cruz, N.K. 2003. *Constraints on Women Entrepreneurship Development in Kerala: An Analysis of Familial, Social, and Psychological Dimensions*. Kerala Research Programme on Local Level Development, Centre for Development Studies, Thiruvananthapuram, Discussion Paper [53]. Available at: http://www.esocialsciences.com/data/articles/Document1138200590.5478479.pdf [accessed: 8 July 2010].

Ganesan, S. 2003. *Status of Women Entrepreneurs in India*. New Delhi: Kanishka Publications.

Government of India. 2001. *Census of India 2001*. Government of India, Ministry of Home Affairs. Available at: http://www.censusindia.gov.in/ [accessed: 8 July 2010].

Hofstede, G. 1991. *Cultures and Organizations: Software of the Mind, Intercultural Cooperation and its Importance for Survival*. London: McGraw-Hill International (UK) Ltd.,London.

Hollander, B.S. 1990. Women, Family Culture, and Family Business. *Family Business Review*, 3(2), 139–151.

Jaffe, D.T. and Brown, F.H. 2003. When Succession Crosses Genders. *Family Business Magazine*. Available at: http://www.dennisjaffe.com/articles/WhenSuccessionCrossesGenders.pdf [accessed: 7 July 2010].

Khaleej Times Online. 2009. *The Continuous, Growing Role of Women in Indian Family Business*. December 3. Available at: http://www.khaleejtimes.com/biz [accessed: 8 July 2010].

Kluckhohn, F. and Strodtbeck, F. 1961. *Variations in Value Orientations*. Evanston: Row, Peterson.

Lalitha Rani, D. 1996. *Women Entrepreneurs*. New Dehli: APH Publishing Corporation.

Manimala, M.J. 2002. *India Report 2002*. Global Entrepreneurship Monitor (GEM) and Indian Institute of Management Bangalore. Available at: http://www.gemconsortium.org/download.asp?fid=298 [accessed: 7 July 2010].

Mutharayappa, R., Choe, M., Arnold, F. and Roy, T. K. 1997. *Son Preference and Its Effect on Fertility in India*. National Family Health Survey Subject Reports, International Institute for Population Sciences (Mumbai, India) and East-West Center Program on Population (Honolulu, Hawaii, U.S.A.),

No. 3, March, 1–35. Available at: http://www2.eastwestcenter.org/pop/misc/subj-3.pdf [accessed: 8 July 2010].

Naskar, S.N. 1996. *Foreign Impact on Indian Life and Culture (c. 326 B.C. to c. 300 A.D.)*. New Delhi: Abhinav Publications.

Pawar, S. 2009. *Family Business; Has a Future in India?* Sterling Institute of Management Studies, National Centre for Rural Development (NCRD) [online, 26 June 2009]. Available at: http://www.scribd.com/doc/16691629/Family-Business-in-India [accessed: 8 July 2010].

Ramachandran, K. 2005. *Indian Family Businesses: Their Survival Beyond Three Generations*. Working Paper, Indian School of Business, Hyderabad.

Sharma, D.D. and Dhameja, S.K. 2002. *Women and Rural Entrepreneurship*. Chandigarh: Abhishek Publications.

Vera, C.F. and Dean, M.A. 2005. An examination of the challenges daughters face in family business succession. *Family Business Review*, 18(4), 321–346.

Walokar, D.M. 2001. *Women Entrepreneurs*. New Dehli: Himalaya Publishing House.

Watts, G. and Tucker, J. 2004. A Systernic View of the Succession Process. *Families in Business*, May–June, 14, 16–17.

Note

The authors had a very tough time in finding a daughter–successor in a family business. Many of the instances mentioned in literature review were approached but they did not cooperate, mainly on the grounds that they were only managing the business and that they were not the successor in the family business. The authors approached various government bodies such as the Ministry of Micro, Small and Medium Industries and District Industry Centres to get the contacts of female entrepreneurs who have inherited businesses from their fathers. The government agencies held no such database but they helped by providing data of small- and medium-sized enterprises operating in the country. The authors contacted a large number of such entrepreneurs and inquired about their succession plans. Here, one interesting fact to be mentioned is that many of these entrepreneurs retorted by saying "why would their daughter take over their business? At best she would own her husband's business." This finding is very much in line with the literature on Indian cultural ethos and succession system. Finally, the Indian Industries Association (IIA) helped us by providing information about a Kanpur-based firm which was jointly managed by father and daughter. They passed on the contact numbers and names of the owners (names have been changed at the request of the respondent). The authors deeply acknowledge the support provided by all the agencies and especially by IIA and the respondent entrepreneur for her cooperation.

CHAPTER 3

Lebanon: Father–Daughter Succession in Family Business within a Middle Eastern Culture

JANINE SABA ZAKKA AND JOSIANE FAHED-SREIH

Literature Review and Authors' Commentary

A family business is usually established and owned by a member of or the whole family. It is financed by the family, and managed by family members, which creates interdependence between the family and business. Succession in a family business is an important process needed to maintain the continuity of the family in the ownership of the business. Family relations, culture, and traditions affect and sometimes constrain the succession process. This case study presents an overview of the culture and business laws in Lebanon and the Arab world that govern the work of females, and the effect of the country and region's culture and laws on the female role in leading a family business. As a result, the father–daughter succession process is described in the context of the above factors. Two cases that describe father–daughter succession in a small family business and a big family business transferred into a family-owned corporation are used to demonstrate the succession process to a daughter. These studies show the importance of the continuity of the family business, and the social, cultural, family, and internal business factors that face a daughter when she takes over the business.

Historic and Demographic Review on Lebanon

Lebanon, a small country located on the eastern coast of the Mediterranean Sea, does not possess natural resources; hence services and agriculture are major sectors in the country. The Lebanese people have practiced entrepreneurship since the Phoenician traders who sailed from the Lebanese shores to sell their goods in different countries around the Mediterranean. Throughout its history, Lebanon has suffered from frequent invasions and civil wars that drove the Lebanese to seek safety and financial refuge in different countries. Lebanese immigrants reached the Americas in the 1900s where they established their own family businesses to earn a living for the family.

Since Lebanon is a small country, most industries are dominated by family businesses which constitute 86 percent of the private sector, and account for 1.06 million of 1.24 million jobs (Fahed-Sreih, 2006).

Family businesses are distributed among the different sectors in Lebanon in the following ratios (Fahed-Sreih, 2006):

Agriculture	60%
Manufacturing	53%
Trade and Services	62%
Lebanese Banks	43%
Operating Banks	24%

It should be noted that the banking sector employs 29 percent of the working labor in Lebanon. Being the major type of business, the contribution of family business to the Gross Domestic Product (GDP) in Lebanon by industry sector is as follows:

Agriculture	8%
Manufacturing	16%
Banking Sector	67%
Construction	9%

Effect of Arab and Lebanese Cultures on Working Women

Most Arab countries are governed by Islamic law (Sharia), which imposes certain practices on women especially in areas of inheritance, divorce, marriage, and child custody rights (Jamali et al., 2005). Traditionally, females in most Arab societies are viewed in the context of traditional roles of mothers and home caretakers who are not allowed to work outside the home. In some Arab communities women have to be accompanied by a male relative if they are to establish their own business (Charbaji, 2009) and they have limited access to credit.

Lebanon is an Arab country in the Middle East, and is affected by the culture of the region concerning the treatment of women and their role in society. Women are faced with the influence of laws set by the government, the influence of religious traditions, and the influence of the family and the local community. The Lebanese society is a mixture of 17 religious sects divided between Muslims and Christians. Due to this social diversity and Lebanon's openness to the west, women in Lebanon have been allowed to assume functions outside the context of their homes. Nevertheless, religious leaders set laws that govern the lives of the majority of the Lebanese people. These laws are unfair to women in some sects in the areas of inheritance, work, and marriage. Men are considered the head of the family and society. As a result, some Lebanese women face restrictions on their behavior and they have to assume their traditional role of caretakers at home (Jamali et al., 2005).

On the other hand, the migration of Lebanese men during the civil war to the Arab Gulf countries, North America, and Europe, and the economic condition prevailing in the country resulted in a shortage in the working force that was compensated for by introducing women into jobs that are traditionally occupied by males. As a result, there was an increase in the enrollment of women in higher education institutions. At the Lebanese American University, for example, females are approximately 49 percent of the student body.

With Lebanese women pursuing higher education, the number of women in employment increased. Nevertheless, Jamali et al. (2005) state that Lebanese woman managers feel that they are marginalized and excluded from corporate developmental assignments and training which are provided exclusively for males. In addition, the culture of many organizations does not accept gender interaction (Ibid.).

Lebanese law concerning women's rights to education, health, and law was recently modified. The official report on follow-up of the implementation of the Beijing Platform for Action (1995) and the outcome of the twenty-third special session of the General Assembly (2000), by the National Commission for Lebanese Women states the following progress in the areas of women and education, health, and law:

- Officially, women are treated equally with men as far as their legal competence to enter into contracts and administer their property is concerned.
- Under the Trade Act, as amended, women have the right to enter into contracts involving credit, real estate, and other property. They may also engage in commercial transactions without spousal permission and in their own name. Allowances and end-of-service benefits are equal for men and women.
- Women may dispose of their possessions without male intervention. They therefore sell, buy, and relinquish such possessions, whether they became theirs before or after marriage, without the prior consent of a spouse, father, or legal guardian.
- Women are equal with men before the courts. Legal proceedings may therefore be brought by or against them and they may also lodge complaints in their own name. Women have the right to testify before courts and government institutions and their testimony receives the same consideration as that of men.
- Lebanese law makes no distinction between women and men in matters of loans and mortgages.

(NCLW, 2004:8)

Nevertheless, Lebanese women are still faced by glass ceilings and lower pay than men in some business sectors, and very low participation in public institutions: there are five women out of 128 members of the parliament, two women out of 736 heads of municipal councils, no woman yet as head of the Engineers' Union, no woman yet as head of the Physicians' Order, one woman was elected twice as president of the Pharmacists' Order, one woman was elected once as the president of the Dentists' Order, and this year a woman was elected for the first time as president of the Bar Association. However, this year, the Lebanese Government suggested a 20 percent participation quota for women on municipal councils. This suggestion is not yet adopted by the Lebanese members of parliament as a law. In addition, The HDR (2008) estimates that the economic activity rate of women in 2007 was 32.4 percent as compared to 41 percent for men.

Female Entrepreneurship in Lebanon

Lebanese women with university degrees, who also gain experience in the market through employment, are qualified to start and run their own businesses. In addition, the limiting factors that women encounter through employment drive them into starting up their businesses. Jamali (2008) reported that gender and pay discrimination and glass ceilings drove women to establish their own businesses. In addition, women entrepreneurs benefit from the time flexibility they enjoy as entrepreneurs to take care of their families and thus find a balance between work and family (Ibid.).

It was noticed that most female entrepreneurs finance their business by the use of family funds due to lack of support from private and governmental financial resources (Jamali, 2008; Weeks, 2009). Weeks (2009), reports that self-financing hinders female entrepreneurship business growth. Weeks (2009) reports that 51 percent of the female entrepreneurs in her study sought external financing, but most of them were denied financing from a formal financial institution. A report by the IFC (2007) showed that borrowing by Lebanese female entrepreneurs is 35 percent of the total borrowings as compared to 60 percent for the Arab World. In addition, the IFC (2007) noted that the majority of Lebanese female entrepreneurships are clustered in the services and small trade industries and that they have smaller-size businesses than males.

Succession in Family Business

Family business in Lebanon and the Arab World is believed to be a way to enhance a family's social standing rather than a money generating activity (Fahed-Sreih, 2006).

Families in Lebanon are experiencing greater geographical dispersion, more freedom of choice, and changing gender roles in the family and the business. Choosing among heirs used to be done in a non-professional way. The eldest son, who might not be qualified, takes over the business and leads it to financial losses and in some cases to bankruptcy. As a result, succession in some cases has caused tension and separation among family members and even brothers.

Family companies devise policies stipulating that family members who desire to work in the business should work outside the family company prior to joining the business as this allows them to understand how they stand in the job market and gives them the experience of being an employee. This would help them tremendously in knowing how to treat their own employees once recruited into their family companies.

Father–Daughter Succession in a Family Business

In the past when a daughter, especially in the Middle East, showed interest in the family business, she was directly discouraged as the business is usually inherited by males. Things are changing nowadays but not to a great extent. Some families, depending on their culture, may include females in the business in ownership and to a lesser extent in leading positions. In a study conducted at the Institute of Family and Entrepreneurial Business at the Lebanese American University on whether females can take ownership positions in the business, more than 50 percent said yes (Fahed-Sreih, 2008). But moving from verbal approval to reality is a different issue. A majority also showed tolerance to females taking leading positions in the family business. However, wage differentials are always an issue in the Middle East, but the gap narrows as females go up the ladder in the company (Fahed-Sreih and Sharifi, 2009).

The Case Study

Succession from father to daughter is presented as cases in two family businesses: a small recently established business, and a large old family-owned corporation.

A SMALL BUSINESS

"Le Blanc Catering" (LBC) was established in the summer of 2008. The family owns 65 percent of the company and a partner owns 35 percent. The partner used to work in a small catering firm, and always had the ambition of establishing his own business but did not have enough financial resources. The chance came when he met the head of the family. The head of the family liked the business, and after evaluating its future prospects, was convinced that it is a good investment. He offered to finance a new catering business to be established between him and the caterer who would become a partner. The partner would have a share of the firm and also would be the manager as he is an expert in the field. The head of the family manages the finances and the accounting records of the business.

In 2010, the head of the family had health problems, and hence he planned his succession with his partner. The business was growing and he wanted someone from the family who is trustworthy to handle the details of the daily work. The head of the family belongs to the old school that believes that women are incapable of handling any kind business. But, since the family had only girls and no boys, the plan was that one of his daughters would join the firm at entry level to learn the business just like a fresh graduate. The daughter holds a BA and an MA in Education with no experience in the catering field. She worked in an educational institution for two years. The family encouraged the decision, and there was no rivalry from other family members. In addition, the daughter's fiancé encouraged her to take this big step in her life by joining LBC and leading it to more growth. The daughter, who likes the catering business, after thorough thinking, quit her job and joined LBC. Now she feels that the business is her home.

THE SUCCESSION PROCESS

When the daughter joined the business, she went through a training process supervised by the partner who welcomed her presence in the business. At first, she observed the employees to learn their jobs, then moved through the different departments and worked with the managers to learn all aspects of the work. First she started learning the executive assistant work, moved on to the assistant operation manager, then to the operation manager, then to the purchasing and public relations and marketing departments.

Nevertheless, the training process was not easy for the daughter. One challenge was that the employees, who are non-family members, were hesitant in providing information about their jobs because they felt threatened that the daughter might take their jobs, although this is not why she joined the business. Other employees would not voluntarily provide any information or instructions to the daughter unless she asked about all the details of their jobs. Another challenge was that she had to handle the different personalities, moods, and age groups of the employees and managers, which took a lot of effort. The daughter believes that the negative attitudes of the staff are not due to gender issues, but only due to job insecurity on the part of the staff members. In addition, the father is not working in the business anymore which reduces the conflict between him and his daughter. The father does not interfere with the training of his daughter; he refuses to help her even if she asks for his help.

The daughter is already planning her future role in the business which she is learning by training on the job from the lower to the higher levels in the business. She knows that once her training is complete, she will have full understanding of the business and will be able to assume her role as a major owner and manager of the business. She also believes that in the meantime she has to work on her relations with the staff of the business to gain their trust, respect, and cooperation as the non-family employees should feel that they have secure jobs with a promising future. At the same time, the daughter accepts her father's authority and refusal to help her in her initial steps in the business, although she missed getting some training and advice from her father at least at the initial stage of her entry into the business.

The daughter sees the business growing every year which requires more staff. She believes that more than one strategy is needed and innovation is a necessity to face the competition in the market. The partner is very cooperative with the daughter and the employees. The partner respects the daughter and treats her equally.

A LARGE BUSINESS

The company will be called ALJ to protect confidentiality. The information about this company is obtained through interviews with the current owner, and a previous research paper about the company entitled "Father, Daughter and Grand Children: The Growth of a Family Business" (Ghattas, 2007).

ALJ was established in Beirut by the father in 1945 as a customs clearing firm. Over the years this family business grew to become an international transport company. The daughter, who is an only child, took over the family business after the death of her father and led the company from a single ownership to a family business and then to a shareholding corporation. The firm currently employs more than 150 employees, around ten of whom are related to the owner. The firm, under the leadership of the daughter, expanded its activities to include sea freight, air freight, land transport, customs clearance, projects and heavy lifts, packing and moving, and warehouse and distribution. The firm has branches in Lebanon, Cyprus, Syria, Iraq, Jordan, Turkey, and Bulgaria.

THE SUCCESSION PROCESS

The father, who was the founder of the business, had an authoritarian style of management. This resulted in a low feeling of belonging to the business by the employees, which led to an atmosphere of ambition, but with loyalty to oneself, and aiming at material success. Nevertheless, the father, with his autocratic management style, was a fair and generous man. He paid his employees well and he drove the business to success and growth.

When the father got sick, he started planning for his succession. As he had an only child, a daughter, he chose her to be his successor. The father belonged to a religious and social environment that would not allow and accept a girl who is an only child to inherit from her father, and definitely would reject her running the business. The father had full confidence in his daughter, and hence challenged his environment and appointed his daughter as manager of the firm. His autocratic personality blocked all protests and challenges from his environment.

The daughter started working in the business after she graduated from university; she started as a department clerk and then climbed the ladder, thus gaining information on all aspects of the business, in order to be ready to take over after father's death. The daughter generated a family atmosphere in the business. She is described by the employees as a modest and polite person who is always ready to help them in any matter. She cares for the employees. This attitude by the daughter created a feeling of belonging among the employees and increased their loyalty to the daughter and the business. This was a main factor that enabled the daughter to expand the business further on the international stage. The daughter's husband supported her and helped her in implementing her management style as he had a personality similar to his wife and had the same educational background.

With the expansion and diversity of the business both nationally and internationally, the daughter faced serious competition and knew that she and her husband had to take measures to face it. They felt that they could not manage the business by themselves, and at that time the eldest daughter of the family was not interested in joining the business, and the son was not yet ready for such a job. Here the decision to incorporate the business was made.

The daughter, her husband, and their three children remain the main owners of the business. A minority group of family members were admitted as shareholders due to the need for additional financing and expertise to help in the management of the business. At this stage the son was not yet admitted to the business. His parents would not allow him to assume a full-time position until he completed his education at a reputable university in order to be qualified to face the challenges in the market. They refused to give him privileges just because he is the son of the owners. They wanted him to earn his position in the business.

The daughter in this case had the support of the family members and of her husband. With her intelligence and character she gained the trust and support of the employees who not only did not feel threatened, they felt secure in a family atmosphere.

Discussion and Conclusion

Family business is common in many countries, especially in the Middle East. This type of business is owned, operated, and financed by the family. Succession in a family business is maintained by transferring the ownership of the business to a next generation family member, usually a male.

Female entrepreneurship and its challenges has been the subject of previous literature. The issue of working females is handled differently by cultures. While working women are accepted by some cultures, they are not appreciated or accepted by others. Factors such as religion, traditions, and country-specific laws determine the boundaries within which women can work.

Females in Lebanon have come a long way to reach their present status of having the right to work, to own a business, to be equal to males by law, and the right to education. Hence the number of women earning university degrees and entering the business world as employees and entrepreneurs has increased. With this changing role of women, succession in family business took a new direction. Daughters are qualified to be entrusted to run the family business after their fathers, and they are doing their job in a very efficient and successful way. But this is mostly the case if the family does not have male heirs.

The two cases presented in this study are representative of succession in a family business to the daughters. The two women were chosen to take over the family business after their fathers because there were no male heirs in the family which agrees with Fahed-Sreih (2008) and they are trusted by their fathers. The succession planning was done because in both cases the fathers were sick.

This study confirms the effect of the Lebanese culture and laws on female entrepreneurs. Daughters inherited the business of their fathers in the absence of males. They are allowed by the Lebanese laws to lead a business with all the legal requirements of this job. However, the daughters had to adopt a management style that would satisfy their environment in order to gain the trust that would provide them with the support to manage the business.

Culturally, in the Middle East, daughters do not try to be pushy with their fathers, as their brothers might do. They try to streamline the company by being tolerant and even fond of their fathers' authority. The desire to serve their family, which they usually do outside the family business, is the motivating drive and factor that goes beyond gaining control and power. So, daughters look at ways in which they can gain trust which is considered the way to give them control in their family enterprises. Daughters feel responsible and dutiful to their fathers, and to their families, when they take over. What is important to note is that trust and respect are at the root of success of daughters taking over from their fathers.

In the LBC small business case, the daughter was appointed as the successor but had to learn directly from the leader of the business and the other managers and staff before going to office. The learning phase had to take place in order to develop the skills of the future successor and to shape behaviors in the appropriate and required manner. She was accepted by the family members.

On the other hand, ALJ which represents the large organization, can provide various positions for family members who can grow in the system of their organization, and assume higher positions later if they are qualified. A system of policies and procedures is usually in place in large organizations to ensure proper functioning. At ALJ this system was not present. The father insisted on giving the business to his daughter and he made sure that all legal and religious barriers were surpassed so that his daughter would become the CEO of the business.

Most family members who are expected to become future successors need to be shown what is expected from them. Leaders who are in office and in power should show and teach their future successors the behaviors that are most crucial to their success and to their organization's success. The daughter and her husband at ALJ apply this opinion to their children. Family members have the option of getting to the top because they inherited their position. Hence at ALJ, a family company, the daughter and her husband believe that to lead their businesses professionally and to avoid problems that might challenge their business, they should employ their family members in positions that they find suitable and compliant with their qualifications and then train them to assume more responsibilities in their family companies and let them earn their position through hard work.

The limitations of this case study are that it discusses two female entrepreneurships and the lack of male heirs in the families in both cases. Although female entrepreneurships in Lebanon are common, not all function smoothly as seen by the two examples in this study. Some female entrepreneurships face pressures from family members, or from their environments, or suffer from financial problems with no support from the families. In addition, it is not evident whether the same fathers mentioned in the cases of this study would transfer the business to the daughters in the presence of qualified sons.

It is recommended that future research on father–daughter succession includes case studies on families that have both sons and daughters in order to monitor and analyze the decision of the father, and to study a bigger number of female entrepreneurships to obtain information that can be generalized to the country.

References

Charbaji, A. 2009. The Effect of Globalization on Commitment to Ethical Corporate Governance and Corporate Social Responsibility in Lebanon. *Social Responsibility Journal*, 5(3), 376–387.

Fahed-Sreih, J. 2006. *Handbook of Family Business and Business Consultation: A Global Perspective*. Binghamton: International Business Press.

Fahed-Sreih, J. 2008. Distinctive Trends, Challenges, Problems and Opportunities facing Family Businesses in the Middle East, in *Family Business Models from Around the World*, compendium on family owned businesses — Culturally Sensitive Models of Family Business in the Middle East, edited by V. Gupta. Hyderabad: The Icfai University Press.

Fahed-Sreih, J. and Sharifi, H. 2009. Wage Discrimination in Lebanon as related to Experience and Education: Is it Allocative or Evaluative? *International Journal of Business and Emerging Markets*, 2(2), 131–146.

Ghattas, R. 2007. Father, Daughter and Grand Children: The Growth and Survival of a Family Business. *International Journal of Business and Economics*, 6(1), 88–95.

Human Development Report (HDR). 2008. *Gender Related Development Index*. New York: United Nations Development Program.

International Finance Corporation (IFC). 2007. *GEM Country Brief–Lebanon 2007*. International Finance Corporation, World Bank Group, Washington, DC.

Jamali, D. 2008. Constraints and Opportunities Facing Women Entrepreneurs in Developing Countries—A Relational Perspective. *Gender in Management: An International Journal*, 24(4), 232–251.

Jamali, D., Sidani, Y. and Safieddine, A. 2005. Constraints Facing Working Women in Lebanon: An Insider View. *Women in Management Review*, 30(8), 581–594.

National Commission for Lebanese Women (NCLW). 2004. *Official Report on Follow Up of the Implementation of the Beijing Platform for Action (1995) and the Outcome of the Twenty-Third Special Session of the General Assembly 2000*. Beirut, Lebanon.

Weeks, J.R. 2009. Practitioner Section Women Business Owners in the Middle East and North Africa: A Five Country Research Study. *International Journal of Gender and Entrepreneurship*, 1(1), 77–85.

CHAPTER

4 Malaysia: The Challenge of Father–Daughter Succession in Malaysian Family Business

NORASHFAH H. YAAKOP YAHAYA AL-HAJ AND
AHMAD HJ. ZAINUDDIN

Values Guiding Malaysian Culture in Business

Since the beginning of its history, Malaysia has been a meeting place for a diverse range of cultures and religions. As a result of these external influences, a new unified but distinguished Malay culture has emerged. Contemporary Malaysia represents a unique fusion of Malay, Chinese, and Indian traditions, creating a pluralistic and multicultural nation that has its character strongly rooted in social harmony, religion, and pride in its ancestral background. With such a rich cultural heritage, acquiring the relevant skills and cultural knowledge in order to conduct business in Malaysia is crucial to success.

Following years of confrontation in search of independence, Malaysia was established in September 1963 through the union of the Independent Federation of Malay, the former British colonies of Singapore and the East Malaysian States of Sabah and Sarawak. Over the last few decades the country has evolved from a successful producer of raw materials to a multi-sector economy. Today, Malaysia offers a unique blend of old traditional culture and new technological innovations. As the Malaysian market continues to develop and prosper, it is becoming increasingly valuable for those entering into business in Malaysia to be aware of the cultural dimensions that shape the fabric of this country

A study by Best and Williams (1997) and one by Ismail and Ibrahim (2008) show that some women leaders assume traditional roles such as "mother" and "teacher" so that society will be more tolerant and accepting of their leadership. The theory of social conditioning explains that because society conditions women to be gentle and nurturing, they behave as such. Bruni et al. (2004) acknowledge that women often have to resort to alternative leadership styles possibly because social expectation makes it difficult for them to wield formal authority in organizations. Having said that, there are women leaders (typified by the "boss" personality) who are not afraid to exercise their formal authority. This is quite likely in the Malaysian society which is moderately masculine (Hofstede, 1998) and thus allows some degree of gender role equality.

Malaysian women's participation in commerce may exist in any of the four categories of employment status, that is, as an employer, an employee, an "own-account" worker, or an unpaid family worker. As indicated in a Malaysian Labour Force Report (Department of Statistics, 2004:44), out of the total working female population in 2003, 77.5 percent were paid employees, 11.7 percent were own-account workers and 9.6 percent were unpaid family workers. Only 1.2 percent were categorized as employers. For men, the percentages were higher for the employer and own-account worker categories but lower for employees. The fact that the number of unpaid female family workers is almost five times higher than it is for males is particularly disturbing. One possible reason for this is that Malaysian women are being exploited and made to work for free by their own family members.

Commentary on the Culture of Family Business in Malaysia

Since independence, most Malaysian companies are controlled by foreigners from European countries, particularly the UK. However, the trends of family businesses have now also evolved to local participation amongst Malaysians. Family control in Malaysia increased from 57.7 percent to 67.2 percent. To illustrate, 67.2 percent of shares are owned by family firms, 37.4 percent are in the hands of only one dominant shareholder and 13.4 percent are state controlled (Ibrahim and Samad, 2010). Thus, family controlled seems to dominate and control the Malaysian capital market. The list of the 40 richest Malaysians in 2009 was dominated by family (as issued by the Malaysian Business in the February 2009 edition). From the list, 28 out of the 40 richest people are family based and account for 70 percent of the top 40 (Ibid.).

Family businesses, whether large or small, play an important role in economic development. During the last decade the combination of economic development, new technologies, and increasing market opportunities, plus the participation of a new generation of family members, have together contributed to the increased vitality of family businesses. They have become more sophisticated about management. There is an increased awareness of the challenges and opportunities that exist in balancing the business requirements and opportunities against the family needs and wants when faced with structural pressures in the reality of the business environment. The family system puts priority on emotional concerns, family needs and maintaining stability. The business system puts priority on business performance, business demands, and managing change. What needs to be put in place is a parallel strategic planning process. This represents an important change in thinking about how families view themselves.

On the whole the family has certain core values. Thus, on the one hand, challenges come from how family businesses translate their core values into a management philosophy that meets the needs of the business, while on the other hand, strategic thinking for the business requires family commitment. Both family and business must share a common future vision. In order to be successful when formulating business development plans, family businesses must fit in with the family enterprise continuity plan. Few cases of family businesses provided in this chapter will highlight the firm, the succession process and the entrepreneur, the cultural dimensions and their role in father–daughter succession

A study on succession planning in Malaysian family firms and its implication on business performance found that preparedness of the successor/heir, family relationships, and planning and control activities contributed significantly to business performance (Ismail and Mahfodz, 2009). Previous research shows that there are ongoing issues for family firms, and succession planning is certainly one of the most critical issues in the operations and continuity of a family firm. However, relationships within the family are highly associated with firm performance most positively and significantly (Ibid.). It was also found that some forms of formal succession planning in many family firms in Malaysia do exist (Ibid.).

Case Study 1: Jalur Setia (M) Sdn Bhd

In this case study "Jalur Setia (M) Sdn Bhd" has been inherited by the owner's daughter, Mastura binti Najami. Jalur Setia is a company specialized in printing graphics, signboards, light box, exhibition billboard/backdrop, road signs, brass/bronze/aluminium/plastic signs, promotion items, poster, stickers cut, rubber stamp, lamp post banners, banners, and other advertising products, situated in Kota Kinabalu, Sabah, Malaysia. Jalur Setia (M) Sdn Bhd started as a small company in 2005 with a capitalization of RM 1,000,000. Despite being small, the company created a powerful competition with other non-Bumiputera companies in a similar business field. Nonetheless, the company remained strong due to its robust supply chain and its relationship amongst workers and business communities is the primary reason for its success today. In addition, support from the government to encourage business in Bumiputera companies plays a role in catalyzing operational success and independence for sustainable growth in Jalur Setia (M) Sdn Bhd. After more than five years of operation, Jalur Setia (M) Sdn Bhd's regular clients are mostly from government and government-linked agencies, that is, UMS, UiTM, JAKEL, MARA, FAMA, MRSM, and many others.

THE SUCCESSOR'S EDUCATIONAL BACKGROUND

The successor holds a degree in information engineering systems. She is the only daughter in the family but has other brothers. Recently, she has managed her father's company accounts as a family business. In terms of education, the highest qualification achieved amongst the siblings (herself and her older brother) is a Bachelor's degree from a local university. The relationships amongst the siblings have been close whether at the office or at home. At first, the daughter did not wish to enter her family business because she wanted to focus on her studies, but then she realized she would be chosen anyway to continue the business as a result of her qualifications and capability; for this reason she decided to learn from her father the practical ways of how to manage a business.

Along with informal and on-the-job training, she gained knowledge and experience from her father and brothers, making her more confident to manage the business herself. The most critical aspect of the business is managing the customers and suppliers. In a team atmosphere, they took the initiative to develop strong branding and positioned strategic planning for their products and services to the extent of seeking assistance from third parties such as consultants, employees, and clients. They believe family, client, and employees play an important role and influence in the family business that Mastura inherited. Mainly, she acquired the recipe and knowledge about the business through her father, even though her father does not have the highest education level; his extensive experiences in business are priceless. He always stresses the importance of communication with customers and develops strong bonding with them to the degree of some becoming very good friends.

Mastura, as the daughter–successor did not encounter serious difficulties during the transition process but, when she was a beginner, she was faced with difficulties in understanding the business route. A common problem encountered was in communication with clients. The method that was used in her family business is simple: if you are hard working and have a desire to learn about the business, then you are already in the business. As an example, her younger brothers (who are still in secondary school, and during their free time go to the office) at this time did not know about management and they started from the bottom. The styles of management she embodies are leadership skills, punctuality, hard work, and a friendly environment.

The strategies frequently used by the successor are maintaining good relationships with the clients, a desire to try, and a willingness to take risks in business. The reason she joined the business is because of the responsibility toward family. Since this business is the only source of finance for her family, they need to work hard and collaborate amongst themselves in a team atmosphere. For now, she still finds it difficult to deal with clients and is consistently learning to overcome her weaknesses. At times she prefers to handle the company accounts rather than dealing with the clients; however, this will not be a sustainable strategy to develop her family business. As such, she regularly seeks help from her father and brothers for decisions and advice related to clients.

As she sees it, the best thing that she is grateful for about being the successor is the liberty of managing through her instinct and way, and not being led by others. She started to become familiar with the entire financial source of the business during her university days. She exposed herself to such experiences during her semester breaks, when she worked at the office as usual which is doing the company account, as she herself continued to do the job after she graduated. At the stage of learning, she would also learn from other companies and gain experiences from them to improve her entrepreneurial skills. She discovered that such learning opportunities helped her when she assumed responsibilities within her father's business.

Mastura believes that most conflicts that arise between business and family can be settled at home. Even though they are busy in their daily life, at the end of the week they usually take part in family activities to strengthen ties between siblings. The family members have enlisted advice from experts on the way forward so as to plan for handing over from the founder to the successor. Mastura says, "One or more family members in the family firm, there are advantages and disadvantages, of course." In her opinion, it is good to let the child or family successors continue a family business because it is less risky, and more predictable and worthwhile in terms of ownership. All the effort and hard work will be protected and maintained by the family's own successors. However, it will be difficult if their child or other successors have their own interests and/or wants. From her personal advice, Mastura suggests that the predecessor should give the chance to his or her child so as to have their own experiences because later on he/she will realize their responsibility toward the predecessor on their own.

As Mastura noticed, difficulties faced by the successor usually originate from gender issues/power struggle issues/personal conflicts within the family; in contrast, the daughter–successor stated that no such things as gender or power struggle issues have happened. She says this is because they believe that this is for their whole family's engagement and future endeavors. Her father always said that all his effort is for his family. The only problem will be the expectations that the predecessor (her father) will dictate from his successors; this in itself can cause conflicts. So, in Jalur Setia (M) Sdn Bhd, Mastura's father revealed this through knowing and discussing how best the drivers of the company can work together effectively. Thus, there will be no issues of forcing his own child to do things his way, it's all about making decisions together; but for once, he will explicitly announce his wishes to each one of the children that he wants his children to continue what he did best before.

Mastura's father encouraged his children to be involved in the business by exposing them to the business world at a very young age so they would develop an interest in the dealings. Mastura agrees with this strategy, if predecessors have the intention of letting their children take over the business (just as her father did), because it will provide benefits in the long run, but it must be done from a very strategic point of view. Like herself, even though she was not fully equipped with knowledge about the business, at least she learned the traits in phases long enough for her to ready herself in creating a sustainable and smooth transition process. She stated that her experiences of being a daughter–successor and a women leader in the family firm are not very common in the Malaysian culture. But for herself, she respects all men as she respects her brothers and her father. The woman's life changes once she gets married because she has responsibilities toward her marriage. Men, on the other hand, need to work harder once they have their own family. However, in business, there are no such differences. As long as you work hard and have the desire, then you will get the benefits. On the aspect of her business future plans, she wants to expand her business by opening up a new branch in Sarawak in five years' time.

Case Study 2: Seri Optical House (M) Sdn Bhd

"Seri Optical House (M) Sdn Bhd" is managed by Ms Woo Xiao Cheng, appointed through the father–daughter succession concept. The company is an optical chain store specializing in frames, contact, and optical lenses, and is situated in Shah Alam, Selangor, Malaysia. The daughter–successor took over her family business because of the good relationship with her father whereby they can easily discuss the business. Her brother, who is a civil engineer, also helps her with family business operational issues. She decided to join the family business when she was in college, where she was given the chance to expand her family business even without a formal transmission plan agenda. Ironically, the chance came along when the family decided to open a new branch at Giant Hypermarket and needed a person to manage it; she was the one chosen. Because of that opportunity, eight years ago, she decided not to further her studies in the UK and instead to manage their second branch within Giant Hypermarket; up until now she has not faced any serious problems or obstacles in expanding the business.

The whole family discussed together a business expansion strategy before deciding to take the move of starting a new branch within the Giant Hypermarket and to appoint Ms Woo Xiao Cheng as the manager. She took up the offer with lots of motivation and seeks only family members' advice. She believes that to be successful a person must be committed, with an open heart to search, and able to face any problems—these are also the criteria of a successful successor. She also respects the opinion of experienced individuals, especially when being a junior in cases of making better decisions. Even before deciding to take over her family business, she sought advice from senior business players and believes that having proper qualifications is an important prerequisite. As she said, "Education is one of the best ways to help us to face the challenges in the competitive world." She will not compromise on not having a proper education as this will be the first stage of entering the business world. Nonetheless, in her understanding, there are two methods of adaptation to the family business; the first is to learn and start from the bottom up and the second is not to feel shy to ask around.

Ms Woo Xiao Cheng has been lucky not to have been faced with any serious challenges so far, and the plan to open a small business within Giant Hypermarket has been growing steadily. Her serious efforts are focused on trying to improve her business and to create more profit in addition to not compromising with building a strong customer base. So far, she deals with these challenges through self-learning: reading books, best practice gathering, and trying to see how others are doing in the same field, by being sincere and not cover charge her customer, always giving them good advice and, most importantly, by being hardworking.

Mostly, she enjoys the ride of being a successor of the family business. The conflict that arises between business and family is difficult, but someone has to make final decisions based on the best interest for the company. She gives this advice to any founder who wishes to plan the succession of one or more family members to be involved in the family business: to have a clear job scope for everyone and, no matter what happens, everybody has to sit down and discuss without any prejudice. In cases when conflict arises and oneis required to resolve it, a clear job scope and communication flow will assist employees with whom to refer to and discuss with, and whom to listen to—and who will make the final decision.

Sometimes conflicts will occur when both generations have grown up in a different environment with a different educational background. As in olden days, most of the businessmen enjoyed success as a result of their hard work and now the new generation believes in a different business strategy. The right time for the founder to step aside and make way for the next generation is only when the younger generation is mature enough to handle these problems and has the ability to expand and maintain profits for company. Ms Woo Xiao Cheng suggested that the founder has to trust the next generation and openly face changes and try to adapt and implement new ideas, as long it helps to improve the company. From her experience, she still thinks there are glass ceilings for women in most countries, but in the new generation she does not agree that we have to choose the successors according to gender, but rather according to their ability to handle challenges and bring the company to a better success, which is what matters the most.

References

Best, D.L. and Williams, J.E. 1997. Sex, Gender and Culture, in *Handbook of Cross-cultural Psychology*, Volume 3 Social Behavior and Applications (pp. 163–212), edited by J.W. Berry, M.H. Segall and C. Kagitcibasi. Needham Heights: Allyn and Bacon.

Bruni, A., Gherardi, S. and Poggio, B. 2004. Entrepreneur-Mentality, Gender and the Study of Women Entrepreneurs. *Journal of Organizational Change Management*, 17(3), 256–268.

Department of Statistics, Malaysia. 2004. *Labour Force Survey Report, Malaysia, 2003*. Putrajaya. p. 44.

Hofstede, G. 1998. *Masculinity and Femininity: The Taboo Dimension of National Cultures*. Thousand Oaks: Sage.

Ibrahim, H. and Samad, F.M.A. 2010. *Corporate Governance and Agency Costs: Evidence from Public Listed Family Firms in Malaysia*. Proceedings of the International Conference on Business and Economic Research (ICBER), Malaysia, 15–16 March, 2010. Available at: http://www.internationalconference.com.my/proceeding/icber_proceeding/PAPER_097_CorporateGovernance.pdf [accessed: 8 September 2010].

Ismail, M. and Ibrahim, M. 2008. Barriers to Career Progression Faced by Women: Evidence from a Malaysian Multinational Oil Company. *Gender in Management*, 23(1), 51–66.

Ismail, N. and Mahfodz, A.N. 2009. Succession Planning in Family Firms and its Implication on Business Performance. *Journal of Asia Entrepreneurship and Sustainability*, V(3), December.

CHAPTER 5

Pakistan: Father–Daughter Family Business Succession in Pakistan: A Case Study

SHEHLA RIZA ARIFEEN

Introduction

Family firms are an important part of Pakistan's economy. Nearly 80 percent of all listed companies on the stock exchange of Pakistan's largest city and commercial district, Karachi, having family involvement of some sort while almost all, unlisted (private) firms can be classified as family firms (Zaidi and Aslam, 2006). Succession is a critical issue in family firms (Handler, 1994) as it involves the transfer of leadership, thereby ensuring the continuity of family ownership (Davis, 1968). Though research on father–son succession in family business has been conducted in Pakistan (Afghan and Wiqar, 2007) no research has been carried out on father–daughter succession.

Literature Review

Within the area of family businesses, the topic of succession occupies approximately one-third of the family business literature (Sharma et al., 1996). Research has focused on succession planning as being crucial to the continuity of a business (Miller, 1993; Ocasio, 1999; Pitcher et al., 2000). Some studies show that few family firms survive more than one generation (Birley, 1986; Kets de Vries, 1993) with only 30 percent of family businesses surviving past the first generation (Beckhard and Dyer, 1983; Dyer, 1986). The literature suggests that succession is a course of action that encompasses many activities (Handler, 1994; Sharma et al., 2003). One of these is the continuous training of the successor from childhood to adult years (Sharma and Rao, 2000) including the absorption of information about the business during family discussions in the home (Cabrera-Suarez et al., 2001). The succession process is also described as incorporating sequence, timing, technique, and communication (Dyck et al., 2002). Sequence includes selection and training of successor and "ensuring the successor has the appropriate skills and experience to lead the organization in its next phase" (Dyck et al., 2002:144). Training helps in the transfer of firms' specific knowledge to successors by founders thereby maintaining competitive edge in family firms (Cabrera-Suarez et al., 2001).

Succession planning is the deliberate and formal process of transferring management control from one family member, the founder, to another family member, the successor (Sharma, 1997). While some literature stresses the importance of this formal process (Christensen, 1953; Trow, 1961; Ward, 1987) some academics suggest that succession planning is actually left to chance (Rue and Ibrahim, 1996; Leon-Guerrero et al., 1998; RoyNat Inc., 1998; Sharma et al., 2000). Sharma et al. (2003), drawing on the work of a number of academics (Handler and Kram, 1988; Harveston et al., 1997; Lansberg and Astrachan, 1994; Malone, 1989; Morris et al., 1997; Poza et al., 1997; Rubenson and Gupta, 1996) hypothesize that three factors aid in the succession or transfer of control in a family business. These are the influence of the incumbent's desire to keep the business in the family, the family's commitment to the business, and the propensity of a trusted successor to take over. Further they suggest that all three factors may be necessary to ensure succession, as they state:

> *Incumbents should avoid the delusion that the presence of a trusted successor is all that is required for succession. Without the wholehearted commitment of the incumbent (and the family) to the process, it may be better to plan to sell the business than to plan for the transfer of leadership to the next generation.*
>
> *(Sharma et al., 2003:11)*

The Context

Organizations are affected by the culture of the society in which they operate (Hofstede, 1984). In Pakistan, daughters' participation in family businesses or their succession in family businesses is affected by cultural factors. While family businesses may be the norm, due to the unique socio-cultural and religious environment, very few businesses include women in the family firm. Of the few women listed as directors or executives in family businesses, their role is largely confined to silent shareholder or non-active executives (Zaidi and Aslam, 2006). Women entrepreneurs do not enjoy the same opportunities as men due to the entrenched nature of roles based on traditions and socio-cultural values (Roomi and Parrot, 2008).

Gender role expectations are played out along traditional lines in Pakistan (Arifeen, 2008), men traditionally take up roles outside the home while women are restricted to work within it (Duncan et al., 1997). Of the few women who opt for participation in the workforce, the majority is restricted to working in the fields. Lack of higher education coupled with social stigma about working out of home results in few women entering office work either in clerical, managerial roles (Arifeen, 2010), or business. "The sons of the family are expected to act responsibly and to assume leadership when the time arrives, and the daughters are expected to be married off and honorably start a new life in a new home" (Afghan and Wiqar, 2007:9). A further issue that conspires against women in family firms in Pakistan is the inheritance laws. Under Sunni Islamic law, male heirs are entitled to twice the inheritance of their female counterparts following the demise of a male (Afghan and Wiqar, 2007). However, a father–owner may transfer all his shares/equity to a daughter during his lifetime, as a gift or *hiba* thereby blocking the Islamic inheritance law that would otherwise come into effect. Most people prefer to abide by the inheritance laws and exercise *hiba* only if no male heir exists in the family as under Sunni Islamic inheritance laws, male descendents of the deceased (example, a surviving brother) becomes heir to the majority of the inheritance.

The Case Study: Establishment of the Family Business

Seema Jaffer is currently the only female CEO of an advertising firm in Pakistan. The company, "Bond Advertising (Pvt) Ltd," was established by her father, Jamshed Qureshi. He began his career at the age of 19 in 1963 after acquiring a Bachelor of Arts Degree from Karachi University, in economics. He got a job in an advertising agency in Karachi. He was hired as a trainee and, within a year, he was promoted to branch manager. The branch grew to be one of the biggest in Pakistan, but when the director resigned Qureshi was overlooked.

> *They didn't promote me. So that's when I decided I had to do something else. So the choice was, either I get another job or start my own agency. So I gave it a thought and decided to start my own agency. It was a very hard decision because you know, when you are employed somewhere, you are getting regular money, but I felt I could do it. It was just a gut feeling, that I could do it.*

Jamshed Qureshi did not have capital to start out with as he belonged to a family that were mainly professionals and employed in the service sector. However, he had a good reputation in the media, consequently, he didn't need much in the way of capital as, at that time, advertising was mainly print-based with some radio and outdoor advertising. He started his business with three employees in April 1965 while a number of his clients decided to transfer their business to him rather than to stay with his former employer. However, the initial year was tough, a war broke out between Pakistan and India and most advertising work dried up. It took his company a year to slowly recover, even then finances were severely constrained.

FATHER AND DAUGHTER

Jamshed Qureshi married at the age of 19. His first child, a daughter, Seema, was born before he turned 21 years old, in 1963. However, his wife passed away eight months after the birth of the couple's son, and second child, Imran. Seema was just four years old. At the time, Qureshi's sister moved in with them to help raise the two children until she got married many years later. This help gave him more time to spend with his young family including his daughter.

> *She was the first child. A first child is much closer to a parent always. And I had more time to bring her up as well. I had a lot of time for bringing them up and I was very close to them.*

Seema attended the Convent of Jesus and Mary and excelled at school and sports, winning along the way a children's singing show broadcast on national television. Eventually, when she was older she left home to study a Bachelor's degree in the USA in 1983. When she returned from the US in 1986 after completing her undergraduate studies, she intended to work for a year or so in Pakistan and then go back and do her master's. However, her father had other ideas as he explained:

> *I always wanted Seema to take over eventually from me. This was in my mind always, because even when she was studying in school, she used to come to office and I had given her a table and she used to sit with me in my room and I would tell her that she would pick up things and learn … when she came back after studies she was double minded or she was not keen to come back into the agency since she had done development economics, so she wanted to go in the UN or World Bank. So it was difficult and I sort of kept on pressing her to come and work with me. She started working and I think it was a very difficult period because I was so used to controlling everything myself. The whole agency was centered around me.*

However, Qureshi was conscious of the fact that he had to let Seema learn by experience. A large and lucrative project for full-page calendars proved to be a turning point, as Seema, who requested that she manage and controlled the project, impressed her father with her competence.

> *I started to realize, I was holding too many things in my hand. I said to Seema, "Okay you have freedom to do things but come and discuss things with me as I have a wealth of experience which nobody else can give you." I think that was a starting point or a change. She slowly took over and now she runs it fully. I don't interfere with anything. She comes to me when she needs help.*

THE DAUGHTER'S PERSPECTIVE

Seema joined the business in 1986. At that time the number of employees was around 20. She started from the copy department, and went through all the departments of the agency. She wanted to earn the respect of her father and did so by emulating his tough work habits and grueling schedules. She found he was a hard act to follow.

> *I started picking up responsibilities. I think the relationship kind of evolved and as he started trusting me more, he gave me a lot of space to do what I wanted to do. That was one good thing. I took on more and more responsibility over the last eight years or so. It just happened and there was no formal kind of announcement. I think there was trust and respect.*

The period also coincided with meeting her future husband and then eventually her marriage. She married in 1989 and continued working for Bond Advertising as Seema Jaffer. In the advertising industry, at that time, there were some women working but they were older than Seema and mostly working in the creative field as they wanted to avoid client interaction. The presence of these few women provided a sense of comfort to her, in spite of the fact that very few of them worked in the management side. Seema did not face any problems dealing with clients, partly because of Qureshi's strong standing in the advertising industry.

THE SUCCESSION

Seema became more and more involved in the company under her father's mentorship.

She started looking into everything herself and slowly I sort of slipped out of it. She sort of took over. It was a very smooth thing. Neither of us knew how it happened. I was involved in other activities and I think that gave her a window of opportunity to take over some things and keep doing it herself. Since she was doing alright, I never interfered.

Seema's brother, Imran, returned from USA after completing his education in accounting. He was aware that his father expected him to join the family business. He joined Bond Advertising (Pvt) Ltd and after few years realized he had no interest in advertising. He felt he was better at numbers and logic and was not comfortable with the creative side of advertising. His interest lay in information technology. Some opportunities evolved in this area and he set up an information technology business with both his father and sister as shareholders. Gradually he found that he had less time for advertising and focused all his energies on establishing his IT business. In contrast Seema learnt everything. Consequently, the transition from a junior employee to CEO was smooth mainly due to Seema understanding what her father expected of her. While Seema upheld the values her father had instilled in both his children; hard work, integrity, and empathy with people, Seema's management style was very different from her father's:

I don't like being chained to my desk, which is the old way of working. I use technology, using blackberry and the email. I delegate much more than he ever did ... definitely ... I do delegate much more. The team that I inherited, they were very loyal ... and I put in my own team and my own resources also over the years. I am much more of a team player.

Seema felt that her succession into the advertising business was a gradual process that was not formally planned:

I didn't think I was entitled to it. Imran (my brother) was given a choice. But he chose not to get into advertising. I mean, the option was always there and it wasn't like there wasn't room enough for both. He'd just decided to do something different. He did spend some time in advertising. He didn't like it and figured that's not something he wants to do ... I do enjoy it ... I spend most of my waking time here ... and if I didn't, I think I'd go nuts. It is difficult for somebody whose baby it is, to give up and step back.

Discussion

In Pakistan, family businesses "adhere to Islamic inheritance laws during the succession phase and in the division of business assets among the successors" (Afghan and Wiqar, 2007:22). It is therefore generally taken for granted that the son or sons will eventually take over the business. Often the only son is given no choice. He is groomed and conditioned early in life to accept the responsibility. If the son expresses an interest in some other occupation he is pressurized to give up the idea and take over the family business. In case of multiple sons, most businesses absorb all the sons unless an offspring expresses disinterest in the management of the business. Then a consensus is reached within the family as to who will manage and own the business. Our case study is significant because the father in his life time decided to hand over the business to his daughter while a surviving son was present. One of the factors that may have contributed to this decision is the lack of interest shown by the son in the advertising business. However, unlike Pakistani fathers he did not insist that his son should focus on the advertising business and nor did he encourage his daughter to focus on her husband and children. It seems Jamshed Qureshi did not have the traditional mind set generally found in Pakistani society. He did not differentiate between his son and daughter and expected both to take a role in the business.

Nonetheless, it would appear that the choice of who should take over the reins of the family business may have been made very early on in this case. Qureshi's habit of bringing his daughter to the office, even when in school, his insistence that she join the family business upon her return to Karachi, and his monitoring her development within the business, all point to the idea that Seema's father may have decided that his daughter would be the next successor early in her young life.

Grooming and mentoring is critical to succession planning (Sharma and Rao, 2000; Cabrera-Suarez et al., 2001; Dyck et al., 2002).This is also accompanied by a process of socialization that includes many activities (Handler, 1994; Sharma et al., 2003) and continuous training from childhood to adulthood (Sharma and Rao, 2000). There are also indications in our case study that the socialization process to groom the heir apparent also started at a young age. This is in keeping with research by Longenecker and Schoen that suggests that the process of grooming can take place over a long period, as they state:

> *Parent–child succession in the leadership of a family-controlled business involves a long-term diachronic process of socialization, that is, family successors are gradually prepared for leadership through a lifetime of learning experience.*
>
> *(1978:1)*

Entering the family firm at an early age is an important contributor to the successful succession process (Goldberg, 1996). In this way future leaders of the firm can be groomed so that they have the skills and experience necessary to take over (Fiegener et al., 1996; Sharma et al., 2003).

Formal education also contributes positively to the succession process (Fiegener et al., 1996; Goldberg, 1996). In this case the father–owner ensured both continuous training and a formal quality education by sending his only daughter abroad at a time when it was very uncommon in Pakistan. Literature also points to a hierarchical adjustment of roles between the founder and the successor in the family firm (Hollander and Elman, 1988; Handler, 1990) with the successor moving from having little or no role to becoming the leader of the firm. In our case study, Seema moved from having a small role in the business to becoming CEO of the organization. Previous research points to the process of succession-planning being largely under the control of the incumbent leader (Christensen, 1953; Lansberg, 1988; Malone, 1989), who due to certain psychological barriers (Kets de Vries, 1993; Davis, 1968; Handler, 1990, 1994) has difficulty in dealing with succession. In this case study, the father had no such issues. He desired to keep the business in the family whether it was his son or daughter. He had no psychological barriers with respect to a daughter taking over and had the vision to realize that the success of the family firm lay in the ability to transfer knowledge and skills to his daughter. She was available, capable, and groomed.

The survival of a family business and the transformation from one generation to the next is dependent on the unity of the family members. Succession in Bond Advertising

(Pvt) Ltd was not an issue as Jamshed Qureshi, Imran, and Seema accepted that Seema was the successor. Seema and her father understood each other well and she seemed devoted to both her father and the business. Therefore the existence of a trusted capable successor in the shape of Seema who was committed to retaining the business in the family contributed toward a smooth, conflict-free succession. The entire family and stakeholders were united in ensuring the continuity of the family business, and this is important to the succession process (Sharma et al, 2003).

Limitations and Future Research

A major limitation of our study is that it is based on one case study only. Nonetheless, it is important to note that father–daughter succession in family businesses is a rarity in Pakistan, an exception rather than a rule. The double constraint of gender role socialization and a patriarchal culture, coupled with Islamic laws of inheritance, favor the son as a successor. Therefore, it is difficult to find businesses of father–daughter succession. Of the few businesses identified in Pakistan of father–daughter succession, the daughters inherited the family businesses on the demise of the father as they were the *only* next of kin. In these cases, the fathers, in their life time, would have taken steps to circumvent the Islamic inheritance laws from coming into effect on their demise. In our case study, the father is alive and he chose his daughter as successor in the presence of a surviving son. This study recognizes the critical role of the founder–father, in breaking away from traditions and socio-cultural norms and highlights the responsibility of the founder–father in the succession process. Qureshi's professional educated family background seems to have played a role in his non-traditional thinking. He accepted the fact that his son was not interested in the advertising business and encouraged his daughter instead to play an active role, eventually handing this business on to her. While it would be difficult to generalize from a single case this study nevertheless provides a rare opportunity to take a look at father–daughter succession in Pakistan.

Future research needs to be conducted in traditional societies, particularly within Muslim societies, to identify factors that contribute toward daughters taking a more active role as successors despite the strength of cultural attitudes in such communities.

References

Afghan, N. and Wiqar, T. 2007. *Succession in Family Business of Pakistan: Kinship Culture and Islamic Inheritance Law*. CMER Working Paper [07-54]. LUMS. Pakistan.

Arifeen, S.R. 2008. The Influence of Gender Role Identity on the Advancement of Managerial Women in Pakistan in *Engendering Leadership: Through Research and Practice*, edited by J. Hutchinson. Conference Proceedings, Perth, July 21–24, 2008. Perth: University of Western Australia, pp. 41–54.

Arifeen, S.R. 2010. The Development of Managerial Women: An Exploratory Comparison of Malaysia and Pakistan. *The IUP Journal of Management Research*, 9(2), 21–36.

Beckhard, R. and Dyer, W.G. 1983. Managing Continuity in the Damily-Owned Business. *Organizational Dynamics*, 12(1), 5–12.

Birley, S. 1986. Succession in the Family Firm: The Inheritor's View. *Journal of Small Business Management*, 24(3), 36–43.

Cabrera-Suarez, K., de Saa-Perez, P., and Garcia-Almeida, D. 2001. The Succession Process from a Resource- and Knowledge-Based View of the Family Firm. *Family Business Review*, 14(1), 37–48.

Christensen, C. 1953. *Management Succession in Small and Growing Enterprises*. Boston: Division of Research, Harvard Business School.

Davis, S.M. 1968. Entrepreneurial Succession. *Administrative Science Quarterly*, 13(3), 403–416.

Duncan, L.E., Peterson, B.E. and Winter, D.G. 1997. Authoritarianism and Gender Roles: Toward a Psychological Analysis of Hegemonic Relationships. *Personality and Social Psychology Bulletin*, 23(1), 41–49.

Dyer, W.G., Jr. 1986. *Cultural Change in Family Firms: Anticipating and Managing Business and Family Transitions*. San Francisco: Jossey-Bass.

Dyck, B., Mauws, M., Starke, F.A. and Mischke, G.A. 2002. Passing the Baton: The Importance of Sequence, Timing, Technique, and Communication in Executive Succession. *Journal of Business Venturing*, 17(2), 143–162.

Fiegener, M.K., Brown, B.M., Prince, R.A. and File, K.M. 1996. Passing on Strategic Vision. *Journal of Small Business Management*, 34(3), 15–26.

Goldberg, S.D. 1996. Research note: Effective successors in Family-Owned Businesses: Significant Elements. *Family Business Review*, 9(2), 185–197.

Handler, W.C. 1990. Succession in Family Firms: A Mutual Role Adjustment between Entrepreneur and Next-generation Family Members. *Entrepreneurship, Theory & Practice*, 15(1), 37–51.

Handler, W.C. 1994. Succession in Family Business: A Review of the Literature. *Family Business Review*, 7(2), 133–157.

Handler, W.C. and Kram, K.E. 1988. Succession in Family Firms: The Problem of Resistance. *Family Business Review*, 1(4), 361–381.

Harveston, P.D., Davis, P.S. and Lyden, J.A. 1997. Succession Planning in Family Business: The Impact of Owner Gender. *Family Business Review*, 10(4), 373–396.

Hofstede, G. 1983. The Cultural Relativity of Organizational Practices and Theories. *Journal of International Business Studies*, 14(2), Special Issue on Cross Cultural Management, (Autumn), 75–89.

Hollander, B.S. and Elman, N.S. 1988. Family-Owned Businesses: An Emerging Field of Inquiry. *Family Business Review*, 1(2), 145–164.

Kets de Vries, M. 1993. The Dynamics of Family Controlled Firms: The Good News and the Bad News. *Organizational Dynamics*, 21(3), 59–68.

Lansberg, I. and Astrachan, J.H. 1994. Influence of Family Relationships on Succession Planning and Training: The Importance of Mediating Factors. *Family Business Review*, 7(1), 39–59.

Leon-Guerrero, A.Y., McCann, J.E., III and Haley, J.D. Jr. 1998. A Study of Practice Utilization in Family Businesses. *Family Business Review*, 11(2), 107–120.

Longenecker, J.G. and Schoen, J.E. 1978. Management Succession in the Family Business. *Journal of Small Business Management*, 16(3), 1–6.

Malone, S.C. 1989. Selected Correlates of Business Continuity Planning in the Family Business. *Family Business Review*, 2(4), 341–353.

Miller, D. 1993. Some Organizational Consequences of CEO Succession. *Academy of Management Journal*, 36(3), 644–659.

Morris, M.H., Williams, R.O., Allen, J.A., and Avila, R.A. 1997. Correlates of Success in Family Business Transitions. *Journal of Business Venturing*, 12(5), 385–401.

Ocasio, W. 1999. Institutionalized Action and Corporate Governance: The Reliance on Rules of CEO Succession. *Administrative Science Quarterly*, 44, 384–416.

Poza, E.J., Alfred, T. and Maheshwari, A. 1997. Stakeholder Perceptions of Culture and Management Practices in Family and Family Firms—A Preliminary Report. *Family Business Review*, 10(2), 135–155.

Pitcher, P., Cherim, S. and Kisfalvi, V. 2000. CEO Succession Research: Methodological Bridges over Troubled Waters. *Strategic Management Journal*, 21(6), 625–648.

Roomi, M.A. and Parrott, G. 2008. Barriers to Development and Progression of Women Entrepreneurs in Pakistan. *Journal of Entrepreneurship*, 17(1), 59–72.

RoyNat Inc. 1998. *Who'll Step Up when You Step Down?* Fall newsletter.

Rubenson, G.C. and Gupta, A.K. 1996. Winter. The Initial Succession: A Contingency Model of Founder Tenure. *Entrepreneurship, Theory & Practice*, 21(2), 21–35.

Rue, L.W. and Ibrahim, N.A. 1996. The Status of Planning in Smaller Family-Owned Business. *Family Business Review*, 9(1), 29–43.

Sharma, P. 1997. *Determinants of the Satisfaction of the Primary Stakeholders with the Succession Process in Family Firms*. Doctoral dissertation, University of Calgary.

Sharma, P., Chrisman, J.J. and Chua, J.H. 1996. *A Review and Annotated Bibliography of Family Business Studies*. Boston: Kluwer Academic Publishers.

Sharma, P., Chrisman, J.J. and Chua, J.H. 2003. Succession Planning as Planned Behavior: Some Empirical Results. *Family Business Review*, 16(1), 1–15.

Sharma, P., Chua, J.H. and Chrisman, J.J. 2000. Perceptions about the Extent of Succession Planning in Canadian Family Firms. *Canadian Journal of Administrative Sciences*, 17(3), 233–244.

Sharma, P. and Rao, A.S. 2000. Successor Attributes in Indian and Canadian Family Firms: A Comparative Study. *Family Business Review*, 13(4), 313–330.

Trow, D.B. 1961. Executive Succession in Small Companies. *Administrative Science Quarterly*, 6(2), 228–239.

Ward, J.L. 1987. *Keeping the Family Business Healthy: How to Plan for Continuing Growth, Profitability, and Family Leadership*. San Francisco: Jossey-Bass.

Zaidi, R. and Aslam, A. 2006. *Managerial Efficiency in Family Owned Firms in Pakistan — An Examination of Listed Firms*. CMER Working Paper [06-51]. LUMS, Pakistan.

CHAPTER

6 Philippines: Father–Daughter Succession in Family Business: A Philippine Case Study

ANDREA L. SANTIAGO

Introduction

The dominance of family businesses in the Philippines is unmistakable. While there is no local study that has presented hard evidence on its magnitude, one can readily surmise from the profile of registered businesses that at least 95 percent of businesses are family-owned. This is no surprise coming from a country of over 7,100 islands whose economy is propelled by enterprising individuals who are motivated by the need to survive (Marcucci, 2001).

The profile of registered businesses shows that 99 percent of about 780,000 registered businesses are classified as micro, small or medium (NSO, undated). Moreover, 80 percent of these businesses are either owned or managed by women (Medina, 2001; Sereno, 2010). There are also unregistered businesses recognized by society as comprising the informal sector that contributes 30 percent to Gross Domestic Product (GDP) (ILO, 2002). More than 70 percent of this sector is controlled by women (Diaz, 2001). Clearly, women play a dominant role in the Philippine economy. This fact has come into being because the role of the Philippine woman (Filipina) in business as well as in politics is unlike many countries, where women are still struggling to be recognized. For instance, the country has already been led by two female presidents. Certainly at one point in history, the Filipina held the traditional role of homemaker and while she still does so today, her access to education has allowed her to assume many positions away from the home.

The story of the Filipina and how she has evolved has been written in many ways. Yet, her relationship with her father in a business setting has not been given that much attention. This case study aims to shed some light on that relationship and how it impacts on business inheritance.

Literature Review

THE PHILIPPINE CULTURE

Oriental yet western, traditional yet modern: the Philippine culture is anomalous. The country is located in Southeast Asia but the culture cannot be described as entirely Asian. There are three major nationalities that have shaped Philippine culture: the Spanish colonizers, the American liberators, and the Chinese entrepreneurs. With their entry emerged the "mestiza" or half-breed class who fused their own cultures with that existing in the country. It may thus be misleading to speak of a homogenous culture although two strong values stand true: the clan-like nature of the family and religiosity (Medina, 2001).

The family institution in the Philippines is extended to include relatives through consanguinity and affinity. This extended clan-like nature of the family is a defining characteristic of Filipino culture and society (Medina, 2001; Miralao, 1997). Strong family obligations are a reality governing Filipinos' life in ways that they do not in western society. Family members are expected to respect and care for their relatives, especially the old and disadvantaged.

After the family, the second most important value of Filipino culture is religiosity (Miralao, 1997). The Philippines is the third largest Catholic nation in the world, and the only one in Asia, with over 90 percent of 84 million Filipinos born and raised as Roman Catholics. The religion was brought in by the Spaniards who used Catholicism as a means to subjugate the locals during their 300-year rule (Illo, 1999). God is so central to the Filipino family's life that misfortunes in life are often explained as being part of God's plan. This faith together with family kinship has been used to explain the Filipino's resilient behavior (Medina, 2001).

THE STATUS OF WOMEN IN PHILIPPINE SOCIETY

Prior to the rule of the Spaniards, Filipinas were active contributors to the economy. This did not appeal to the Spaniards who again used religion, this time to tame Filipinas (Brewer, 2004). Filipinas regained their supremacy with the liberalization by Americans in the 1930s (Angeles, 2004; Illo, 1999). Breaking out of the role of dutiful daughters and eventually doting housewives and nurturing mothers, Filipinas emerged to become active participants in income generation (Medina, 2001). They hold an equal share in national employment and even occupy 47 percent of senior positions, the highest percentage from a base of 36 countries (Grant Thornton, 2009).

According to a recent study by the National Commission on the Role of Filipino Women (NCRFW), Filipinas enjoy greater equality than their Asian counterpart, being equally educated as the male counterpart. They gained their right to vote relatively early in 1937 and their human rights were consciously being protected and supported by gender-sensitive legislation (Feliciano, 1994). In the latest Global Gender Report of the World Economic Forum, the Philippines maintained its index of 0.758 although dropped from rank 6 to rank 9 out of 134 countries (Hausman et al., 2009). Its gender equality rating is so high that it even outranked the UK and the US. Despite this, Filipinas continue to be responsible for the home (Angeles, 2004; Illo, 1999; Makil, 1995; Sevilla, 1995). Husbands have begun to share in the household chores but the traditional role of child-rearing and managing the kitchen are still the responsibilities of mothers and wives (Medina, 2001). It is fortunate that working mothers are supported either by the extended family or household help.

FATHER–DAUGHTER SUCCESSION IN PHILIPPINE FAMILY BUSINESS

The actual numbers of women who have inherited or are poised to inherit their family's business are undocumented (Malaya, 2004). There has been simply no local survey that has focused on female successors, let alone one that examines father–daughter succession. Nonetheless one can ask: are Filipinas likely to inherit the businesses of their parents if there is a male alternative?

In a collectivist society where family unity, harmony, and respect for elders are given the highest regard, one can only surmise that daughters will defer to the wishes of their parents (Medina, 2001). The selection criteria may differ per family but choice by gender may be the least concern. Thus, it is expected that unlike many of the Asian counterparts, a daughter need not worry that she will not be selected simply because she is female.

The Case Study

How do I balance my father's legacy and the fact that the business is not making money?

Edna Martinez Sahkrani inherited the management of her father's tree plantation business when he passed away in 2004. The tree plantations were established after her father Ruben closed the fishing operations after some 40 years in existence.

Ruben and his siblings built a very successful fishing business. From a one-boat outfit in 1947, RJL Martinez Fishing Corporation (RJL) peaked in the 1980s to become a 100-fleet operation supported by two ice plants, a shipyard, and over 1,000 employees. The boats traveled to the south and the north of the Philippines where fish were plentiful to Navotas, the biggest fishing port in the country.

Edna remembers the bigger boats catching approximately 100–150 tons of fish daily, translating into sales that hit about USD 18 million annually in absolute 1980 prices. The consumption of petrol was so high that the company was paying USD 3–5 million yearly. With that volume, the business was probably the biggest and most modern at that time. For this reason, the family is still remembered in Navotas and in Palawan.

> *My father was a righteous individual who managed his business honorably despite the many opportunities to do illegal activities that would have allowed him to sustain the fishing operations. But ours is a business of nature and when over-fishing became rampant and the El Niño phenomenon began, there were simply no fish to catch. With a grave heart, my father slowly sold assets to support the development of fish pens in Laguna Lake. It was shortly after that time that my father reinvested his funds and purchased tracts of land in Puerta Princesa, Espanola, and Brookes Point all in the province of Palawan where he planted over 100,000 acacia mangium and mahogany seedlings in a span of four years. That is the business my father passed on to the family and where I assumed managerial responsibility.*

Edna is the youngest of the three children of Ruben Martinez and Mena Constantino. Her brother, Wilfrido, currently resides with his partner in the United States. Her older sister Emma lives with her family in Iloilo, located in the Visayas region, 300 miles south of Manila, the Philippine capital. Edna stays in Manila but shuttles back and forth from Hong Kong as she helps her second husband in his textile business. Her 86-year-old mother has lived with her ever since her father passed.

Assuming responsibility over the family's business is not something that Edna wanted. She did not really agree with her father's penchant for reinvesting his wealth into risky ventures when he could have readily retired. Twice she disappointed her father and was practically estranged from him. In the end, she realized she was the only one her father relied on to carry his dream and it was only to her that he would pass on the business.

Edna and her siblings were not initially involved in the family's fishing business since it was not a place for children. Her uncles, Jose and Luis, as well as her mother were the active family members. When her elder brother Wilfrido became an adult, he chose not to be directly involved. But that was probably mutual. Instead, he managed Mar Tierra, a trading company that initially handled the tuna exports of RJL and later traded and exported molasses. RJL invested in Mar Tierra, giving it a 42 percent stake in the business. Later, her elder sister Emma was tasked to manage the company assets in Iloilo together with her husband. It was only in May 1980, when Edna was 30, that she finally decided to work for her father.

The trust Ruben gave Edna, treating her as his "right-hand man," made her siblings conclude she was the favorite child. But Edna believes it must have been circumstance. She relates how her father was greatly disappointed with her brother Wilfrido, who grew up with an aunt in Malabon, a city adjacent to the fishing port. While in his aunt's care, he was exposed to neighborhood gambling and became distracted by the pleasures of the world.

Emma is the next in line, but Edna explains that her sister was not as focused on the business as she was. Emma was, and is, more into social networking and civic-oriented activities. She has been very active with the Rotary Club in Western Visayas and became the governor of the district two years ago.

This left Edna as Ruben's last hope in identifying a next generation family member to train and take over the family business. She was obedient yet tough, so after graduating with honors from Maryknoll College, a private women's college in Manila, she became the successor apparent.

Edna recalls, "My father was beaming with pride when he pinned the medal on me during graduation. At that point he wanted me to join the family business. Alas, that was his first disappointment with me."

About six months after graduation, Edna decided to marry and live with her husband in the US. Her father was furious. He didn't like her husband and it also meant Edna was going to be far away from home. During her marriage, her parents would encourage her to return to the Philippines where life was more luxurious. In Manila, she wouldn't have to cook, wash clothes, or clean up on top of having to earn a living.

Family pressures put a toll on a marriage that had a weak foundation. Five years into the marriage, and with Edna's third child barely nine months old, she decided to call it quits. She filed for divorce late in 1979. As soon as she returned to Manila, Ruben asked her to join him in RJL; she quickly accepted.

Edna worked with her father for ten years and saw it peak, then decline. She was a silent worker but got things done. She at once noticed that the operations were growing big but administration remained the same. "It's like a girl who has outgrown her dress," she quips in her native language. "Naturally, as one physically grows, the dress should be changed. If not, it bursts in its seams. It was tough to get my uncles to adjust to a new system, but it simply had to be done."

The entry of a new generation usually brings a fresh set of ideas. But moving from an informal to a formal system can be challenging for all. This has led Edna to conclude that "running a family business is more emotional than it should be. It's unlike the corporate world. But I suppose emotions can't be helped, although I believe they can be controlled."

Edna's assertiveness and detachment from emotions probably stemmed from how she was raised and her few years abroad. Since her father worked 12-hour days and her mother worked the night shift, they were hardly present to supervise the children. Edna learned to become independent and when she lived in America she became even more independent. She found her strength by observing her parents manage the home and business, and from eventually taking charge of the household and working full time while residing in the US when her ex-husband could not provide enough for her and her children.

Edna is an intelligent, hard-working woman. She is a tough lady, who for ten years worked in a man's world. The fishing business is by no means a place for women, at least not on the ships.

There was a time I rode one of the vessels that disembarked from Zamboanga. I was the only female in a boat of fishermen. I was totally out of place. But I wanted to understand the fishing operations so I suffered through the inconveniences. Then, out in the open seas, our captain was alerted about a possible attack from local pirates/terrorists. Fearing for my safety, the boat made an unexpected u-turn and dropped me back to Zamboanga. I never rode another fishing vessel again!

Edna stuck it out with her father for as long as she could. But she reached her breaking point. When all the signs indicated that the fishing business could no longer be profitable, she wanted her father to sell the business and enjoy the wealth he still had. But Ruben was a dreamer. He wanted more things. Thus for a second time, Edna became alienated from her father. When he refused to listen to her logical explanations as well as pleas from a concerned daughter, she quit on him. "My father was furious! For ten years, he didn't speak to me. He probably felt betrayed."

However, Edna felt vindicated. In time, Ruben realized that he had to leave the fishing business before it financially drained him. He was not about to get into the smuggling business, an open secret in the fishing industry. He did everything legally – in great contrast to how his father gained his wealth. Thus from his share of the fishing business, he decided to invest in land. "I don't know what came over him. He probably drove along the highway and was impressed by the beauty of Palawan."

Palawan is one of the most picturesque places in the Philippines. It boasts of having pristine beaches, living corals, and lush mangroves. In 1967, it was proclaimed a Fish and Wildlife Sanctuary. In 1993, two properties in the province were designated as World Heritage Sites. For this, the province is being positioned as the top eco-tourism destination in the region.

I never saw the place until I took over. It is awesome! The sight is breathtaking. The locals love it. It is no wonder Brookes Point won an award under the Clean and Green program

> *spearheaded by then First Lady Mrs. Amelita Ramos. But to get there! That's something else. I have had to hire a van for a considerable amount and travel about three to four hours on a road that can get quite bumpy.*

Edna is actually in a quandary. In early 2002, her father had to undergo a heart bypass. The operation went well but to Edna it was a signal for her father to stop working. In January 2004, she broke the ten-year silence by offering to manage the tree plantation.

Ruben was ecstatic when Edna told him she would take care of the plantations. Was it the return of the prodigal daughter? Ruben then gathered enough strength and for one last time visited the tree plantation. He stayed for a week and returned to Manila with bilateral pneumonia.

"I was unaware that he went on his trip, since I had gone through with my surgery," Edna relates. "My father visited me in the hospital in a wheelchair and I chided him about it. A week later, he died. He was 84."

During the eulogy, Edna commented how she believed her father just waited for her to accept the responsibility before passing. She remembers clearly telling those who were present, "I promised him I will take care of his legacy."

However, the reality is stark. During Edna's trips to the plantation, she noticed that the trees were not getting any stouter. In 12–15 years, the diameter should be about 16–18 inches but the trees were quite scrawny despite their maturity. Edna spent a lot of time and money to determine what was wrong with the place and even invested in a satellite study. The same findings kept being reported. The soil quality was not appropriate for the trees since it was sandy and clayish. It had too many minerals for trees to grow healthy, but too few minerals for the plantation to be converted into a mining field. She tried planting pineapple, not for the fruit but for its fiber. However the leaves turned red because of the high iron content. "What am I to do with the plantation?" Edna laments.

> *I could probably sell the land to someone interested to turn it into a palm oil plantation but that needs a mill and who in his right mind will invest millions in a mill at this time? I am running out of options. I promised to preserve my father's legacy but keeping it won't give me back healthy returns!*

As Edna continually ponders what to do, one of her daughters, Karen, eggs her on to continue.

Edna recalls that when her father was alive, he would write to his granddaughter and so Karen felt close to him. Thus, she was badly affected when he passed away. She then felt it was her mission to save the plantation and even took a six-month course in forestry just to understand the forestry business. During that time, she had conversed with experts who advised her to consider soil enhancement. She broached the idea to Edna who balked. "Do you know how much it costs to treat the soil? I am not that wealthy. I don't think I should be putting in more money into the plantation."

However, Karen thinks otherwise. Thus Edna feels quite torn.

> *Now I have to deal with two things—my father's legacy combined with my daughter's determination to preserve it against the harsh reality that the plantation is not going to yield much. I could just harvest the trees and probably recover some of the millions the family has spent. The truth is—there are nights I can't go to sleep, thinking of what my options are.*

Should Edna fulfill her promise to a man no longer on this earth? Or should she be practical and for a third time, turn her back to her fathers' dream?

Conclusions

Edna wanted to tell her story to illustrate how succession may not always be successful if the business itself is not on solid ground. This may occur regardless of whether the business is transferred to a male or female heir. The decision, however, to preserve her father's legacy is tougher for her as a daughter who made a promise to a sick father.

Edna was always considered the successor-apparent but her need for self-identity prevented her from accepting the responsibility early on. She wanted to be a wife, and then a mother, but she eventually returned to being a daughter. By that time though, she knew who she was. While she shadowed her father in all his tasks, she didn't live in his shadow. She was and continues to be her own woman. But then, she is a Filipino woman and she must battle with the strong family obligations that made her accept, in the first place, her role as the successor.

Perhaps if Edna was a male, then the refusal to work in the family business and eventually take over may have prevailed. In the end, Edna, with the compassion associated with women and as a loving daughter, realized that her father needed her and thus she took up the cudgels. Despite her own angst, her father will always remain her father and she, a loving daughter.

Directions for Future Research

In the father–daughter literature, Edna's story is no different from daughters who must make themselves visible to their father and who at the same time must ensure their independence. Like many daughters, she too had to balance her own desire to raise her family and to be the obedient daughter. But what makes Edna's story interesting is that she inherited a business whose viability is in question. She thus faces challenges different from a daughter inheriting a going concern. It would thus be worth exploring how sons would handle the same scenario. Would they undertake the same soul-searching that Edna is going through and would that promise to a dying man weigh just as heavily? This definitely brings to light an aspect of father–daughter succession that may as yet be unstudied.

References

Angeles, L. 2004. Women's Roles and Status in Philippine History: The Socio-Historical Context of Women's Organizing in *Women's Studies Reader* (pp. 33–48). Manila: Institute of Women's Studies, St. Scholastica's College.

Brewer, C. 2004. Contact and 'Morals' in *Women's Studies Reader* (pp. 3–32). Manila: Institute of Women's Studies, St. Scholastica's College.

Diaz, P. 2001. Women Entrepreneurs in the Informal Sector in *Holing Up Half the Sky: Success Stories in the Economic Empowerment of Women* (pp. 71–21), edited by H. Fajardo and E. Panlilio. Manila: Zonta Foundation Philippines.

Feliciano, M. 1994. Law, Gender and the Family in the Philippines. *Law and Society Review*, 28(3), 547–560.

Grant Thornton. 2009. *Global Survey: Women Still Hold Less Than a Quarter of Senior Management Positions in Privately Held Businesses*. Available at: http://www.grantthornton.com/portal/site/gtcom/menuitem.550794734a67d883a5f2ba40633841ca/www.internationalbusinessreport.com [accessed: 8 April 2010].

Hausman, R., Tyson, L. and Zahidi, S. 2009. *The Global Gender Gap Report 2009*. Available at: http://www.weforum.org/pdf/gendergap/report2009.pdf [accessed: 21 March 2010].

Illo, J. 1999. Fair Skin and Sexy Body: Imprints of Colonialism and Capitalism on the Filipina, in *Women and Gender Relations in the Philippines* (pp. 47–56), edited by J. Illo. Quezon City: Women's Studies Association of the Philippines.

ILO. 2002. *Women and Men in the Informal Sector*. Available at: http://www.wiego.org/publications/women and men in the informal economy.pdf [accessed: 8 April 2010].

Makil, P. 1995. Philippine Studies of Women: A review, in *The Filipino Woman in Focus: A Book of Readings* (pp. 143–152) (2nd Edition), edited by A. Torres. Manila: University of the Philippines Office of Research Coordination.

Malaya, M. 2004. *A Gender-Based Analysis of Performance of Small and Medium Printing Firms in Metro Manila*. Unpublished dissertation, De La Salle University, Manila, Philippines.

Marcucci, P. 2001. *Jobs, Gender and Small Enterprises in Africa and Asia: Lessons Drawn from Bangladesh, the Philippines, Tunisia and Zimbabwe*. SEED Working Paper [18], International Labour Office, Geneva.

Medina, B. 2001. *The Filipino Family* (2nd edition) Manila: The University of the Philippines Press.

Miralao, V. 1997. The Family, Traditional Values and the Socio-Cultural Transformation of Philippine Society. *Philippine Sociological Review*, 45(1–4), 189–215.

National Statistics Office (NSO) (undated). *Establishments in the Philippines in 2000*. Available at: http://www.census.gov.ph/data/sectordata/2000/establishments00.html [accessed: 9 April 2010].

Sereno, L. 2010. *Data-Based Programming of Policies and Support for MSMEs*. Presented at a round-table workshop with the same title on March 30, 2010, Asian Institute of Management, Philippines.

Sevilla, J.C. 1995. The Filipino woman and the family, in *The Filipino Woman in Focus: A Book of Readings* (pp. 38–58) (2nd Edition), edited by Amaryllis Torres. Manila: University of the Philippines Office of Research Coordination.

CHAPTER 7 United Arab Emirates: The Al Jaber Group: Traditions and Transitions in a United Arab Emirates Family Business

KATTY MARMENOUT, ELIZABETH FLORENT-TREACY AND MANFRED KETS DE VRIES

The Abu Dhabi Context

Abu Dhabi is the capital of the United Arab Emirates (UAE), a small country in the Arabian Gulf which has seen spectacular economic development since its inception in 1971 thanks to the discovery of oil. It has witnessed a transition from a rural, tribal society to an urban and industrialized one in one generation. While many multinational corporations (MNCs) have entered this flourishing market, the number of expatriate workers (both skilled and unskilled) has increased dramatically, creating a truly multicultural society with around 200 nationalities represented. The drawback of this fast development is the marginalization of the local Emiratis who currently represent only 17 percent of the total population.

Although the UAE economy has developed quickly in the service and knowledge-based industries, the labor market is still largely governed by a low-cost paradigm. The supply of cheap labor (both skilled and unskilled) from the Indian subcontinent and South-East Asia, and expert labor from the west, combined with the recent programs of "Emiratization" aiming to transfer skills and knowledge from the expatriate to the national workforce, has created a complex business context (Abouzeid, 2008). Solid legal frameworks and sound regulatory systems are still lacking in the UAE (Hanouz et al., 2007). In addition, autocratic leadership has contributed to the creation of a fast-paced, but also uncertain, legal environment (Giuffrida, 2008).

A particular difficulty related to conducting research in or interpreting research about the UAE is to establish whether the frame of reference is the local Emirati population or the market, country, or society as a whole. With limited data available from national statistical reporting and confusion about the population segments it covers, secondary data need to be evaluated with care. Less than 2 percent of Emirati nationals (both male and female) are employed in the private sector (Abdulla, 2006). The banking industry is a notable exception as banks are held to a quota system based on an increasing percentage of Emiratis each year (currently 38 percent). Other private sector organizations need to employ 2 percent of local nationals in their workforce. However, despite fees and visa restrictions on expatriate employees many MNCs do not employ any Emiratis (Abouzeid, 2008).

In the UAE, therefore, business practices are influenced not only by the local culture but also to a large extent by the cultures of the expatriates each organization employs. The Emirati work context takes into account religious practices, such as availability of prayer rooms and opportunities to take breaks at prayer times. Business hours may also be shortened for religious observance during Ramadan. Traditions and the Muslim faith may also limit cross-gender interaction between men and women at work. Overall, the rapidly developing Emirati society is greatly affected by foreign cultural influences. Recent findings indicate that certain values and attitudes may be changing (such as increased individualism) but others remain deeply held, such as the Islamic work ethic (Whiteoak et al., 2006).

Women in the Middle East

It has been argued that the major fault line in the divergence of views between the Middle East and the west is based on the status of women (Metcalfe, 2007). In western debates, Middle Eastern women are often regarded as oppressed and victimized, but also as more admirable and hard-working than their male counterparts (Essers and Benschop, 2009). Although 75 percent of all UAE local university students are women, only 14.7 percent of Emirati women were in full-time employment in 2003 (Abdulla, 2006). Indeed, the World Economic Forum (WEF) Gender Gap report indicates that high educational achievements are not reflected in the work sphere (Hausmann et al., 2007). In Egypt, official female employment rates are 22 percent (Service, 2006), whereas in Lebanon rates are closer to 30 percent, with female employees making up 90 percent of the workforce in the banking sector (Dima Jamali and Assem, 2005).

Although the constitutions of most Arab nations acknowledge equality between men and women (UNDP, 2005), personal status laws are largely inspired by Islamic law. "Arab personal status laws remain conservative and resistant to change because a number of Arab States are reluctant to develop a national personal status code. Instead, they leave matters entirely to the judiciary, which is heavily influenced by the conservative nature of classical Islamic jurisprudence (*fiqh*)" (UNDP, 2005:19). Equality of inheritance remains rare (daughters inherit only half the share of their brothers) perpetuating unequal treatment between men and women, and diverges from the Qur'an's provision for equality between human beings.

Women's dress codes and traditions differ greatly within the region. Whereas some Middle Eastern women may argue in line with feminist movements that covering ones hair (wearing *hijab*) is oppressive, many women consider this way of dressing to be part of their tradition and their faith (Metcalfe, 2006). Indeed, wearing the *hijab* can be a reflection of one's commitment to faith and modesty, or an essential part of one's identity (Essers and Benschop, 2009). In the UAE, for example, Emirati women wear their traditional *Abaya* with pride and decorate it with fashionable beads and glitter, whereas in Saudi Arabia, where Islamic dress is required by law, it is perceived oppressive. Thus Saudi women remove their *Abaya* when in a female-only environment.

While gender segregation in the workplace is strictly observed only in Saudi Arabia, certain professions may be dominated by either males or females in line with perceived appropriateness to for their gender (Metcalfe, 2006). Although the late UAE ruler Sheikh Zayed was lauded for his support for women's advancement, he also encouraged women to take up roles "suitable to their nature" (Gallant, 2006). The confinement of women to traditional roles may also be attributed to the fact that it is often considered *haraam* (a sin) for women to interact with men other than their close relatives (Metcalfe, 2006). Finding a "respectable" career is therefore important for women in the Middle East (Gallant, 2006). Whereas there is some evidence that women are increasingly making their mark in atypical professions (Nammour et al., 2008) and role models are starting to emerge (Leading Businesswomen in the Arab World, 2008), still, the majority of women are employed in the public sector as teachers or clerical workers (Abdulla, 2006).

The Case Study: The Al Jaber Family Business

OBAID KHALEEFA JABER AL MURRI: PATRIOT, PATRIARCH, FOUNDER, AND FATHER

"Al Jaber Group" is an Abu Dhabi-based privately owned company, founded one year before seven sheikhdoms came together in 1971 to form the UAE. Obaid Al Jaber's business in the 1970s consisted primarily of basic earth-moving and transportation. But Al Jaber was a visionary leader. When Obaid Al Jaber founded his construction company there was virtually nothing but thorny paths in the country—the first road had been paved only nine years earlier. Al Jaber gained a good reputation in the contracting business, and as oil revenues increased in the UAE in the following decades, Al Jaber Group was in a good position to take on more important projects and the company grew apace with the development of Abu Dhabi.

By the late 2000s, Abu Dhabi controlled an estimated one-tenth of the planet's oil reserves and had nearly USD 1 trillion invested abroad. Al Jaber Group, by 2008, had divisions capable of handling large-scale construction projects, logistics, oil and gas services, shipping, landscaping, industrial development, and trading, with a total turnover of USD 2.5 billion in 2008 and over 50,000 employees. In the nearly 40 years since it was created, the Al Jaber Group had built 5,000 kilometers of roads, thousands of villas, and a second runway at Abu Dhabi International Airport. The Group owned the world's largest crane, capable of lifting 3,000 tonnes; thousands of heavy construction vehicles, scores of supertankers, and a kilometer-long pier.

A LEADERSHIP TRANSITION BEGINS

One of the most important developments for the Al Jaber family occurred in 2004, when Obaid Al Jaber bought out his partners and created a holding company. He made this decision, he said, to prevent disputes in the future and to begin the process of a fair, balanced, and transparent transition to the next generation of family owners and directors. He also wanted to safeguard his ability to act quickly, independently, and flexibly.

A second significant family event occurred in 2006, when his eldest daughter Fatima joined the business as Chief Operating Officer (COO) after working in the Abu Dhabi public sector for 18 years. As the new COO, Fatima was to be responsible for the operations of all the subsidiaries in the Group. Her brother Mohammed, Group CEO, was responsible for strategy, finance, and transactions. The Al Jaber Group was henceforth fully owned by the family. These announcements provided a strong signal to the market that, while new blood had entered the family business, continuity was also assured with Obaid Al Jaber maintaining an active role as the chairman and Mohammed in the role of CEO. Their father had already begun to think about the leadership transition. Obaid Al Jaber insisted that he would not focus on financial and technical performance when choosing a successor but rather on the individual's ability to interact ethically and wisely with a diverse group of employees. He believed that the most important quality in a leader was what he called "a clean heart"—if one's heart is not pure, this will be reflected in the poor quality of one's work.

Obaid Al Jaber advised his children that the younger ones must learn and the older ones must listen:

> *I said to Fatima and Mohammed, join the company and take responsibilities, but listen and learn as if you were in school. Leadership doesn't take place behind closed doors in an office; it requires knowledge of your people, and the ability to motivate people at all levels of the organization to perform their duties faithfully and to solve their problems before the problems become complicated. If you treat people fairly, they will be loyal; if you mistreat them, this will affect the company's interests and performance.*

FATIMA AL JABER

Fatima grew up in the construction business. As a child she was interested in her father's work and often went on site visits with him.

> *My father was very busy, as you can imagine, but he used to take us on tours of his worksites and I learned a lot about his business. He would talk about what he had built and describe his new projects. At that time it was all a bit hard for me to understand—but my knowledge accumulated over the years. Even though we didn't have a great deal of time together, I think back now about the quality of the time we had together to talk about his business.*

It therefore seemed natural that she would go on to study architecture and engineering.

With her father's encouragement, she was one of the first students to earn a degree in architectural engineering from Al Ain University, the UAE's first university founded in 1977. After her graduation in 1987, she worked with the Abu Dhabi Government in various capacities. She reached the level of Assistant Undersecretary for Technical Services at the Abu Dhabi Public Works Department and later served as Undersecretary for the Building Projects Sector of Abu Dhabi Municipality, a significant achievement for a woman in the UAE in the traditionally male domain of civil engineering.

Fatima joined the family business in mid-2006. This was never an obligation, she said, but a matter of choice. It was a real change. She went from working in the public sector to the private sector, and in terms of contracting for major projects, from being the client to being the supplier. While the dynamics of the family business were different, she was confident that she had made the right move. Although she was a family member, she was seen as bringing strategic skills to the organization. One Al Jaber executive said, "I think there are very few people in the Gulf who have her level of technical and commercial experience. And for a woman to have reached the level of success that she has in this market is unique, for sure."

In an organization where "everyone wants to see her for five minutes every day," she did her best to keep her door open. She was considered by her employees to be approachable, fair, and genuine, and they also described her as "a nice person" who took the time to deal with their requests. They respected her for her willingness to get her hands dirty, with site inspections a regular part of her routine. Some described her as a tough leader who also had a sense of humility, aware of her duty to her company and her country, and with an evident gratitude for her blessings in life. She also earned the respect of her father and brother as a key executive in her own right.

Although Fatima Al Jaber was by no means the first woman engineer to be COO of a multibillion-dollar construction conglomerate, when placed within the context of the UAE her accomplishments made her a pioneer. She knew her own mind, and her husband and brother and—even more importantly—her father, supported her as she chose her own path. Many people, including Fatima herself, commented on her father's open-minded and generous support of his eldest daughter, both early in life as he took her along on sites visits, and later when he included her in meetings with high-level government officials where she was often the only woman present. In one of these meetings, a high-ranking UAE official told Obaid Al Jaber, "Your daughter is a contribution to society."

The blessing of her father and her brother in a culture where women traditionally did not take a visible, public role was, she said, one of the keys to her success. About herself, Fatima said simply, "I was born to work. I like success, achieving goals, and going beyond what I thought possible. I have to feel passionate about what I do. But I also like to be surrounded by nice people and good feelings."

TRADITION, FAMILY, AND FAITH

As much as her role as COO meant to Fatima Al Jaber, she was equally conscious of the importance of her role as a mother to her five children, and the strong foundation of her extended family. She felt the tension of balancing the traditions of home and faith in a world that was changing rapidly. Growing up in a large, traditional family, she was the oldest of nine children, four boys and five girls. She was born in Al Ain, the lush oasis region of Abu Dhabi Emirate. In traditional Emirati families, the grandmother is regarded as the senior lady of the household. This was true in the Al Jaber family home: "I was raised by my grandmother; she was the one who made decisions." When Fatima was ten years old, her father moved the family and his construction company to Abu Dhabi. The reassuring presence of her beloved grandmother made the transition to a new life in Abu Dhabi easier for Fatima. Looking back, Fatima felt that she had had a very happy childhood. Fatima was very proud of being a good student and had wanted go abroad to university, but as she was the eldest she had no brothers or sisters in other countries who would be nearby to watch over her. Therefore, her father told her, "No, Fatima. I think it will be too difficult for you to go alone, since you're the oldest one. Try one year here at Al Ain University, and then we can discuss it again if you are not happy." In fact, Fatima did like it, and as she later said, "I forgot all about going abroad. I never remembered to go back and remind my father about his promise to reconsider."

After graduating she did not consider joining the family firm. The Government of Abu Dhabi was at the time looking for talented Emiratis to be involved in the first stages of massive infrastructural development of the Emirates. Schools, roads, hospitals, post offices, and banks, among other projects, were being designed, planned, and constructed. Fatima was in the right place at the right time. She recalled:

> *I just went from one section to the other to get more experience in each area: design, construction, supervision and tendering, contracts. Over a period of several years I gained experience in these different specializations of the construction industry. I worked on hospitals, mosques, government buildings—all the different kinds of building needed in a growing city. I met a lot of experienced people: consultants from all over the world, contractors from different backgrounds, colleagues from other departments and ministries.*

The main thing Fatima learned in those years was the importance of coordinating and working in teams:

> *You cannot build a building without the cooperation of many different people, from the architect to structural, electrical, and mechanical engineers, and all the other planners. It's really about teamwork; you cannot begin the project until you have built the team around you.*

After beginning her professional career, Fatima continued to live at home:

> *Our way of life is that the girl stays with her family until she gets married and moves with her husband to a new home. I stayed with my family until I got married in 1995. I was 30 when I got married. My mother was worried because in the UAE girls usually marry when they are 24 or 25. She thought it might be too late for me!*

Fatima's parents had suggested that she marry a young man of their choice when she finished high school, but she said no.

> *I wanted to finish university. They said, "Okay, if you don't feel comfortable with it, fine." I lived a life where we didn't have so much pressure about what to do; we had some freedom to say loudly what we thought, and to decide for ourselves. I have honestly never had pressure to follow my parents' decisions for me. But I would never embarrass my family.*

Eventually Fatima met her future husband through her work (he later started his own company). Fatima was the first of the Al Jaber children to have a professional career. At the time of their marriage, she had reached the managerial level. Her new husband felt it would be better for her to stay at home. She told him, "I'll think about it. Maybe I can do it. I'll try." But one year later she told him: "I'm going crazy!" She had her first daughter but then decided that the agreement was no longer in place and went back to work. As COO of Al Jaber, Fatima admitted that maintaining a balanced life was a perpetual challenge and often stressful.

When her children were small it was easier for her to spend time at work—she had household help, nannies, and her mother to watch over them. But as her children grew older, they noticed when she wasn't there. She would get phone calls from them asking where she was and when she was coming home. "I'm trying to be a good mother; I try to be there for them. But it's not easy with five children. It's a full-time job. I would love to stay at home and just do everything for them, but honestly, it's not me. I cannot." As a compromise, Fatima would be in her office from 8:30 am to 4:30 pm, with longer days twice per week.

She developed her own way of working to allow her to be more efficient in addition to her reasonable working hours. Like most working parents, she learned to juggle. Sometimes her mother reminded her: "You are leaving your children unattended and I don't like that. You have to come home." Fatima was reassured by her mother's advice:

> *It's nice in a way; my mother can alert me about things which I might not have noticed, I get so immersed in work. She makes sure I don't stay at work too late; she even talked to my father. This is the nice thing about family. We take care of each other. That's really an important part of having a family business—you know it's not only business.*

BUILDING A ROAD FOR THE NEXT GENERATION TO TRAVEL: BALANCING LOVE AND WORK

Obaid Al Jaber was, first and foremost, Fatima's father. During the time when she worked for the Abu Dhabi Government, he also became her mentor. But when she joined the family company as COO, she had to adjust to working with her father in a third role: that of Chairman of Al Jaber Group.

> *In my previous job I reached a point where I felt I couldn't advance any further. I told my father and he said, "Why don't you come and join us?" I felt so proud! When I finally did join Al Jaber Group, it was difficult to figure out how this relationship with my father would work. And I think we are still working on developing this new relationship. If my boss—who is also my father—has a vision and focus based on his greater experience, then I should really respect that. So I'm learning how to work with him as an entrepreneur and my father.*

Fatima knew that any potential clash among family members is always sensed by employees. When she first joined Al Jaber, she felt that employees were trying to figure out who was really in charge: was it her or her brother, the CEO? They would ask her brother to confirm her decisions. She had to make it clear to everyone that she, her brother, and her father each had their own role and responsibilities:

> *It happens that people around us try to create jealousy and tension between us. It took me some time to understand that if we have a clash in the business it will be reflected in our family relationships also, so I go about things in such way that I don't create pressure or tension among family members. Everybody has his own style of management. I cannot be the same as my brother, and he cannot be like me. Sometimes we differ, sometimes we agree, but I don't want differences to turn into clashes between family members.*

Fatima saw the issue of balancing love and work within the Al Jaber Group as one of her highest priorities. Her brother Mohammed had always worked in the family company, but Fatima had joined the company later, bringing in her own ideas and opinions. It was never easy for her to insist on change without first considering her father's and brother's position. She would tell herself, "No, I have to think differently. We are brother and sister, we cannot battle this out." Fatima's brother was the eldest son in the Al Jaber family. In the Emirati culture this meant that her brother would become chairman after her father. Her brother would inherit the leadership and would make the final decisions.

> *I'm not really thinking about [who takes the lead]. I'm just trying to be as productive as I can in my family organization. That's my goal and I'm trying to make it clear for everybody. I'm not here to control everything because this is not my way and I think women don't tend to do it this way. I just like to do my job in a comfortable way; I like to have a good team that can really be productive. So finding my role wasn't easy, you know, and it's still not.*

RE-ENGINEERING FOR THE FUTURE

Over the years before she joined the company, people had got used to reporting to her father or her brother. Fatima realized that the most important first step for her was to build trust and create teams, something that she already had a great deal of experience in.

> *I represented a new hierarchical layer in the organization. It takes a while for people to accept this. First they have to trust me, then they have to change their habits before we can change the culture. People who had worked here for 20 or 30 years wanted to pick up the phone and talk to my father, as usual. Why should they bother to talk to me?*

Fatima decided that the best thing for her to do was to go out into the field and learn about what people were doing. She gave them a clear message: "If you want to talk to my father, go ahead, I'm not bothered. As a member of the Al Jaber family, I just want to improve the business." The restructuring process took three years and spanned across HR policies through factories and fleet management.

A TRANSITION BEGINS

As the first decade of the millennium drew to a close, the Al Jaber Group and the Al Jaber family were nearing parallel transitions: the transition from founder to second generation leadership was beginning to take shape at the same time as the Al Jaber Group itself was undergoing a transition from a construction company to a fully diversified global group. These transitions would inevitably have an effect on the Al Jaber's family and professional relationships. Fatima knew that her father trusted her and her brother, but he preferred to continue to grow the Al Jaber Group in a measured, cautious way. For his children, the pace of growth sometimes felt slow. "He is testing us," Fatima knew. "He has told us that each person must deserve the place he is sitting in." The three family members agreed fully on one thing though: "We must respect each other. We cannot afford to fight."

The Al Jaber Group was part of a holding company wholly owned by Obaid Al Jaber. Although the founder was still in control, the family was also testing the holding company "in pilot operations," as Fatima said, to see if it would continue to be appropriate for the family and the business:

Will the holding structure we have currently in place still work for us when the founder is no longer in control? We have a board but is this board capable of taking decisions without the founder? Do we understand the nature of the businesses that we are taking decisions about?

She also put a high priority on clarifying the family's roles and responsibilities as owners in the future:

Do we understand each other, we brothers and sisters? If we sit together, can we agree on one logical decision, or we will end up having clashes as we used to do as brothers and sisters growing up? So this is my worry now. This is something I am already aware of as I work with my brother the CEO. What will happen in the future, if all the other brothers together must take a decision for the business? Within the family we need to also do a bit of restructuring to enable us to look toward the future, to be able to take the right decisions, in the right environment.

Looking back over her often challenging transition into an executive position in the family company, Fatima admitted that during her first year she had considered leaving, but in the end decided to stay:

It was a hard decision. I evaluated all the other options: I could start my own company, I could work for other companies, I could just take a break. But then I said, "You know, if I don't work on the restructuring of the company and the family, nobody will, because nobody understands my family the way I do." I decided that, with the help of people around me, I could really have an effect on the restructuring of the business. And I could also help my family to go to the next stage of family business ownership.

For Fatima, this family responsibility fell naturally to her. Men were less interested in such things, she felt, or rather they tended to let family events unfold without intervening.

Women really care about creating the whole environment. I'm passionate about my family business, and I need to have a role in continuing the success of my family business. And I owe my family; they have given me so many good things. We can have a family business after my father. We don't have to sit and worry that the family business will not continue. I think that because I'm the oldest child I will always have a large share of responsibility. And as a businesswoman I want to show people that women in this region have many opportunities and can run their own life. I want other families who own businesses to understand that being a woman is not a restriction; a woman can be a productive member of a family business. Maybe people will tell me, "Fatima, you don't have to do all of this." But I think that my children will benefit. They will share the successes of the family business one day.

LOOKING FORWARD

Fatima Al Jaber looked to the future with great enthusiasm and some trepidation. She was in her early forties, a phase in the human life cycle when she would begin to transition from being her father's daughter to having more senior-level responsibilities within Al Jaber Group and within her extended family. Al Jaber Group was also approaching a transition phase in the entrepreneurial lifecycle that would take it from a founder-led organization to a second generation owner–leadership group consisting of nine Al Jaber siblings.

Moreover, these personal and organizational transitions were occurring in the context of the high-speed transformation of the UAE during a global economic financial crisis. As she reflects on her future role in society, she is confident that her contribution as a role model "just being there" can encourage other women to engage a path filled with worthwhile opportunities and challenges.

Time will tell, but it seemed that Fatima Al Jaber was indeed the right woman, in the right place, at the right time. The game has just started to get interesting.

References

Abdulla, F. 2006. Education and Employment among Women in the UAE. *International Higher Education*, 45, 9.

Abouzeid, R. 2008. Job Training for Emiratis 'Fails in Key Subjects'. *The National*, August 25.

Dima Jamali, Y.S. and Assem, S. 2005. Constraints Facing Working Women in Lebanon: An Insider View. *Women in Management Review*, 20(8), 581–594.

Essers, C. and Benschop, Y. 2009. Muslim Businesswomen Doing Boundary Work: The Negotiation of Islam, Gender and Ethnicity within Entrepreneurial Contexts. *Human Relations*, 62(3), 403–423.

Gallant, M. 2006. Five Case Studies of Emirati Working Women in Dubai—Their Personal Experiences and Insights. Unpublished PhD Thesis, University of Southern Queensland. Available at: http://eprints.usq.edu.au/1425/ [accessed 31 July 2011].

Giuffrida, A. 2008. Investors Stuck in Cul-de-sac. *The National*, December 29.

Hanouz, M.D., Diwany, S.E. and Yousef, T. 2007. *The Arab World Competitiveness Report*. World Economic Forum.

Hausmann, R., Tyson, L. and Zahidi, S. 2007. *The Global Gender Gap Report 2007*. World Economic Forum.

Leading Businesswomen in the Arab World. 2008. *Financial Times Special Report*.

Metcalfe, B.D. 2006. Exploring Cultural Dimensions of Gender and Management in the Middle East. *Thunderbird International Business Review*, 48(1), 93–107.

Metcalfe, B.D. 2007. Gender and Human Resource Management in the Middle East. *The International Journal of Human Resource Management*, 18(1), 54–74.

Nammour, M., Gokulan, D., Agarib, A. and Zain, A.A. 2008. Women Make their Mark. *Khaleej Times*, September 19.

Service, E.S.I. 2006. *The Egyptian Women and Economy*.

United Nations Development Programme (UNDP). 2005. *Arab Human Development Report*. New York: United Nations Publications.

Whiteoak, J.W., Crawford, N.G. and Mapstone, R.H. 2006. Impact of Gender and Generational Differences in Work Values and Attitudes in an Arab culture. *Thunderbird International Business Review*, 48(1), 77–91.

PART III Africa

CHAPTER 8

Egypt: Lessons from a Father's Culture and Life Values: A Female Entrepreneur Builds her own Family Firm in Egypt

SAM ABADIR, DAPHNE HALKIAS, DESPINA PRINIA,
MIRKA FRAGOUDAKIS AND PATRICK D. AKRIVOS

Introduction: Cultural Values Regarding Gender Roles in Egypt

Egypt has undergone a series of successive invasions or conquests, each of which has impacted Egypt's cultural and social fabric. Egypt's contemporary culture is thus a mixture of a multitude of elements, shaped by the progression of historical events (with the Paranoiac model still subconsciously active), which has contributed to the development of Egypt's current atmosphere. The cumulative effect of the historical transformation of Egypt has consequently created an environment in which, at present, a woman's rights are caught in a contradictory cultural foundation.

The decades of the 1950s and 1960s particularly marked the climax of an upsurge of the liberal movement for women's rights in accordance with the socialist transformation in society introduced by the new political regime. With this new regime came legal equality for all citizens. Women began to enjoy their rights to a similar extent as men, in all spheres of life (for example, education, employment, politics). Thus, the gender gap during this period was undeniably reduced, though not eliminated. One must mention that the newly introduced socialist ideology was able to reconcile its doctrines with Islam, going so far as to claim Islam as the religion of socialism. This strong support developed out of the prevailing influence of liberal Islamic thought.

The global trend focusing on women's rights has cast Egyptian women into the midst of international currents emphasizing the role of women in development. This trend calls for the guarantee of women's rights in society. Still, it seems that the liberal trend has been reversed on the basis of misinterpreted religious grounds. Consequently, as the vulnerable group in society, women have fallen prey to setbacks in their rights.

Unfortunately, religion is often used as a pretext for these setbacks. Various opportunities, which had become available to females, are now being questioned.

The reactionary tide, gaining impetus over time with the increasing political, economic, and social problems, has aggravated the pre-existing inequality between males and females. In a traditionally male-dominated culture, the previously reduced gender gap has once again widened in response to the strong reactionary movement (El-Safty, 2004).

The Culture of the Coptic Christians

The culture of the Coptic Christians is quite comparable to western Catholic practices and is also familiar in an Islamic cultural context. The Coptic community, which is quite insular (similar to other minorities), correlates the survival of its individuality with the roles of its female members. Regarding the minority, the construction of a NeoPharaonic Nation seemed an urgent matter, regarding the eradication as a race, therefore placing an emphasis not solely on the reproductive responsibilities of Copt women. A woman was therefore not only to bear children but must herself be intelligent, proficient, and skilled, to bring up the future sons of the nation. In the Coptic family as a microcosm of the nation, "There is no advancement to the nation except with the advancement of women."

The issue of schooling as a variable of the womans' role in Egypt has tipped the scales in support of women entering enterprise activities. Egyptian legislation supports the right of education for women. However, this right was slowly adopted, because it contradicted the cultural value of female seclusion in the earlier, more traditional days of the Ottoman Turkish restrictions on women. A mother's education, however, improves only the likelihood of current enrolment for female children, with no significant effect on male children. The influences of gender on schooling attainment in Egypt, in addition to the child's gender, have also been other household-specific gender variables such as female headship and maternal education levels.

Cultural Variables Influencing Female Entrepreneurship in Egypt

A logical sequence of expansion in female education deals with the development of employment opportunities for women. Whereas historically and traditionally, women were restricted to stereotypically female jobs (for example, teacher, nurse), new occupational prospects have emerged. The number of women in the labor market has thus increased, covering all occupational fields. One significant variable leading to the wider access of females in the labor market is the support of a legislative system guaranteeing their equality in both hiring procedures and wages (El-Safty, 2004).

According to 2006 Egyptian Labor Force Survey statistics (Ministry of Finance, 2007), "There are some 630,000 woman-owned micro and small enterprises (MSEs) in Egypt." This is an impressive number in absolute terms but not so impressive when compared to the number of male-owned MSEs. Of the total MSE population, women make up less than 17 percent. This means that men outnumber women by a ratio of more than five to one. In most countries around the world where such data is available, the average proportion is closer to two to one, suggesting there is potential in Egypt for a higher number of women entrepreneurs.

In Egypt's private sector, only 15 percent of workers are women. Not being in the workforce at all means that women do not have much opportunity to gain business skills and experience or to be exposed to ideas for developing products and services to fill unmet needs or gaps in the marketplace. International research on the background of entrepreneurs reveals that public sector employment does not provide a very strong incubation environment for emerging entrepreneurs compared to employment in the private sector, especially, employment in small or medium enterprises. Therefore, "entrepreneurially speaking" Egyptian women are at a disadvantage.

Findings from a comprehensive survey of the MSE sector carried out in 2002 and 2003 by the Economic Research Forum (ERF) (Ministry of Finance, 2007) suggests that, compared to male-owned MSEs in Egypt, women's enterprises are started with a considerably lower level of capitalization; are more highly concentrated in the trade sector (where barriers to entry are low); more likely to have only one worker; more likely to have outside establishments in the informal sector; and less likely to be exporting. In addition, they have less access to formal technical, business management, and entrepreneurial training, business development services (BDS), and finance, coupled with a lower average level of education and higher illiteracy rate than men. So from a business growth perspective, Egyptian women MSEs are also at a disadvantage.

Egypt is a nation of very small enterprises. In the MSE sector, only 3 percent of male-owned enterprises have over ten employees; for women-owned enterprises, it is less than 1 percent. But this means that close to 60,000 of the 630,000 women-owned MSEs are in the small enterprise category (with between ten and 49 employees). With respect to women's entrepreneurship in Egypt, there appear to be two major challenges. The first is to create a cultural, social, and economic environment that is more favorable to the emergence of women as entrepreneurs, and the second is to ensure that women who already have their own enterprises have adequate access to the resources and supports needed for sustainability and growth, that is, financing, technical and business management training, information, BDS, business networks, and technology. Without addressing these challenges, the Egyptian economy will not be able to benefit from the latent and untapped economic and entrepreneurial potential of the half of its population represented by women!

Promotion and awareness-raising are among the most critical elements in changing the environment for women's entrepreneurial activity. This is true in any country, as it is for Egypt. It involves creating heightened public awareness of the role of women in entrepreneurial activity and the contribution they make to the economy and to society in general, and promotion of entrepreneurship as a viable and feasible employment opportunity for women. An important vehicle for creating this awareness is the profiling of successful women entrepreneurs who can serve, not only as credible role-models for other women, but also to challenge some of the myths and widespread misperceptions regarding women's capabilities as economic generators.

The Case Study: Agricool Egypt

THE ENTREPRENEUR

This case study of father–daughter succession is a bit different that most such narratives where the daughter becomes the second, third or fourth generation business successor of her father. This narrative focuses on the life story of Wafaa Rizkalla and the cultural values she attained from her father which directly influenced her growth into a successful female entrepreneur living and working today in Cairo, Egypt. Though Wafaa's father was never an entrepreneur himself, she credits him as a role model for the cultural values and work ethic she has lived by in becoming a successful business woman and being the first generation of her own enterprise activities. In this unique case study the daughter succeeds her father in his attributes, values, culture, inspiration, and vision of life's path to build her professional identity and family business.

Wafaa Rizkalla, a 49-year-old Coptic Egyptian, is CEO of a company which imports equipment from Europe for poultry farms and greenhouses. The company's main office is located in Cairo and the company's store is in the city's outskirts. She is married and has two sons, a 20 year old and a 15 year old. Wafaa spent her childhood years traveling in many Arab countries as well as in Italy and Switzerland due to her father's occupation as an International Labor Organization expert for the United Nations Development Programme (UNDP). Because of the frequent changes of location, Wafaa and her sisters attended several English and international schools and were educated both in English and French. After high school, Wafaa chose to study Fine Arts in Cairo, not fully realizing the entrepreneurial road that laid ahead in her life.

HIGHER EDUCATION AND THE BEGINNINGS OF ENTREPRENEURSHIP

In 1980 Wafaa returned to Egypt to study at university and for the four following years she shared her time between Egypt and Italy. In 1985 she decided to permanently settle in Egypt and started working for an Italian company in the field of poultry equipment. At the same time she continued her studies on a Master's Degree in Islamic Art and Architecture, History of Art and Miniature Painting at the American University of Cairo, which she acquired in 1991. A few years later, in 1996, Wafaa became a partner of the Italian company she was working for and it was that firm that gave her the necessary resources to open her first office. As a partner, Wafaa was working closely with her Italian counterpart, a man of advanced age who in 2003 withdrew from the enterprise due to health problems. The next couple of years were a very trying time for Wafaa's career since her partner's poor health, along with the bird flu epidemic, forced her to shut down her company.

However, being driven and ambitious, Wafaa did not give up working entirely. Because Wafaa has always been sensitive to the problems in her community she turned her attention to a charitable organization for people with impaired vision and blindness, which is one of the most crucial health issues plaguing Egypt today. Wafaa helped raise funds to provide surgical treatment for at least 3,000 people, "those most in need," to restore their sight. Indeed Wafaa is a person who enjoys to work, is focused on her goals and works diligently to ensure the final result of her plans. She admits that, "If I would have not started in the equipment field I would have done something else. I would have bought an oven to make handmade artifacts or modern art on metal. Fine arts are what I studied."

It wasn't long before the bird flu epidemic subdued and many of Wafaa's former associates in Italy contacted her, offering to supply her with equipment so she could start up her business. She decided to start an entrepreneurial family business where she would be the first generation, followed by her son and his progeny in the future. She recalls, "I knew the field of poultry equipment from previous employment and did not want to start something new. I knew where I was going." Therefore, in 2007, Wafaa launched her own company: Agricool Egypt.

THE BUSINESS

Agricool Egypt specializes in equipment imported from Italy for poultry and greenhouse cooling and ventilation systems, along with all other equipment related to the field. Despite working alone, Wafaa has on several occasions collaborated with similar businesses such as Agricule Group in the United Arab Emirates and Syria. Agricool Egypt is run solely by Wafaa who is the CEO and in charge of every managerial aspect of the company, even deal making and marketing. The company's store occupies one employee while the installation of equipment is assigned to freelance contractors.

Even though Wafaa was no stranger to this line of work, being in charge of her own company meant she had to fight very hard to gain her clients' trust. She recalls, "I faced many problems because people thought I had second quality merchandise as I was selling at low prices, so I had to constantly prove myself in the business." Another issue that Wafaa came across as a female entrepreneur in Egypt is that "clients think because I'm a woman, it will be easy to push me and get a better price." Wafaa managed to turn this into an advantage for her business: "I use that to spread my work and obtain the reputation of being less expensive with good quality equipment!" As a result of the economic crisis, most customers in the equipment field began trying to save money by purchasing low-quality, inefficient products whereas Wafaa made it her goal as a businesswoman to promote and sell high-quality heavy-duty equipment at low prices.

Wafaa describes launching her business and maintaining it as a challenge especially because of her gender. As she says, "The first year was very difficult due to being a woman alone in a field of men! But I was able to go through 2008 without major damages, 2009 was better and I feel 2010 will be even better!" Being a woman running her own successful family business in Egypt is a constant battle for Wafaa since, as she says, "I do not have a problem being a woman in Egypt but I do have problems in the field since it is a male-dominated field ... I am the only Egyptian woman selling equipment in this field." As far as being the head of the company she adds that, "Since oriental and traditional employees hardly accept a woman as a boss, now I deal with very young people and I'm as senior to them as their mothers." In regard to other women who aspire to become entrepreneurs, Wafaa suggests, "Women need to start businesses in a field they are comfortable with and not push themselves, otherwise they will be frustrated." Furthermore, in her experience as an entrepreneur, Wafaa has adopted the following business attitude: "My challenge is to grow while keeping a low profile not to (provoke) male competitors ... I think I am very successful because I am not overwhelmed by my ambitions. I do not want to eliminate competition. I want to be reliable, credible, and supply good equipment."

HER FATHER'S INFLUENCE

Wafaa's upbringing was very much influenced by her father. She grew up in several Arab countries as well as in Italy and Switzerland due to her father's nature of work. Wafaa's father was a university graduate who started his career as an employee for the Egyptian Ministry of Industry. He worked in Syria for a few years as part of the Egypt–Syria partnership during the union with Syria and returned to Egypt in 1961 to resume his duties while collaborating on a project for UNDP. It was the project manager who recommended that he work for UNDP and his first mission was as an

International Labor Organization (ILO) expert in Sudan. In his line of work, Wafaa's father was highly appreciated and very sociable. He continued to work in smaller international projects even after retiring, since he had great cross-cultural appeal to professionals in his field.

In regard to their family life, Wafaa describes her father as the main authority figure in the house: "When I was young I obeyed his orders, no discussion." She and her sisters however were treated as individuals and not minimized because they were girls. They were expected to successfully graduate from university, start work, and assume adult responsibilities. Unlike her sisters, who are also raising their own families, Wafaa is the only one to assume such a demanding job as being a woman entrepreneur. Her older sister is an employee at an auditing firm and her younger sister, who holds a degree in psychology, is presently not working and is a full-time mother. Wafaa's mother, who used to be a French teacher and holds a MA in French Literature from Switzerland, stopped working to raise her daughters and help them with their frequent cultural adjustments resulting from her father's many work-related relocations.

Wafaa's entrepreneurial activities do not appeal to her mother and sisters. They think she's become nervous and opinionated and that she does not need to work, instead she could stay home and look after her husband and two sons. Her mother disagreed with Wafaa's decision to start her own business; she preferred the safety of being a salaried employee for her daughter. However, now she trusts her and seeks her help for official documents and managing her finances. Fortunately, Wafaa's husband does not share their point of view. Being an associate of several international firms, he encourages his wife, shares her concerns, and offers advice.

Wafaa, as a female entrepreneur and CEO of her own firm, has role modeled her father's work ethic and values as her guide. Early in her career, while she was still collaborating with her Italian partner and wanted to open her first office, her father was by her side supporting her. She recalls, "When I started my work I turned to him for advice. He helped with my first business plan and the presentation for a loan to the bank." Wafaa also recalls some difficult times that the family went through, specifically the Christmas holiday when Wafaa was 23 years old and in her senior year at university. The family had gathered at the airport waiting to welcome her father from a business trip to Rome when they were informed that he had suffered a heart attack. That was a turning point in Wafaa's life because her perception of her father as a strong authority figure and esteemed professional was challenged in a shocking way. For the first time saw him in such a fragile state. This altered her view of life as a process that runs like a well-oiled machine to one of unexpected and sudden changes and downturns. Wafaa's father slowly recovered over the following year but did not resume working at the same pace again.

Even though her father passed away before the launch of the new Agricool Egypt, Wafaa admits to being influenced by him in a very important aspect of her profession. "I watched my father work in different environments, cultures, and with people of varied backgrounds. He respected people's beliefs and thus gained their trust. That's how I learned to respect time and people." Furthermore she admits she owes to her father "my communication skills and spirit to work in diverse situations and the ability to endure difficulties." Wafaa's father was supportive in another very important aspect of the business: finances. Wafaa used her inheritance to launch Agricool Egypt since her previous work in the field had not been profitable enough to help start the business.

ENTREPRENEURIAL CONTINUITY INTO THE NEXT GENERATION

Wafaa is the mother of two sons. Her oldest son is 20 years old and is attending the American University of Cairo majoring in Political Science and her younger son is 15 years old and attending high school. Wafaa was fortunate enough to not have experienced any conflicts in being a mother and CEO of her own business. She retains a positive work/life balance by prioritizing, being very organized, and naturally enjoying working and being on the move.

Wafaa's sons are used to seeing their mother at work. They are beginning to get involved in the family business by regularly coming to the office and greeting the long-term clients. Wafaa's younger son is very interested in entering the business and often goes to the company's store to watch the work and try his hand at equipment assembly. He is very sociable and well liked by the business' constituents. However, Wafaa does not want him to enter the business until he finishes high school and his army service. She prefers to help her son learn more about their field of work and then decide whether he wants to enter the family business or continue his studies in another direction. Wafaa trusts her older son to succeed her, continue, and expand the family business into the next generation. Her only concern, however, is whether she will face any conflicts within the succession process with her son in her dual roles as CEO and mother. In regard to her own continuing role as the company's CEO she admits, "I do not know for how long I will continue working and when I will stop. It is a very rewarding occupation but with many of problems. My challenge is to continue growing in all aspects of my life."

Conclusion and Discussion

The presented case study is unique in many ways. Not only does it present the entrepreneurial spirit of a woman in Egypt, but also of a minority, namely the Coptic Christians, and the women's unique and active role within that culture. The study presents a woman who has moved beyond stereotypical female jobs and into a male-dominated business. It is also an impressive case of succession, where succession is not an enterprise per se, but a succession in ethics, values, and lifestyle that culminated in the creation and maturation of a family business run by an Egyptian woman.

In interviews with the subject, it became clear that the influential factors to her entrepreneurial spirit were the family's educational level, her international exposure, and the inspiration of her father's culture and life values. In her desire to become a female entrepreneur and open her own family business, she needed time to gain her mother's and sisters' approval as well as that of a predominately male-dominated market. She follows her father's inheritance in that she leaves her sons the freedom to become their own persons, before deciding if they want follow the family business. It is still too early for any serious succession planning. The entrepreneur wisely waits for the successors to approach the family business rather than assigning them predetermined roles.

Future Research Direction

Egypt is a country where business and entrepreneurship changes and develops faster than society and culture can keep up. There is a need for comparative research among female entrepreneurs of all cultural/social group represented in Egyptian society. This comparative research, although taking into account quantitative approaches, should go beyond the statistical approach of measuring patterns of entrepreneurship in Egyptian family business with a female CEO, and also focus on how economic and non-economic policies involving public services and private organizations, have or not helped Egyptian women grow into entrepreneurs and lead their own family businesses.

Future research is to explore the wider trends among female minority entrepreneurship and compare that to the entrepreneurship of the majority of female-run businesses. Factors to be considered are international exposure and higher education, as well as the educational background of the parents. It is also important to explore how these factors influence the choice of business and how many of these female-run businesses are successions from pre-existing businesses, as in the case of our subject's business succeeding a business that went bankrupt and closed for a short period of time before she revived it. Finally, this case outlines a direction for future research that is not only limited to Egypt but globally applicable: mother–son succession across cultures.

Reference

El-Safty, M. 2004. Women in Egypt: Islamic Rights Versus Cultural Practice. *Sex Roles: A Journal of Research*, 51(5/6), 273–281.

Ministry of Finance, 2007. Egyptian Women Entrepreneurs: Profiles of Success. Egyptian Ministry of Finance and Ministry of Investment. Available at: http://www.sme.gov.eg/English_publications/Profiles_of_Success_Eng.pdf [accessed 2 August 2011].

Further Reading

Armanios, F. 2002. 'The Virtuous Woman': Images of Gender in Modern Coptic Society. *Middle Eastern Studies*, 38(1), 110–130.

Dancer, D. and Rammohan, A. 2007. Determinants of Schooling in Egypt: The Role of Gender and Rural/Urban Residence. *Oxford Development Studies*, 35(2), 171–195.

Guenena, N. and Wassef N. 1999. *Unfulfilled Promises: Women's Rights in Egypt*. Cairo: Population Council: West Asia and North Africa Regional Office.

Henderson, R.P. 2005. The Egyptian Coptic Christians: The Conflict between Identity and Equality. *Islam and Christian-Muslim Relations*, 16(2), 155–166.

International Finance Corporation. 2007. *Gender Entrepreneurship Markets*. GEM Country Brief–EGYPT 2007.

International Labour Office. 2007. *ILO Activities in Africa 2004–2006*. Eleventh African Regional Meeting, Addis Ababa, April 2007.

Ministry of Finance. 2007. *Egyptian Women Entrepreneurs. Profiles of Success*. SMEPol Project, March 2007.

United Nations Capital Development Fund. 2003. *Microfinance Sector Development Approach*. March–April 2003.

CHAPTER **9**

Nigeria: Sociological Issues in Father–Daughter Business Succession in Nigeria

CHINEDUM U. NWAJIUBA AND CHINYERE A. NWAJIUBA

Introduction

Family businesses have a relatively long history in Nigeria dating close to a century. The introduction of the formal economy as a result of colonialism has existed in some parts of Nigeria since the late nineteenth century. These businesses range from small-scale manufacturers, trading, and service sectors. In some cases, especially around the costal trading cities such as Lagos, Porthhacourt, and Calabar—all lying by the Atlantic—some business have been inherited by siblings up to the second and third generations. Most of these successions have been to sons. Rarely is that the case with female descendants, daughters. Searching for answers as to why almost only male descendants, especially sons, inherit businesses is the objective and challenge of this chapter.

Literature Review and Theoretical Framework

A search through the literature shows a dearth of materials explicitly dealing with father–daughter business inheritance. This suggests gaps in knowledge that require research to fill in. Such studies would have to deal with the extent of existence of family businesses that have transcended generations and been passed on to daughters. Such studies will necessarily also dwell with a temporal focus but also across sectors of the economy, and with a spatial component across the geo-cultural diversities of Nigeria. The issue therefore involves elements of originality in methodology, conceptualization, and execution.

Succession, in the context of family business, is defined as the actions and events that lead to the transition of leadership from one family member to another (Sharma et al., 2001). In the context of this paper, it entails the transfer of a commercial investment of any type from the owner to his or her survivors. As observed by Ukaegbu (2003), it could be a transfer to members of a nuclear family in a monogamous household such as a wife and children, or members of a compound family in a polygynous household, namely wives and children. Furthermore, survivors could also be members of the extended family such as uncles, aunts, nephews, nieces, cousins, and in-laws. In Nigeria, entrepreneurial succession in most cases usually follows the guidelines of inheritance. The father bequeaths his business(es) to his offspring. The focus of this paper is on father–daughter business succession. The subject of father–daughter succession in enterprises is both in the realm of business and economics, but also has sociological and cultural aspects. Various shades of gender theories are very relevant to this. Nigeria is a highly patriarchal society where men dominate many spheres of women's lives (FMWASD, 2006). Business succession is evidently an aspect that typifies the subordinate role of women.

According to the BNRCC (2010), gender is described as the socially constructed roles and responsibilities of men and women, and boys and girls which may vary over time. These may differ across societies, cultures, and families. "Gender roles" refers to different learned behavior expected of men and women. The concept of gender is important because it is at the core of gender analysis—revealing how women's subordination is socially constructed and therefore, can be changed. Gender inequality is not biologically predetermined, and nor is it fixed. The concept of gender is therefore an analytical tool for understanding social processes. This is distinct from sex which describes the biological or physiological differences between male and female, men and women, boys and girls. These differences are universal and are determined at birth. Sex and gender are therefore not synonymous. Roles are defined by gender by the society in which they belong. For example, in some societies men are expected to farm, while in others it is the responsibility of women.

Traditional configurations of gender roles often mean that women have multiple responsibilities in the home, at the workplace, and in the community. These many demands often leave women with less time for political involvement, and less opportunity to actively participate in decision-making processes that impact on their lives, their environment, and their aspirations (Fordham, 2001). Changes in gender roles often occur in response to changing economic, natural, or political circumstances, including development efforts. Both men and women play multiple roles in society. The gender roles of women may be identified as reproductive, productive, and community managing roles, while men's are often categorized as either productive or involved in community politics. Men are often able to focus on a particular productive role, and play their multiple roles sequentially. Women, in contrast to men, must often play their roles simultaneously, and balance competing claims on time for each of them. Productive roles refer to the activities carried out by men and women in order to produce goods and services either for sale, exchange, or to meet the subsistence needs of the family.

A number of lessons are evident from the positions espoused by the BNRCC (2010). First is the dynamic nature of gender roles. That is that changes can come with socio-economic and political circumstances. What these mean is that though daughters inheriting family businesses from fathers is currently an exception, changes could come with time. The disadvantaged economic and financial position of women is very well evident in the literature. Choksi (1995), however, described this as a worldwide phenomenon in which women have limited access to financial services, technology, and infrastructure. They are engaged in relatively low-productivity work. This view is similar to that of Hesse (2005) who notes that women's financial dependence on men brings about gender inequality. In Nigeria, men in this case may not necessarily include fathers, but more often husbands or any other relationships.

Anyafulu (2010) percieves some of these issues as discrimination against women and defines it as a human rights issue. In Africa, she says, women suffer scandalous deprivation and denial which they often bear in silence. This she attributes to discriminatory laws regarding inheritance and property rights, and use of communal lands. It also manifests as limited access to employment in formal and informal sectors as well as limited access to education and training of women.

The issue of women's disadvantaged positions in inheritance is not limited to the formal and business sectors. Even in the informal and rural non-farm sectors this is even more the case. Ohajianya et al. (2010), in a study of the agricultural sector in Imo state in southeast Nigeria, found the same trend in the agricultural sector. Though women are commonly engaged in farming, especially arable food crops production, only about 9.2 percent of the women obtained farmland through inheritance, and these were all widows using their late husband's lands, as the culture barred women from inheriting family land. In such circumstances, as female land ownership is limited to being a result of the death of their husbands, such lands are held in trust or at the pleasure of their male children. However, 51.5 percent of the women obtained land from purchase (Okoh, 2010). This points to an emerging properties market that offers women the opportunity to own land.

Nature and Characteristics of Family Business in Nigeria

Family businesses in Nigeria contribute significantly to the Nigerian economy both in terms of the Gross Domestic Product (GDP) as well as a source of employment and income. With a strong informal economy, a lot of the activities are at the family level. Activities they engage in range from manufacturing to services; this specifically includes bakeries, clothing and textiles, stationeries, trading, and hoteliers (Okoh, 2010).

Family businesses are a prime source of employment. This is no mean contribution to the Nigerian economy where unemployment in urban areas is estimated at over 50 percent. The gender disaggregation of unemployment shows, however, that more males than females may be unemployed (see Table 9.1). This is partly attributed to a number of factors including the gender roles of males and females, which commonly precludes or limits male involvement in certain activities. Nigerian woman are commonly found in microenterprises requiring minimal financial resources but often employing skills that may nearly always be acquired by women. Commonly, these are in the fashion, textile, and cosmetics activities (Okoh, 2010).

Table 9.1 Unemployment rate by sex in Nigeria (1999–2000)

	1999	2000	2001	2002	2003	2004	2005	2008	2009	% change 2008–2009	% change 1999–2009
M	53.6	52.9	54.8	53.4	54.1	54.5	53.7	57.0	58.1	1.9	8.3
F	46.4	47.1	45.2	46.6	45.4	45.4	46.2	55.4	56.7	2.3	22.1
Nigeria	12.5	18.0	13.6	12.6	11.2	11.0	10.8	12.9	13.6		

Sources: Central Bank of Nigeria (various years). Statistical Bulletin, Abuja: CBN

Yet female entrepreneurship in Nigeria is not new. It has probably been around as long as male entrepreneurship in some parts of Nigeria. The nature of female entrepreneurship has also been dynamic, changing over time and diversifying into areas that were hitherto dominated by males. In nearly all these cases, there are no common examples of daughters inheriting businesses from their fathers. Most intriguing is that even in businesses owned and operated by females, the preference is for their sons to inherit those businesses from their mothers.

Succession and continuity in family business is very important in Nigeria. It is the ambition of virtually all Nigerian entrepreneurs and business owners to raise a biological successor from their family. The successors have to be males and not females. Hence, businesses are rarely inherited by daughters. This pattern tallies with the case of rural farm families where the prime resource is the land. The land is virtually never inherited by daughters, especially in the ancestral home lands, but sometimes this may occur with purchased urban lands. The surprise is the carry-over to non-traditional assets such as family business. This shows the continued entrenchment of core traditional values with the emergence of non-traditional assets such as family businesses.

WHY FATHERS DO NOT HAND OVER BUSINESSES TO DAUGHTERS: FACTORS AFFECTING FATHER–DAUGHTER SUCCESSION

A number of factors have been identified as affecting father–daughter succession in Nigerian family businesses. These are:

1. *Nigerian culture and its influence on family business.*
   It may be unconventional to state a Nigerian culture. Nigeria is a fairly huge country with about 150 million people with significant diversities. There are some 250 ethnic groups, with different languages. There also two major religious groups—Christians and Muslims—and some traditional religion adherents. Such diversity does not lend the country to easy cultural characterization. Yet, some commonalities do exist. The most important of these is the premium on male children who are seen as the holders of the family tree, name, and assets. In contrast, the females are seen as ultimately belonging to another family as a result of marital practices. As a result, family businesses are seldom passed on to daughters.

2. *Religious factors in family business.*
   Nigeria is an intensely religious society with two dominant inclinations—Christianity and Islam. Both, however, are as a consequence of European colonial influences from the southern coasts and an Arabic influence from the northern arid areas. These have lasted about two centuries and have severely shrunk the influence of traditional religious practices. In both instances, however, both religions have not altered the gender roles, on the contrary rather, reinforcing them. For instance, in the predominantly Islamic areas, especially in the north of Nigeria, a woman's involvement in economic activities may be limited. This so-called "glass ceiling" may be inferred as being very prevalent in Nigeria. Even in formal paid employment, women could be disadvantaged as some employers are reluctant to employ women. Gender disparities are still very glaring in Nigeria (Okoh, 2010).

3. *Women entrepreneurs would rather handover to sons.*
   Women entrepreneurs control just 1 percent of the manufacturing sector in Nigeria. Enterprises owned and managed by women are small with low success rates (Achoja and Eyaefe, 2010). Despite these low levels of participation by females as entrepreneurs, the propensity is not to have those businesses inherited by daughters. An interesting dimension to entrepreneurship and business inheritance in Nigeria, therefore, is that even female business owners would rather have their businesses inherited by their sons and not their daughters. The prevalent attitude is that women perceive sons as being more capable at succeeding them and as also at keeping the business(es) within the family.

4. *Lack of interest and capability.*
   Since succession is the act or process of one person taking the place of another in the enjoyment of, or liability for, his or her rights or duties or both (Webster's, 1993 cited by Ukaegbu, 2003), some daughters may want to inherit the wealth of their fathers because of the resources and use it as mere entitlement for their daily living and comfort. This line of logic considers that they may not be interested in or capable of carrying out the responsibilities of the business. She may not be ready to be the risk bearer, increase and manage wealth and set and implement goals.

Limitations and Future Research Directions

The first limitation of this narrative springs from the lack of literature and previous research on the subject of father–daughter succession in local family businesses. There have been some of changes and advances in the roles of women in Nigeria. Yet, despite changes in several other aspects of life and living in Nigeria, not much has changed in the attitude to inheritance. There is also lack of real world cases relating to father–daughter business inheritance in Nigeria that can be examined ethnographically. Nigerian researchers aspire to continuing research work in family business to enlighten and bring to the cultural dialogue the issue of father–daughter succession in Nigerian family businesses.

References

Achoja, F.O. and Eyaefe, J.A. 2010. Repositioning Women Entrepreneurs in a Depressed Global Economy: The Nigerian Experience in *Engendering Policy for Attainment of the Millennium Development Goals in* Nigeria (pp. 98–104), edited by R. Okoh. Asaba, Nigeria: Rural Linkage Network.

Anyafulu, B. 2010. Human Rights and Violence Against Women: A Faceless Struggle in *Engendering Policy for Attainment of the Millennium Development Goals in Nigeria* (pp. 47–55), edited by R. Okoh. Asaba, Nigeria: Rural Linkage Network.

Central Bank of Nigeria (CBN). Various years. *Statistical Bulletin*, Abuja: CBN.

Building Nigeria's Reponse to Climate Change (BNRCC). 2010. *Gender and Climate Change Toolkit*. Ibadan, Nigeria: BNRCC/NEST.

Choksi, A.M. 1995. Foreword *Development in Practice: Toward Gender Equality*. Washington: The World Bank.

Federal Ministry of Women Affairs and Social Development (FMWSD). 2006. *National Gender Policy*.

Fordham, M. 2001. *Challenging Boundaries: A Gender Perspective on Early Warning in Disaster and Environmental Management, UNDAW, Environmental Management and the Mitigation of Natural Disasters: A Gender Perspective*. Report of the Expert Group Meeting, Ankara, Turkey, November 2001, New York, USA.

Hesse, A. 2005. Towards a Feminist Human Rights Perspective. *Poverty, Inequality and Insecurity*. Brussels: Wide. p. 42. Available at: http://www.iiav.nl/ezines//email/DawnInforms/2005/November.pdf [accessed 02 August 2011].

Ohajianya, D.O., Nwaiwu, I.U. and Osuagwu, C.O. 2010. Analysis of Factors Affecting Income of Women in Agricultural Production in Imo State Nigeria, in *Engendering Policy for Attainment of the Millennium Development Goals in Nigeria* (pp. 91–97), edited by R. Okoh. Asaba: Nigeria: Rural Linkage Network.

Okoh, R. 2010. Engendering Policy for Attainment of the Millennium Development Goals: An Overview in *Engendering Policy for Attainment of the Millennium Development Goals in Nigeria* (pp. 5–15), edited by R. Okoh. Asaba, Nigeria: Rural Linkage Network.

Sharma, P., Chrisman, L., Pablo, L. and Chua, I. 2001. Determinants of Initial Satisfaction with the Succession Process in Family Firms: A Conceptual Model. *Entrepreneurship Theory and Practice*, 25(3), 17–25.

Ukaegbu, C.C. 2003. Entrepreneurial Succession and Post-Founder Durability: A Study of Indigenous Private Manufacturing Firms in Igbo States of Nigeria. *Journal of Contemporary African Studies*, 21(1), 4–5.

PART IV Europe

CHAPTER 10 France: Father–Daughter Succession in France: The ONET Group Case Study

KATIA RICHOMME-HUET AND JULIEN DE FREYMAN

Introduction

Is a cross-gender team spanning two generations (Jaffe and Brown, 2003), such as father and daughter, able to run a family business effectively? This is a key question, despite the fact that Schumpeter (1934) considered that heirs tend to destroy family businesses through inappropriate management methods (Cater, 2006). In France, family businesses account for 60 percent of the gross national product (IFERA, 2003), however the country is faced with a paradox: whereas 39 percent of owners (KPMG, 2007; PWC, 2006) express the desire to keep the business within the family, at 7.2 percent (Transregio, 2006), the proportion of successors in the next generation willing to take over is the lowest in Europe.

There are a variety of reasons for this lack of interest among both men and women as potential successors. These include business and capital transfer taxes, the complexity of the legal rules, funding sources, the lack of anticipation, and the change in work–life balance (Mellerio Report, 2009). Nevertheless, the gender barrier is an aggravating factor (Dumas, 1998): whereas women are given credit for just over 32 percent of entrepreneurial activities in France (GEM, 2007), few daughters succeed their fathers (Bayad and Barbot, 2002). Therefore, in France, men probably have less to worry about and less to prove. By focusing on the case of a granddaughter–successor who took over as President of ONET SA, this case study illustrates some of the cultural and social attitudes that make it difficult for women to climb the family business ladder.

Literature Review

Up until recently, French authors have mainly focused on semantic and managerial aspects of family business (Caby and Hirigoyen, 2002; Allouche and Amann, 2008), or considered the origins and nature of the pros and cons of such businesses (Arrègle et al., 2004; Arrègle and Mari, 2010). However, an increasing number of scholars are beginning to explore the problems surrounding family business succession (Begin et al., 2010; De Freyman and Richomme-Huet, 2010). While there is established research on preferences for male successors (Dumas, 1989), research on father–daughter succession is only just beginning to emerge. For example, Bayad and Barbot (2002) consider the particular difficulties experienced by women successors and suggest further work on the father–daughter succession process in unlisted family businesses. Other scholars confirm the close interconnection between the managerial and ownership dimensions of family business succession and exemplify how difficult it is for women to be recognized as acceptable, credible, and legitimate successors (Barach et al., 1988). In their study of a father–son–daughter triad within a family business succession context, Richomme-Huet and De Freyman (2005) showed that the presence of a "committed" daughter in the family business added to this complexity. The importance of cultural variables in the father-to-daughter succession process were further underlined by Barbot et al. (2004).

The Case Study

ONET SA GROUP: BRIEF HISTORY OF THE FIRM: FROM THE MARSEILLES DOCKS TO NUCLEAR POWER STATIONS

In 1860, Hippolyte Format set up his own business, called "Maison Format." It specialized in the handling of sacks of commodities and the provision of cleaning services to mills on hillsides close to the Port of Marseilles. In 1924, his grandson, Hippolyte Reinier, developed and mechanized the cleaning activities, which became the company's core business (renamed "ONET" in 1950). He also set up subsidiaries in other cities (Lyon and Nice), regions (Savoie and Languedoc-Roussillon), and bordering countries (Switzerland, Monaco, Belgium, Luxembourg, Spain, and Italy). The company moved from being a local operation to an international operation in three generations.

In 1973, with Louis Reinier (Hippolyte's son) at the helm, new services were introduced based on consultancy. By 1987, nearly 10 percent of the capital was floated, the Reinier family remained the majority shareholder with 87 percent of the shares. From that point onward the company increased its operations through the acquisition of innovative companies (Telem in the field of electronic security and Comex in the field of nuclear industry) and competitors (Entreprise Ferroviaire-Safen in the cleaning sector) as well as establishing international partnerships with, for example, Mitsubishi, AECL, ENS, and NUKEM. The ONET Group is now a major player in the corporate services sector, with a turnover of over 1.2 billion euros, more than 55,000 employees distributed across a network of 300 local branches, and a head office in Marseille.

THE SUCCESSION PROCESS AND THE GENERATIONAL OVERLAP

In 1978, Hippolyte Reinier (third generation successor) decided to retire. He separated the succession of the company into two different processes: whereas the ownership was handed over to his children (his son Louis Reinier and his daughter Janine Reinier-Fabre, the fourth generation), the management was split between Louis Reinier (his son) and Paul Fabre (Janine's husband). Hippolyte also appointed a right-hand man: "When he was making decisions on who would succeed him, he called on Max Massa to drive the business, which meant that there were three people taking decisions for the company."

The process of succession can be costly in financial terms. As this was the case in previous successions, it became an important issue for the current generation because there was a belief that poor handling could affect the company's valuation and in addition have tax implications. To minimize potential problems the two owners (Louis and Janine) and their families (namely Reinier and Fabre) decided to start the ownership succession process early; and in order to determine the correct company value, they floated ONET on the Stock Exchange (in June 1987) to value the company at the current market price.

In 2004, the company's governance was reorganized to prepare the succession from the fourth to the fifth generation. Louis had one child and potential successor, Elisabeth Reinier, while his sister Janine Reiner Fabre had three children, Anne Fabre, Françoise Fabre, and Marie Fabre-Grenet. The holding company "Financière Reinier," created in 1990, was merged into ONET SA, to enable the creation of two new separate holding companies: Holding Fabre with the members of the Fabre family (Janine and her husband and their three daughters and Roland Grenet, Marie's husband) and Holding Reinier with the members of the Reinier family (Louis, his wife, and their only daughter Elisabeth Coquet-Reinier). Roles were shared equally in the holding company, the supervisory board, the board of directors, and the executive board. This structure operated until 2007—this was the year that heralded a final break between the two families. The Fabre family sold its shares to the other side of the family after an uneasy relationship, and this cleared the way for Elisabeth Coquet-Reinier to become chairman of Holding Reinier in October 2007, which now holds 100 percent of the ONET SA capital.

SUCCESSOR IN WAITING

When Elisabeth Coquet-Reinier joined the company in 1977 at the wish of her grandfather, her first job was to sort the mail. She was paid the guaranteed minimum wage, even though she had four years of higher education under her belt! She was strongly encouraged by her grandfather Hippolyte to study economics, with a view to entering the family business: "You will study economics; you will take all the time you want but you will take over the business!" Elisabeth explains, "For my part, I wanted to do research, I was a scientist! To him, I was the oldest of the four cousins, 'the family son' and I had to take over the firm." She gave up her personal plans, obtained her degree, and gained work experience within the family business whilst studying for a master's degree in 1977.

In time, and step by step, Elisabeth created her own jobs and departments, for example, Control and Audit, and Communication, and began to build her career experience in her own way, even though this meant at times demonstrating her own frustration, as she says: "With every outburst I climbed a rung on the ladder." It seems that for Elisabeth her early years in the company were ones of emotional turmoil:

> *I don't believe they saw the progress I was making; I carved out my own niche. However, for ten years, it was a constant struggle and every evening I asked myself what on earth I was doing in this firm. It was my mother who said: 'Hang on in there, hang on in there!'*

Despite the support of her grandfather and his wish to see her take over the company one day, at times it seemed that her gender undermined the support she received from her father and uncle: "My father and my uncle were not very 'feminist'! They were in fact very, very macho ... so, a woman ... They had no confidence in me at all! For them, it was not my role." Elisabeth's strategic response was to alternate between "outbursts" and "diplomatic silence," so as not to "rock the boat."

However, by 1991, she had become a company executive in charge of management control and audit. She continued to make her mark against the backdrop of a male-dominated business. From 2007, following the sale of the Fabre family shares, the ownership structure was to become much simpler and clearer.

CULTURAL DIMENSIONS AND FATHER–DAUGHTER SUCCESSION IN ONET SA: SUCCESSION PLANNING

Ownership succession was planned to limit the impact of high taxation and to keep voting rights. Indeed, when Hippolyte died, the cost of the succession led Louis and Janine to favor another valuation method (by floating on the stock market) to transfer "bare ownership" to their children in the form of shares (49.99 percent and three lots of 16.67 percent). In line with their parent's wishes, Elisabeth and her cousins had little decision-making power during this period, despite being members of various management boards, in fact her three female cousins had no management role at all.

Elisabeth was viewed as a legitimate successor as a result of her grandfather's wish to see her take over the family business. Therefore, her coronation was supported by the whole of the Reinier family. They had decided unanimously to take out a loan to purchase the Fabre shares up for sale. It was also supported by all the employees who followed Elisabeth in her plans for the future. She recounts: "It seems silly to say so, but I had the same philosophy as my grandfather, which was not necessarily the case of the son-in-law or indeed my aunt."

The presence of Max Massa, called on by Hippolyte to manage the family business, made Elisabeth's succession easier since he set himself up as her mentor: "Mr. Massa was my Pygmalion: he took me with him everywhere; he took me on site visits; he took me to see customers. He was my mentor!" He holds 0.4 percent of the capital in his own right and 0.43 percent with other employees.

RIVALRY, DISCRIMINATION, AND GENDER STEREOTYPE

Family rivalries were often limited, thanks to the family pact that guaranteed a board place and holding from each branch of the family. Nevertheless, differences in points of view persisted and were not always settled. By asserting herself, Elisabeth turned some members of the Fabre family against her. However, she observes: "In family businesses, you don't talk of rivalry; it never goes that far and that's the key to their success." Professionally, Elisabeth considers that she had to behave in ways which would reflect and protect the values of the family. She deliberately refrained from taking positions or making changes in order to "tread carefully so as to avoid conflicts." Conflict was not tolerated in the family: "It was about being a team from start to finish; there was no room for individuals." Conflict was only conceivable in the work context, provided it was quickly resolved so as not to "jeopardize the company. Everything is interconnected, especially in a family firm."

The fact of her gender added other difficulties that Elisabeth had to face: "I heard a lot of people say: 'you're a woman, it's not your place', so I asked myself a lot of questions both about myself and my abilities." After the death of her grandfather (who was at the heart of her career plan), it became more difficult and complex to rally effective support from members of the two families. A form of discrimination against Elisabeth developed more easily and was clearly connected to gender stereotyping:

> *To begin with, in their eyes, the fact that I had three children meant that I didn't have time to work as well as bring up children. And I was a woman as well! Lastly, I didn't have a background of top-level higher education in business management or engineering! Had I been a boy, I wouldn't have gone through the same experience at all. Not at all! Well, I don't know whether it's good or bad but I do know that for a start they would have respected me more and that it would have been less difficult for me to learn the ropes!*

At one point Elisabeth found herself facing two choices: to either accept playing second fiddle or to boost her chances of becoming the successor. She finally opted for the second option: "Precedent was on my side, I knew the firm inside out and I saw that there would be a problem (for example, with the son-in-law's management), that I couldn't let it happen." It would take her 30 years of patience, presence, skill, and tenacity to be seen as the natural and obvious successor. "I slammed a lot of doors, I shouted a lot in the corridors ... it's not at all what you should do but I did it anyway!" Succession has finally indeed refocused things on one family and around Elisabeth: "With the remaining family, we are so used to saying things to one another's face that we never get into conflict."

Discussion and Conclusions

The literature on family business succession refers to a combination of conditions favorable to the "coronation" of women successors (Vera and Dean, 2005). They are referred to as successors by default (Bayad and Barbot, 2002), and "invisible" candidates (Dumas, 1989); they are rarely associated with being the "natural" solution, and must often rely on the absence of a son or one that is disinterested in succession. The ONET case does indeed confirm that the absence of a male candidate may be a necessary and conducive condition to the emergence of a female successor in France (Dumas, 1989; Constantinidis, 2010). However, it also shows that it is not sufficient as a condition, as despite the presence of a son-in-law, Elisabeth was eventually able to take over. Some personality traits (character, determination, patience, and so on), skills (managerial, human, entrepreneurial, and so on), and support (family and non-family) are also required for the female successor (Constantinidis, 2010).

The importance of the ONET case is that it shows that female successors may have to become invisible for a time during their quest for succession. This may also be the case when the decision on how the female successor enters the family business is not hers to make. Furthermore, invisibility may be a strategy that allows women to quietly but steadfastly develop the skills and experience they may need to eventually become a serious contender. Elisabeth herself suggests a deferred strategy, as she put it, "Don't join the family business immediately after finishing your studies. Start out somewhere else, gain some knowledge and work hard before you join the company."

The case shows how challenging it is for a female successor (Dumas, 1990) to dissociate family and business in her relationship with her father (convergence of the woman's role and place within the family and the company). It is nevertheless important to note that Elisabeth was selected by her grandfather as the key successor because she was the first-born of all children in the fifth generation. Her gender seemed less important as there were no sons from whom to select. However, the transition is not necessarily a smooth or automatic process and females may have to work harder to prove themselves and their competence. According to Barbot et al. (2004), the daughter must prove her competence to her father and to other family members. Furthermore, she also needs to affirm her independence toward her father, a characteristic typical of western culture (Dumas, 1990). However, the ONET case shows us that intra-family conflicts, often brought up in the literature, are not necessarily the most destabilizing since "family pacts" can, in France, give rise to inter-family tensions that are much more destructive for the female successor.

Limitations and Future Research

This chapter sought to highlight, within the scope of a French context, some of the particular issues related to a family business handover to a female successor, and to emphasize some aspects of the complexity arising from the "father–daughter" relationship. The ONET case study, using secondary data and an interview with its leader, revealed some strategic decisions, interpersonal relationships, and cultural behavior that can influence the outcome of the successor's challenge. However, these results need to be put into perspective as they are based on a single case study; however, these results provide some insight into an area in which there has been extremely limited research to date. We suggest further research could focus on the decision on the method of succession and inter-family conflict management.

References

Allouche, J. and Amann, B. 2008. Nature et Performances des Entreprises Familiales, in *Le Management, Fondements et Renouvellements* (pp. 223–232), edited by G. Schmidt. Paris: Sciences Humaines.

Arrègle, J-L, Durand, R. and Very, P. 2004. Origines du Capital Social et Avantages Concurrentiels des Firmes Familiales. *M@n@gement*, 7(2), 13–36.

Arrègle, J.L. and Mari, I. 2010. Avantages ou Désavantages des Entreprises Familiales? *Revue Française de Gestion*, 200(Janvier), 87–109.

Barach, J.A., Gantisky, J.B., Carson, J.A. and Doochin, A. 1988. Entry of the Next Generation: Strategic Challenge for Family Business. *Journal of Small Business Management*, 26(2), 49–56.

Barbot, M.C., Bayad, M. and Bourguiba, M. 2004. *Transmission, des PME Familiales: Etude Exploratoire de la Relève Père-Fille en Tunisie*. Actes du Séminaire 'l'Entrepreneuriat en Tunisie, Quelles Recherches? Quelles Formations?', ENIT, Tunis, 29–30 April.

Bayad M. and Barbot M.C. 2002. *Proposition d'un Modèle de Succession dans les PME Familiales: Étude de Cas Exploratoire de la Relation Père-Fille*. Congrès International Francophone sur la PME, HEC Montréal.

Begin, L., Chabaud, D. and Richomme-Huet, K. 2010. Vers une Approche Contingente des Entreprises Familiales. *Revue Française de Gestion*, 200(Janvier), 79–86.

Caby, J. and Hirigoyen, G. 2002. *La Gestion des Entreprises Familiales*. Paris: Economica.

Cater, J.J. 2006. *Stepping Out of the Shadow: The Leadership Qualities of Successors in Family Business*. Unpublished Thesis, Louisiana State University.

Constantinidis, C. 2010. Entreprise Familiale et Genre. *Revue Française de Gestion*, 200(Janvier), 143–159.

Cédants & Repreneurs d'Affaires (CRA). 2006. *Observatoire CRA de la Transmission des PME-PMI*. Available at: http://www.cra.asso.fr/Observatoire-de-la-transmission [accessed: 12 July 2010].

De Freyman, J. and Richomme-Huet, K. 2010. Entreprises Familiales et Phénomène Successoral. *Revue Française de Gestion*, 200(Janvier), 161–179.

Dumas, C. 1989. Understanding of Father–Daughter and Father–Son Dyads in Family-Owned Business. *Family Business Review*, 2(1), 31–46.

Dumas, C. 1990. Preparing the New CEO: Managing the Father–Daughter Succession Process in Family Businesses. *Family Business Review*, 3(2), 169–181.

Dumas, C. 1998. Women's Pathways to Participation and Leadership in the Family-Owned Firm. *Family Business Review*, 11(3), 219–228.

International Family Enterprise Research Academy (IFERA). 2003. Family Businesses Dominate. International Family Enterprise Research Academy. *Family Businesses Review*, 16(4), 235–240.

Jaffe, D.T. and Brown, F.H. 2003. When Succession Crosses Genders. *Family Business Magazine*, Spring. Available at: http://www.dennisjaffe.com/articles/WhenSuccessionCrossesGenders.pdf [accessed: 13 July 2010].

KPMG. 2007. *L'Entreprise Familiale: Une Entreprise Décidément pas Comme les Autres*. KPMG Entreprises.

Mellerio Report. 2009. *Transmission de l'Entreprise Familiale*. Rapport à Hervé Novelli, Secrétaire d'Etat chargé du Commerce, de l'Artisanat, des Petites et Moyennes Entreprises, du Tourisme, du Service et de la Consommation, Octobre.

PWC (PriceWaterhouseCoopers). 2006. *Enquête sur les Entreprises Familiales Françaises*. Available at: http://www.pwc.fr/enquete_sur_les_entreprises_familiales_francaises2.html [accessed: 13 July 2010].

Richomme-Huet, K. and De Freyman, J. 2005. *La Triade Père-Fils-Fille dans la Succession Familiale: Une Approche par le Récit de Vie*. Actes du colloque L'entrepreneuriat: des enjeux, des stratégies et des hommes, Brest.

Schumpeter, J. 1934. *The Theory of Economic Development. An Inquiry into Profits, Capital, Credit, Interest, and the Business Cycle*. Cambridge: Harvard University Press.

Transrégio. 2006. *Enquête sur la Transmission d'Entreprise dans Sept pays Européens*.

Vera, C.F. and Dean, M.A. 2005. An Examination of the Challenges Daughters Face in Family Business Succession. *Family Business Review*, 18(4), 321–345.

CHAPTER **11**

Germany: Family Business Paradox and Gender Role Strain: An Example of Father–Daughter Succession from Germany

CHRISTINA ERDMANN

Introduction

This case study will show how a female German successor faced the fundamental paradox of family business (Simon et al., 2005; von Schlippe et al., 2008) and gender role strain (Levant and Philpot, 2006) during her succession process. The integration of both concepts has not yet been achieved in research on female succession. Rather they are discussed either in the family business research (von Schlippe, 2009) or marital and family therapy research (Levant and Philpot, 2006). It will become obvious that withstanding the fundamental paradox of the family business system as well as overcoming traditional role convictions is a challenge to both the father–predecessor and the daughter–successor. It will also become clear that traditional, gender role-related convictions still influence succession processes by daughters in today's Germany.

Literature Overview

FAMILY BUSINESSES: THE PIVOT OF GERMANY'S ECONOMY

In Germany family businesses are an important part of the country's economy. Depending on the definition, up to 95 percent of all German businesses can be categorized as family enterprises (Institut für Mittelstandsforschung, 2007). Family businesses realize approximately 40 percent of total revenue in Germany and provide almost 60 percent of all jobs that are subject to social insurance contribution (Ibid.). Approximately 70,000 to 110,000 businesses (Klussmann, 2008; IFM, 2010) in Germany will be transferred in the next five years, and 90 percent of all family-owned businesses look for a family member to take over the business (Freund, 2001).

FEMALE SUCCESSORS IN GERMAN FAMILY BUSINESSES

In entrepreneurial families succession by the eldest son had been standard for generations (Erdmann, 1999; Erdmann, 2010, Schäfer 2007). Continuity of the business was intertwined with continuity of the entrepreneurial family. Female succession was an uncommon exception to that rule (Isfan 2002, Schäfer 2007). Sometimes a business was closed when there was no son was around to take it over rather than looking for "unconventional options," for example, succession by a daughter. In most cases such an option was not within the realm of consideration.

In modern Germany this mindset seems to be changing. In recent years many daughters of business families have taken over a business from a father or a mother, and in the media there are a lot of reports about successful female successors (for example, Klussmann, 2008, Stern, 2005). People are also aware of specific circumstances for women when becoming entrepreneurs or successors (Voigt, 1994). Special programs are in place to promote women to managerial jobs, or support them when founding their own (small) business (Bundesministerium für Bildung und Forschung, 2008) or to take over businesses from incumbents or non-family owners (Bundesweite Gründerinnen Agentur, 2010).

However, taking a closer look at individual cases, female leaders as successors is still not standard. Although women today represent around 45 percent of the working population (Bundesministerium für Familie, Senioren, Frauen und Jugend, 2009), only one-tenth of all successors are women (Bundesweite Gründerinnen Agentur, 2010). Arguments against women as successors still seem to stem from a very traditional understanding of the female gender role (see Figure 11.1).

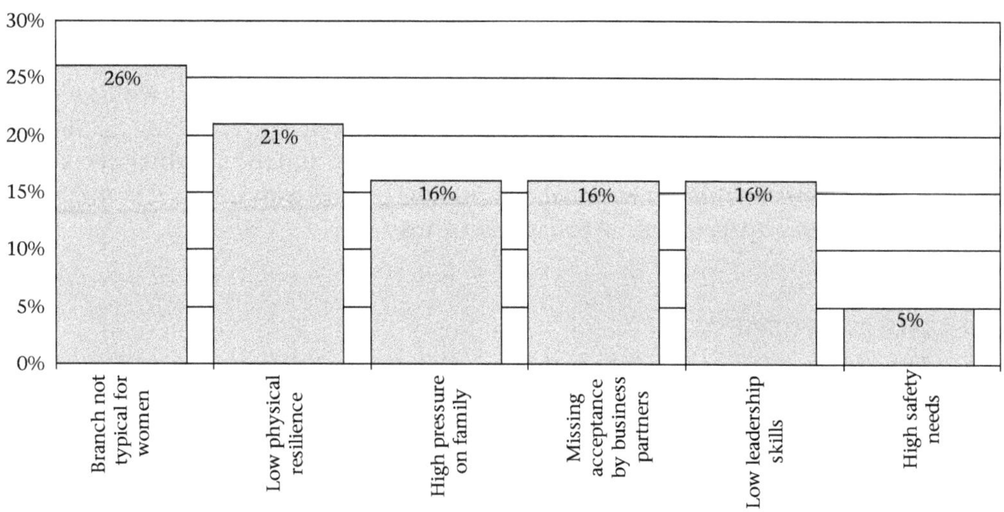

Figure 11.1 Main arguments against women as successors

Source: Bundesweite Gründerinnen Agentur (2010), translation by CE

PREPARATION FOR SUCCESSION AND GENDER-RELATED OBSTACLES

Often female successors have not been prepared in advance to take over the business (Keese, 2002). Sechser (2009) notes that by gaining qualification and self-confidence, daughters must first emancipate themselves from their role of being "just the daughter" to being the daughter working as top manager or CEO in the family business (Ronke, 2008). Although they are often willing to take the leadership role, many daughters still encounter resistance in their own families, facing gender-related prejudices or a patriarchal family culture (Haubl and Daser, 2006). Daughters are likely to encounter the kind of resistance that sons would not and thus find that this must support their own interests and exert more force than a son would have to. They are more open to accepting their father as their advisor after succession is in place. Moreover, they tolerate and accept a father's influence to a larger extent than a son would be likely to accept (Angelopoulou, 2008; Klussmann, 2008).

PARADOXES IN FAMILY BUSINESSES

The case presented here will show how the successor and the incumbent are captured in paradoxical needs of their family system and the enterprise system which they are not able to dissolve.

In the agrarian, pre-industrialized society, "the family" and "the business" were one unit. Because of industrialization both systems grew apart and different rules for behavior and decision making emerged based on different systems of logic (Simon et al., 2005:31). Behavior patterns appropriate in one system might not be in the other. These patterns are contradictory and cannot be harmonized (see Table 11.1).

Table 11.1 Family system and enterprise system

	Family System	Enterprise System
Access	Birth, matrimony, adoption	Entry, employment
Exit	Not possible	Possible, depending on contract
Communications	Attachment communications	Decision communication
Ways of communication	Barely formalized, oral, hardly hierarchic	Formalized, written, hierarchic
Decision	Broad room for negotiation, rather consent-oriented	Sparse room for negotiation, hierarch-oriented
Importance	The individual person (not exchangeable)	Function, competence (the individual is basically exchangeable)
Currency	Love, attachment, faithfulness, loyalty, survival	Manpower, commitment, competence
Adjustment	Appreciation, recognition, affiliation (long-ranging, e.g. for decades)	Money, salary (short-termed, and mid-term—if applicable: career options)
Criteria for Justice	Equality: everyone gets the same, or: everyone gets what they need "distributive justice"	Inequality: position and salary depending on output, competencies and commitment in the network) "initial justice"

Source: von Schlippe and Klein (2010), translation by CE

In non-entrepreneurial families the two systems are separate. Individuals follow the rules of both systems according to their respective situation. Entrepreneurial families, though, are not able to make this distinction: in family business both systems are intertwined daily (Simon et al., 2005:34). As a consequence, those families face a paradox. What might be adequate behavior in one system can be completely disproportionate in the other, but they have no chance to set one system aside: their day-to-day business and family activities intertwine. For example, the role of the successor as CEO will carry different behavioral expectations than the role of daughter. Successful family businesses utilize this paradox as a driving force, following the family logic in some instances and the enterprise logic in other situations (Simon et al., 2005:34). They deliberately negotiate the respective terms and needs of these situations again and again.

THE GENDER ROLE STRAIN PARADIGM

The question of succession by daughters in Germany is still influenced, if not limited, by a "dominant patriarchal idea of the social structure" (Breuer, 2009:329, translation by CE). The case presented here offers an example of a female successor's efforts of finding her own way into effective succession and leadership in a strongly traditional environment. These convictions often cause strain related to the gender role (Levant and Philpot, 2006), and seem to amplify the difficulties entrepreneurial family members already face because of the paradox described above.

The psychological perspective of gender role identity paradigm assumes a person has an inherent need to meet traditional gender roles. These needs have both biological and social roots. Successful personality development included gender role identity (Levant and Philpot, 2006:304).

In contrast, the gender role strain paradigm proposes that appropriate gender roles are determined by the prevailing gender ideology ... and are imposed on the developing child by parents, teachers, physicians, and peers—the cultural transmitters who subscribe to the prevailing gender ideology (Levant and Philpot, 2006:305).

This constructivist perspective on gender roles assumes that gender roles are psychological and socially constructed entities that can be learned—and changed. The case presented in this chapter offers an example of such change and the underlying learning process. It also demonstrates which difficulties the daughter–successor faced that can be allocated to either discrepancy strain, dysfunction strain, or trauma strain (Levant and Philpot, 2006).

- *Discrepancy strain* might be "experienced by an individual who does not perceive herself to fit to the mold of the 'ideal women'" (Levant and Philpot, 2006:309). This kind of strain is related to standards of beauty, marriage, and motherhood, and the so-called "Superwoman Syndrome."
- *Dysfunction strain* may arise after a woman has "attained the socially reinforced personality characteristics, values, and roles appropriate for the ideal female, because the standards themselves are associated with negative outcomes" (Levant and Philpot, 2006:311).
- *Trauma strain* occurs "when a woman suffers trauma in the process of gender socialization" (Levant and Philpot, 2006:313), which might occur, for example, in the form of devaluation and role restriction.

It becomes obvious that the female successor interviewed for this case study experienced the paradox described above as well as other forms of gender role strain (albeit she did not use the word "strain" explicitly to describe her situation).

The Case Study

The interviewer met with the female successor in her office in her construction company. The interview was conducted in German. This account is as literal as possible while maintaining the spirit of the discussion. Names and specifications have been adjusted to protect the identities of the parties.

THE BUSINESS: LEADERSHIP STRUCTURE

Wilhelm Hartmann founded the business in 1910 in a mid-size town in the Ruhr Area in western Germany. The company then was handed from father to son for three generations. Today Wilhelm's great-granddaughter Martina (39) is CEO. In 2009 the company had 100 employees and a revenue of 25 million euros. The particular year marks the most successful one in the company's history.

Walter Hartmann, Martina's father, took over the business from his father in 1968 at the age of 27. In 1994 Walter set up an advisory board that he chairs. In 1998 a non-family member CEO was appointed who had been a long-time company employee. This CEO, Thomas Winter, reported directly to Walter Hartmann. In 2004, Martina, Walter's eldest daughter and member of the fourth generation, joined the business at her father's request. As will become clear from the interview, this was not an invitation to succession but presumably an expression of Walter's concerns about his daughter's future situation at that time.

> *I believe, my father offered this job to me not preferentially in terms of "She will be my successor." Above all, he was concerned I have a job after my divorce. He did not doubt my competencies. But he is very patriarchal in his thinking, so from his point of view, succession is a job a woman shouldn't do.*

Since 2004, Thomas Winter and Martina have shared the leadership function. While he is responsible for all technical issues, Martina focuses on acquisition, client service, human relations, and strategic development of the company. Both are the main contact persons for all general foremen and construction managers working in the company.

OWNERSHIP STRUCTURE

Although Martina leads the company, Walter remains the only shareholder as had his father and his grandfather. In the 1990s Walter received a very attractive offer to sell the business—which he dismissed: "He did not find an answer to what he would do after selling the business. So he didn't sell. If I had not come, he would have continued to be the leader behind the CEO." The present ownership structure will change in the near future. At present Martina and her father are negotiating a new contract, and Martina is sure about the outcome:

> *Shares will be distributed 30:30:30:10. My father, my sister, and I will have 30 percent each, and Thomas Winter will get 10 percent. I will buy out my sister as soon as possible. My goal is to get all shares except Thomas Winter's 10 percent. I will not be able to get my father's shares very soon, but that might simply be a question of time.*

Martina negotiates with tenacity: "The first draft of the new contract was not acceptable to me. In the end, I would have had no say, the decision-making power would have been completely in my father's hands as it was before."

AN EXAMPLE FOR THE FAMILY BUSINESS PARADOX IN THE HARTMANN COMPANY

When Martina had been asked by her father to enter the business she had relocated to her parent's place having gone through her divorce only some months before. Her two small daughters stayed with her and she had decided to go "back to my roots, where my family and all of my friends live." Until that time she had essentially lived the life of a traditional wife and mother, as seen below.

When she entered the family business, she noted:

> *My father made a big mistake in not informing the employees what I would be doing. Mr Winter knew only that I was about to start working in the company. "By the way, my daughter is about to work here!" He only gave me general directions on what he expected from me.*

Walter Hartmann's behavior is a typical expression of the paradox entrepreneurial families often face. From a family system's perspective, his behavior is very logical. In the situation dealt with here, he acted as a father—barely formalized, oral, regardless of hierarchies, putting the individual (his daughter) in a position which ensures her survival in terms of occupation and income (see Table 11.1). The problem with this behavior is that he showed family-related behavior in the enterprise system. Acting as a normal employer with his daughter (giving clear advice to the CEO and informing the employees about his daughter's entry in the business) would probably not have met his convictions about loyalty and love within his family.

On the other hand, Martina as the newly employed daughter had different expectations. She had expected to be introduced as any other employee. Having this in mind, she behaved in terms of the enterprise system and not mainly as the proprietor's daughter. "I did not know this. I didn't know that my father did not tell the others the work he thought I should do." The absence of an appropriate mixture between enterprise- and family-related communication with his employees caused a lot of conflicts for Martina in her daily work.

> *I faced big problems, especially when it came to whether I got acceptance for my decisions. I believe that in my first two years no one took me seriously. But then I decided not to be content with that situation ... I started to call for changes, especially in terms of structure and development. We had to change things together, and I showed them that it worked. I acquired new clients, and they realized that I knew what to do.*

It became obvious that Martina was seen as the "little daughter" in the beginning when she was brought to the business and introduced by her father from a family system perspective. She was able to leave that role behind as soon as she started to behave from the enterprise system perspective. This does not mean that she no longer sees herself as her father's daughter. Instead, getting the recognition and the respect of the employees shows that she had found a way to combine the needs and characteristics of both systems in her own way. "I know that I have achieved a lot in the years since I am here. I have improved things, and I will go on with that. I want the recognition for what I do. Basically, this is a beautiful gift, when I get the respect and thanks of my employees."

A lot of other examples concerning this paradox can be found in the interview, mainly focusing on the communication issue between father and daughter or predecessor and successor. For example, Martina points out that until today there are heated discussions with her father: "In the first years we were at loggerheads with each other. But today I am able to show great patience and endeavor, let this kind of struggle pass by and try to find my own way." Due to limited space in this study, this issue will not be discussed here but will be the subject of further research.

AN EXAMPLE OF GENDER ROLE DISCREPANCY STRAIN FOR MARTINA

At the beginning of her marriage, Martina submitted herself to a traditional way of living. "I married very early and had my first daughter at the age of 22. I followed my husband to his hometown because he wanted to live nowhere else. When he decided to go the United States of America (USA) to continue with his studies, I interrupted my own studies." During that period she lived a traditional role allocation. Succession "was not up for debate." Throughout the interview a lot of statements can be found that express her own tradition-oriented perspective as well as her father's traditionalistic attitudes and convictions about women's role.

However, Martina is not a traditional woman to the core. Her biography forced her to find her own individual way in terms of motherhood, marriage, and as an active business woman.

When she and her husband left the USA after two years, the family settled in a country close to Germany. Her husband pursued his career there. Martina started to continue her own studies again. "I had my second daughter when I had restarted my renewed studies and was in the middle of my second state examination." Then she began her legal clerkship and "commuted between two places of residence. Three to four days per week I lived at my parent's place in the Ruhr Area together with my daughter, doing my legal clerkship ... while the rest of the week I was with my husband abroad." With her divorce some years later it became clear that the idea of living a traditional life as wife and mother would not work for her any longer. In the interview she offers no background of the divorce, but it is very likely that after the divorce Martina suffered from discrepancy strain in terms of motherhood and marriage. "With two small children one had to think about how to rearrange one's life again and was forced to develop a new structure."

Martina faced this kind of strain later also. She wants to be a good mother for her two daughters but also a successful business woman. She is very aware that, despite the demands of these roles, it "was clear that I benefit from a kind of 'family bonus' [when entering the father's business]. I would never have to argue if I suspended work unexpectedly, for example, because one of my children was sick." Levant and Philpot (2006:310f.) mention the "superwoman syndrome" wherein women try to fulfill the demands of the traditional female gender ideology as well as of the modern (business) woman. It seems to be typical for entrepreneurial women to not see themselves as "superwomen" but think of this doubled demand as normal. However, this group of demands, deriving from different roles, lead to role overload which contributes to dysfunctional strain as well as trauma strain from role restrictions (see below).

DYSFUNCTION STRAIN FROM DEPENDENCE

This kind of strain cannot be identified directly from the interview. However, Martina talks about how she wants her daughters to be independent referring to her own feelings of dependence on her husband as well as on her father:

> *From my life story, I think of independence as one of the most important issues in one's life. And my children are brought up that way. They should never be hooked on something or somebody. I hope they never make themselves dependent on a man, for example, a husband.*

Her convictions do not only lead to a general statement about independence, but to very precise and practical ideas for the future:

> *Once my own daughters become mothers themselves I will pay for child care from the very first day. They will be able to continue with their work … of course we have a totally different family life compared to other families, where a traditional role allocation exists.*

DYSFUNCTION STRAIN FROM ROLE OVERLOAD

Martina has worked in the business for six years now. During that period of her life she suffered from "a lack of communications with my father" and saw herself in "a defensive position, working in structures dominated by men." She also expresses clear convictions about how to bring up her two daughters who are teenagers today. Amongst other aspects mentioned above, she points out that, "I follow my daughters very closely and care for them intensively, but at the same time I allow them freedom." There are hints in the interview that her attention to detail as well as the combination of her demands affected Martina. Again there are no direct hints of strain from role overload but indirect indications can be found indicating she had a hard time meeting all the requirements of her different roles. For example, there is a small remark about her daughters which may point to a reinforced commitment as a mother after her divorce: "After having relocated to my family's place I sorted out things. I "leveled" and "re-oriented" my children …" Meanwhile things seem to have become smoother. For example, Martina speaks about trouble she experienced in the office and how talking with her daughters helps: "I discuss these issues with them, and my elder daughter is really tough, compared to her I am Snow White." Martina also says that things have improved at the office. She talks about exposures that can be interpreted as strain from role-related demands: "For a year it is really okay. I can rest easy and I sense that they [the employees] are glad that I am here." But she is aware that the role demands are huge: "To be a part-time entrepreneur is just as impossible as it is to be a part-time mother. You can't do that."

TRAUMA STRAIN FROM ROLE RESTRICTION AND DEVALUATION

In the interview, two of the aspects of trauma strain defined by Levant and Philpot (2006) are evident: role restriction and devaluation.

Martina's father Walter seemed to have clear concepts about the role of his daughters on the succession issue. In the interview Martina reports that he was convinced both daughters would marry one day and stop working then. She sees her father's thinking anchored in a traditional role perception. "He was not against me in terms of succession. But rather than thinking of my sister and me as potential successors, I believe my father for all of his life hoped for an appropriate son-in-law." The idea of the appropriate son-in-law came within reach when Martina's twin sister Silvia got engaged. Her fiancé worked in the business, but when he and Silvia broke the engagement her former fiancé left the business. Even in this situation, Walter did not consider one of his daughters as successor. With this he expresses a clear role restriction for his daughters:

> *Rather he had the idea of merging the business with the construction company of his cousin and started negotiations with him. But it did not work, because both men did not come to agreements about legal and leadership issues. This idea had just been dropped when I entered my father's business.*

There are a lot of other remarks in the interview which make clear that Walter had neither Martina nor Silvia in mind when thinking about succession—if he thought about that at all. Like many other daughters from family businesses, she thinks of her father as a consummate entrepreneur "who did everything but has difficulties in handing over." This issue seems to be directly connected to the question of trauma strain by missing recognition for Martina, and devaluation of her worth.

The issues of devaluation and role restriction seem to be closely linked in this case. Not thinking of Martina (or Silvia) as a potential successor can be interpreted as a kind of devaluation of the whole person and the talents she might have for that role. If one takes "appreciation" as an antonym for "devaluation," the interview gives another example of the devaluation Martina experienced. Asked whether Walter ever expressed pride and appreciation about Martina and her achievements, Martina pointed out, "He did not tell me that he was proud of me. I know that he tells other people, but never to me."

Discussion and Conclusions

As can be clearly seen from the interview, both Walter and Martina followed several options in their lives which did not work out. Walter tried to find a male successor using different approaches. This wish was grounded in his traditional understanding of the (restricted) role of females. His daughter's fiancé, sons-in-law, or even merging his business with his cousin's company were more likely to fulfill his "inner picture" of good succession than the appointment of his own daughter. When both daughters married he had to realize that none of his sons-in-law would work for him. Having tried out other options, Walter had to admit that none of those could be realized successfully, but even then he did not see his daughters as successors. Getting Martina into the business in the first place had nothing to do with succession. From his personal point of view, he saw himself as a good father (family system perspective), generous and liberal in offering her a job. He faced a kind of constant threat to his traditional role model and perhaps to his self-perception, though, when Martina started to take over responsibilities based on her own decisions.

Martina also saw herself in a traditional female role for long time, but during her marriage she learned that this option would not work for her. Following the traditional role of (house-) wife and mother made succession impossible. At the same time this had been the loophole to eventually get her father's acceptance in a field which he always considered as "adequate" for women. Like her father, Martina had to realize that traditional concepts did not work for her either. Getting Martina into the business meant saying goodbye to traditional role thinking for her father, as well as for Martina. Being trapped in the paradox between the demands of the family system and enterprise system, Martina experienced years of operating in unclear roles and various kinds of strain from this.

Limitations and Further Research

The case presented remains preliminary as it is based only on a single interview with the daughter. However, as a biographic narrative, it serves its function quite well. The family business paradox as well as the impact of traditional role thinking is clearly demonstrated. Further interviews with Martina's father and especially with Thomas Winter, the non-family CEO, would allow for enhanced insights into the father–daughter communication and the "inner logic" of the succession process.

The linkage between the family business paradox and the gender role strain paradigm in general has not been discussed in family business research so far. Although a limited number of examples from the interview were illustrated here, it is clear that both concepts help to explain the difficulties a female family member may have on becoming the successor in a family business.

Further research should be done on the issues discussed above. Are there specific problems for female successors that arise from the family business paradox? Are there differences originating in gender issues when looking at the variables of the family system and the enterprise system? Which types of gender role strain derive mainly from one system, which are linked to both? A cooperation of family business research and family therapy research might provide deeper insight into these aspects.

Moreover, the interview conducted for that case study suggests that the gender role strain paradigm is applicable not only in the field of marital and family therapy research but also in the family business context. Further research is needed to support this idea. Further research should also be conducted to find out whether there is a typical distribution of the different strain modes for entrepreneurial women. A combination of qualitative and quantitative research based on a larger scale of probands or interviewees may give further scientific insight into circumstances that daughters in family businesses face when becoming successors.

References

Angelopolou, A. 2008. Generation Tochter. *Magazin Wirtschaft*, 3, 18–20.

Breuer, F. 2009. *Vorgänger und Nachfolger—Weitergabe in institutionellen und persönlichen Bezügen*. Göttingen. Vandenhoeck & Ruprecht.

Bundesministerium für Bildung und Forschung (eds). 2008. *Power für Gründerinnen. Maßnahmen zur Mobilisierung des Gründungspotentials von Frauen*. Berlin: Bundesministerium für Bildung und Forschung.

Bundesministerium für Familie, Senioren, Frauen und Jugend (eds). 2009. *Unternehmensnachfolge durch Frauen*. Berlin: Bundesministerium für Familie, Senioren, Frauen und Jugend.

Bundesweite Gründerinnen Agentur 2010. *Unternehmensnachfolge durch Frauen—Daten und Fakten II*. Stuttgart: bga-Publikationen Nr. 28.

Erdmann, C. 1999. *Unternehmer und Nachfolger. Die Entstehung von Nachfolgebereitschaft*. Wiesbaden: Deutscher Universitäts-Verlag.

Erdmann, C. 2010. Unternehmerfamilien und Nachfolgebereitschaft. Erziehung von Unternehmernachkommen im Spannungsfeld zwischen Familie, Unternehmen und Eigentum. *Familiendynamik*, 1(35), 40–48.

Freund, W. 2001. Frauen in der Unternehmensnachfolge, in *Jahrbuch zur Mittelstandsforschung* (pp. 43–62), edited by Institut für Mittelstandsforschung. Wiesbaden: Schriften zur Mittelstandsforschung Nr. 106.

Haubl, R. and Daser, B. 2006. *Familiendynamik in Familienunternehmen: Warum sollten Töchter nicht erste Wahl sein? Abschlussbericht des ersten Projektabschnitts*. Frankfurt am Main: Bundesministerium für Familie, Senioren, Frauen und Jugend.

Institut für Mittelstandsforschung (eds). 2007. *Die volkswirtschaftliche Bedeutung der Familienunternehmen*. Bonn: IfM Materialien Nr. 172.

Isfan, K. 2002. *Unternehmensübernahmen durch Frauen—Zur Sicherung des familieninternen Generationenwechsels*. Wiesbaden: Deutscher Universitäts Verlag—Gabler Edition Wissenschaft.

Keese, D. 2002. Geschlechtstypische Nachfolgeprobleme in Kleinen und Mittleren Unternehmen. *Wirtschaftspsychologie*, 4, 34–38. Available at: http://www.wirtschaftspsychologie-aktuell.de/Material_4_2002/02-Schwerpunkt06-keese-04k2.pdf [accessed 22 August 2011].

Klussmann, S. 2008. *Töchter der deutschen Wirtschaft*. München: Finanzbuch-Verlag.

Levant, R.F. and C.L. Philpot. 2006. Conceptualizing Gender in Marital and Family Therapy Research: The Gender Role Strain Paradigm, in *Family Psychology* (pp. 301–329), edited by H.A. Liddle, D.A. Santisteban, R.F. Levant and J.H. Bray. Washington: American Psychological Association.

Ronke, C. 2008. Die Geschwister Steigenberger—Die drei vom Zimmerservice, in *Töchter der deutschen Wirtschaft* (pp. 127–133), edited by S. Klussmann. München: Finanzbuch-Verlag.

Schäfer, M. 2007. *Familienunternehmen und Unternehmerfamilien. Zur Sozial—und Wirtschaftsgeschichte der sächsischen Unternehmer* 1850–1940. München: Beck.

Sechser, E. 2009. *Wenn Töchter Weiterführen*. Wien: Institut EUF.

Simon, F., Wimmer, R. and T. Groth 2005. *Mehr-Generationen—Familienunternehmen. Erfolgsgeheimnisse von Oetker, Merck, Haniel u.a*. Heidelberg: Carl-Auer.

Stern. 2005. Töchter an die Macht! *Stern* (May 28). Available at: http://www.stern.de/wirtschaft/job/nachfolge-toechter-an-die-macht-538938.html [accessed: 20 May 2010].

Voigt, M. 1994. *Unternehmerinnen und Unternehmenserfolg. Geschlechtsspezifische Besonderheiten bei Gründung und Führung von Unternehmen*. Wiesbaden: Deutscher Universitäts Verlag.

von Schlippe, A. 2009. Psychologie der familieninternen Nachfolge in Familienunternehmen in *Familienunternehmen in Recht, Wirtschaft, Politik und Gesellschaft. Festschrift für Brun-Hagen*

Hennerkes zum 70. Geburtstag (pp. 39–55), edited by R. Kirchdörfer, R. Lorz, A. Wiedemann, R. Kögel and T. Frohnmayer. München: C.H. Beck.

von Schlippe, A., Nischak, A. and El Hachimi (eds). 2008. *Familienunternehmen Verstehen. Gründer, Gesellschafter, Generationen*. Göttingen: Vandenhoeck & Ruprecht.

von Schlippe, A. and S. Klein 2010. Familienunternehmen—blinder Fleck der Familientherapie? *Familiendynamik*, (35)1, 10–21.

CHAPTER 12 Greece: Dreams of My Father: A Father–Daughter Succession Story in a Greek Family Firm

DAPHNE HALKIAS, ELEANNA GALANAKI,
NORMA A. JUMA AND PATRICK D. AKRIVOS

Introduction: Values Guiding Greek Culture

The Greek culture is guided by a historical duality—a complex mixture of character constituents that have resulted from Greece's location between east and West and from the combination of classical with modern elements in the Greek national character. The four centuries of Ottoman rule imparted to Greek institutions a structure radically different from what is the norm of the west. The Greeks have maintained their ethnic identity through long-lasting foreign dominations by enveloping themselves as a group with the cultural values of the importance of religion, the strength of the family institution, and the love of independence (Papalexandris, 2006).

The Greeks are beholden to their Greek Orthodox Church and its clergy for the major role it played in the revolution for independence and in preserving Greek language, culture, and tradition through centuries of foreign occupation. Religion is closely linked with being Greek since 97 percent of Greeks report to be Greek Orthodox Christians. Aside from the Greek Orthodox Church, the social entity that protected its members against unfavorable or hostile elements throughout Greece's modern history has been the family (Papalexandris, 2006).

In general, Greek independence is balanced by collectivism in many other domains, such as personal relations, family, and even employee–employer relationships. In the majority of Greek families, parents still strive to the maximum of their ability to provide their sons and daughters with property, education, employment, or to finance some entrepreneurial activity, hence the large numbers of small family-owned firms. Climbing the social ladder to gain community recognition also explains the great value Greeks and their families attach to higher education, which is believed to be a prerequisite for success, social status, and economic prosperity (Papalexandris, 2006).

Values Guiding the Entrepreneurial Business Culture of Greeks

Overall, the readiness of Greeks to engage in entrepreneurial activities is further strengthened by the considerable degree of social mobility in Greece. With no line of separation between classes, there is high expectation among family members and one's social network for success. Greeks are fiercely competitive in grasping business opportunities. This explains also the preference for ventures that allow a high margin of profit (trade, shipping) and the "dream" to seek opportunities abroad. A strong belief in independence makes those who work in the private sector willing to work for themselves. About half of the Greek labor force is self-employed and 90 percent of Greek firms have fewer than ten workers (Papalexandris, 2006).

The reality of the global recession has changed the face of entrepreneurial culture for Greek family firms. Because of economic fears brought on by the country's economic collapse, Greek family businesses are turning their profit sights inward and adapting more conservative attitudes on regional expansion. This recession-fueled trend is highlighted in the disappointing aspect of new ventures appearing in Greece which consistently focus on the internal market and satisfying domestic demand. Seven in ten enterprises do not expect to have or spend money to find and service any clients from abroad and will exclusively appeal to domestic customers. This is the lowest such statistic in Europe, as the relevant European mean is estimated at 48 percent, and is intimately connected with the retail nature of the majority of Greek enterprises. A small percentage of the order of 21 percent state that up to a quarter of their customers could be from abroad and are generally in the manufacturing and services sectors; 8 percent state they expect over 25 percent of their customers to be foreign, and these are chiefly tourism-oriented enterprises and thus are bound by nature to have foreign clients (GEM, 2008).

Female Entrepreneurship in Greece

Greece is relatively advanced in terms of gender equality in the workplace and business women are treated fairly and with respect. It is, however, important for women to maintain a professional approach and distance with male colleagues. Despite the relative increase in female entrepreneurship, Greek women report their quality of life appears to have deteriorated due to their need to combine work and family obligations. Greek women usually find themselves within family-owned firm holding positions involving marginal power or responsibility while key leadership positions are held by male family members (Katz, 2008).

The high levels of early-stage entrepreneurship in Greece in the past years fed the pool of established business, which has risen since 2006. Specifically, the percentage of the population aged 18–64 years who are owners or co-owners of a business in operation for over 3.5 years exceeds 13 percent, the highest in Europe. This is explained by the high levels of self-employment in Greece. Thus, in totality and taking into consideration all categories of businesspeople, 18.7 percent of the population aged 18–64 (nearly 1.3 million individuals) was involved in some sort of venture in 2007. This statistic is the second highest, after Iceland, in 2007, not only among European countries that have an average of 11.3 percent but also among all high-income countries. These facts characterize Greece's entrepreneurship as chronically "shallow"; new ventures appearing each year do not tend to populate the entirety of the "value chain" leading to the final product, but rather chiefly on the chain's final link (GEM, 2008).

It is within the last decade that the proliferation of national grant schemes, EU-funded initiatives as well as small business loans targeting women, has propelled an increase in Greek female entrepreneurship (Halkias et al., 2010). The involvement of women in businesses is increasing and more specifically, in the family firm. There is scant extant literature on gender issues in the Greek family firm ownership and management, even though the global rise in female entrepreneurship and self-employment has been quite dramatic (Pyromalis et al., 2004).

Early-stage entrepreneurship in Greece is distributed between the two genders in a 70 to 30 male-to-female gross imbalance. When examining the numbers of women in established entrepreneurship and family firms (ventures functioning for over 3.5 years), the gender disparity is eliminated (Papadosifakis, 2008). However, the divide becomes apparent again when investigating importance attached to social capital—a salient feature of new venture creation—where women are less likely than men to have connections with potentially beneficial networks (Halkias et al., 2010).

It should be noted, however, that employment issues in Greece are complex and cannot be approached solely by studying the official data. Family ties, which remain strong in Greece, continue to provide protection to family members facing employment problems. As a result, the official data may give a false picture of employment, because many people, usually women, who are underemployed under the protection of the family, are seeking work. However, such people are officially classed either as "self-employed" or as "helpers in the family business." Moreover, major difficulties arise when recording "atypical" forms of employment, which often involve female employment. The phenomenon of undeclared work, particularly in family firms, which also involves female employment, merits special mention (Global Business Culture Consultancy Report, 2009).

For Greece to maximize the economic potential of female entrepreneurship, policies and structures need to be devised and deployed that are, and more importantly are seen to be, enhancing rather than hindering development. In addition to direct funding or capital support, business mentoring and education are also needed. The success of the enterprises owned or inherited by women, and even men, is potentially compromised by the lack of business expertise. Programs that provide training in strategic planning, marketing, logistics, and financial management are all needed (Halkias et al., 2009).

The Culture of the Greek Family Firm

An important characteristic in Greek societal culture is the distinction between in-group and out-group, which affects significantly the ways in which Greeks relate to others. The in-group usually includes family, relatives, and friends and there is a lot of protection, trust, support, and cooperation between its members. The out-group is often viewed with hostility and relations with out-group members are often characterized by suspicion and mistrust. In Greek communities social relationships can become polarized, being either positive or negative with no room or neutral gradation between the two (Papalexandris, 2006). It is this value that rigidly guides the various processes flowing through the Greek family firm, including the succession process (Kelafas, 2008).

As with many other southern European countries, business structures in Greece have traditionally veered towards the strictly hierarchical. Most organizations are either government-run or family-owned firms with a tendency towards a patriarchal, hierarchical approach to management. The Greek economy has always been characterized by small, family based and managed enterprises or self-employment—with a large service sector supporting a small manufacturing basis (Katz, 2008). In the Greek family firm, members of the workforce and staff, for the most part, depend on the discretionary judgments of the owner and his relatives for their well-being. Although this tendency still somehow exists today, increased company size, social awareness, and questioning of authority has caused owners and their families to introduce new work practices to ensure cooperation and weakening antagonism, a characteristic often seen in both industrial and peer relations within firms (Papalexandris, 2006).

Succession Issues in the Greek Family Firm

Succession in Greek family businesses can be tricky to navigate—and even to survive—due to the same cultural values that have helped Greek culture survive all the strife and conflict of their modern history. Greeks are known as having "strong family ties." In particular, Greek parents go to great pains to secure a "future" for their children. They value education of their children as a means for securing a life better than their own. Still Greeks also frequently practice Kanutism, the futility of trying to avoid the unavoidable. "Suggestions from friends and advisors that we must plan for the day where somebody else will sit in our chair or stand behind our counter are brushed away liked contaminated food. We tend to believe that always bad things happen to others but never to us. We are invincible. We are immortals. We will be around forever!" (Kefalas, 2009).

With regards to the role of gender in the succession process, literature repeatedly cites that male offspring are favored in the succession process within family firms (Allen and Langowitz, 2003) regardless of suitability (Miller et al., 2003). In Greece, the "glass ceiling" or perceptual barriers to women's advancement to senior management positions in family firms still exist (Stavroulakis, 2001; Halkias et al., 2010). Yet, progress has been made over the past 15 years as noted in a study published in 2009 which indicates greater presence of women in managerial positions in Greece while satisfaction with leaders does not appear to be significantly correlated with gender (Galanaki et al., 2009).

The Case Study: Autokinitistiki S.A.

THE FAMILY FIRM HISTORY

This is a story of father–daughter succession that spans four generations. At present, this is a third generation firm at the brink of transferring the reins to the fourth generation. The firm was founded in the 1930s. The firm produces common platform spare parts for vehicles and it has also diversified into the real estate business. The initial intention was to produce interchangeable spare parts for vehicles irrespective of model or brand. The founder left Greece in 1928, a business trip rarely heard of during that time period among Greeks. His goal was to be educated in the necessary technology to build his auto parts business.

During his travels Vasilios visited Citroen, a major French automobile manufacturer. Back then, the auto parts market was highly monopolized. Upon his return to Greece, he formed a company and it became a representative for Citroen in Greece. The company mainly produced spare parts known as *soustes* or leaf springs. During the Second World War, Greece found itself under occupation by Nazi Germany. During the German Occupation, the company was forced to produce ammunition for the invasion force.

The founding entrepreneur, Vasilios, was killed in the Second World War. In 1945, upon the death of the founder, the founder's son, Athanasios, and his brother, Dimitrios, took over the company. Athanasios was 25 years old and knew very little about his own father and even less about the business because he lived with his mother after his parents divorced. In 1947 Athanasios and his brother restructured the company. They invested in a piece of real estate of about 5,000 square meters at Leoforos Athinon, a central point of commercial activity in Athens, and created a new factory. Family strife led to a split of the original company. Athanasios built his first factory at Leoforos Athinon while Dimitris took over another building they owned in the same area of Athens. In 1962 Athanasios assumed the sole management of the company and made it a Limited by Shares Company, known as "Anonymos Etairia," in Greek Law. During that same year he built a new factory and a colossal commercial building known as Kiffisou Central Station which today is partly the depot for KTEL, the Greek national bus transit system that connects almost all cities and towns of the Greek mainland, at Kifissou Central Station. The space covered approximately 30,000 square meters. As the years moved on the company developed: in 1987, new facilities for the factory were built. In 1998, a fourth facility was built to shelter the manufacturing processes in the commercial area of Thebes. At that point, the company maintained the previous sites. Today, only the Thebes facility operates as a leaf spring manufacturing line.

THE FATHER–DAUGHTER SUCCESSION PROCESS

Athanasios had two daughters and no sons. The elder daughter, Yolanda, is ten years older than her sister, Diana, and therefore she would be the first child as successor to enter the family business. Their mother, Maria, was a homemaker and had very little interest in the day-to-day operation of the business. Athanasios consulted with his wife on critical issues but she was not directly involved in the management of the family business. By the time Yolanda was 18 years old, Athanasios expressed concerns about the succession plan. However, Yolanda was not pressured to join the company at that time. She got married in 1974 and worked at her in-laws' family business.

Over the years Yolanda kept up with the growth and development of her father's businesses. In 1989, and after her divorce, she joined the family firm. She says:

> *... I entered the family business with zest. I was alone with two young daughters and I needed to enter the business at a full-time professional level in order to financially support my children. Maybe my dedication, my need and my desire to support the company for the good of the whole family can be attributed to the fact that I am the eldest child.*

In 1994, at the age of 35, Yolanda suddenly found herself CEO of the family firm after her father suffered a debilitating stroke. Athanasios retired at the age of 74 in 1994 due to health concerns. Even in his failing health, the transfer of management was definitely a challenge for the father. The family often referred to the business as his "third daughter." It was extremely difficult for him to let go and turn over the management of the company to his eldest daughter. What supported father and daughter during this emotionally difficult transition was that ultimately Athanasios saw much of himself in his daughter and had confidence in her abilities as CEO. This confidence in Yolanda to successfully succeed him as CEO helped him to let go of the reins of power and authority without conflicts from the family, as the younger daughter was completely in agreement with her father's decision.

There was never any written formal succession plan in place. Yolanda consulted with her father on various issues but she was given autonomy to lead the family firm after her father's retirement. The succession plan was a given in this family so nobody really talked about it and no third party was ever involved in the succession process. Yolanda remarked that "... if we would have been unwilling to join the family business, it would have been a catastrophe." Initially the father owned 100 percent of the shares but he later converted the sole proprietorship to an "Anonymous Etairia," thereafter he distributed the shares as required by law. He allotted 30 percent of the shares to his wife, 30 percent to himself, and 20 percent to each to his two daughters, Yolanda and her younger sister, Diana. Athanasios's health was on a continuous decline after 1994, and upon his death in 2006, all the family firm's shares were equally distributed among his wife and two daughters. Today, Yolanda is the CEO of the company. However, she and her sister, Diana, have equal decision-making power at the firm. The sisters consult and jointly make critical strategic decisions together. It is fair to state that the succession from the second to the third generation was smooth and without conflict despite the lack of a formal succession plan.

ROLE OF SPOUSE IN THE SUCCESSION PLAN

Yolanda believes that involving in-laws in the family business complicates issues. In her opinion in-laws are outsiders and they may be more willing to take risks and splurge at the company expense. She in fact remarked that "we were lucky we never involved our husbands ... the husbands, no matter how good they may be, do not know the history of the company. They will have demands which may not fit with the company." She also worried about the spillover effect between work issues and family life. These are issues the third generation will discuss with the upcoming fourth generation who may hold a different opinion.

THE FOURTH GENERATION

Roselita, Yolanda's older daughter, took courses in economics at high school (the American Community Schools of Greece) to find out if she was interested in further studies in this area. She preferred physics and later majored in Mechanical Engineering at Tufts University in Massachusetts, USA, and is currently finishing her PhD. Yolanda did not want to make the children feel obligated to join the business. Having felt pressured to take over her father's business herself, she did not want that for her children. It turned out that Roselita majored in a field related to the family business' core product line. Roselita has continued to live in the US and pursue graduate studies there for the past ten years and has shown an interest in the developments taking place within the family business. Yolanda also has a younger daughter, Mirka, who majored in Psychology at the

American College of Greece and is now pursuing postgraduate work as a Researcher at The Center for Young Entrepreneurship and Family Business at the University of Bergamo in Italy. Mother and daughters favor that as any possible daughter successors they should first pursue experience outside the family firm.

The family recognizes that the fourth generation succession plan will be far more complex than the previous generations simply due to the sheer number of potential successors. At the moment, Yolanda and her sister Diana hold the leadership positions at the firm. In addition, Diana has two sons: Anastasios, who completed business studies at Queen Mary University in London and is finishing an MBA at Imperial College in London, and, Athanasios, who has majored in Computer Science at Brunel University in the UK and will soon begin his Masters degree. At present, Anastasios is the only fourth generation successor who is actively involved in the daily operation of the family firm. Yolanda exclaims that "... having two successors in the business worked out okay. Now there will be four family members vying for control and authority plus spouses ..."

Yolanda wonders if some of the successors will look beyond the family business for a professional career. She clearly understands that succession is a gradual process but there is no clear explicit formal plan in place. She emphasizes that all the fourth generation members must be treated equally and the responsibilities and equity should be equally distributed. She remarked that, "I do not fear the process of succession. What I fear is the personality clashes when having more than one head of the company." Clearly the CEO believes that a formal succession plan is not as critical as an open and honest collaborative and cooperative relationship among the four heirs.

THE DAUGHTER AS CEO AND ENTREPRENEUR

Dreams of my father

Yolanda's father, Athanasios, involved his children either directly or indirectly in the business at a very early age. Yolanda's earliest memory is when she was four years old and often listened in on her parents' conversations. After hearing such conversations she sought clarification on what the parents discussed. She says, "I feel very much tied to my father's dreams. He often said that the company is his life-long creation that cannot be left to chance. I could never give this company up and sell it or pass it to outsiders."

Her father also taught Yolanda the value of maintaining a degree of flexibility and being responsive to emerging opportunities in the local and regional market. She recalls how her father told her that, "You cannot be an entrepreneur and be rigid." Athanasios did not believe in taking uncalculated risks such as gambling or gaming in the stock market. He believed in operating an honest business and he kept proper accounting records. He did not cheat on his taxes or on anybody. He valued his employees. Yolanda's father impressed upon her that even during extreme hardship she must pay the employees first then other creditors. According to Athanasios an entrepreneur should be the last one to be paid. If nothing is left he reckons, "Then do not eat."

Athanasios, as a traditional Greek father, taught his daughters the value of keeping strong family bonds. After Yolanda's engagement her father called her aside and told her that no matter what she must be home by 9:00 pm—no excuses. Later in life Athanasios would sum up his achievements as having a good family and a good business. He asserted that there is "no use for a successful business if you do not have a happy family life."

My father's university of life

Yolanda is multilingual but she did not further her formal education. She married young and joined her husband's jewelry business. It was certainly very different from her father's business but she learnt how to interact with customers. Her father-in-law taught her the virtue of listening to people without interrupting or volunteering unsolicited advice. She says that the jewelry business calls for one to be discerning and this proved a useful skill to her later as CEO and entrepreneur.

At the age of 12 her father took Yolanda on a business trip to promote the leaf springs business and to introduce her to the Greece he knew. They took a tour through the mountains and rivers. She fondly recalls those memories which laid the foundation of her own parenting skills. Over the years she consulted with her father regarding her children's education and other key parenting issues. For instance, her father did not allow her to go to Italy to study History of Art but he advised her to let Roselita go to the USA for further studies.

Differences in management style

Yolanda describes her father's management style as austere and authoritarian. He let everybody know exactly what needed to be done, when he needed it, and how he needed it done. During their younger years Athanasios often told his children that they were lazy and never got things done in a timely manner. Athanasios had two advisors but he always made the final decision. Yolanda agrees with the father that you cannot afford to have too many voices making strategic decisions for the company. She narrates an encounter with an employee who kept comparing his experience at the family business to that at a multinational. She asserts that, "There is no relation between multinational and family business ... they have different structures ..." In terms of management style, however, Yolanda has a more participatory approach. She is of the opinion that she has to be respectful to those who preceded her at the company. She speaks to them in second person plural as dictated by the Greek custom of formal, business language.

Yolanda also describes her father as a risk taker. She views herself as risk adverse. Her father once told her that if he was as conservative as she he would have never achieved what he did. Yolanda however believes that the times have changed. The investment opportunities in the 1950s to the 1980s are not the same in the contemporary business environment. She argues that when she took over the reins in 1994 it was a period of sustainability and slow growth. In 1962 when other businessmen were busy buying real estate around Ambelokipi and other central areas of Athens, her father was buying land in Kiffisos which is located south of the city in an underdeveloped suburban area. Many wondered why he was wasting money on what they perceived as agricultural land while the real money was in houses and apartment buildings around secure neighborhoods such as those surrounding the US Embassy in the center of the city. Athanasios, however, bought 30,000 square meters at Kiffisos with the deep conviction that the land was bound to appreciate in value. It turned out that he was correct.

CULTURAL DIMENSIONS

Traditionally, the Greek cultural context of the auto mechanic industry does not favor women making sales calls or entertaining clients. This is still the case to a certain degree today especially in male-dominated sectors. When Yolanda and Diana took over the business they devised a system of having a sales force that visited with and entertained the clients. They always maintained the formal business language with the clients. While their father was still living clients consulted with him. These steps were necessary given that their primary industry is male-dominated.

Some directors left the company or retired when Yolanda became the CEO. Yolanda attributes this to a generation gap between her and the older members of the company. However, she pointed out that not all older people left the company. Some stayed on and built a mutually respectful relationship with Yolanda and Diana, even though they had not been used to answering to women.

Yolanda, due to her upbringing, has a strong affiliation with her parental roots. She speaks fondly of her ethnic group, the Epirotes. She reckons that Epirotes have a more developed sense of creativity and keenness in trade and commerce. She has embraced her father's charitable work in Zitsa Ioanninon, her ancestral home.

FUTURE DIRECTIONS

Yolanda pointed out that they will continue to diversify into areas where they have core competence. They will also continue to be conservative with their cash flows. They will also maintain a comfortable buffer in order to build a cushion for the economic downturns.

Conclusion and Discussion

The case study presented in this chapter highlights a father–daughter family business succession story within the context of the Greek culture of the past several decades. The firm was founded over 80 years ago and is now led by a daughter–successor who shares decision-making power with her sister—the third generation of the family firm. Whereas the second to third generation transition seemed fairly seamless, that was not the case during the transition from first to second generation. Family strife caused a split in the initial firm. History may repeat itself during the transition to the fourth generation if an explicit succession plan is not put in place. The lack of an explicit succession plan may cause some significant issues—including clashes of gender—if not addressed by a specific business plan given the sheer number of potential successors.

Some of the issues highlighted in this case are rather unique. The father did not have any male heirs. Would things be different if he did? The daughter states that the father did not believe in gender differences when it came to business acumen. However, it is clear that the daughters were expected to maintain a professional approach and distance when dealing with male clients. Moreover, some of the senior male executives left the company when the daughter took over the management.

The fact that the daughter–successor, Yolanda, considers in-laws as outsiders is very much attune to Greek cultural values pertaining to the in-group and out-group. In terms of the organization structure and the management philosophy, Yolanda's generation has made the transition from an outright autocratic style to some degree of participatory management.

Future Research Directions

This case is consistent with the extant literature but at the same time there are very distinct issues that may inform further research in this area. For instance, it would be interesting to conduct a comparative study between father–daughter successions where there is a probable male heir and those where there is none. We hypothesize that the gender issues may be more of an issue when both male and female successors exist. The fourth generation succession where two females and two males are probable to succeed their mothers, the two sisters, will make for an interesting longitudinal case study in family business succession in three-year intervals over the next two decades.

References

Allen, I. and Langowitz, N. 2003. *Women in family-owned businesses*. Boston: Babson College/ MassMutual Financial Group.

Galanaki, E., Papalexandris, N. and Halikias, I. 2009. Revisiting Leadership Styles and Attitudes towards Women as Managers in Greece: 15 Years Later (May 1, 2009). *Gender in Management: An International Journal*, May 2009. Available at: http://ssrn.com/abstract=1420666 [accessed: 28 August 2010].

Global Business Culture Consultancy Group. 2009. *World Business Culture: Report on Greece*. Available at: http://www.worldbusinessculture.com/Business-in-Greece.html [accessed: 29 August 2010].

Halkias, D., Nwajiuba, C., Harkiolakis, N., Clayton, G., Akrivos, D. and Caracatsanis, S. 2009. Characteristics and Business Profiles of Immigrant-Owned Small Firms: The Case of African Immigrant Entrepreneurs in Greece. *International Journal of Business Innovation and Research*, 3(4), 382–401.

Halkias, D., Thurman, P., Harkiolakis, N., Caracatsanis, S.M. (eds). 2010. *Female Immigrant Entrepreneurs: The Economic and Social Impact of a Global Phenomenon*. Farnham: Gower Publishing.

Ioannides, S. and Tsakanikas, A. 2008. *GEM Greece 2007: Executive Summary*, in Global Entrepreneurship Monitor (GEM) Global Report 2008, edited by N. Bosma, Z. Acs, E. Autio, A. Codura and J. Levie. Boston: Babson College/Global Entrepreneurship Research Association.Katz, L. 2008. *Negotiating International Business*. Charleston, SC: Booksurge Publishing.

Kefalas, A. 2009. *Successful Greek Business Leaders in Greece and the United States: A Comparative Study of Two Cultures*. Unpublished Research Project Proposal submitted to Terry College of Business, University of Georgia, USA.

Miller, D.L., Steier, L. and Le Breton-Miller, I. 2003. Lost in Time: Intergenerational Succession, Change and Failure in Family Business. *Journal of Business Venturing*, 18(4), 513–531.

Papadosifakis, E. 2008. The Rapid Development of Greek Entrepreneurship, in *Trade with Greece*, pp. 72–77. Available at: http://www.acci.gr/acci/LinkClick.aspx?fileticket=6UjGQPr2N1I%3D&tabid=383&mid=177&language=en-US [accessed: 28 August 2010].

Papalexandris, N. 2006. Greece: From Ancient Myths to Modern Realities, in *Global Leadership and Organizational Behavior Effectiveness* (pp. 767–802), edited by J.S. Chhokar, F.C. Brodbeck and R.J. House. New Jersey: Lawrence Erlbaum Associates.

Pyromalis, V., Kalkanteras, T., Rogdaki, M. and Vozikis, G. 2004. *An Integrated Framework for testing the Success of the Family Business Succession Process According to Gender Specificity*. Proceedings of the Allied Academies International Conferences, Maui, Hawaii, 2004.

Stavroulakis, D. 2001. *Employment and Working Relations in Greece according to Gender Specificity.* Eurofound: The European Foundation for the Improvement of Living and Working Conditions. Brussels, 2001.

CHAPTER 13

Italy: The Challenges of Father–Daughter Succession in an Italian Family Business

LUCIO CASSIA, ALFREDO DE MASSIS AND FEDERICA GIUDICI

Introduction

Family businesses play a pivotal role in all European countries. This is particularly true in Italy, where a study conducted by Aidaf (Italian Association of Family Enterprises) and the Bank of Italy (2004) shows that family businesses represent 93 percent of the nation's companies and employ 98 percent of the workforce in manufacturing companies with fewer than 50 employees (European Commission, 2008). This evidence appears to be closely linked to the fact that family businesses are mostly small and medium-sized enterprises (SMEs) and that they account for 99 percent of Italian firms (Istat, 2008).

The importance of succession and continuity in family business is due to the fact that they contribute to maintaining the national level of entrepreneurship (Ampò and Tracogna, 2008). According to the Global Entrepreneurship Monitor (Bosma and Levie, 2009), Italy is characterized by a low level of "early-stage entrepreneurial activity," defined by the number of individuals involved in new entrepreneurial initiatives in a year. To enable the existing businesses to survive intra-family succession is therefore a crucial issue in the Italian economy in order to protect the degree of national entrepreneurship.

The following analysis investigates the succession process characterized by the *transition of leadership from a father to his daughter*, focusing on the relationships among the actors involved, the way the succession process takes place, and the main issues emerging. The aim is to detect the presence of cultural elements specific to the Italian context that may influence this process.

The Italian Culture and its Influence on Family Business: A Review of the Literature

The management and organization of national companies are influenced by the social and cultural aspects of the country in which they are located. According to Masino (2008), it is possible to identify three main aspects of the Italian culture that have influenced the domestic economy. First, the influence of the public government, which has traditionally contributed to protecting the entrepreneurial environment from very real international competition, thus favoring the diffusion and persistence of the family business type of firm. Secondly, one must consider the great importance of the family unit in the Italian culture, and, thirdly, the relevance of the local communities that provide the social and cultural background conducive to the birth and growth of firms. Castagnoli (2006) identifies the crucial role of the Roman Catholic culture in shaping the Italian entrepreneurship system. In particular, he stresses the real and symbolic importance of the family as the main determinant of the diffusion of family businesses in the Italian economic context. The persistence of family capitalism could be explained, according to Casson (1999), by the reduction of transaction costs provided by the nature of the relationships among family members. In order to maintain this advantage, the dynastic motivation of future generations is important in managing the family business. This need also affects women's roles in the firms: women have traditionally played an informal role in family business (Dumas, 1992); however, the current need to guarantee the dynastic continuity of family firms is increasingly contributing to the emergence of female entrepreneurship (Castagnoli, 2006). According to Unioncamere (2007), 20.1 percent of Italian family firms have a female CEO; nevertheless, the percentage of female CEOs is in inverse proportion to the company size: medium and large family firms account for 13.9 percent of female CEOs, and this percentage is reduced to a mere 2 percent of companies ranked in US Top Fortune 2000 (Università Bocconi-AidAF, 2008).

The management of the succession process is one of the most important concerns in family businesses (De Massis et al., 2008; Chua et al., 2003; Bauer, 1993; Handler and Kram, 1988); this problem is especially relevant in the Italian context, where family businesses make up about 70 percent of the national Gross Domestic Product (GDP) (Cerif, 2008). Corbetta and Montemerlo (1999) suggest that the issue of succession is likely to be more challenging in Italy than in the United States of America (USA) for four main reasons: (a) Italian family firms are characterized by a "rigid" ownership structure since family assets are concentrated in the family business equity; (b) boards of directors tend to be basically close to non-family members, even if the presence of outsiders can be very helpful during a succession process, for example, in evaluating and training potential family members and in facilitating parent–child communication; (c) key decision-making teams are also less open toward external members; and, (d) Italians tend to postpone succession issues, both those related to the management of the succession process and to its planning.

FEMALE ENTREPRENEURSHIP IN THE ITALIAN CONTEXT

Entrepreneurial initiatives led by women are mainly located in the northern part of Italy and operate in the industries of manufacturing (48.4 percent) and personal services (32.1 percent) (Centro Studi Sintesi, 2006). Among the main reasons expressed by Italian women for undertaking an entrepreneurial activity is the need or desire to continue the business of a relative. Some bodies of research (for example, Centro Studi Sintesi, 2006) show that different motivations to become an entrepreneur correspond to different modes of starting up an entrepreneurial activity: the majority of women succeeding a relative in the family business identify the desire to ensure family continuity as their main motivation; on the other hand, women starting a new business are mainly motivated by the desire for autonomy and the wish to achieve high levels of income.

The main problems faced by female entrepreneurs tend to be concentrated in the early stages of their leadership; the most critical issues are the difficulties in obtaining recognition of their authority by their firm's stakeholders, to balance and reconcile the demands of family and work, and to acquire new customers (Centro Studi Sintesi, 2006). Songini and Gnan (2009) points out that small and medium-sized family businesses are a favorable environment for the removal of the so-called "glass ceiling" (Hymowitz and Schellhardt, 1986), but only in those cases in which the woman is a member of the board of directors or function director.

Finally, a survey conducted by Montemerlo et al. (2009) on 1,776 Italian family firms indicates that family ownership is a positive determinant of female involvement in top management teams and helps family women overcome potential obstacles they may encounter during their career (for example, the special challenge to meet family and job needs); in particular, the need to ensure the continuity of the family business seems to lead family owners to encourage the firm to recruit the most qualified family resources, regardless of the gender. On the contrary, non-family women do not seem to be favored by the family nature of a firm.

FATHER–DAUGHTER SUCCESSION IN THE ITALIAN CONTEXT

There is a lack of studies related to the peculiarities of father–daughter succession in the Italian context. Furthermore, conflicting results emerge from the few works that, albeit marginally, deal with this issue. A study by Ampò and Tracogna (2008) on 358 small and medium family businesses in the district of Trieste (Northern Italy) shows that the impact of the successor's gender is a relevant matter in the succession process: 6.7 percent of the entrepreneurs interviewed cited as a justification for the lack of succession to the next generation the fact that they operate in an industry that does not properly fit the gender of their son or daughter. Therefore, the successor's gender appears to be a significant factor affecting decisions related to the succession processes of Italian family businesses.

Todd (1983) has identified four different types of families, basing his analysis on two main aspects: (a) the level of freedom/authority, which describes the nature of the relationship between parents and children; and (b) the degree of equality/inequality, which identifies the attitude of the parents toward the children and is measured through the observation of the succession's rules being adopted. The study shows that Italian families are characterized by a high level of equality with different levels of authority ("community family" and "egalitarian family" types). The succession process in Italian family businesses seems therefore to be characterized by a high sense of equality in the treatment and evaluation of the children, with no significant differences of treatment between male and female heirs.

The Case Study

The following sections describe the father–daughter succession process in an Italian family firm, the "Nuova Termostampi Spa." Qualitative evidence was collected through personal in-depth interviews, informal conversations, and personal observation (Yin, 1994). We interviewed the CEO of the company, Mrs Marinella Manzoni, and her nephew and possible future successor, Marco Manzoni. The interview was based on a semi-structured questionnaire specifically designed to gather detailed information on the history of the firm, the succession process that led to the leadership of the founder's daughter, and the cultural aspects related to the new director's leadership.

The interviews were then combined with secondary source data, such as available company documents, family information, and other available information pertinent to the firm and its succession process. These sources were used to verify the interview data and ensure objectivity in the data collection process. The use of multiple sources of data allowed the triangulation of evidences (Yin, 1994) and ensured that our research followed established data-collection practices and contributed to the long tradition in management research to advance theory building based on case study.

A BRIEF HISTORY OF THE FAMILY AND THE FIRM

Nuova Termostampi Spa is a medium-sized family firm located in Bergamo and operating in the plastics industry and active in mold construction for plastic molding as outsourcers. The company currently employs 83 people and had a turnover of 13 million euros in 2009. It originally served clients in the electronic industry, but has progressively expanded its client portfolio to customers in the automotive, mechanical, consumer electronics, and design industries. Today, Nuova Termostampi deals with both molds design and production and with thermoplastic and thermoset molding and assembly of components.

The company was founded in 1962 by Alessandro Manzoni, who had previously worked with molds production in SAIBI; in the mid-60s the firm, originally named "Alessandro Manzoni," appeared as a small craft business constructing molds with a dozen employees. In the mid-70s the company innovated its production process by initiating the activity of compression molding of thermosetting materials; during the 80s, the firm began to specialize in the molding of thermoplastic materials and started the injection molding of polyester resins. These continuous innovations were mostly promoted by Gianrenzo Manzoni, the founder's son, who joined the business in 1974 with a share of 25 percent and, in 1976, at the age of 25, took the baton of the family business after the unexpected loss of his father. Gianrenzo led the firm's great period of expansion, but he died prematurely in 1996, succeeded by Marinella, the founder's daughter and his sister, who assumed the leadership of the business. She continued the consolidation and growth of the company, culminating with the opening of a new production plant. Since 2005, Nuova Termostampi also has a Romanian branch where labor-intensive activities are carried out.

The Manzoni family tree and the key events in the history of the family business are reported in Figure 13.1 and Table 13.1.

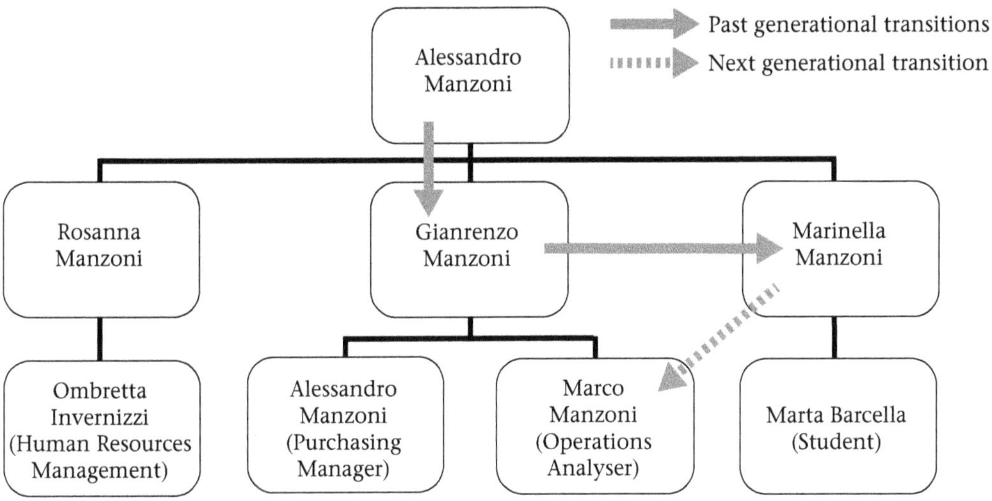

Figure 13.1 Manzoni family tree and successions

Table 13.1 Key events in the history of the family business

Year	Event
1962	Foundation of the company—production of molds for thermoplastic materials
1974	Entry into business of thermoset compression molding—Gianrenzo acquires 25 percent of the firm
1976	Death of Alessandro Manzoni and **succession to the son Gianrenzo**
1980	Extension of production plants and transfer of the company location to Dalmine
1982	Entry into the business of thermoplastics molding
1990	Start of injection molding of polyester resins
1993	New production plant in Treviolo (Bergamo)
1996	Death of Gianrenzo and **succession to Marinella**
1997	Expansion of the plant in Dalmine (Bergamo)
2005	Relocation of the establishments in Lallio (Bergamo), opening of a subsidiary in Romania

The current organization chart of the firm is reported in Figure 13.2.

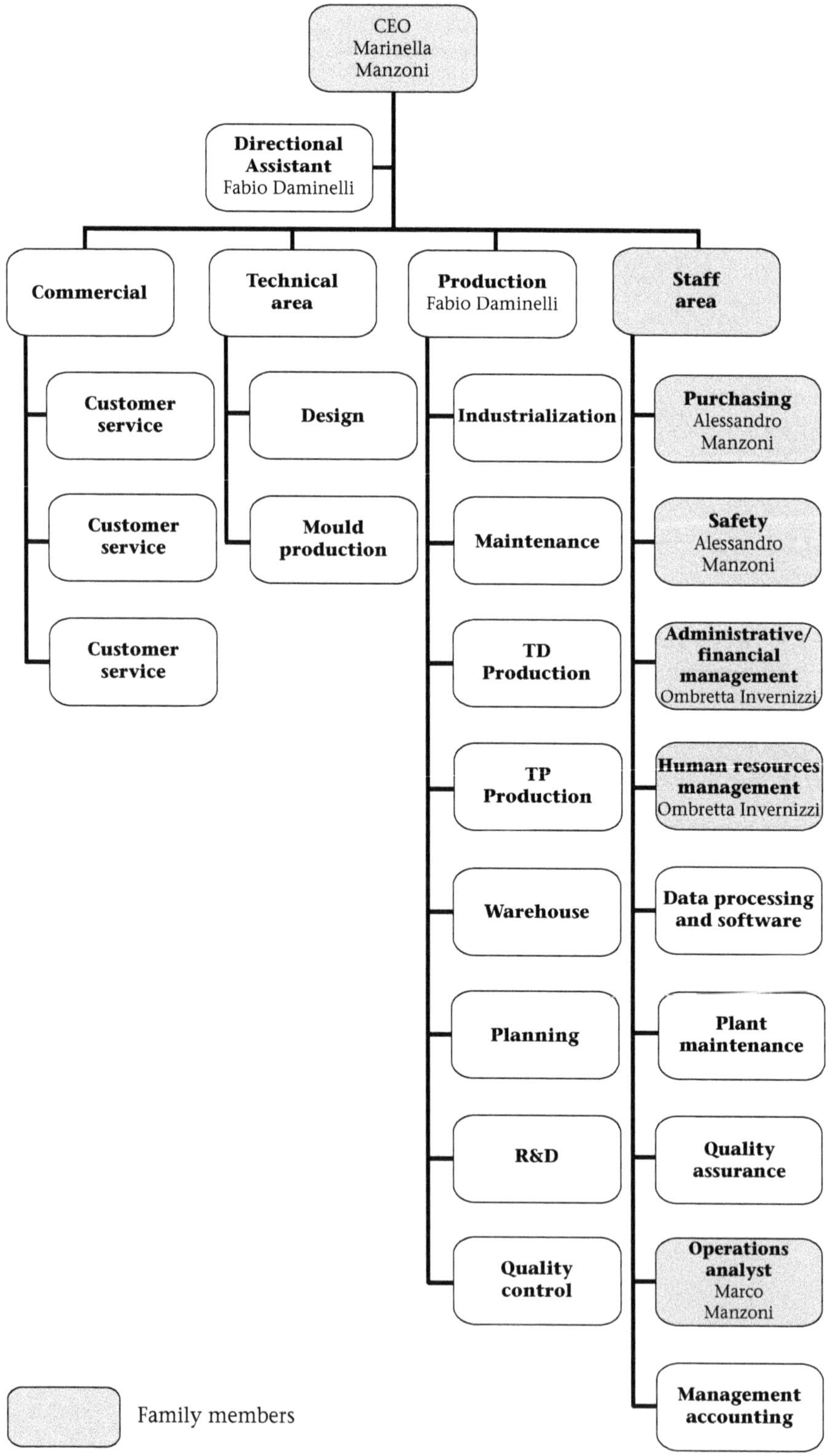

Figure 13.2 Organizational chart of Nuova Termostampi Spa

THE SUCCESSION PROCESS

The succession process in Nuova Termostampi is a particular example of father–daughter succession. In fact, the daughter was a teenager when her father died, and the only heir designated to lead the family business was Gianrenzo. In order to be prepared to succeed his father, he had followed a path of technical studies, aimed at developing technological and production skills related to the family business. The father recognized his son Gianrenzo as the unique heir both for character's affinity and because he was the only one possessing strong technical skills. Furthermore, Gianrenzo was the only male member of the next generation and, in the family culture, the only possible heir of the father. Even if the eldest daughter, Rosanna, had been working in the family business in accounting and administration roles, she had never been seen as a viable heir by her father, mainly because she was a woman, was married, and did not possess strong technical skills.

In 1974, Gianrenzo joined the company and benefited from his parents' donation of 25 percent of the firm's shares. After the sudden and unexpected death of his father, Gianrenzo had to manage the succession without a prepared plan and in a challenging period for the firm, since the company had undertaken ambitious investments to expand business activities and support technological innovations. His sisters supported him by absolving him of secondary activities: Gianrenzo outlined the strategic guidelines for the firm and was focused on technical issues; Marinella dealt with production, customer management, planning, and scheduling; and Rosanna continued to manage the administrative and financial duties.

In 1996, Gianrenzo died and the problem of succession again emerged unexpectedly in a delicate period of significant change for the company that had made huge investments to support the expansion of its production plants. Also, in this case, the succession process had not been planned. Marinella, the youngest sister of Gianrenzo, was the only one of the two sisters to have shown a strong commitment to leading the family company. After careful evaluation of her new responsibilities, she therefore assumed leadership of the firm.

THE FOUNDER'S DAUGHTER AT THE HELM OF THE FIRM

The entrepreneur at the helm of the firm is Marinella Manzoni, the youngest daughter of the founder, Alessandro. She has been working in the family business since she was a child. Her mother taught her the importance of work; in particular, she emphasizes that her personal relationship with her father was strongly influenced by the family business and the role of her mother: "My mother used to tell us that we should not give any concern to our father because he was already busy enough with work" and, again: "My mother was always repeating that the business was the main and most important issue in my life."

While working in the family business, Marinella obtained an accounting diploma. Her aspiration was to become an interpreter since, given the natural preference of her father for his male child to be potential successor, she did not catch a glimpse of career possibilities in the family business. After her graduation, waiting to start a course to become interpreter, and strongly influenced by her mother, Marinella worked in the family business as an accountant. She soon became interested in a wide set of issues not only related to her direct task: she coded the drawings and the products and was concerned with planning and price forecasting, showing a marked curiosity and the desire to continuously understand the dynamics within the family company. The interest accrued during the first months of work in the firm convinced Marinella to continue to operate in the family business, sharing management responsibilities with her siblings and dealing with production planning, pricing, and management of relationships with customers and suppliers.

Marinella's relationship with her brother was characterized by complementarities and cooperation, even if frictions between them sometimes occurred due to the fact that Marinella tried to gain independence and explicitly criticized some of Gianrenzo's decisions. She describes herself in this way: "I felt weak but not impressionable by my brother; I reasoned with my head and I wanted to fully understand everything." Marinella stresses that the relationship with the family became more difficult after the birth of her daughter since Gianrenzo did not accept a partial commitment due to her new family needs. Shortly before the death of her brother, Marinella had even developed the will to leave the firm because she felt the need to dedicate more time to her family and because her relationship with Gianrenzo had become jeopardized.

Cultural Dimensions and their Role in Father–Daughter Succession

This section is structured in order to present different cultural aspects that may influence the father–daughter succession process, derived from the literature starting from the studies of Dumas (1989). For each cultural aspect, we have identified and analyzed the impact of the main issues emerging from the case study.

REASONS TO JOIN THE COMPANY

Marinella decided to succeed her brother mainly for social ethics reasons; she is aware that the destiny of more than 40 people and their families depends on the future of the company. During the years, the main goal pursued by the successor through her choices has been the "preservation of the family name," that she identifies in the maintenance of an ethical behavior, the supply of real quality, the attention to products and customers, and in assuring a long-lasting intergenerational continuity to the business. She says with understandable pride: "What moves us isn't just money," stressing that the reasons for the development of the family business are not merely economical, but also social and tightly bound to the local environment in which both the family and the firm are located. According to her, even her father Alessandro Manzoni had decided to start the family business not only for an economic aim, but motivated by the desire for autonomy. Marinella did not decide to take the baton of the family business for the aspiration of self-affirmation or the desire of personal achievement. She started working in the firm as a clerk and chose to become president of the company only when painful and unexpected events occurred; this empirical evidence is consistent with the existing literature (Dumas, 1989) arguing that critical events increase the possibility for a daughter to be seen as a viable heir.

FATHER–DAUGHTER RELATIONSHIP

The daughter describes her father as a "very good and calm person," even if she had not established a strong relationship with him since he was too often busy with his work; the presence of the family business seems to hinder the father–daughter relationship because the father figure almost completely overlaps with the firm, while daughters are only marginally involved in the family business.

However, we have little information about the relationship between Marinella and her father because Alessandro died when she was only 14. According to Dumas (1989), a duality issue usually emerges in the father–daughter relationship, since the father expects his daughter to behave both as a businesswoman and as his "daddy's little girl." In the present case study, this problem seems to partially emerge in the relationship between the brother and the sister: Marinella says that the fact that she acted on her own and approached in a critical way the decision-making processes of the firm caused irritation between her and her brother.

BEING A VIABLE SUCCESSOR AND WOMEN'S "INVISIBILITY"

Barnes (1988) argues that sons, even if younger, are often chosen as successors instead of the older sisters. At the death of her father, the elder sister had not been considered as a viable successor. Similarly, Gianrenzo never saw any of his sisters as possible successor; Marinella succeeded him as the new leader only because of his sudden loss and the parallel unavailability of other possible heirs (the eldest son of Gianrenzo, Alessandro, had not shown interest in taking over the leadership of the firm and the other son, Marco, was still too young).

The principle of the first-born has therefore not been followed in the two past successions: in the first father–son succession, for reasons related to the gender of the first-born (Stavrou, 1999); in the brother–sister succession because the former's eldest son was not significantly interested and committed to managing the family firm.

DISCRIMINATION AND GENDER STEREOTYPING

Vera and Dean (2005) underline that gender discrimination is stronger with external stakeholders than with people within the family firm. This is consistent with the emerging empirical evidence since the entrepreneur has identified in the interactions with customers the main events of gender discrimination, while the discrimination was lower with the firm's employees. Marinella states that she often felt uneasy and uncomfortable as a woman, when she faced meetings with exclusively male customers and competitors or where the few women were the secretaries of her interlocutors. With regard to this aspect, she criticizes the fact that, in Italy, technical roles are almost exclusively occupied by men.

In the post-succession period, the attitude of external stakeholders has been highly discriminatory toward the new female entrepreneur. In particular, many customers expressed their mistrust: "Remember that we don't believe in women," and they threatened to stop their commercial relationships with the firm since they did not believe in a woman's ability to manage what was considered a typically male business. The entrepreneur clearly admits this attitude: "I don't know if this would have happened if my name was Mario." She stresses that this behavior, although latent, continues to persist even today, despite her management capabilities having been fully demonstrated in the field.

THE "GLASS CEILING"

Several authors (Gillis-Donovan and Moynihan-Bradt, 1990; Hollander and Bukowitz, 1990; Rodriquez-Cameron, 1989; Nelton, 1986) argue that women working in a family business often feel invisible to the eyes of the other members of the family and of the firm. Marinella claims that she has never been considerably interested in entering the family business since she did not see in the firm big opportunities for growth and personal accomplishment because her father had never seen her as a possible heir and Gianrenzo evidently showed his intention to be succeeded by one of his two sons. Furthermore, when Marinella expressed her interest in the family business and strived to better understand the internal dynamics of the company, she often clashed with her brother and his collaborators; also, her attempts to propose improvements for the company were rarely taken into consideration.

OWNERS' WILLINGNESS TO RELINQUISH CONTROL

Given the nature of the case analyzed here, there is no significant empirical evidence related to the typical difficulty of the incumbent to leave the family business (De Massis et al., 2008). We are not able to understand whether this problem would have emerged because of the premature death of the founder Alessandro and of his son Gianrenzo. However, during the interview Marinella clearly expressed her total inclination to let go and pass the baton to her nephew as soon as he will be ready to lead the family firm.

The entrepreneur also underlines her strong propensity for effective delegation of responsibilities and states that women are more likely to delegate because: "The female psychology is different from the male one: for women it's easier to understand people and to identify the most suitable individuals to which to delegate the business tasks." This delegation-driven leadership style led Marinella, in 2004, to appoint for the first time a non-family member, Fabio Daminelli, as Directional Assistant in charge of personally supporting the CEO to carry out her top management role. Marinella openly criticizes the typical tendency of Italian male entrepreneurs to excessively centralize all decision-making processes in their hands, avoiding any kind of delegation and favoring the proliferation of the owner-managed firm.

DIFFERENCES BETWEEN MALE AND FEMALE LEADERSHIP

Dumas (1989) argues the presence of differences between male and female behavior within the family business system. Marinella declares:

> *The succession evidently entailed the shift to a very different leadership style. It was a shock for the employees; my brother was a centralizer and charismatic leader; on the contrary, I have a different and less imperative management style: I used to explain to employees why they should do what I ask them.*

These different leadership approaches may be caused by intrinsic differences between the nature of women, characterized by a need for interaction and collaboration, and men, who are basically more independent individuals (Dumas, 1989).

Marinella also says that an important reference point for the company fell down after her brother's death, and she was not able to replace it:

> *I don't consider myself as a real business woman, but rather as a good manager. My brother was a businessman: he developed innovative ideas and was very creative; on the contrary, my distinctive skills consist of in the ability to identify the most suitable person to execute each business activity and in a great aptitude to motivate people and foster strong commitment in the workforce.*

According to the entrepreneur, the crucial aspect in the management of a family business is to make people work together, minimizing potential conflicts and driving them toward common corporate objectives; the importance of collaboration and interaction among the employees determines the propensity of Marinella to delegate decision-making responsibilities: "I'm very pleased if someone gives me a hand in taking decisions; I don't know if I would have been able to succeed during the years if I had been alone." The entrepreneur has therefore been able to recognize and admit her need to be supported in the exercise of leadership in order to overcome potential issues, especially related to technical aspects because, unlike her brother, she does not possess the strong technical skills needed to guide the company.

NON-FAMILY MEMBERS' RIVALRY

Dumas (1989) states that the entry of a daughter into the family business is usually hindered by non-family members more strongly than in the case of a son because his entry is expected. Marinella has therefore powerfully sought the cooperation of the internal stakeholders, meeting the employees and technicians who had previously worked with her brother in order to obtain their support, because she was aware of an essential need for their assistance. Marinella says that her employees were not easily convinced that she was the right person to succeed her brother because she was a woman, but they did not have any alternative and were consequently forced to trust her. The entrepreneur recognizes that even today, after almost 14 years, some employees still remember Gianrenzo's leadership style and recall his memory when they face Marinella's decisions on which they do not agree.

MANAGERIAL AND PATRIMONIAL TRANSFER AND FAMILY MEMBERS' RIVALRY

The transfers of managerial control and ownership have occurred simultaneously in both the past succession processes since they were both determined by the sudden and unexpected death of the respective incumbents. As far as ownership is concerned, the daughters possess a minority stake, while the shares of the son, already the main shareholder since the father's death, was further increased by his mother's legacy. The inequity in the way of treating the son versus the two daughters was frequently a source of disappointment. This empirical evidence is consistent with research by Friedman (1991) stating that the explicit preference of the parents for the son is a recurrent cause of conflicts between male and female heirs in family business. In the case of Nuova Termostampi the main conflict episodes involved, in particular, the elder sister of Marinella: "My sister has always felt excluded from the family business, more than me because she was the eldest daughter and hardly accepted the appointment of her younger brother as the new leader."

At the death of Gianrenzo, his shareholding was split between his wife and his two children, and two non-family members were included in the board of directors in order to protect the interests of his wife and children.

MANAGEMENT OF WORK–FAMILY CONFLICT

The desire to become a mother seems to clash with the professional activity for a woman entrepreneur (Cole, 1997). This is supported by the findings of our case study: when Marinella succeeded her brother, she decided to stop having other children. The entrepreneur says that her husband did not interfere at all with her decision to take over the leadership of the family firm. However, she considers the Italian sexist culture, according to which the tasks of taking care and bringing up the children are almost entirely a mother's responsibilities, as the main cause of the difficulties to conciliate the two roles of mother and entrepreneur. The entrepreneur is firmly convinced that being a mother represents an undoubted advantage for women, because it enables them to have greater sensitivity and ability in the management of human resources; this is explicitly recognized by Marinella as an element that proved to be very useful in the management of the family business.

Cole (1997) identifies another important issue related to the work–family conflict, that is, the "double message," on one hand, the woman is pushed by her family to become a mother; on the other hand, she is required to keep up her commitment to the company. In the case study, this phenomenon occurred with Gianrenzo: when Marinella became a mother, he did not accept the reduction of her commitment to the family business.

The entrepreneur has pointed out that an important difference between men and women is that women do not match their personal achievement with their firm's performance: "My personal fulfillment doesn't overlap just with the development of the firm, maybe because I'm a woman before an entrepreneur." This attitude may be another source of friction between the role of the entrepreneur and the role of the mother and the wife played by women in the current society.

Discussion and Conclusions

This case study is related to a family firm that is successfully led by a woman entrepreneur. It has allowed for the identification of some factors, specific to the Italian culture, that have influenced the succession process and the development of the present family business.

First, it is possible to observe how the founder of the firm and his whole family have been extremely involved in the family business, to the point that the father figure was almost completely overlapped with the firm. Also, family relationships seem to be constrained by the needs of the firm. This predominance of the family business over individuals' lives reveals itself in the fact that, for instance, the entrepreneur has abandoned her personal career aspirations outside the company in order to support the family members in the management of the firm. The crucial role of the business in individuals' lives may appear in conflict with the central importance traditionally attributed to the family in Italian culture; such contradiction is, however, overcome if one considers the fact that it is probably the nature of the family firm that justifies and determines its preponderance on the lives of family members.

This is the reason why the intention of successors to ensure the continuity of the family business is an overwhelming and decisive motivation to join the company; this motivation has driven the successor to take the helm of the firm even if she is a woman entering an industry traditionally reserved for men. The taking over of the leadership role is even more critical for women, because of the propensity of parents to educate sons and daughters in different ways. In particular, the son is typically brought up with the aim of developing skills and competences useful to succeed his father at the head of the firm; the daughter, on the contrary, is usually involved in the family business only in secondary roles.

The emerging empirical evidence seems therefore to suggest that in the Italian culture there are activities and industries best suited to one gender and not to the other, and there is diffused conviction that the business approach, the leadership style, and the skills of an individual depend not only on his or her own individuality, but also, significantly, on his or her gender. In particular, according to the findings of this case study, it seems that women pay more attention to relational aspects and show high propensity to delegate tasks and activities, while men are characterized by a more centralized and authoritarian leadership style.

Another important issue regards the figure of the mother in the work environment: the Italian culture, while recognizing the crucial role of the family in the lives of individuals, delegates its management almost exclusively to women; even the care and the growth of children is mostly delegated to the mother (and not to the father). For this reason, discrimination against women is even more evident when the woman is also a mother, so that she is frequently forced to face the mutually exclusive choice between being engaged in the work or in the family activity. This problem does not appear when the entrepreneur is a man: the case study has shown that it is more likely that the family adapts itself to the needs of the working husband or father rather than the opposite.

Probably, the fact that women are primarily required to manage the family and that daughters are not raised with the idea of succeeding their father in the leadership of the business, partially explains why a woman entrepreneur is often not fully recognized in her role or she does not consider herself totally suitable to autonomously lead a company. This is consistent with the case study findings related to the female propensity for delegation and to the need of a woman entrepreneur to be supported by another individual in the leadership of the firm.

Limitations and Future Research Directions

This case study can be considered a first attempt to fill the shortage of data and studies focusing on the phenomenon of father–daughter succession within the Italian context, with particular regard to the cultural variables affecting it. Considering our focus on only one single company and the limited number of empirical studies in the Italian landscape, we consider our findings in need of further empirical investigation. Future research could be aimed at further investigating the cultural variables affecting the father–daughter succession process in the Italian context on a wider empirical base, using either qualitative or quantitative methods. Further qualitative studies would be useful since the cultural dimensions affecting the phenomenon are many and complex (Yin, 1994). However, large-scale quantitative studies are also necessary in order to allow for the statistical generalization of results.

Such future studies could be aimed at identifying, among the cultural variables influencing the father–daughter succession process, which ones are actually determined by the peculiarities of the national culture and which ones are simply aspects specific to the case analyzed. Future research efforts could also aim at identifying whether and how the impact of cultural variables on the father–daughter succession process is influenced by other factors, for example, the size of the family firm, its geographical location, or its industry.

References

Ampò, A. and Tracogna, A. 2008. *Successione Imprenditoriale e Prospettive di Continuità Nelle Piccole e Medie Imprese*. Trieste: EUT Edizioni Università di Trieste.

Banca d'Italia. 2004. *Proprietà e Vontrollo delle Imprese Italiane. Cosa è Cambiato nel Decennio 1993–2003*. Milano: Banco d'Italia.

Barnes, L.B. 1988. Incongruent Hierarchies: Daughter and Younger Sons as Company CEOs. *Family Business Review*, 1(1), 9–21.

Bauer, M. 1993. *Les Patrons de PME entre le Pouvoir, l'Entreprise et la Famille*. Paris: InterEditions.

Bosma, N. and Levie, J. 2010. *Global Entrepreneurship Monitor 2009 Global Report*. London: Global Entrepreneurship Research Association. 72 pp.

Casson M. 1999. The Economics of the Family Firm. *Scandinavian Economic History Review*, 47(1), 10–23.

Castagnoli A. 2006. Behind the Family Firm: women Entrepreneurs in Italy XIV. Conference paper presented at the *International Economic History Congress*, Helsinki, 21–25 August.

Centro Studi Sintesi 2006. *Sintesi del Rapporto sul 1° Osservatorio sull'imprenditoria Femminile: Caratteristiche e Problematiche*. Available at: http://www.artigiani.vi.it/DocRepository/donne/DYNXPDOC_120_6405.pdf [Accessed 15 August 2011].

CERIF (Centro di Ricerca sulle Imprese di Famiglia). 2008. Le Imprese di Famiglia: Imprenditori è il Momento di Lasciare il Testimone? *Convegno CERIF*, November 21.

Chua, J.H., Chrisman, J.J. and Sharma, P. 2003. Succession and Nonsuccession Concerns of Family Firms and Agency Relationship with Nonfamily Managers. *Family Business Review*, 16(2), 89–107.

Cole, P.M. 1997. Women in Family Business. *Family Business Review*, 10(4), 353–372.

Corbetta, G. and Montemerlo, D. 1999. Ownership Governance and Management Issues in Small and Medium Size Family Business: A Comparison of Italy and the United States. *Family Business Review*, 12(4), 361–374.

De Massis, A., Chua, J.H. and Chrisman, J.J. 2008. Factors Preventing Intra-Family Succession. *Family Business Review*, 21(2), 183–199.

Dumas, C. 1989. Understanding of Father–Daughter and Father–Son Dyads in Family-Owned Business. *Family Business Review*, 2(1), 31–45.

Dumas, C. 1992. Integrating the Daughter into Family Business Management. *Entrepreneurship Theory and Practice*, 16(4), 41–55.

European Commission. 2008. *Overview of Family Business Relevant Issues*, European Commission. Available at: http://ec.europa.eu/enterprise/policies/sme/documents/family-business/index_en.htm [accessed: 8 July 2010].

Friedman, S.D. 1991. Sibling Relationship and Intergenerational Succession in Family Firms. *Family Business Review*, 4(1), 3–20.

Gillis-Donovan, J. and Moynihan-Bradt, C. 1990. The Power of the Invisible Women in the Family Business. *Family Business Review*, 3(2), 153–167.

Handler, W.C. and Kram, K.E. 1988. Succession in Family Firms: The Problem of Resistance. *Family Business Review*, 1(4), 361–381.

Hollander, B. and Bukowitz, W. 1990. Women, family culture, and family business. *Family Business Review*, 3(2), 139–152.

Hymowitz, C. and Schellhardt, T.D. 1986. The Glass Ceiling: Why Women can't Seem to Break the Invisible Barrier that Blocks them from the Top Jobs. *The Wall Street Journal*, March 24, 1.

Istat. 2008. *Rapporto Annuale*. La situazione del Paese nel 2008. Available at: http://www.istat.it/dati/catalogo/20090526_00/rapporto_annuale_2008.pdf [accessed: 7 July 2010].

Masino, G. 2008. Culture and Management in Italy: Tradition, Modernization, New Challenges, in *Gestion en Contexte Interculturel: Approches, Problématiques, Pratiques et Plongées*, edited by E. Davel, J.P. Dupuis and J.F. Chanlat. Canada: Presse de l'Université Laval et Télé-université UQAM Québec.

Montemerlo, D., Minichilli, A. and Corbetta, C. 2009. *The Determinants of Women's Involvement in Top Management Teams. Opportunities or Obstacles from Family-Controlled Firms?* Available at: http://www.ifera2009.org/ [accessed: 7 July 2010].

Nelton, S. 1986. *In Love and in Business. How Entrepreneurial Couples are Changing the Rules of Business and Marriage*. New York: JohnWiley.

Rodriquez-Cameron, L.M. 1989. *Wives and Mothers in Family Business*. Doctoral dissertation, University of Southern California.

Songini, L. and Gnan, L. 2009. Women, Glass Ceiling and Professionalization in Family SMEs. *Journal of Enterprising Culture*, 17(4), 497–525.

Stavrou, E.T. 1999. Succession in Family Businesses: Exploring the Effects of Demographic Factors on Offspring Intentions to Join and Take over the Business. *Journal of Small Business Management*, 37(3), 43–61.

Todd, E. 1983. *La Troisieme Planete*. Paris: Empreintes.

Unioncamere. 2007. *Rapporto Unioncamere 2007*.

Università Bocconi-AidAF. 2008. *Giovani e Donne Nelle Aziende Familiari: Una Ricerca Esplorativa*. Cattedra AidAF-Alberto Falck.

Vera, C.F. and Dean, M.A. 2005. An Examination of the Challenges Daughters Face in Family Business Succession. *Family Business Review*, 18(4), 321–345.

Yin, R.K. 1994. *Case Study Research, Design and Methods*, 2nd Edition. Thousand Oaks: Sage Publications.

CHAPTER 14 Russia: Father–Daughter Succession in a Russian Family Business: A Case Study

EVGENY POLYAKOV AND NATALIA VINOKUROVA

Lev Klimenko Ltd. was established in April 1992 as a family-owned business and as one of the first private patenting bureaus in Russia. It survived a loss of the founder and is currently owned and run by the daughter of the founder who inherited the business in January 2002. The case study offers some insight into the main phases of a succession process pertinent to the business environment, history, and cultural values of Russia, as well as the factors which are relevant for succession planning and management. It may help managers of family businesses understand how to plan and successfully manage the succession process in order to survive generational change accompanied by the management of gender change.

The Business Culture of Russia: A Review of the Literature

The free market economy is still developing in Russia. According to Bosma and Levie (2010), Russia has a very low level of entrepreneurial activity. Given that in the UK only 17 percent of the original small business stock is still in business after ten years (Barclays Bank, 2006) and that in Russia these figures are not yet available, these long-term survivors are of interest. The carrying capacity of small and medium-sized enterprises (SMEs) in many economies is about 95 percent, defined as their percentage share of business ownership form. The situation in Russia is radically different due to its communist heritage (Day et al., 2007).

Early-stage entrepreneurial activity and established business ownership is relatively low in Russia (Bosma and Harding, 2007). Russia is the tenth lowest in early-stage entrepreneurial activity out of the 42 countries surveyed and the lowest for established business ownership. As a result of the 2008 financial crisis, there have been mass redundancies and, associated with these, an increase of entrepreneurial activity in Russia in the past few years. However, only 4 percent of individuals who set up a new business in 2009 were women (Bosma and Levie, 2010). According to Verkhovskaya and Dorokhina

(2009) and Allen et al. (2008), Russian women are more active in a stable business and less active in start-up activities.

Men are more inclined to see opportunities in the environment and to give a more positive evaluation to external conditions for starting a new business. Men are more optimistic in evaluating the knowledge and experience necessary for starting a new business and have less fear of failure. Men are more often ready to take risks—the fear of failure prevents 53 percent of men and 68 percent of women from starting a business (Bosma and Harding, 2007). However, although men start a new business more readily, they are not always more successful than women.

Russian business mentality is also restricted by power distance. Individual responsibility or individual entrepreneurial activity is more difficult to develop in countries with a high index of power distance. According to Hofstede (1986) and Elenkov (1998), this index in Russia is 88, power relations are paternalistic and even autocratic with individual mentality being suppressed by the director's opinion.

Family Business in Russia Today

Kaledgyan (2010) noticed that the prosperity of Russia is closely connected with the development of the business of such famous families as Demidovy, Stroganovy, Eliseevy, and so on. The tradition of development has discontinued for some time but recently there has been an interest in developing the tradition once again. There are more than 15 million family firms in the United States of America (USA) and only 2 million throughout the whole of Russia. Kaledgyan (2010) gives some reasons for this:

- The first generation of Russian businessmen had no experience of father-next generation succession of family business. Russian business is more a brothers-in-business rather than father-and-son business.
- Russia still has no family business legislation (Salahova, 2009).
- Russia is an unstable country for the development of SMEs.
- Governmental programs and governmental policy prevent the development of any kind of family business (Verkhovskaya and Dorokhina, 2009).

Family businesses share common characteristics and face common problems, among which generational change is recognized to be the most relevant (Bigliardi and Dormio, 2009). Turning the business over to children without creating chaos depends on how well the owners prepare themselves and their child for this transition (Johnson, 2010). Although the majority of fathers would prefer that their son or daughter take over the business and carry on the family legacy, this is not always the best option available. It is argued that when the son or daughter isn't ready, then there should be a board of directors and the owner should solicit its input and recommendations. Hiring a consultant may be an option for doing an assessment of not only junior but other executives in the organization who may be qualified for the succession.

Family business continuity from the founder generation to the second generation in terms of succession has been discussed by Kansikas and Kuhmonen (2008) who reviewed and combined family business succession and evolutionary thinking in organizational and economic change to understand the nature of family business succession. However, one of the key elements of family business remains life goals which are substantially influenced and impacted by parents, mentors, and influential "others" (Moyer and Chalofsky, 2008).

Given the tough economic environment, family businesses don't need only interested successors to remain financially viable, but also a firm grasp of what the business is worth as well as a structured succession plan for turning the enterprise over to the next generation (Jacobs, 2009). The heir's life goals may need to be seriously reconsidered and they need to ensure that they possess the correct knowledge, skills, abilities, and attitude to take advantage of the opportunities and sometimes unexpected duties placed before them. In addition, relationships in the family exert a strong impact on the success of the business.

Family businesses constitute a substantial if not the largest proportion of economically active SMEs in Russia (Barkhatova et al., 2001). Russian pre-revolutionary history brings multiple examples of successful family businesses; however, this segment is currently in its embryonic state (Kihlgren, 2002; Vinokurova et al., 2005).

The Case Study: A Family Patenting Business

Adapting Russian legislation to the standards of international law became extremely urgent in the early 1990s as a result of the fundamental changes taking place in the country's social and political order. Changes to the intellectual property legislation became a focal point of this process. The Russian Government had decided to bring together a team of specialists with experience in this area with an aim to: (a) develop new draft legislation; and (b) create the State Institute of Patent Attorneys, an arrangement similar to that which exists in all developed countries. One of the invited individuals was Lev Klimenko. By that time, he had over 20 years of experience in managing the Department of Innovation, a license department in the Division of International Cooperation of the Ministry of Petrochemicals and Refining. His daughter Tatiana comments: "My father received the task of creating a department of patent attorneys, to develop curricula and train new staff members."

The first students of the faculty were mostly former Soviet patent specialists involved in research, design institutes, and big enterprises with patent offices. New legislation that was introduced in 1992 destroyed the monopoly of "Soyuzpatent" in the field of services for national industrial property protection outside Russia. In 1992, several private firms of patent attorneys were established. One of them was Lev Klimenko Ltd.[1] As Russia by that time had only recently entered the path of free enterprise, the newly born businessmen were not familiar with such concepts as exclusive rights, trademarks, and patents. Therefore, education became the first priority objective for Lev Klimenko Ltd. as company managers needed explanations as to why it is necessary to register a trademark and why the design or a model should be protected by a patent.

The firm was widely involved in educational seminars, participated regularly in exhibitions, and contributed to a newspaper column, "Business Lawyer." However,

1 The firm was founded by the Institute for Intellectual Property, one private firm, a professor of Moscow State University, a legal consultant, experts of FIIP, and first patent agents. Originally, the father had 85 percent shareholding. When the daughter succeeded the firm she received 94 percent of shares. Currently, she has 100 percent ownership of the firm.

free competition developed very fast and made protection of exclusive rights related to intellectual property very topical in just a few years. In the past, people mostly asked for help after suffering "injury" due to stolen designs, technologies, and so on. At the present time, the firm's clients often request an assessment of possible risks to protect their rights and gain maximum benefits.

The founder of the firm, Lev Klimenko, graduated from Moscow State University in 1958 with a law degree. He later received a second degree in management. He was called a "walking encyclopedia" and was an extraordinary intellectual. His elder daughter, Tatiana, says that "apart from the best education received from the top university, this was due to his extreme sense of purpose, anxiety for knowledge, and real love for work."

Lev Klimenko used to say to his daughter that "every new generation in a family should be more educated than a previous one, to know more and to be more skilled."

Tatiana comments on this: "My father's general level of erudition was so high that at the age of 46 years I am still striving to achieve it."

Lev Klimenko told Tatiana that "one can do 'pseudo-business' and business, but only deep knowledge multiplied by proven experience may bring a person to the level of a 'real expert'."

Knowledge and experience made him a leader. He was followed and his opinion was always taken into consideration.

Tatiana was always keen on education. Her relatives made her believe that it is a shame to study poorly. She finished her school with excellent grades. Then, she entered the Chemical and Technological Faculty of the Oil and Gas Academy named after Gubkin. In 1986, Tatiana graduated with the diploma and qualification of an engineer. Straight after the Academy she started her employment at the All-Union Institute of Organic Synthesis. "Everybody predicted for me a scientific career. But after two years of work I understood that due to the perestroika, research and science were of no interest and I decided to obtain a degree which would be in higher demand."

Even for Tatiana, a 24-year-old girl, it was clear that the country was losing its huge scientific potential. People who secured the ownership of property, often with a deficit of knowledge, or education, sometimes very primitive and ignorant, rushed to quick money. They were not interested in a long-term investment in science and research. Directors of privatized research and scientific project institutions were more interested in providing their sites for rent than paying for scientists and researchers. All connections between enterprises, producers, and institutes that developed new technologies were broken.

The collapse of the USSR several years later fostered the breakdown of these connections. Research institutes' employees with high-level education and intellect were forced to work as sales assistants and taxi drivers just to be able to feed their children. Thus, they changed their business and professions for "pseudo businesses." Most of them changed their qualification to accountants as this profession was in high demand. Another problem which occurred was that not every person who dealt with science could overcome his/her ego and start working as a sales assistant or a hairdresser. Someone who considered it possible to continue professional activity abroad left the country. It would be wrong to say that they "escaped" in search of a better life. Many of them were forced to do it.

Tatiana was still a young girl when she understood that enterprises will not survive for a long time if they use only their old research works. The younger generation did not want to go into science but rushed into the fields of finance, trade, and business services.

There was a dramatic absence of demand for science for ten to 15 years. As a result, the connection between the younger and older generations was lost. Currently, a certain need for qualified engineers and scientific experts is growing.

When, in 1988, Tatiana decided to obtain another promising qualification of a marketing expert, the word "marketing" was so novel for Russia that the national register of qualifications did not have the term "marketer" in their books. That is why after two years of studies Tatiana received a Degree of Economics in International Economic Relations.

I felt my father's guiding hand during all my studies. When I was writing my first dissertation my father advised me not to follow blindly but to conduct a patent search for the topic of my work. He even asked his colleague to teach me how to use the archives of the patent library. I was the only student from my university who completed a patent search in all the developed countries worldwide. My dissertation made a sensation.

For her second dissertation, Tatiana's father suggested a topic related to the international transfer of technologies and knowledge-based calculation of license reward. She gave it to her father for a review. He read it and threw it away saying, "and now we will write together."

After these words, I was furious and indignant for a long time, and then even cried, realizing that I was completely unable to resist my father's will. There were many tears in my childhood and teenage years when I was re-writing essays torn by my father! Only when I had grown up did I understand how important these night watches were. My father was never sorry for this process and was very persistent. Now when some old staff members of our small firm tell me "you wrote it as your father" it is the best praise for me! It means that I wrote something really brilliant.

After Tatiana gave birth to her son in 1993, her father was possessed with the idea of making his first grandson a successor to his business. Lev Klimenko told Tatiana that her son should be the successor of his business but because of his young age he saw Tatiana as an intermediate link. By that time, Tatiana had already gained technical and economic degrees, but her father tried to persuade her to also complete a law degree. At that time she was well aware of the fact that advocacy could be her career.

When Tatiana graduated from the second academy and received a good opportunity to begin her new career, she was a marketing director in several companies. After maternity leave she had to start looking for another place of work. Her father recommended his firm of patent agents which was an established family business by that time. Her mother and sister persuaded her to follow the advice of her father. Thus, Tatiana started her work in her father's firm in 1996. In the beginning, she was responsible for public relations. At the same time, she learned the business of patent agents.

Our family learned about the illness of my father in 2000. It was cancer. My mother decided to never tell the truth to him. After the surgery my father was informed that it was a gastric ulcer. After the operation doctors gave a very sad forecast that he could live for only two to four months.

Surely Lev Klimenko could guess about the real diagnosis but he decided to play up to the family's decision. The relatives pleased themselves that their lie was successful whereas Tatiana's relations with her father were like a game: "I know that you know that I know." Her father lived for two years after the operation. After the operation he started to work very hard and these were two years of titanic work. They were the most active years of his work as he was afraid to be too late in completing something very important.

During the last year of his life he began to implement his idea of setting up an Expert Institute of intellectual property. He described this idea very precisely and it was actively supported. People followed him and asked many questions after his public speeches. In half a year, Lev Klimenko set up the Expert Institute of intellectual property and started to hire specialists. His idea was so attractive that even academics from the Russian Academy of Science decided to join this Institute. Unfortunately, he could not realize his project to the full. Thus, there are still no independent experts for the legal protection of intellectual property in Russia. Expert Institute is working now, but only as a firm of patent agents.

Unfortunately, I could not realize the grandiose idea of my father. Every day I think about it and understand the necessity of the realization of this idea but one has to have a huge intellect, be very experienced, and have the charisma of my father to implement it in practice.

Close to the father's death, there were no doubts concerning the successor in the family. Tatiana's education and experience of working for the firm made her the sole candidate and only possible option. After graduating from the State Finance Academy, her younger sister had made a very fast and successful career in banking. Giving up her job and retraining for another job did not make sense.

Half a year before his death, Lev Klimenko gave his daughter Tatiana all his shares in the closed corporation as a gift. Up until the last days he was chief executive officer. However, his death was unexpected even for the employees who saw him every day. He had many plans when celebrating the New Year in 2002. Everybody felt very confident and protected under his management. That is why when after the holidays Tatiana came back and declared that, on behalf of her father, she would act as a CEO, everybody was surprised. On January 18, 2002, Lev Klimenko passed away.

Soon after, one of the employees recognized that Tatiana was very scared and did not know what was going on at that time. Tatiana had to learn many things and was extremely grateful to the colleagues who supported her.

One thing still concerns me. My father was not only an incontestable authority, but also liked to teach people, especially young people. I think I have not got that experience and knowledge which I could and must have taken from him. Now, after all these years I am more self-confident, but back in 2002 I constantly appealed to my father when I did not know what to do … All the time I mentally asked him what to do, what he would have done in my place. Now such questions do not come up, but when I do something well, I always think my father would be proud of me. And this thought gives me comfort.

The company lost a lot after the founder's death but Tatiana managed to preserve the mental and ethical norms brought by her father who was an author of the ethical code of the patent attorney association. Since the company is rather small, the family type of relations exists in it and everyone is aware of each other's lifestyle and problems.

This style of relations at work is very comfortable for employees but still implies certain concerns for the employer. In a big company the director ranks high and is distant from the staff, whereas in a small company it is expected that the executive, being aware of the troubles the employees face, makes concessions to them, even at the expense of their work.

> *Due to the nepotistic character of relations inside the company, my father could not turn down requests from the staff which sometimes sounded speculative. I remember my thoughts back then: "For God's sake, I do not want to love these people so much that I could not turn down a request." But, unfortunately, in the course of time I drifted into the same type of relations. That is why I consider the main problem to be not the fact that in some cases the executive is a woman, but that I cannot distance myself from the subordinates.*

Ten years ago, the Russian Agency for Patents and Trademarks founded the Russian State University of Intellectual Property where judicial and economic faculties for high school graduates were formed. Both departments prepare experts–practitioners in the area of intellectual property protection and management. Thus, a new succession planning stage is on the way in Lev Klimenko Ltd. Tatiana followed the advice of her father and generated an interest in the legal profession in her son:

> *My son has been working for our firm every summer since he was 15 and he has been doing it with pleasure. He accumulates the necessary knowledge and experience. Recently he claimed that I gave him tasks which were too easy, and he wanted to do something more serious. By the time of graduating from the University he will already have long-term working experience in the patent business. He has a good chance to become a good specialist and a worthy successor to the business of his grandfather, whom he has always loved dearly and has been deeply proud of. I hope that my son will continue conducting the family business in a proper way applying mental and ethical norms brought to the company by his grandfather.*

Conclusion

As it can be seen from the Lev Klimenko example, path dependency (Rosefielde, 2005) affects the development of family businesses in Russia and has not made any positive contribution to the change of a masculine society with highly autocratic management structures. A situation of uncertainty does not allow for any planning—not only for business succession but also the support of the operational and tactical activities of companies.

Tatiana, daughter of the business founder, did not obtain a law degree, which seemed to be a prerequisite for her becoming a successor, and she could not acquire one due to having a small child. However, and in addition to this, Lev Klimenko's educational approach has severely affected her self-confidence during her formative years. She lacked initiative and had always been guided by her father. When it came to her assuming the business she was not prepared for this and was constantly in need of her father's advice and support.

Up to the year 2000 there was no succession planning in place. Apart from the transfer (no legal documents had been prepared to this effect before the death of Lev

Klimenko) of the company's shares, there was no attempt made to prepare the successor for the efficient management of the company. That is the reason why the employees of the firm were so surprised when Tatiana announced herself to be the new CEO in January 2002. This illustrates the lack of succession planning in the given example and confirms some of the theoretical propositions mentioned earlier. One of the reasons for a lack of succession planning may also be a polychronic Russian culture which makes the succession process almost impossible in a highly destabilized environment.

References

Allen, I.E., Elam, A., Langowitz, N. and Dean, M. 2008. *The GEM Global 2007 Report on Women and Entrepreneurship*. Global Entrepreneurship Monitor, New York.

Barclays Bank. 2006. *Small Firms in Britain, 2006: A Review by Barclays Local Business Banking*. London: Barclays Bank.

Barkhatova, N., McMylor, P. and Mellor, R. 2001. Family Business in Russia: The Path to Middle Class? *British Journal of Sociology*, 52(2), 249–269.

Bigliardi, B. and Dormio, A.I. 2009. Successful Generational Change in Family Business. *Measuring Business Excellence*, 13(2), 44.

Bosma, N. and Harding, R. 2007. *GEM-Global Entrepreneurship Monitor 2006 Results*. Babson College/ London Business School/ Co-Sponsors, USA/UK.

Bosma, N. and Levie, J. 2010. *Global Entrepreneurship Report*. Global Entrepreneurship Monitor, New York.

Day, J.C., Polyakov, E. and Day, J. 2007. *Understanding Inter Generational Family Business Success: A Qualitative Approach Using a Local Sample*. Proceedings of the XII April Economic Conference, Omsk State University, 16–17 April, 2, 239–242.

Elenkov, D. 1998. Can American Management Concepts Work in Russia: A Cross-Cultural Comparative Study. *California Management Review*, 40(4), 133–162.

Hofstede, G. 1986. *Culture's Consequences. International Differences in Work-Related Values*. CA: Sage Publications.

Jacobs, D.G. 2009. Securing Your Future. *Landscape Management*, 48(2), 14.

Johnson, R. 2010. Family Succession—The Final Challenge. *Supply House Times*, 52(11), 122.

Kaledgyan, S. 2010. Family Business: Historical Heritage or New Horizons? *Personal Money* [online, 19 April 2010] Available at: http://www.personalmoney.ru/snwsinf.asp?id=1259674 [accessed: 7 July 2010].

Kansikas, J. and Kuhmonen, T. 2008. Family Business Succession: Evolutionary Economics Approach. *Journal of Enterprising Culture*, 16(3), 279.

Kihlgren, A. 2002. Small Business in Russia: A Case Study of St. Petersburg. *William Davidson Working Paper*, Number 439, University of Michigan, USA.

Moyer, S.K. and Chalofsky, N.E. 2008. Understanding the Selection and Development of Life Goals of Family Business Owners. *Journal of Enterprising Culture*, 16(1), 19.

Rosefielde, S. 2005. Illusion of Transition: Russia's Muscovite Future. *Eastern Economic Journal*, 31(2), 285–299.

Salahova, L. 2009. Notes on Family Business in Russia. A presentation [online, 22 February 2009] Available at: http://www.pravis.ru/index.php?page=publications&id=64 [accessed: 6 July 2010].

Verkhovskaya, O. and Dorokhina, M. 2009. *GEM Report Russia* [online] Available at: http://www.gemconsortium.org/document.aspx?id=950 [accessed: 6 July 2010].

Vinokurova, N., Ollonqvist, P., Holopainen, P., Viitanen, J., Mutanen, A. and Gerasimov, Y. 2005. *Challenges in Roundwood Trade between Finland and Russia—A Cultural Approach*. Working Papers of the Finnish Forest Research Institute 7.

CHAPTER 15

Spain: Father–Daughter Succession in Spain: Success Factors in a Male-Dominated Sector

MARÍA CRISTINA DÍAZ GARCÍA AND
ÁNGELA GONZÁLEZ MORENO

Introduction

In Spain, 85 percent of firms are family firms, employing almost 14 million individuals (70 percent of the private employment), with a turnover rate that is equivalent to 70 percent of the Gross domestic product (GDP) and accounts for 59 percent of the country's exports (Instituto de la Empresa Familiar, 2009). The generational change is the main threat that family firms have to deal with and, unfortunately, the most influential cause of business failure. The statistics, with respect to the succession process, are not promising; since the analysis of the 1,000 largest companies in Spain in 1972, 1982, and 1992 shows that the percentage of family businesses has declined steadily (40 percent, 23 percent, 17 percent, respectively) in each of those years (Gallo et al., 1996).

In Spain, the primogeniture criterion has been widely used over time, probably because of its convenience, exempting parents of the responsibility of selecting the most qualified child. However, this approach underutilizes a key resource for the family business: the skills and abilities of the daughters. Therefore, in a recent survey, this criterion appears to be in clear decline, since the process of professionalization leads family businesses to choose the most qualified family member (Barbeito et al., 2005).

Very few studies focus on the unique impact of a cultural context of family firms around the world but, despite similarities in economic and family spheres in western countries, it is probable that female entrepreneurial activity and family business activity would take different forms in different cultures.

Therefore, the present research explores the impact of culture on the process of father–daughter succession of family businesses in Spain with a case study approach. With this we contribute to a deeper understanding of how a planned succession that provides the female successor with an active role in order to hone the experience she has gained outside the firm is determinant in contributing to the legitimacy and credibility of the female successor, especially within a male-dominated sector.

We will present a review of literature regarding female entrepreneurship, family business succession, and socio-cultural impact on business. Following that is a case study on a female successor in a Spanish family firm. In the final sections, the conclusions are presented together with the recommendations for future research.

Literature Review

According to Mejías (2001), socio-cultural values in Spain are dominated by the importance given to the family, since it is the realm where the values are transferred from one generation to the next. Women are generally more intensively affected by the stereotypes and pressure of social roles. In Spain the roles ascribed to women are considered to be more conventional and less disruptive of the established order. In this line, Martín (2005) argues that despite the fact that the prejudice to choose daughters as successors has diminished there still remains a gap in achieving effective equality. He states that, frequently, the son is selected as the successor based on family and social arguments, even when admitting that the professional profile and the character and commitment of the daughter would be more appropriate for the firm. In these cases, the parents take an approach tainted by protective machismo which is meant to "protect" the daughters from the perceived "toughness" of entrepreneurial leadership.

Socio-cultural values have a pronounced impact on the choice of successor and the quality of the interpersonal relationship between the predecessor, the successor, and the members of the family. Martinez et al. (2007) interviewed daughters in family firms, observing that the majority of them have a positive view of their professional career in the family firm and have had a successful socialization into the family firm. Furthermore, the family support, especially from parents, is highly valued as the factor that leads them to assume leadership of the firm. In their study, two main problems for female successors were observed: first, the lack of training in both managerial capabilities and technical processes, in which the sons are generally trained, and second, that there was a lack of succession planning, as it is considered a taboo issue to discuss as a family.

Therefore, it seems that the managerial competence of the successor is highlighted as a key success factor in the planning and in the successful completion of the transfer, together with integrity, trust, and the respect from stakeholders (Astrachan et al., 2008).

This previous managerial competence can be highly improved with the active role of the successor in the family firm, therefore, it is important that the father trusts the capabilities of his daughter and explicitly defines her role in the firm with a carefully designed succession process. According to Astrachan et al. (2008), the implication of the successor in strategic planning can derive numerous benefits. First, they obtain the knowledge related to the business model of the firm and the dynamics of the sector. Second, they gain their own vision for making decisions and develop more commitment to the firm. Third, it contributes to facilitating a significant improvement of the interpersonal relationships in the firm, between the next generation members, parents, and children and family and non-family members. Finally, the successors gain respect from others, meaning that their legitimacy and credibility is reinforced, since others can evaluate their performance, managerial, and human capabilities.

Case Study[1]

In deepening our understanding of father–daughter succession in the Spanish context, we have conducted an in depth explorative case of a father–daughter succession that is passing successfully. We believe that, in reviewing this case, other women can learn from the interviewee's experience to make their career paths more effective and their businesses more successful.

Back in 2000, Julian decided to found his firm within the real estate development and construction sector. He had experience as a business owner in the same sector and took the risk to abandon his previous established firm to create one on his own. His primary motivation for taking this risk was that "he perceived an entrepreneurial potential in some of his children that he did not want to waste." With time, the activity of the firm was diversified to the distribution of kitchens furniture (2003) as well as a real estate agency (2005). The capital of the firm is divided in seven equal parts for the parents, three sons, and three daughters. One of them is Maria, who will succeed her father in the near future by taking on the leading role in the firm. She currently participates in the patrimony and active management responsibilities within the firm.

FAMILY FACTORS ON THE CHOICE OF THE SUCCESSOR AND INTERPERSONAL RELATIONS

When Julian founded the firm, all six brothers and sisters were working or studying, so he told them that, despite the fact that they were all shareholders, they had to decide who wanted to participate actively in the management of the firm. This participation would be based on merits according to their profile. Therefore, they had to plan a clear distinction of roles and responsibilities, that is, make an ordered approach to a family firm protocol. Maria refers to it in the following quote:

> *In that protocol we decided which posts we, as shareholders, were willing to hand over to family members, which responsibilities would be a part of those posts and, furthermore, the formal relationships that were going to exist ... the family decided that my profile was the most appropriate to be the manager of the firm, and this was decided from the first moment since we all voted the decision and it was accepted by unanimity ... the reason was my entrepreneurial spirit, I am very similar to my father, I have always stood out for being self-assured, for having initiative ... but I was conscious of my lack of training in the business realm and, therefore, I took an MBA and several courses related with the construction sector ... I educated myself as much as I could and when I started managing the firm I learned more than ever.*

According to Maria, the reason behind her election has been her complicity and the character similarity to her father. She sees her father as a role model who has given her the necessary freedom to find the possible solutions, instead of simply suggesting the solutions to her, which could have reduced her legitimacy in the firm.

> *Shareholders are always looking forward to explore new opportunities, and we have an amazing entrepreneurial spirit in this firm; we have little fear! My father has always had very clear*

1 The interviewee and her father have been given fictitious names to protect their identity.

ideas; he sets up a business and molds it in a masterful way; he is so talented! I lack many years of experience ... I admire so much the way he is capable of outlining a business, that is, in very little time he has everything thought out and structured and makes everything so easy for you ... my father is the engine that gives me a tremendous security to start.

Where the conflicts between family shareholders can sometimes lead to bad performance and deficient leadership abilities, the female successor in this case has an extraordinary relationship with the family shareholders. All members of ownership have accepted her role. If there are issues, she confronts problems with other family members in an objective way:

For example, now that I am the manager of the group and I have four brothers and sisters working for me, they have had to understand the difference between a Sunday meal in my grandfather's house and an intense work meeting. In the work context, I may have to confront them about something that is not appropriate or when an objective has not been achieved, and they have to accept it as another employee.

In this case, the family shareholders are not a source of conflict but instead a source of support in order to make important decisions that will impact the interests of all of them.

The most important thing that you need from your shareholders is that they believe in you, that when you suggest a new business opportunity or an important change in any of the business units they support you. In the meetings I have never found any hindrance, they always say "let's do it," they assume that we (my father and I) are here to decide how the firm should grow and, for me, that is the most important thing; it is my family, isn't it? And if I find that anyone is not satisfied with my management I would be very personally affected. For the moment, I am lucky because they are satisfied and always support me; this is why I am very motivated.

LESSONS FROM THE SUCCESSION PROCESS: THE ACTIVE ROLE OF THE SUCCESSOR

Through this case, we see that being in an active role in the company, before assuming total control of the firm, contributes to a successful succession. Maria has had the opportunity to learn and exercise the managerial capabilities in decision making, since from the first moment the firm has had a deliberate strategy of diversification. This fosters the creativity to develop a number of different alternatives and the discipline to evaluate the options and select the most appropriate; it is something that it is learned by doing.

From the beginning we had in mind that we were a very big family with some people willing to participate in the project and if we concentrated only in one activity it was not possible to participate as we wanted. My father told us: "A firm grows or dies, and we can't stagnate since we can have good results in one activity. Eventually, an economic cycle will come and lead to the firm's death, and if we do not diversify and grow, we are not going to achieve what we want." ... the diversification is a responsibility that the two of us have assumed, every time that we spot an opportunity we make an analysis and ... if it is interesting we begin to mature the idea. He has more experience and, therefore, proposes very interesting aspects, but I contribute also as much as I can.

In addition, she has had to change her way of making decisions from the manner that she had when she was employed as a manager of another firm. That is, she has learned that she has to adapt her outside experience as a manager to her new position as business owner, where she is the main responsible person of all the decisions taken by the firm which have an impact on its survival and the employees' well-being.

> *I had work experience managing large teams, making decisions with intensity and promptness that made me a rather aggressive executive ... because the position demanded that from me. When you arrive to a managerial position as the one I have now, where everyone looks at you and judges you 24 hours a day, you have to transform yourself in the opposite, you have to be a calm person, which makes very well-thought out decisions ... it might seem that you have just made them without thought, but actually you have thought about them at home. You develop abilities to take decisions quickly but in any moment you might show that they have not been planned, that you improvise.*

Also with Julian's mentoring, Maria has improved her skills to manage a project, her negotiation abilities to obtain resources, and has honed her ability to participate in teamwork; developing her leadership and communication capabilities to achieve consensus and trust. This led her to achieve legitimacy and credibility in the eyes of her father, employees, financing providers, and society as a whole.

> *I had worked as an employee for eight or nine years. That experience helped me a lot. First of all you are able to empathize with your employees and that is critical for good communication and mutual understanding, since I can demand a lot of my team. But my team also demands from me several things that if you have not been in the other side I think you can't perceive. Second, I entered a very masculine sector and I had to gain the respect of others by working hard, I had to set a good example and had the necessary empathy with my employees so that they realize that I respected and valued them and I understood their situation.*

That is, the value of her outside experience has increased exponentially with her active role in the firm, conferring legitimacy on her. However, another source of legitimacy that cannot be discounted is that conferred by the founder's attitude toward the successor:

> *My father is essential; he is the face of the firm. This is a sector in which you need tremendous credibility, since it is a multimillion euro industry. Therefore, if the banks do not believe in the integrity and professionalism of the business owner they are not going to lend you the astronomic amounts of millions of euros that you need to start a real estate development. Hence, his presence is critical for me, because without him the firm would be nothing. Little by little during my seven years in the firm I have had to gain the respect of the financial entities and the social and labor environment that surround my firm. I have had to enter business associations so that people would not see me as "Julian's daughter" since this was the way they recognized me during the first three years ... he has invited me to enter in the first place, has given me the initiative and the defence of the projects, so that people could see that I was not only the girl by his side who was still learning ... two years ago, I was awarded as a young female business owner and in my discourse I expressed my gratefulness to him for having distanced from me enough in order that others saw me ... that is what he has done and it has been done intentionally.*

This gained legitimacy undoubtedly increased the self-confidence of the successor:

> *Business owners really do not retire, but he is 62 years old and he does not want to be present in every important thing and in the day-to-day management ... I believe we are ready to make the leap to the stage where I am responsible for everything and I am the face of the firm ... but for now he is still here, therefore, until he does not leave the directorship we are not going to know if I have achieved that credibility. I am conscious of that.*

There is a final factor that also contributes to Maria's legitimacy as an executive of this company. Maria was appointed for the role before starting a family of her own—she now has three children all under the age of six — and this fact has contributed to her ability to balance her roles as manager and mother:

> *My role requires me to participate in business associations; this means that when I finish at 8:30 pm I have to attend a meeting until 11:00 pm. This is what conflicts me, but, since I arrived to the position before becoming a mother, I have always known what my position involves ... there are times when I am tired, but I cannot be surprised because it was my choice.*

The greatest barrier to her legitimacy has been achieving the balance between the past legacy and the new guidelines for the future. Maria has been able to decide which traditions to maintain and to what extent innovations could be incorporated into the firm, maintaining an appropriate relationship between the past and the future of the firm. In this case, she admits this is the only difficulty she has encountered as a successor, stated in the following quote:

> *I am not my father; I have my own style for doing business. The fact that the firm was up and going for two years and some months before my arrival implied that I had to adapt to a certain culture, a way of using technologies, ways of working, mechanisms to relate with the departments, and so on ... I have had to modify them little by little with diplomacy and showing first that the changes were going to work. Then, in a way it is an advantage, because you enter in a comfortable way, learn at your rhythm, and do not have to make decisions from the first day but, on the other hand, afterwards it takes a little of effort to impose your own managerial style.*

Discussion and Conclusion

From the narrative we can observe the dynamic dimensions of the succession process, during which the roles of the two main types of actors, predecessor and successor, evolve in an intertwined way.

The smooth transition is certainly favored by the lack of conflict within the family and firm. In the property realm no problems have arisen since members of the family have the same share of capital and Maria was selected unanimously as the successor. In the managerial realm the succession was carefully planned to provide the successor with the knowledge along with the legitimacy and credibility of the firm stakeholders. Furthermore, her people-centered managerial qualities seem to be central in minimizing conflicts among family members.

Both the clarity in the factors for choosing the daughter as the successor, which leads to unanimity in her selection, and the planning of the succession, which gives the daughter an active role, can prevent the female successor from encountering particular barriers when taking over the family business.

That the successor obtains legitimacy and credibility is extremely important for the performance and survival of the family firm, but is even more important when the successor is female and, furthermore, in a male-dominated sector such as construction. Therefore, the planning of the succession, that allocated an active role to the female successor, enables her to obtain different capabilities. This shows her competence to the stakeholders and provides her with legitimacy, in line with the findings of previous research. The greatest barrier to legitimacy is solving the great tension of balancing the past legacy with future growth and change. This step is really critical for successors and a tough balance to find.

Although other problems might arise, they cannot overshadow the satisfaction that comes with leading the team that keeps the family legacy growing. Within these problems, an example is the economic crisis that Spain and especially the construction sector have been undergoing since 2008. In Spain the age of retirement is 65 years old, this means that the stage of the succession coined "joint kingdom"[2] will last at least three years more. However, the crisis might enlarge this stage, because in this moment of uncertainty and financial problems the legitimacy of the founder is more necessary than ever. Precisely, the firm is trying to overcome the crisis by diversifying its activity, inspired by the founder, Julian, who has taught his daughter the importance of growth and change. Entrepreneurship is a driver for family firm longevity.

Recommendations for Further Research

We believe that this case highlights the impact of industry on succession success, particularly in the case of father–daughter transfer in future research. In an industry which is male-dominated, we might expect more legitimacy and credibility problems with stakeholders that could have threatened the transition process. However, this has not been the case in our example. Despite the constraints of the well-defined occupational norms (structure), individuals (successor and predecessor) have agency to actively perform their subject position.

Researchers have to be conscious that since subjects are constituted socially and in turn construct social reality, the social construction of reality has to be understood in a reciprocal mode between structure and agency (Ahl, 2007). Therefore, researchers in future studies have to be sensitive to both institutional influences and female agency, which position them differently in terms of how they address their gender construction within their particular contexts (Shaw et al., 2009). In this line, it could be fruitful to research the role of outside experience in female leader development and her legitimacy building or how the timing in accepting the managerial responsibilities and having a family can alter the perception of conflict, that is, lack of work–life balance.

2 This expression comes from 'Regné conjoint' used by Bayad and Barbot (2002).

Future research could also benefit from further exploring the learning process between the founder and the successor, in terms of how the entrepreneurial spirit is passed on from the first generation to the following ones.

References

Ahl, H. 2007. Sex Business in the Toy Store: A Narrative Analysis of a Teaching Case, *Journal of Business Venturing*, 22(5), 673–693.

Astrachan, J., Marchisio, G. y Mazzola, P. 2008. Planificación Estratégica y Desarrollo del Espíritu Emprendedor en la Siguiente Seneración in *Transformarse o Desaparecer: Estrategias de la Empresa Familiar para Competir en el Siglo* (pp. 253–264), edited by J.M. Amat, J.I. Martínez and J. Roure. XXI, Barcelona: Deusto.

Barbeito, S., Martínez, M. and Guillén, E. 2005. La Planificación del Proceso de Sucesión en la Empresa Familiar Gallega. *Anales de Economía Aplicada* (XIX Reunión Anual de Asepelt), Junio, Badajoz.

Bayad, M. and Barbot, M.C. 2002. *Proposition d'un Modèle de Succession dans les PME Familiales: Etude de cas Exploratoire de la Relation Père-Fille*. Congrès International Francophone sur la PME 2002, HEC Montréal.

Gallo, M.A., Cappuyns, K. and Estapé, M.J. 1996. La Empresa Familiar Entre las 1000 Mayores Empresas de España in *La Empresa Familiar*, 5, Estudios y Ediciones IESE.

Instituto de la Empresa Familiar. 2009. Available at: http://www.iefamiliar.com/organizacion/datos.asp [accessed: 15 July 2010].

Martín, V. 2005. *La Mujer y el Liderazgo en la Empresa Familiar*. Boletín nº 30, *UNILCO SEG*,

Martinez, R., Hernández, M.J. and Poza, J. 2007. Trayectoria Profesional de las Hijas en la Empresa Familiar: De la Infancia a la Sucesión in *Conocimiento, Innovación y Emprendedores: Camino al Futuro*, edited by J.C. Ayala and Grupo de Investigación FEDRA (Family Enterprise Development Research Applications) (coord.). Universidad de la Rioja.

Mejías Valenzuela, E. (Dir) 2001. *Valores Sociales y Drogas*, FAD, Fundación la Caixa.

Shaw, E., Marlow, S., Lam, W. and Carter, S. 2009. Gender and Entrepreneurial Capital: Implications for Firm Performance. *International Journal of Gender and Entrepreneurship*, 1(1), 25–41.

CHAPTER 16 Scotland/United Kingdom: Driving a Scottish Family Business Forward: From Faither to Wee Lassie

STUART GRAHAM AND CLAIRE SEAMAN

Introduction: Scotland and its Family Businesses

Scotland provides the cultural backdrop to this chapter for a *faither* (Scots spelling of "father") to *lassie* (a Scots term for "daughter") succession. These differing terms in Scots dialect highlight the condition of Scotland as part of a larger state, the United Kingdom, but with very distinct cultural identities which vary across regions of Scotland. The cultural and regional identities of Scotland play a key role in this case study—as the backdrop against which the father–daughter succession developed and as an influencer for the business. Whilst Scotland is a *country,* with its own distinctive cultural facets, it should be borne in mind that, "Scotland is a *nation,* but not a *state*" (McGarvey and Cairney, 2008:1). Although Scotland is not a state in legal terms, it has acquired a degree of "political independence" (Dinnie, 2002) by the re-establishment of the Scottish Parliament and Government in 1999.

Despite Scotland's relatively small size, when measured by population, 5.1 million, it has a predominant number of family businesses within its geographical boundaries. Whilst authoritative statistics are scarce, estimates suggest that Scotland has in the region of 60,000 family businesses, accounting for 85 percent of private enterprises in Scotland, employing 50 percent of its private sector workforce (Stepek and Laird, 2007). With a focus on one such Scottish family business, and associated cultural influences, this chapter explores the father–daughter succession experience through the daughter's narrative account.

Cultural Variables and Scottish Family Business Succession

The interaction between Scottish culture and the environment for family businesses is in itself of interest, and at one level could be seen to create the environment within which any succession process happens. Key to understanding this process is the concept of "layers" of culture. The importance of culture and structure for entrepreneurship has been highlighted by a number of authors (Davidsson, 1995) though empirical research remains scarce.

LAYERS OF CULTURE

Whilst Scotland has a significant proportion of family businesses, there is nonetheless, "sparse research" (Seaman and Graham, 2009:231) relating to them within the academic literature of a general nature, or with any specific focus upon father–daughter succession and cultural variables. In recognition of such limitations, for the purposes of this study, Hofstede's six "layers of culture" (1991:10) are adopted to frame a commentary of potential socio-cultural variables of relevance to a Scottish father–daughter succession.

NATIONAL CULTURE

Although Scotland has a degree of autonomy to manage its own affairs, there remains a strong sense of rivalry based upon past conflicts and strong cultural differences between "England and the Scots" (Usunier and Lee, 2005:10). In considering Scotland's cultural heritage, McCrone et al. recounted quotes from their respondents such as: "There is a different cultural heritage, a different background. The attitudes are different, the thinking is different. Our educational standards are higher" (1995:170). Despite the passage of time, such national "mental programming" (Hofstede, 1991:10) continues to influence both family and business attitudes to some degree.

REGIONAL CULTURE

Whilst there are socio-cultural variations at a national level within the UK, in terms of "a strong North/South paradigm" (Usunier and Lee, 2005:234), the same distinction is also appropriate within Scotland; including distinctions between the Highlands and Lowlands and rural and urban communities. There is also a distinction made within the Lowlands between east and west, where the focal points tend to be Edinburgh to the east and Glasgow in the west. Glasgow is Scotland's largest city, with a past steeped in a world renowned reputation in heavy industry, ship-building in particular. Today, having rejuvenated itself, it represents a vibrant modern city. However, despite Glasgow's reconstruction over several decades, it is still often referred to as "macho" city, meaning, "the most violent city in Western Europe" (Craig, 2010:131).

GENDER

Coutts identifies the lack of research into the "unique contribution" made by women in family businesses (2005:11). The socio-cultural variable of gender is of major significance to Scottish family businesses as there is still a legacy of the role of women in domestic settings and work related activities.

GENERATION

The family values guiding the business have a major part to play in succession planning. In a research study where Scottish family enterprises were included, it was found that "some preferential treatment" was given to family members in regard to employment and management practices (Cromie et al., 1999). Whilst such findings have been identified as commonplace within a diverse range of situations, the fact remains that a key socio-cultural influence in Scottish family firms is a strong commitment to "kith and kin."

SOCIAL CLASS

Different class cultures are associated with social classes in most countries. Education opportunities and occupations/professions are key differentiators. In considering social mobility in Scotland, Payne points toward different patterns compared with England based upon Scotland's "separate culture and historically subordinate relationship to England resulting in distinctive employment opportunities" (1987:2).

ORGANIZATIONAL CULTURES

The social systems within organizations are critical features influencing how the enterprise functions. This is particularly important in respect to family businesses where issues relevant to "business" and "family" values may need to change for a variety of reasons, not least of which in a succession.

Whilst the notion of differing "layers of culture" is a useful means of categorizing varying influencing factors, applying them to particular instances of family business development is somewhat more problematic in practice. However, they are utilized in a general manner within the following case study to identify issues of cultural significance to the succession process.

Case Study: Scottish Chauffeur-Drive

The case study presents a daughter's account of her experiences and recollections associated with the succession to managing director of her father's business established some 40 years previously. The daughter's own narrative gives voice to her biographical story and highlights issues associated with cultural relevance.

FROM SMALL BEGINNINGS TO LARGE BUSINESS

> *My dad had two siblings, a brother and sister brought up by his parents in a very poor area of Glasgow quite close to here. My father and his brother bought the business in 1966. I think they were just presented with this opportunity in their early twenties ... they thought, well why not? ... my dad then just found his niche ... he's not amazingly well-educated but he's got a very good business brain ... just taught himself how to do things and built the business from a very small business, three taxis ... we've now got over 50 cars in the fleet in two cities. It's gone from quite a small business to a very successful and very large business.*

This opening account of her father's background and achievements reveals the daughter's real appreciation of the entrepreneurial spark so often ignited within the first generation of a family business. In cultural terms, recognition is given to the social standing of her father and his immediate family at a time when Glasgow was a home of heavy industry, and a time when associated cultural aspects were shaping its reputation as a "macho" city. The opportunistic nature in which the business was acquired may also point toward escaping from the drudgery of heavy industry and allowing the brothers to work together in order to move their generation toward a greater level of affluence.

Today the business has a workforce of over 20 and a turnover in the millions (GBP). The chauffer drive-centered business has luxury cars including Mercedes, Daimlers, Jaguars, and high-end "people carriers." The company promotes itself a:

> *Scotland's number one chauffer-drive service ... it was just a phrase that my dad started putting in literature a very long time ago ... [but] we are number one if you look in terms of size ... the longest established ... dealing with all the top hotels ... we are number one ... my vision for the future would be to carry on the tradition ... but I am aware that the market is just going to contract ... we need to find other avenues to do what we do ... maybe move into events management, organizing logistics.*

Conscious of the "tradition" built by her father, her horizons are now more strategic, reflecting perhaps "generational" differences.

Whilst Scotland, and many of its "national" cultural values, are part of the company's tradition, cultural features at a "regional" level must also be maintained. The business has been expanded to include an Edinburgh base in addition to the one in Glasgow. This was achieved by acquiring an Edinburgh company.

> *It's very important to us that we're perceived as being an Edinburgh company in Edinburgh. We have an Edinburgh phone number that gets diverted here [in Glasgow] ... we were aware of the fact that we had to be seen to be an Edinburgh company, not a Glasgow company who went to Edinburgh.*

GROWING UP IN A FAMILY WITH A BUSINESS

What was it like being a child in a family that owned a business?

> *When you're a child, it's just normal; you don't really think it's unusual. The only issue I remember, and this is rather a silly one ... Dad was always driving one of the fleet cars, and as a child, it was very embarrassing to be dropped at primary school in a Daimler limousine ... as a very small child, that was just torture.*

This raises the issue of "social class" as an early cultural incident in childhood, potentially having an effect upon how the business was viewed both through the eyes of a child and the symbolism of luxury. "We didn't have an affluent upbringing ... the business only started to do pretty well in the first 15 years." This is the period over which the daughter has been in the company. This may bring into question how the daughter viewed the business and her perceived "social" standing over a period of time; perhaps reflecting a change of attitude from father to daughter.

In these formative years what was the relationship like between father and daughter?

> *Well my mum says my dad and I are very similar and we clashed a lot when I was a teenager ... we're both quite strong-minded but, we've come out the other end of it very strong, but I think more of it was just personality rather than business-driven ... I'm a strong personality and I know what I want, but I go about it in a different way. Dad's quite old school ... shouting at people ... I'm not confrontational, my dad is.*

This characterization of her father being 'confrontational' is the stereotypical profile of Glaswegians, hardened by past decades of heavy toil and cultural masculinity. So how would she describe her management style to running the business compare to her father's?

> *It's not as harsh as my dad's! I would like to think my management style is clear to the staff, what I want them to do, and clear to my clients, what the business stands for and how we go about our business. I try and not have any conflict with the staff. If there's conflict, I will always try and diffuse it, I don't like conflict, I'm not good at conflict.*

How would she describe the organizational culture?

> *I think the culture now is very different to what it was. Our staff retention now is very high, people used to leave all the time ... it was a combination of my dad's fiery temperament, and a women who worked here ... she was a very difficult character ... she was just against change. So the culture, I would say, has changed significantly twice, once when my dad stepped back and then again when this woman left. The staff who've been with us since this woman left are the same staff ... everyone's quite happy!*

FROM UNIVERSITY TO A FALL INTO THE BUSINESS

Returning to the formative years, did the question of her parent's two daughters entering their father's business ever arise?

> *At no point were either my sister (three years younger) or I pressured to come into the business. In fact, it didn't cross my dad's mind that either of us would come into the business ... it genuinely was never discussed when I was at school, university, came out of university, nothing like that.*

So what happened?

> *I kind of, almost fell into it in my mid-twenties. I was the first of my family to go to university ... I was deemed to be intelligent enough to go ... came out and really didn't know what I wanted to do ... went back to university and did a management and marketing program ... and I started doing two days a week for my dad doing marketing.*

As the first of her family to go to university, the daughter brings to the fore cultural recognition of both "generational" and "social class" changes from her parents along with "gender" progression in terms of upward mobility. The move into the business on a part-time "project" type basis is also illustrative of females coming into a family business as a "helper."

I was looking for something to do, it was never something I thought I would do long-term ... It was just a gradual thing that I realized, actually I enjoy working here and my dad and I had a chat about it and decided I would start working in reservations ... did that for five years ... just learning the business from the ground up ... there was absolutely no special treatment at all ... there was quite a lot of friction ... I was young and naïve and maybe assumed that I could come in at some exalted level. I'm so glad I didn't, because now I know the business inside out.

Was the fact that her father was very hard on her because of notions of "gender," which stakeholders may hold in terms of how men and women should behave and styles of leadership associated when a women leads a business?

I don't actually think it's anything to do with me being a woman. I honestly think my dad is, despite old-fashioned notions in some ways, pretty progressive when it comes to men and women and what they're able to do, there was never any doubt in his mind that I could do it ... despite the fact that it's probably quite a masculine business running a car hire business, which is basically what we are, and had I been his son I, perhaps, would have been more involved as a child in cars ... so no, I would disagree with this hypothesis.

FROM PARTNERSHIP TO MANAGEMENT

Then in 1997 my dad said, "We'd like to make you a partner," completely out of the blue, hadn't been discussed at all, he just said, "What do you think?" At that point I said, "Well yes, why not?" So that was also quite a gradual thing, I became a partner, but I didn't really get more involved in management until my dad started to think about retirement ... maybe early 2000. At that point we started looking at the management transition from my father to myself.

So at this stage there was actual recognition and movement in respect to "generational" progression in terms of management and associated cultural change. How did this affect the business?

The idea had always been he would sell the business because there was never any discussion about us (sisters) being part of the business, and I think when they made me a partner in 1997, they realized that that was not going to happen and succession planning began ... I instigated it because I saw it was something that would have to be looked at and no way was I ready to take over, but I knew that it was something we would have to start thinking about. I think their assumption was that [my sister and] I would not get involved; but I think once one of us was involved, it became something that they thought, well we don't need to sell the business now, we can continue working in the business and when we are no longer able or wanting to, the daughter can run it and I think that was also just a gradual thing. I think with family businesses things aren't black and white, I mean, it's very ... yeah, a lot of it's very gradual, the thinking that goes on.

Were there any concerns when you became partner in terms of your younger sister? "That only came up during the succession planning discussion, in terms of ownership of shares and how they would manage that." How long has that been going on for? "Oh years!"

SUCCESSION INTO HER FATHER'S ROLE

Did succession go according to plan?

> *Well, it took a lot longer than I thought it was going to take ... that was procrastination ... he'll only do something if his back's pressed up against the wall ... looking back, I'm glad it took that length of time, we then came to the right decisions.*

While "generational" change has met the expectations of the daughter, in practice things do not always go as planned.

> *I don't think he really wanted to retire; he said to the staff, "don't tell people I'm retired." ... So people even up to three years after would phone and the staff had been instructed to say "he's not here at the moment, can I help you, or can I get him to call you back?" ... that just became completely unworkable ... a lot of succession, I think, is in other peoples' minds ... [if] they don't realize that I'm running the business, then succession hasn't actually happened ... so I am 39 at the moment, so I was 34 when I became managing director, and my father withdrew from the business.*

DRIVING FORWARD

How do you view the business today?

> *I feel very proud of the business and how the business has grown in the last ten or 15 years since I've had an active role in that growth. I'm happy with the way things have gone ... the business is part of our family ... there's a love there.*

Have you thought about succession in the future?

> *I would love my son to run the business, but he's eight months old, so it's a wee bit far off! But ... at some point I'm going to have to think about whether we talk about it, at what age, yeah, there's a whole other thing that I'm going to have to educate myself about.*

Discussion and Conclusions

The case study draws attention to a series of events and experiences associated with a daughter's childhood, adolescence, and adulthood regarding her views and emotions toward her father's business. What is of prime significance is the manner in which future succession was never discussed during the two sister's formative years. Whilst it was assumed by the parents that the business would be sold at some appropriate point in the future, it does nonetheless raise the question of how typical this situation is within family businesses. Whilst the issue of gender is discounted with respect to the daughter's extremely demanding preparation for succession, does the type of business, in terms of masculinity and femininity, exclude serious consideration of children in certain instances? This case illustrates that whilst opportunistic circumstances can lead to unexpected succession, there are real dangers in discounting continuity of the business at any stage in generational life cycles.

Recommendations for Further Research

Specific research focused upon children's perceptions, over progressive periods of their formative years, toward their parent's business would be informative in light of this case study. There is also a need to encourage studies, across the spectrum of family business research, giving attention to Scottish family businesses in an attempt to reduce a significant gap in literature.

References

Coutts. 2005. *Coutts 2005 Family Business Survey*. London: Coutts & Co.

Craig, C. (2010), *The Tears that made the Clyde*. Argyll: Argyll Publishing.

Cromie, S., Adams, J., Dunn, B. and Reid, R. 1999. Family Firms in Scotland and Northern Ireland: An Empirical Investigation. *Journal of Small Business and Enterprise Development*, 6(3), 253–266.

Davidsson, P. 1995. Culture, Structure and Regional Levels of Entrepreneurship. *Entrepreneurship and Regional Development*, 7(1), 41–62.

Dinnie, K. 2002. Implications of National Identity for Marketing Strategy. *The Marketing Review*, 2, 285–300.

Hofstede, G. 1991. *Cultures and Organizations: Software of the Mind*. Maidenhead: McGraw-Hill.

McGarvey, N. and Cairney, P. 2008. *Scottish Politics: An Introduction*. Basingstoke: Palgrave Macmillan.

McCrone, D., Morris, A. and Kiely, R. 1995. *Scotland—the Brand: The Making of Scottish Heritage*. Edinburgh: Edinburgh University Press.

Payne, G. 1987. *Employment and Opportunity*. London: Macmillan.

Seaman, C. and Graham, S. 2009. Creating Competitive Advantage in Scottish Family Businesses: Managing, Sharing and Transferring the Knowledge in *Cultural Implications of Knowledge Sharing, Management and Transfer: Identifying Competitive Advantage*, edited by D. Haromonina. IDI International Publishers.

Stepek, M. and Laird, M. 2007. *SFBA Strategy: A Discussion Document*. Blantyre: Scottish Family Business Association.

Usunier, J-C. and Lee, J.A. 2005. *Marketing Across Cultures*. Harlow: FT Prentice Hall.

CHAPTER **17**

Sweden: Two-Fold Succession in a Family Business Matriarchy: A Swedish Case

CECILIA BJURSELL AND LEIF MELIN

Introduction

This case study from Sweden illustrates three important aspects of succession in family businesses. First, succession processes includes two different dimensions: the transfer of ownership from one generation to the next, and the succession of leadership in the family firm. Second, succession processes includes stages and activities that go on for many years. The case study reported here shows how the ongoing succession process has continued for a period of about 15 years and is yet not completed, Finally, this case illustrates the fact that daughters are considered by the father as being the future owners/ leaders of the family business, but also a situation where daughters take over if there is no competition from sons.

The Swedish Context

In the Swedish society, regulations for parental leave, equal opportunities, and government childcare contribute to a welfare system that aims at supporting women's participation in working life. Today, about a third of all new ventures are initiated by women, 22–28 percent of the companies are led by women and, in 2006, women's businesses employed 418,127 people, 70 percent of the employees were other women and these businesses paid 91 billion Swedish crones (about 9.3 billion euros) in wages (Holmquist and Wennberg, 2010).

The future for women-run enterprises in Sweden is looking good since they have lower numbers for sick leave among employees, the number of women in technological industries at the Swedish business incubators have increased from 10 percent in 2005 to 29 percent in 2008 and at the current rate of development every other business will be run by a woman in 2030 (Ibid.). Assuming that women prefer a feminine leadership style, the Swedish managerial style works well with its action patterns characterized by pragmatic consensus seeking, focus on flexible service orientation and change, active participation and dialogue (Czarniawska-Joerges, 1993; Jönsson, 1995). The Swedish managerial style suggests a process-oriented understanding of leadership (Holmberg and Åkerblom, 2006), which can be seen as an expression of current legislation in combination with egalitarian influences in society.

Contrasting the positive outlook above, research shows that, although the Nordic European countries have a tradition of promoting gender equality, few women sit at the higher levels in organizations (Kantola, 2008). Despite the Swedish high ranks in international indexes of equality, the labor market is characterized by gender segregation (Sundin and Tillmar, 2008). As a result of a subordinate position in society historically, women have not always enjoyed the privilege of being business owners (Holmquist and Sundin, 2002). Still, the notion of the manager/owner/entrepreneur displays gender bias and assumptions of masculinity (Ahl, 2002a and 2002b; Mulholland 1996).

The family business is often characterized as representing a traditional patriarchal structure. Although women have participated actively in family businesses on a practical level, academic research has neglected women as well as female industries (Javefors Grauers, 2002). Production and entrepreneurship are viewed as male territory, which makes women invisible in this discourse (Pettersson, 2002). However, differences can be found as a result of local contexts as well as societal contexts, and women's enterprising can be understood as reflecting patterns of enterprising in society at large (Holmquist and Sundin, 2006; Javefors Grauers, 2004). Family-owned firms constitute about 70 percent of all businesses but a study performed in a Swedish county on privately-owned businesses with more than four employees, showed that only 4.7 percent of the main owners were women (Melin et al., 2004). When a great majority of the firms in Sweden change ownership in the years to come, the main hindrances for women in family firms will be the attitudes and values that daughters are not suitable, interested, or considered as owners of the business (Melin, 2008).

The Swedish Case Study

Louise Attevik is one of the children in the third generation of the Atteviks family business. She represents the family in the operative business of the car dealership where her responsibility is real estate. The family considers it important to have a family representative in the business: the owners should be present in the daily work at the company. Louise holds a Master's degree in Business Administration, specializing in organization and marketing. Whilst continuing her studies, Louise also worked in the family business. After completing her degree, she worked at Mercedes Benz Finance, at a small IT company, and at EON, an energy company. Upon entering the family firm, Louise was assigned a board member as her mentor. Louise says that it is a combination of personality and competence that make the exchange with her mentor fruitful:

> *He has a very nice personality. He is calm, has a lot of experience, and knows the business. He also knows our family well. I can talk to him about family troubles, and I can talk to him about how to approach problems and people in the business.*

Despite an educational background in business, relevant work experience, a family supporting her presence in the firm, and a competent mentor, Louise still has ambiguous feelings for the family firm. She hovers between wanting to run the family firm and considering selling if someone comes along and presents an interesting offer.

THE FIRM

"Atteviks" is a licensed car dealership working with the brands of Audi, Volkswagen, Skoda, and Scania. The firm is situated in Jönköping, a small town in the south of Sweden. Over the years, the firm has grown and has sales and service facilities in seven locations. The company is organized as the Atteviks Bil AB group with two subsidiaries, one for cars and one for trucks. Sigvard Attevik, who started the business in 1945, always put the customer in focus:

> *Already from the beginning, the customer was at the centre of attention. Sigvard found it important to be the first to deliver services that would provide the customer with a feeling of being taken care of.*
>
> *(Atteviks homepage, www.atteviks.se, 16 April 2010)*

The customer orientation is also expressed in the company values that evoke the image that Sigvard built based on honesty and integrity, and that has remained unchanged over the years:

> *Atteviks family values permeate the company and are clear to all employees: keep things in order, sincerity and honesty, listen to customer needs, respect for the individual—no matter income and social status, at Atteviks, all should be received in the same way.*
>
> *(Atteviks homepage, www.atteviks.se, 16 April 2010)*

Owning the business over several generations has provided stability. It is not unusual to find employees who have worked for 30–40 years in the firm, meaning that knowledge and experience is gained, preserved, and shared in the firm over many years.

Another dimension of values is that the company must adapt to the culture in the local community. The Swedish clean-cut ideal from the 1950s works well in a small town where everyone knows one another, and on an organizational level this means that the workshop should be tidy; for example, no junk in the halls and orderly arrangements as a symbolic representation of honesty as the guiding principle. With about 300 employees and a turnover of 1 billion Swedish crones, the third generation continues to work according to these values. At the same time, each generation bring their own leadership style to the firm.

The Attevik Family

Sigvard Attevik started the firm that now is run by the second and third generation. Sigvard and his wife Eira had two children, Anita and Christina. In those days, daughters were usually not considered as successors of a firm in Sweden.

I don't think it ever occurred to my father that daughters could take over as managers in the firm. It didn't occur to me either because I just wanted to get out and see the world.
(Anita Löf, second generation)

Anita settled in the home town of Jönköping while her sister moved to another city. Per-Åke Löf, who married older sister Anita, started working in the firm as an accountant at the request of his father-in-law. When the founder passed away in 1969, Per-Åke stepped in as the CEO of the family business. He remained in that position until one of his daughters took over as the CEO. In the third generation there are four children, Cecilia, Louise, and their cousins Karin and Gustav. In the fourth generation there are seven children (see Figure 17.1).

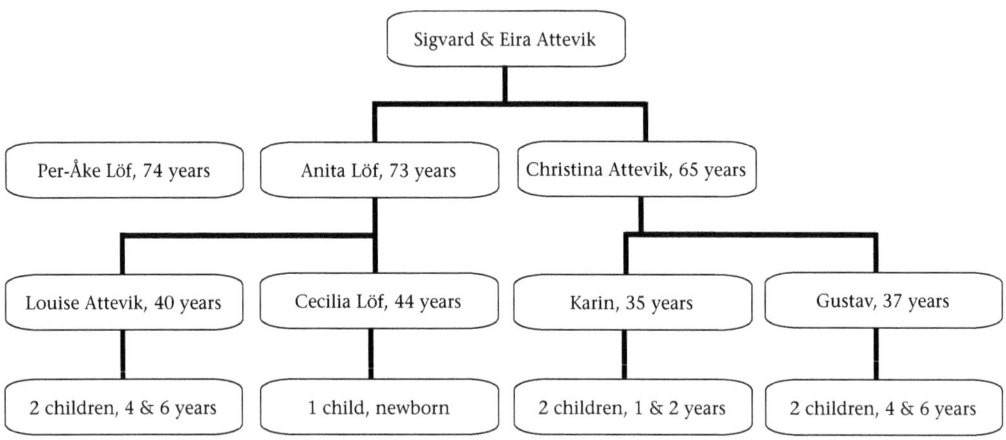

Figure 17.1 The Atteviks family chart

The Succession Processes

The company has been through two succession transitions. The first one was in the late 1960s, and the second one started about 15 years ago and is still ongoing. These transitions both held the succession of leadership and of ownership as two separate but related processes. Below, the two-fold character of successions will be described.

THE SUCCESSION OF LEADERSHIP

In 2003, Per-Åke's oldest daughter, Cecilia, took over the CEO position, after having worked together with her father for a few years. Similar to Louise, Cecilia has a solid education and previous work experience in the motor vehicle industry, in Sweden and abroad. She describes how she hit the "glass ceiling," and to move on in her career she entered the family business. A couple of years after Cecilia became the CEO, the company risked losing a key manager for one of its divisions. In order to retain this person in the firm, Cecilia stepped down from the CEO position and offered it to this division manager, who accepted and stayed with the firm. Later, due to personal reasons, Cecilia wanted to stop working and asked her sister to join Atteviks as the family representative. Their cousins were not asked because they were younger and had not been involved in the business.

> *When she asked me if I could do this I said yes. I think it's interesting, I think it's fun and I think it's important. We have very good managers today in the business but there are rapid changes in the industry. It's important to have a family representative in the business so that we keep updated for the big strategic decisions.*
>
> *(Louise Attevik, third generation)*

Louise had strong support from her sister and father when she entered the firm. When her father had entered the firm, he brought in external competencies and the board became an important arena for company development and ownership discussions. However, Per-Åke soon realized that he and his father-in-law had very different leadership styles. The founder, Sigvard, was the entrepreneur involved in everything that was going on, while Per-Åke was the organizer and engineer, building the company structure over the years. Still, Per-Åke was allowed to work in his own way and to make his own mistakes. When handing over to his daughters, he reasoned in the same way. Louise's mother, Anita, had been a role model by having her own career both as an employee, and running her own business breeding cattle and being active in the local society in addition to being a mother. Anita expects the daughters to take over the firm, but at the same time, she does not believe that they are ready for this.

> *My mother can't understand why you would like to do something else. And it's not like she said "Great that you're moving into the family business" but more like "you probably won't make this on your own, you need help" and it's not because she wants to be mean but simply that she has that attitude.*
>
> *(Louise Attevik, third generation)*

Even though Per-Åke has supported his daughters, they came to a total disagreement on a decision concerning a building in one of the subsidiaries. Since they could not agree, Per-Åke stepped aside and let his daughters do it their way.

> *The reason he left was because he presented us with an ultimatum at a board meeting, "Either we do it my way or I will leave the company" and the rest of the family could not accept it so he left. He is very proud of his girls and he often tells us that he thinks we perform well and take care of this business but he can't manage that we chose to do things in our own way.*
>
> *(Louise Attevik, third generation)*

Today Per-Åke is not involved in the business at all. Sometimes his daughters ask him for advice but mostly he is the grandfather of their children. The succession of leadership is done, even though the daughters are not fully convinced that they will be the ones running the business.

THE SUCCESSION OF OWNERSHIP

The first transition of ownership took place when the founder died and his daughters inherited the firm according to his will. In the current ongoing succession of ownership, the children in the third generation own shares in the business and have been active board members since they started working for the company around 20 years ago. Their mothers still have the majority of votes. So even if Louise is the practicing owner in the daily life of the management group, her mother and aunt still represent the ownership power. The question of ownership is delicate within the family as it provides an opportunity to stay connected to the business. Restructuring board work is a sensitive topic:

> *The question of who will be a board member is a hot potato at the moment. Everybody wants to stay. We have talked about a family council but that doesn't work for us, we never manage to get together. In the third generation we all have small children at the moment and we work a lot and live in different places.*
>
> *(Louise Attevik, third generation)*

The family has tried to add a family council but it never worked out as planned. To have external board members in the group is described as a way to keep a good climate for discussion.

> *Sometimes I feel that as owners, we listen more to external board members than to each other. In the third generation we feel that this is something that we need to work with. I think this is common in a family business since you start out early and in the beginning you sit in and listen to learn. But when are you supposed to start acting? No one tells you when you are ready. I'm actually turning 40 this year, and Karl-Johan Persson was 35 years when he took over a large listed company (H&M). I'm old enough but you will never be grown up in your parents' eyes.*
>
> *(Louise Attevik, third generation)*

One part of the family dimension is how people identify with the firm. Anita has always enjoyed being known as a representative for the family business. Compared to Anita, Louise has always tried to keep a low profile, never using her last name if possible. However, the family values are based on not getting things for free; people should get an education and work hard. The girls have never received a car of their own from the firm. The down-to-earth approach is very much in line with the Swedish mentality that is often expressed by referring to "Jantelagen," the Swedish name for the tall poppy syndrome, a norm guiding social interaction in groups. This ideal that is especially pronounced in small towns and rural areas, is about being hard working and honest. Everybody should be on an equal level and not stand out in the crowd.

The Cultural Dimensions and their Role in Father–Daughter Succession

ASPECTS GENERALLY RELATED TO SUCCESSION

In the succession of leadership, the transfer is described as being managed quite easily. The founder hired his son-in-law and left him to work in his own way, even though the two gentlemen had very different managerial styles. This acceptance was passed on in the next succession: when Cecilia and Louise came to a major disagreement with their father, he stepped aside and let his daughters run the business in the way they preferred. The fact that both daughters were highly educated and had extensive experience in similar industries probably made the decision easier to make. The parent–child relationship was strong enough to separate between a professional and a private level, where he is still a grandfather taking care of his grandchildren. Before leaving the firm, father and daughter worked together for a few years but apart from this practical transfer of knowledge, there were little formal succession activities.

The divisions of ownership and leadership are crucial in order to understand the process of succession. It seems as if ownership has a stronger link to identity issues. Thus, it might be harder to separate from the ownership role. This could have practical as well as psychological explanations. On a practical level, ownership may be a way to guarantee that you will have access to capital when you have retired from the business. On a psychological level, ownership can be linked to the identity of individuals and thus, handing over ownership becomes a question of losing an established identity and needing to build a new one (Melin, 2007).

ASPECTS SPECIFICALLY RELATED TO DAUGHTER SUCCESSION

There has been a shift in how to regard women in business over time. The women in the second generation were not considered as possible business leaders, neither by their father, nor by themselves. For the daughters in the third generation, a career is natural and they have education and previous work experience that has proven quite useful when working in the car dealership. One could have alternative theories that if they had a brother, the daughters would not have been considered as successors on the managerial level. However, they have a male cousin who is not considered suitable for a management position based on his lack of education and work experience. There has been no rivalry between people in the third generation, rather a slight resistance toward being the one taking over.

For Cecilia, eldest sister of the third generation, the family firm provided new opportunities when she hit the glass ceiling in her career. The family agrees that the industry is quite male-dominated but, within the family, being a woman has never been considered a hindrance. When the father had employees with a hostile attitude toward women, his experience was that usually these persons had other attitude problems as well, and thus, they were not good for the firm. Considering a possible work–life conflict, this is something that concerns both women and men in Sweden today.

The outsider position that women still have might provide room for alternative actions not available for males, who are living within the same entrepreneurial and social norms. Cecilia made a spectacular move as a CEO when she decided to step down from that position in order to provide a career opportunity for one of the firm's division managers. To keep this key person within the business she resigned and offered her position to the valuable manager who stayed with them as the CEO.

Research has shown that structural hindrances might explain why daughters do not take over the family firm to the same extent that sons do. The separation between leadership and ownership made in this text suggests that, in the current Swedish situation, women might be considered as business persons while women as main owners are still encountering structural hindrance. Could this be an explanation to why the mothers in the second generation are so reluctant to hand over the shares to the next generation? There are of course no simple answers, but this could be one component to understand resistance in succession when daughters are taking over the firm.

Discussion and Conclusions

Previous literature shows that while women have practical support for participating in business life in the Swedish context, there are still structural hindrances for taking over ownership of the family firm. Based on this case, we suggest that the main learning outcome for both researchers and practitioners would be to recognize the two dimensions of succession. The case presented illustrates succession as a two-fold process within one firm: the transfer of ownership and of leadership in the family firm.

We end with a few lessons learned and some suggestions for future studies. The differences between generations in the case study represents changes in the Swedish society. In the 1960s, women were usually not considered as possible business leaders, while their daughters were encouraged to work in the firm. The changes over past generations are essential for understanding future successions. Another learning from the leadership succession is that the first succession set a norm for how to act in succession; the father referred back to that when he took over from his father-in-law as a model for a pliable succession process. To compare alternative succession models is a promising venue for future research. Furthermore, we argue that it can be fruitful to recognize that a society that, on surface, complies with the ideals of gender equality, such as the Swedish society, still might harbor traditional gender structures that influence activities. Finally, we propose that ownership would imply a stronger connection to identity than leadership and believe the study of what ownership and leadership separately mean in terms of identity construction in family firms would be an important extension of this research.

References

Ahl, H. 2002a. *The Making of the Female Entrepreneur. A Discourse Analysis of Research Texts on Women´s Entrepreneurship*. Jönköping: Jönköping International Business School.

Ahl, H. 2002b. The Construction of the Female Entrepreneur as the Other, in *Casting the Other. The Production and Maintenance of Inequalities in Work Organizations*, edited by B. Czarniawska-Joerges and H. Höpfl. London and New York: Routledge.

Czarniawska-Joerges, B. 1993. Swedish Management. Modern Project, Postmodern Implementation. *International Studies of Management & Organization*, 23(1), 13–27.

Holmberg, I. and Åkerblom, S. 2006. Modelling Leadership—Implicit Leadership Theories in Sweden. *Scandinavian Journal of Management*, 22, 307–329.

Holmquist, C. and Sundin, E. 2002. Kvinnors Företagande—Siffror och Synliggörande in *Företagerskan. Om Kvinnor och Entreprenörskap*, edited by C. Holmquist and E. Sundin. Stockholm: SNS Förlag.

Holmquist, C. and Sundin, E. 2006. Women as Entrepreneurs in Sweden: Conclusions from a Survey in *Women and Entrepreneurship*, edited by C.G. Brush, N.M. Carter, E.J. Gatewood, P.G. Greene and M.M. Hart. Northampton: Contemporary Classics. Edward Elgar.

Holmquist, C. and Wennberg, K. 2010. *Många Miljarder Blir Det … Fakta och Nyckeltal om Kvinnors Företag. Info 0124*. Stockholm: Tillväxtverket.

Javefors Grauers, E. 2002. Från Mjölkaffär till ICA-butik? in *Företagerskan—Om Kvinnor och Entreprenörskap*, edited by C. Holmquist and E. Sundin. Stockholm: SNS Förlag.

Javefors Grauers, E. 2004. Kvinnors Företagande, en Avspegling av Samhället In *Kvinnor som Företagare i Gnosjö pch Jönköping*, edited by C. Holmquist and E. Sundin. Stockholm: SNS Förlag. R 2004:3. NUTEK, Stockholm.

Jönsson, S. 1995. *Goda Utsikter. Svenskt Management i Perspektiv*. Stockholm: Nerenius & Santérus Förlag.

Kantola, J. 2008. 'Why Do All the Women Disappear?' Gendering Processes in a Political Science Department. *Gender, Work and Organization*, 15(2), 202–225.

Melin, L. (Ed.) 2007. *Sensibility and Affection in Succession of Ownership: Guidance on Transition of Ownership and Leadership, in SMEs*. Stockholm: NUTEK (in Swedish).

Melin, L. 2008. Ägarskiften Genom arv Eller Köp—en Möjlighet för Kvinnor in *Sesam* öppna *Dig! Forskarperspektiv på Kvinnors Företagande*, edited by P. Larsson, U. Göransson and M. Lagerholm. Stockholm: Vinnova.

Melin, L., Bjuggren, P-O., Ericsson, A., Hall, A., Haag, A. and Nordqvist, M. 2004. *Ägarskiften och Ledarskiften i Företag. En Fördjupad Analys*. Stockholm: NUTEK.

Mulholland, K. 1996. Gender and Property Relations within Entrepreneurial Wealthy Families. *Gender, Work and Organization*, 3(2), 78–102.

Pettersson, K. 2002. *Företagande Män och Osynliggjorda Kvinnor. Diskursen om Gnosjö ur ett Kvinnoperspektiv*. Dissertation, Kulturgeografiska institutionen, Uppsala Universitet, Uppsala.

Sundin, E. and Tillmar, M. 2008. Organisational Entrepreneurs in the Public Sectors—Social Capital and Gender in *Women and Entrepreneurship and Social Capital. A Dialogue and Construction*, edited by I. Aaltio, P. Kyrö and E. Sundin. Copenhagen: Copenhagen Business School Press.

CHAPTER **18**

Switzerland: Encouraging Success: A Father–Daughter Succession Story in a Swiss Family Firm

CLAUDIA BINZ, SIMONE SCHWEIKERT AND
JENS O. MEISSNER

Introduction

Family businesses are often referred to as the backbone of Swiss economy: almost 90 percent of all companies in Switzerland—of which 98 percent are small and medium-size entreprises (SMEs)—are considered family firms (Frey et al., 2004). The fact that these family-owned businesses account for roughly 60 percent of the Swiss gross domestic product (GDP) (Fueglistaller and Zellweger, 2007) and employ two-thirds of the workforce demonstrates their contribution to a stable, growing economy (KOF, 2002).

Family firms are strongly influenced by the inextricable connection between family and business system (Zahra and Sharma, 2004). This reciprocal relationship expresses itself, for example, in the case of generational transition—the family business succession. There are few other topics in family business research (FBR) that, due to their practical relevance, receive close to as much attention as succession issues (Debicki et al., 2009; Bird et al., 2002; Gibb et al., 1998). A recent study implies that within the next five years, 77,000 (26 percent) family firms in Switzerland will be facing generational transition (CS and CFB-HSG, 2009). Despite the growing number of well-educated, highly qualified women in Switzerland, in the case of family business succession, only a small minority of these family firms are passed on to daughters. The case of father–daughter succession in family businesses has been largely neglected not only in practice, but also in literature (Dumas, 1989).

The objective of this chapter is to shed light on how socio-cultural parameters shape both the societal and familial role of women in Switzerland, and to analyze the potential impact of these parameters on the process of father–daughter succession in a Swiss family business.

Literature Review

The first part of the literature review aims to frame the relevant research within FBR and to provide a definition of the *family firm*. The second part focuses on the main dimensions of Swiss culture and their potential impact on the father–daughter succession process.

Although awareness for the research field has been growing among academics and practitioners in the past decade (Zahra and Sharma, 2004), FBR has been largely excluded from academic research (Litz, 1997) it can therefore be considered an emerging field of study (Bird et al., 2002). Even though family business succession has been the dominant topic in FBR for years, some aspects, such as the role of women in the succession process, have been largely neglected (Dumas, 1989). Considering the increasing economic importance of women, changing family structures and altering work models, this topic needs to be addressed urgently by FBR.

While definitions for family firms abound in the literature, "there is no widely accepted definition of a family business" (Littunen and Hyrsky, 2000:41). These definitional ambiguities hinder the advancement of the field (Chua et al., 1999) because they complicate comparisons across studies and hinder the integration into a common body of theory (Zahra and Sharma, 2004). For this case study we are using the definition of Chua et al. (1999), who propose that a family firm is characterized by "the intentions and vision of a dominant family coalition and the potential trans-generational sustainability of that vision" (Chua et al., 1999:25).

SOCIETAL CULTURE AND WOMEN IN SWITZERLAND

The consensus that societal culture influences entrepreneurial behavior (Chrisman et al., 2002) and activity (Shane, 1992) is highly relevant for this chapter. Theory suggests that societal culture potentially plays an important role in shaping people's perceptions and interpretations of reality. We therefore assume that cultural dimensions in Switzerland have an impact on father–daughter succession processes in family businesses by influencing the actors involved.

Building on Hofstede's five dimensions of culture, House et al. (2002) defined and analyzed nine cultural dimensions in the context of the GLOBE (Global Leadership and Organizational Effectiveness) project in 1993. The study researched the interrelationships between societal culture, organizational culture, and organizational leadership, distinguishing between *As Is* and *To Be* scores: *As Is* scores correspond with the current practice; *To Be* scores reflect the respondent's value orientation (Staeheli, 2003). Figure 18.1 displays the values for the German-speaking part of Switzerland. Implications for the case study are drawn below.

FATHER–DAUGHTER SUCCESSION: IMPLICATIONS FOR THE CASE STUDY

Today, 53 percent of the family firms in Switzerland remain in the family after a generational transfer (ZKB, 2005). Although only 4 percent thereof are currently passed on to daughters (Ibid.), the father–daughter succession topic is becoming increasingly significant. In 2008, the number of female students at Swiss Universities exceeded the number of men for the first time in history. Despite this promising trend the number of women in business is still very low (BFS, 2008).

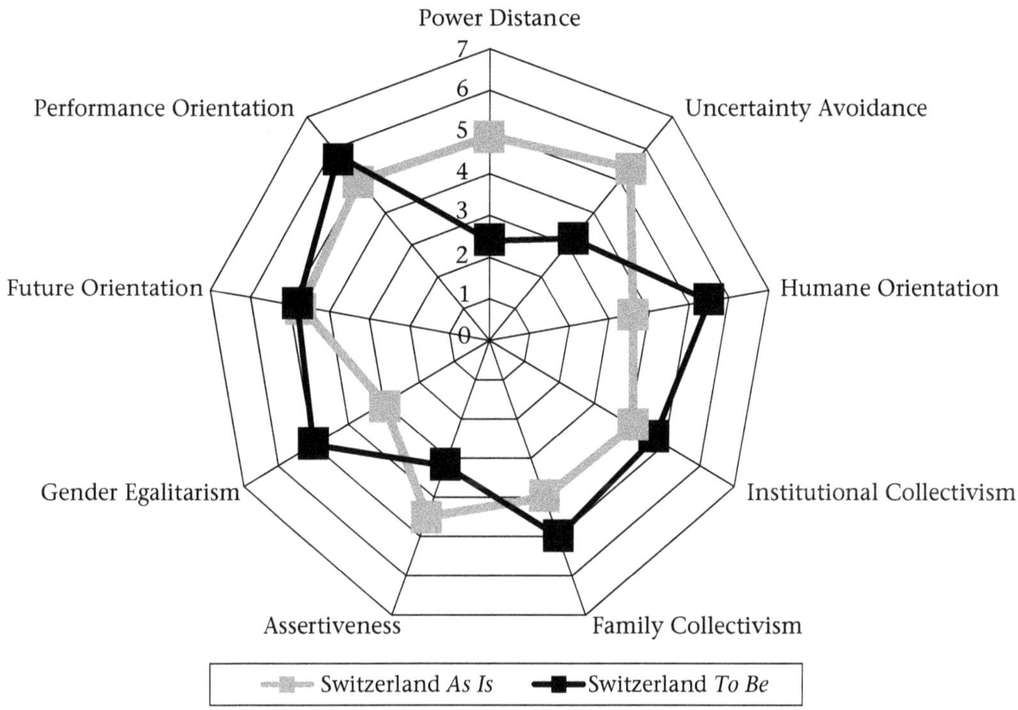

Figure 18.1 Comparison of GLOBE German-speaking Switzerland *As Is* and *To Be* scores

Source: Szabo, Brodbeck, Den Hartog, Reber, Weibler and Wunderer, 2002

Women have typically played an informal role in family businesses (Dumas, 1992)—this is no different in Switzerland. Recent changes in society and family structures, in the educational landscape and the business environment call for an increasing involvement of female successors in Swiss family businesses. Drawing from House et al.'s (2002) GLOBE model and the cultural dimensions defined therein, we conclude as follows with regards to the relevance of socio-cultural parameters for our case study:

- *Swiss society seen as traditionally hierarchical and patriarchal:* Divergent *As Is* and *To Be* scores with regards to *Power Distance* indicate that Swiss society is traditionally hierarchical and patriarchal, but that the Swiss aim to be more egalitarian (which corresponds with the high *Gender Egalitarism To Be* scores) (see also Endrissat et al., 2005).
- *Swiss women seen as traditionally subordinate:* The divergent *As Is* and *To Be* scores with regards to *Gender Egalitarism* also indicates that the perception of women in Switzerland is changing from traditionally subordinate, accepting, and caretaking (rural, collective society) to increasingly emancipated, educated, demanding as well as emotionally and financially independent (urban, individualized society). The traditional image is slowly changing and adapting to the new reality.
- *Family seen at the center:* The high *As Is* and *To Be* scores with regards to *Family Collectivism* indicate that the immediate, or core, family is very important in

> Switzerland. The strong peasant tradition, where the offspring was responsible for their elders' well-being, explains the strong commitment within Swiss families and the still prevailing role of the eldest son, who traditionally became the new patriarch after the father's demise.

After providing this theoretical frame, we now take a look at practice.

Case Study

In 1954, Theo Breisacher emigrated from southern Germany to Switzerland with a mere 100 marks in his pocket and the goal of becoming a successful businessman. In 1966, he bought a decommissioned flooring factory in the picturesque city of Alpnach, in Central Switzerland, and founded the sole-proprietorship called "Alpnach Norm." Today, the company has the reputation of being one of Switzerland's leading producers of high quality, custom-built, innovative cabinet systems. In over 40 years, this simple carpenter's workshop with six workers has developed into a successful group of companies with approximately 160 workers, an annual turnover of 42 million Swiss francs in 2008—and a female owner and manager.

Starting in 1996, at the time of the company's 30th anniversary, Theo's second youngest daughter, Brigitte Breisacher, joined the board of directors of the Alpnach Norm group. Step by step, she took over operations of the company from her then 62-year-old father. In 1999, she expanded Alpnach Norm by opening the kitchen manufactory Alpnach Kitchen Ltd—this venture is what she calls "her biggest success so far." In the same year, at the age of 31, Brigitte Breisacher officially took over the company.

Taking into consideration the rather large Breisacher family—Brigitte Breisacher was the sixth of seven children—it is surprising to hear Brigitte Breisacher say that, "There were never any disagreements about who would eventually take over the company." Today she is the only one in the second generation of the Breisacher family to be working at the company. Brigitte Breisacher knew all along that she wanted to work at her father's company. As a three-year-old, she accompanied her father to his office on Saturdays where she happily arranged paper clips. At 19, she started off as an accountant in the company, and a short time thereafter took over the divisions of marketing and HR. In 2008, Brigitte Breisacher became the sole owner of the family company. She established a holding structure for the Alpnach Norm group, and she bought out her siblings.

This is the story not only of a woman who, with self-confidence, hard work, and a down-to-earth attitude, worked her way up to the top of a traditional family business in rural Switzerland. The case also illustrates the importance of family, and family culture, for the development of potential successors.

ALPNACH NORM, THAT'S ME!

If one were to ask Brigitte Breisacher today, at which point in her life she knew that she would be working in her father's company she would say that for her, there were no other options: "For me, there was only Alpnach Norm, and I always wanted to be my father's secretary." Her strong identification with the company was already noticeable in her early years. She explains that in school she would draw the company's logo on every single drawing she did in her art class. "As a little kid, I identified myself 100 percent with the company"—and this is no different today.

FROM DAUGHTER, TO EMPLOYEE, TO CEO

After her formal scholarly education, Brigitte Breisacher started an apprenticeship at a manufacturer of automatic doors and gates. After a short while, the business was sold to a Swedish conglomerate, and the former owners left the company before the new owners came to take possession of it. Brigitte Breisacher, still an apprentice, was suddenly on her own. She hired new workers, did the accounting, and corresponded with the new owners—at the age of 18. After finishing her apprenticeship, she joined her father's company as an accountant in 1987. Even here, she was not granted any sort of grace period as the hitherto existing accountant surprisingly left the firm just when she joined it. After a brief adjustment period, Brigitte Breisacher took over all responsibility for the accounting at Alpnach Norm. In hindsight, she says, "I was overwhelmed, my father simply threw me into the deep end of the pool, so it was either learn to swim, or drown."

The young woman had to prove her worth from the beginning—not as a daughter, but as an employee: "My father never treated me like a daughter, but instead as an employee—perhaps he was even a bit harsher with me." Today, Brigitte Breisacher feels that this was exactly the right strategy to use in order to gain the respect of the other employees.

From accounting, she moved to sales where she was responsible for the marketing and HR department. When, in 1999, one of the biggest kitchen manufacturers in Switzerland went bankrupt, Brigitte Breisacher and her father decided to buy the assets and built up Alpnach Kitchen Ltd. In addition to her normal duties at Alpnach Norm, Brigitte Breisacher took over several functions at the new firm. Even today, she still leads the sales of the tremendously successful kitchen manufacturer.

THE SUCCESSION PROCESS

Her achievements convinced her father: in 1996, Brigitte Breisacher took over operations of Alpnach Norm. In hindsight, she says, "I came to the point where I had the opportunity to really show what I could do ... I wanted to prove myself by delivering results." She values that true success can only be achieved through an honest effort.

From the time she became president of the board of directors, to the time she took over the entire company, some time passed. In 2007, during the family's yearly ski trip, the father surprisingly announced that the family inheritance would be detailed, and at the same time, the succession of Alpnach Norm would be signed and sealed. Nevertheless, it took another two years for Brigitte Breisacher to take control of the firm.

In May 2009, Brigitte Breisacher established Alpnach Holding Ltd, thereby merging Alpnach Norm Ltd and Alpnach Kitchen Ltd. She took out some credit from her father, and thereby dispensed herself from any obligations she would have to her siblings. Due to a sensational business year in 2009, Brigitte Breisacher was able to repay a large part of her debt to her father in a very short amount of time. On this occasion, the family decided on all modalities with regards to the inheritance: "My father had built up a proper empire—the company, the houses, the business real estate—and therefore, it was really important for him, that everything be handled properly."

When all documents were signed and the handing over of the business was cemented, her siblings reassured her of how proud they were of her. "For my siblings it was always clear—I am Alpnach Norm, and eventually I would take over the company and lead it." Brigitte Breisacher emphasizes that there were "never any internal battles, rivalries, jealousies, or mistrust." She says that her siblings were convinced that she was the only one of them that was fit to do the job, that she was the only one who had the "courage to take over the responsibility, has the demeanor, the knowledge, and the ability to be successful."

When asked about the actual chain of events that led to her being selected as the successor, she states that, "We actually never talked about it." Although Theo Breisacher still keeps his old office at Alpnach Norm, he doesn't really mix himself up in the firm's daily operations anymore.

> *We actually discuss relatively little about what's going on in the company ... on May 23, he said, look this is your company now, I'll stay out of it ... I would never have expected him to be so consistent and actually stay out of it—but to this day, he has kept his word.*

THE BREISACHER FAMILY

The Breisacher siblings grow up in a very traditional family. The mother was always at home for her kids, "She would always keep our father grounded." The parents instilled values like humility, decency, and respect, in their children. They raised them to be open, honest, and transparent; the children were often admonished to never make promises they could not keep. To this day, Brigitte Breisacher holds herself to these values.

According to Brigitte Breisacher, it was really important to her father that his children be allowed to choose their own paths in life. He wanted none of them to feel obliged to work in the family business, if they did not choose to do so by themselves. Both parents never exerted any pressure on their children, not even their only son, who may have traditionally been expected to work in the family's firm. In essence, every one of the children was allowed to pursue their "own individual dreams, wishes, and desires." The Breisachers treated all their children equal.

Brigitte Breisacher is convinced that it was less the social and cultural values that influenced her development, and more the Breisacher family culture. What she considers very significant for her personal development was the encouragement of her parents for all siblings to pursue their own goals. She adds that the Breisacher family solidarity is very strong. "I have a very close relationship with my parents and also with all my siblings." Brigitte Breisacher repeatedly highlights the harmonic family atmosphere, and emphasizes that, "With us, peace in the family is written in capitals, and not only the peace in our family, but also, automatically, our peace at work."

BEING A FEMALE CEO

According to Brigitte Breisacher, it takes quite a lot to be able to operate in such a male-dominated area; she deals with carpenters, architects, and builders. However, she sees no disadvantages, but rather a lot of advantages to her being a woman:

Of course, I am operating in a men's world. But for me, this is actually quite comfortable: I get appointments a lot quicker than most people, and it is also easier for me as a woman to get access to certain circles or to certain people. For me, I can only say that this is very positive.

Nevertheless, she emphasizes the importance of a respectable, business-like appearance for female entrepreneurs: "Obviously it's not enough to just be blond ... you have to know what you are talking about, and you have to be able to deliver on your promises. As a woman, you are often scrutinized more than a man would be."

However, today, Brigitte Breisacher is accepted and respected not only by her suppliers and customers but also by her staff members. She attributes her success partially to her well-founded practical knowledge which she gained through 23 years of combined work with her father. "On the one hand, my father was my greatest role model, and on the other hand my best teacher." Furthermore, she sees her ability to deal with new, unpredictable situations and to fight to achieve her goals as her own personal success factors; these qualities she has had to prove in all her jobs.

LEARNING ON THE JOB

Sometimes, Brigitte Breisacher wrangles with the thought of whether it would have been better for her to have chosen a different educational path in life; that is, to have gone to university instead of doing an apprenticeship. Back then, she says, that wasn't even a question: "I didn't want to study, I wanted to work." To this day, she still stands by her decision; however, over the years, she has continued to educate herself. Since she started working at Alpnach Norm, she has completed various further education and management courses in, for instance, the areas of marketing and corporate governance. This is how she specifically acquires new knowledge, which she needs in order to improve her work. She chooses a targeted number of seminars and workshops to attend. The topics really have to interest her, and she also has to be convinced that the course has a practical application: "I have no university education ... I've acquired all my knowledge through my work experience. I've had to learn to assert myself, in general, throughout my whole life."

Discussion and Conclusions

Taking into consideration the cultural dimensions House et al. (2002) had defined in the context of the GLOBE project, like the authors, one might be surprised by the case study presented. Subsequently, several interesting findings were deduced from the case study, and with regard to the developmental path for a female successor are presented below:

- *Identification:* From an early age Brigitte Breisacher's identification with and commitment to Alpnach Norm was tremendous—and had grown naturally. Her father encouraged her to come along to the office, but never forced or talked her into joining the firm.
- *Development*: By means of working her way up through different hierarchical levels Brigitte Breisacher gained her employees' trust and respect. At a very young age she took on a considerable amount of responsibility, and grew with the challenge.

- *Succession*: The succession process was initiated and carried through by Theo Breisacher; this corresponds with the picture of the *family patriarch* taking decisions. Brigitte and her father actually never talked about the point in time when she would take over the firm. Theo Breisacher felt confident to hand over the firm to his daughter, because the results of her work—over all the years they worked together—had convinced him.
- *Family*: The Breisacher case indicates that an egalitarian, encouraging, and loving family culture potentially supports a smooth succession process in family firms. However, Theo Breisacher had to take into consideration that his approach to encourage his children to pursue their "individual dreams and desires" could lead to the situation that none of his children had decided to take over the family business. The Breisacher case undermines the high scores House et al. (2002) identified for *family collectivism*: the strong solidarity among the siblings as well as the supportive relationship between parents and children impressively demonstrate a family culture of support, love, and encouragement.
- *Female CEO*: While there are some cues that Theo Breisacher ruled both his company and family in a rather *patriarchal* manner, he nevertheless supported his second youngest daughter from the very start and raised and trained her to be his successor. This might explain why Brigitte Breisacher today feels so comfortable in her role as a female entrepreneur—she benefits from certain advantages she enjoys as a woman. However, at the same time, she is highly aware of the potential pitfalls she could encounter because of her being a woman.
- *Education*: Although Brigitte Breisacher knew early on she wanted to take over the firm, she chose not to follow the typical educational path for managers—she learned on the job, but constantly and very specifically continued to educate herself over the years.

Brigitte Breisacher's story does not reflect the assumptions one could derive from studying the existing literature on both father–daughter succession and the perception of the woman in Switzerland. Her story is somewhat of a "best practice example" for both business owners and potential successors.

The case highlights the enormous relevance of the family culture for the succession process. The Breisacher succession was successful because there was a benevolent business owner who was willing to let go once a viable successor had been found; a family culture encouraging personal development of and solidarity among all family members; and lastly because the successor was willing to undertaking continuous and laborious efforts to reach her goals.

Limitations and Future Research Directions

This chapter highlighted the increasing importance of female succession for FBR, and demonstrated, by means of a single case study, a "best practice" father–daughter succession process in a Swiss family firm.

As traditional gender roles are becoming blurred and the number of educated and ambitious women is increasing, the need for further investigation on the specific challenges and opportunities of female succession in family businesses becomes apparent. Interesting questions for further research include characteristics of the family culture and their implications for the succession process, or the educational and professional path of female successors.

However, it must be taken into consideration that "family businesses are not a homogeneous group. What works for one family in a specific situation will not necessarily work for another family in a different situation" (Sharma et al., 1997:17). So while socio-cultural dimensions or family culture might explain certain characteristics of the father–daughter succession process in family businesses, one should be careful assuming that the results are in any way applied to other family firms, and always take into consideration the specific conditions of the family firm studied.

References

Bundesamt fur Statistik (BFS). 2008. *Auf dem Weg zur Gleichstellung von Frau und Mann—Stand und Entwicklung*. Neuenburg: BFS

Bird, B., Welsch, H., Astrachan, J.H. and Pistrui, D. 2002. Family Business Research: The Evolution of an Academic Field. *Family Business Review*, 15(4), 337–350.

Chrisman, J.J., Chua, J.H. and Steier, L.P. 2002. The Influence of National Culture and Family Involvement on Entrepreneurial. *Entrepreneurship Theory & Practice*, 26(4), 113–130.

Chua, J.H., Chrisman, J.J. and Sharma, P. 1999. Defining the Family Business by Behavior. *Entrepreneurship Theory and Practice*, 23(4), 19–39.

Credit Suisse and Center for Family Business University St. Gallen (CS and CFB-HSG). (2009). *Erfolgreiche Unternehmensnachfolge*. Available at: http://www.credit-suisse.com/nachfolge [accessed: 29 June 2010].

Debicki, B.J., Matherne, C.F., Kellermanns, F.W. and Chrisman, J.J. 2009. Family Business Research in the New Millennium: An Overview of the Who, the Where, the What, and the Why. *Family Business Review*, 22(2), 151–166.

Dumas, C. 1989. Understanding of Father–Daughter and Father–Son Dyads in Family-Owned Businesses. *Family Business Review*, 2(1), 31–46.

Endrissat, N., Mueller, W.R. and Meissner, J.O. 2005. What is The Meaning of Leadership? A Guided Tour Through a Swiss-German Leadership Landscape, in *Proceedings of the Sixty-fifth Annual Meeting of the Academy of Management (CD)*, edited by K.M. Weaver.

Frey, U., Halter, F., Zellweger, T. and Klein, S. 2004. *Family Business in Switzerland: Significance and Structure*. 15th F.B.N. World Conference, Copenhagen.

Fueglistaller, U. and Zellweger, T. 2007. Die Volkswirtschaftliche Bedeutung der Familienunternehmen in der Schweiz. *Schweizer Arbeitgeber*, 15(9), 30–33.

Gibb Dyer, W. and Sanchez, M. 1998. Current State of Family Business Theory and Practice as Reflected in Family Business Review 1988–1997. *Family Business Review*, 11(4), 287–295.

Hofstede, G.H. 2001. *Culture's consequences* (2nd Edition). Thousand Oaks: Sage.

House, R.J., Javidan, M., Hanges, P. and Dorfman, P. 2002. Understanding Cultures and Implicit Leadership Theories Across the Globe: An Introduction to Project GLOBE. *Journal of World Business*, 37(1), 3–10.

Konjunkturforschungsstelle der ETH Zuerich (KOF). 2002. *Innovationsumfrage 2008*. Available at: http://www.kof.ethz.ch/surveys/structural/panel/inno_2008 [accessed: 22 March 2010].

Littunen, H. and Hyrsky, K. 2000. The Early Entrepreneurial Stage in Finnish Family and Non-Family Firms. *Family Business Review*, 13(1), 41–54.

Litz, R.A. 1997. The Family Firm's Exclusion From Business School Research: Explaining the Void. *Entrepreneurship Theory & Practice*, 21(3), 55–71.

Shane, S.A. 1992. Why do Some Societies Invent More Than Others? *Journal of Business Venturing*, 7(1), 29–46.

Sharma, P., Chrisman, J.J. and Chua, J.H. 1997. Strategic Management of the Family Business: Past Research and Future Challenges. *Family Business Review*, 10(1), 1–35.

Staeheli, L.A. 2003. Cities and Citizenship. *Urban Geography*, 24(2), 97–102.

Szabo, E., Brodbeck, F.C., Den Hartog, D.N., Reber, G., Weibler, J. and Wunderer, R. 2002. The Germanic Europe Cluster: Where Employees Have a Voice. *Journal of World Business*, 37(1), 55–68.

Zahra, S.A. and Sharma, P. 2004. Family Business Research: A Strategic Reflection. *Family Business Review*, 17(4), 331–346.

Zurcher Kantonalbank (ZKB). 2005. *Unternehmen Zukunft: Generationenwechsel bei KMU in der Schweiz*. Zurichsee Druckereien AG, Zurich. Available at: https://www.zkb.ch/etc/ml/repository/prospekte_und_broschueren/vorsorge/211273_unternehmen.File.pdf [accessed 15 August 2011].

PART V North America

CHAPTER 19

Canada: Gender and Culture in Father–Daughter Succession in the Family Business: A Canadian Case Study

LUCIE BÉGIN, CHRISTINA CONSTANTINIDIS,
DAPHNE HALKIAS AND D.-CLAUDE LAROCHE

Introduction: Values Guiding French-Canadian Quebec Culture

From its foundation, immigration has played a key role in shaping the character of Canadian society. Canadians are not of any one country, race, or heritage. The nation is rooted in multiculturalism which means that immigrants are invited to integrate by bringing in the richness of their own cultural background. Despite their pluralism and maybe because of it, Canadians share some common values such as tolerance and egalitarism, which find their true expression in the Canadian Charter of Rights and Freedoms.

Even if they share Anglo-Saxon roots and a similar lifestyle, Canadians and Americans differ in their values: Canadians tend to be less traditional, more tolerant, less patriarchal in their work and family structures and more orientated toward autonomy and equality. This difference is illustrated, for instance, by the fact that 49 percent of Americans believe "a father must be master of the house" while less than 20 percent of the Canadians agree, and only 15 percent of the Quebecois do (Adams, 2004).

Over the past few decades, as it has been the case in most industrialized countries, values have evolved within Quebec's culture, moving from highly collectivistic and spiritual values to more materialistic and individualistic ones. Specifically, a strong belief held in Quebec is that of equality between individuals and genders.

Gender Issues in French-Canadian-Quebec Culture

Representing more than 50 percent of the overall population in 2009, women in Quebec have been increasingly evolving into a more self-dependent, educated, and dynamic group.

These trends are not coincidental. Women in many parts of the world, just as in Quebec, have been gaining lost ground in regards to their differences with men. Particularly, it has been shown that women are increasingly more educated, competitive with men, and in some cases they are surpassing them in traditional strong holds. This being said, women choose to have different career paths, for instance, a substantial percentage of them decide to follow social and human sciences fields, while men are more frequently present in the natural sciences fields (Conseil du statut de la femme, 2010).

While the civil code has been appropriately modified so as to ensure total gender equality, salary discrepancies have yet to be completely solved, even if the gap has been drastically lessened. Nevertheless, within the population, the notion of gender equality is today well implanted, at least in the recent generations, giving hope for an even more equalitarian society in the future. Therefore, women in Quebec generally function as independent individuals strongly present in the workforce. They are very prompt to work, even when divorced with children, and pride themselves in being independent in their decision making regarding both work and family life (Langlois, 1990).

Female Entrepreneurship in Canada

Women are taking on the risks and rewards of entrepreneurship in ever-increasing numbers. Over the past two decades, Canada witnessed an increase in women's entrepreneurship of over 200 percent. Since 1997, on average, women entered the small and medium-sized enterprise (SME) marketplace at twice the rate per year as men. By 2001, 47 percent of all SMEs in Canada had at least one female owner and women held majority ownership in 18 percent of them (Carrington, 2004).

Research has highlighted that women entrepreneurs in Canada are clearly not homogenous. Canadian women own businesses of all sizes, in all sectors, and in all stages of development. As illustrated, however, the profile of a typical female-owned business does contrast with the average characteristics of a male-owned firm. These differences have an effect on the financial performance of women-owned firms. Statistical profiles alone do not tell the complete picture unless one assumes that both women and men exhibit the same expectations for their business and perceive similar obstacles to reaching those goals. Research suggests this is not the case. In an examination of business owners' perceptions of success, it has been found that female entrepreneurs attribute higher value to maintaining customer and personal relationships, spiritual well-being, and work–life balance (Collerette and Aubry, 1990; Orser and Riding, 2004).

Increasingly, female entrepreneurs are considered important for economic development in Canada. Not only do they contribute to employment creation and economic growth through their increasing numbers, but they also make a contribution to the diversity of entrepreneurship in the economic process (Verheul and Thurik, 2001). Female and male entrepreneurs differ with respect to their personal and business profile: they start and run businesses in different sectors, develop different products, pursue different goals, and structure their businesses in a different fashion (Verheul et al., 2006).

There are notable differences among Canadian women entrepreneurs in terms of their motivation for starting a business, and between the motivations of women and men. For women, different motivations appear to be linked to different types of businesses and economic success (Zinger, 2007; Hughes, 2006). Research has shown that female entrepreneurs in Canada believe that gender diversity in terms of products, processes, forms of organization, and targeted markets is necessary for a selection process where customers are at liberty to choose according to their preferences and where female entrepreneurs learn about what is viable from a technological and organizational perspective. This process, in turn, has led these women to develop a higher quality of entrepreneurship (Verheul et al., 2006).

Family businesses are the backbone of the Canadian economy, generating 45 percent of the Gross Domestic Product (GDP), 50 percent of all jobs, and even 70 percent of new jobs (PriceWaterhouseCoopers Global Family Business Survey, 2007–2008). According to Cadieux et al. (2002), 33 percent of all the family businesses in Quebec are owned by women. Some have been the founders, others have succeeded their parents.

The Case Study

Following in her father, grandfather, and great-grandfather's footsteps, Carole Bellon took over Bellon Industries, the leader in made-to-measure awning and canvas products manufacturing in Quebec, in March 1995. Following her early desire to own and manage the family business, she took her position as an experienced and legitimate successor ahead of other potential candidates. She dynamically undertook all challenges. Her passion, business acuteness, and work ethic, as well as her egalitarian view of society drove her in a non-traditional, non-linear succession process, toward successful leadership and management. She now envisions the future of the family business and thinks about the next generation. At the same time, she is very active in the business community and acts as President of the Chambre de commerce de l'Est de Montréal.

THE BUSINESS, THE ENTREPRENEUR AND THE SUCCESSION PROCESS

Bellon Industries: a brief history

In 1895, Joseph K. Bellon, a Czechoslovakian immigrant, created his business in Montreal. A craftsman by trade, with experience in working with metal and canvas, he opened a roller awning workshop. He was selling awnings to small businesses to protect goods displayed on the sidewalk, along with shade structures, buggy seats, and tents, among other things. Ingenious and with a good business sense, he prospered enough to incite his children to join the family business to help him, either temporarily or on a permanent basis.

His first-born son, Georges, took over the family business in 1935 and decided to focus operations on canvas products and roller awnings. He developed a new market, manufacturing and distributing residential awnings mostly for an Anglo-Canadian clientele, richer than the French-Canadians who preferred the aluminum awnings, which were less expensive and made of a permanent structure. The visit of King George VI in Canada in 1939 was an important moment for the business, as Georges Bellon created and installed different types of banners and decorations for this event, giving the impetus to expand and diversify the business, notably in a whole range of products for camping and sport activities. In 1967, Bellon Industries manufactured most of the awnings for Expo '67, the acclaimed Montreal World Fair, another very lucrative contract. The company grew rapidly during the following years.

When Carole's father, Guy Bellon, took over the business, he decided to sell the camping and sport division for which he had no interest and to concentrate on canvas products. In 1976, the family business won the contract to manufacture most of the awnings for the Montreal Olympic Games. During the 1980s recession, the company faced difficult times, but managed to grow steadily. Soon after, Guy bought another business to complement its existing offer. Carole joined the family business in 1974, first on a part-time basis and, since 1976, full time. She started at the bottom of the ladder and learned all the different jobs in the workshop and the showroom as well as in the office (sewer, clerk, seller, representative, secretary, and so on). During the years with her father, she developed the snow shelter product line in order to keep the business manufacturing/operating during the winter season and keep resources occupied all year long (previously a seasonal type of business).

In 1995, Carole, with some business partners, bought out the family business from her father. Since then, she bought back all the shares of her partners and she is now the sole owner of the family business. "Bellon Industries" employs 75 staff members and subcontractors in Montreal and 12 in a factory in Chambly, located on the south shore of Montreal. Bellon Industries manufactures a large range of products such as residential and commercial awnings, banners, car shelters, industrial shelters, covered walkways, ramps and stairways, industrial curtains, monofilament nets for sport fields, inflatable products, waste lagoon covers, and a large array of custom-made industrial products. Bellon Industries have been growing and flourishing, through product innovation, diversification, and acquisitions. The quality of products and of the customer service has always remained a core value throughout the generations.

Profile of Carole Bellon

Carole grew up in a catholic family, raised by her mother who was at home, with her two sisters, respectively two and nine years younger. Since their early childhood, Carole and her sisters listened to stories of the family business. Each opportunity to help in the business, counting bolt stock, classifying shipping bills, or whatever job that needed to be done, was seen as a rare opportunity to see their father, who worked constantly. Carole's parents separated when she was 15 and the three daughters remained with their mother. They were taught the values of hard work, independence, and autonomy. Carole moved into her own apartment at 18, when her parents divorced.

Most of Carole's high school education was as a resident in the private Catholic school Marie-Clarac in Montreal. After being a day student for one year, she went to the comprehensive school of Anjou where she finished her high school education in 1974. She then studied at Vanier College and completed her post-secondary education at John Abott College, an English language establishment located in the West Island of Montreal. She undertook a Bachelor in Business Administration at HEC Montreal as a part-time evening student while she worked full time in the family business, six days a week. After a year and a half, she had her children and decided to stop her studies.

The succession process

Sharing her father's passion for the canvas industry, Carole joined the family business as a part-time seasonal employee at the age of 16. She began as a secretary, occupied various positions within the family firm, and climbed the ladder progressively. She brought the idea of manufacturing car shelters, to keep manufacturing operations rolling during the winter; expanding efficiencies. Her father remained focused on the awnings, the core business of the company. In 1976, they bought "Canevas Décor Camping," a firm specializing in awnings for camping, and the former owner of that business joined them to become Guy Bellon's right-hand man. Carole was at this point a full-time employee and had already been in the business for six years, but there was as yet no question of her succeeding her father. Nevertheless, she was not happy to see this man taking what she thought was her rightful place. But, rather than feeling like a victim, she decided to learn as much as she could from this man and to show to her father that she was trustworthy and capable. After a while, it appeared that this man was not working as hard as had been hoped, and that did not to sit well with Carole's father, who was very demanding and valued hard work, especially from his management team who needed to set an example. So, this man left the company and created his own business elsewhere. Carole became the general manager and her father's right-hand woman.

Soon after, the second daughter entered the family business, also starting from a secretary position. For her, it was just a job like any other and she had little interest in the business itself. Her attitude was in contrast with Carole's and this became a source of friction in the office. As general manager, Carole was very committed to the company and had embraced her father's values: hard work and high-quality service. She tried to change her sister's ways but without success. She asked her father to resolve the situation by firing her sister but he refused as she was family. Frustrated by the situation, Carole decided to leave the family business and pursue her career as an accounting manager in a large private company. Six months later, her father asked her to come back, after her sister left on her own accord. Carole accepted but under her terms and conditions: "I want the authority that comes with the responsibility; I want my place. Frankly, I want to take your place. That is what I want." From this point, the succession was clearly stated, but the steps and the timing was not determined. Progressively, her father gave her more and more responsibilities. Their relationship changed and adopted a more professional tone.

This shared direction lasted for some years to the great pleasure of both, father and daughter. In 1988, when Carole was ready to take over the business, her father felt too young and did not want to stop. She, along with her father bought "General Canvas," a firm specializing in industrial canvas products and boat tops. Shortly after, Carole decided to have children. When her son was three years old and her daughter one, her father announced that he was ready to sell the business. But the timing was not right for Carole. With her young family and her full-time job, she was not inclined to add on additional business responsibilities. "If you are not capable of waiting a few years, just go. Sell the business to someone else," she said to her father. She even suggested a potential successor to him, who entered the business in order to take it over. Carole left the family business for the second time and found a job as a general manager.

Soon after, at the request of the business's accountants, Carole reconsidered her decision to take over the family business. They told her that she should come back and take over the business in partnership with associates, that way responsibilities would be lessened. So she did. She chose as partners a businessman whose firm had been bought by Bellon Industries and who was an expert in production; a man with strong negotiation and selling experience; and her father's accountants who decided to join as associates as well. They bought her father's business in March 1995 and at the same time merged one of the associate's businesses. This move allowed the business to grow and to acquire complementary competencies. Management transfer occurred simultaneously with the transfer of property. Nevertheless, Carole's father stayed for the transition and remained even when he got sick, and up until his death in September 1997.

Analysis of the Father–Daughter Succession: Gender and Cultural Issues

REASONS FOR JOINING THE COMPANY

Carole aspired to take over the family business at a very young age. At six years old, she loved to give a hand, considering it rewarding. She entered the family firm at 16 with this intention and ambition in mind. The business was always a priority for her, along with her family. Her motivations were mainly her passion for the business and for management, as well as her desire for diversified and challenging work.

RELATIONSHIPS BETWEEN FATHER, MOTHER, AND DAUGHTER

Carole's parents had clearly defined roles. They were traditional and aligned to norms of the times. Carole's father was managing the business while Carole's mother was raising the children. This role distribution had an impact on their respective relationships. Carole believes she shares her mother's work and family values.

Carole affirmed her independence and forcefulness first toward her mother at the age of 16, when she began to work. At 18, when her parents divorced, Carole took her own apartment and ran her own life. At this point, Carole made it clear to her mother that the business and the family were two different things: "Listen, do not ask questions about the business, I will not speak about it, my job is my job, and the family is the family." It was important to draw a line. Nonetheless, her mother was happy and proud that Carole continued in the family business and was successful.

Carole knew her father mainly at work. She helped him in the business since she was a child. Later, she worked with him as an employee, and managed the business with him. Carole's father was quite authoritarian and Carole used to act as a "buffer" between him and employees. But, despite their different management styles and some tensions, they always made a good complementary team.

BEING A VISIBLE AND VIABLE SUCCESSOR

At the beginning, Carole was not considered by her father as a potential successor. Neither did she think that the business would be hers by inheritance. "You must work, you must show to your father or to your mother that you have a desire to take over the business, you must stand out and show an interest." She took action to ensure that her father did not see her as a little child anymore. She showed clearly her interest, she asked her father to take her when he was meeting customers, suppliers, or bankers, and observed and learned from him. She also arrived with new ideas, carefully planned, with strong and organized arguments. Sometimes, there were conflicts between them, as there had been between him and his father before. She always considered that was normal and learned to work in collaboration with him. "I always took my place. It was important for me."

As a woman, there were additional issues to take into account. Carole had to prove to her father that she was capable to do the job as a man, more so because they are in a male-dominated industry. Besides the theoretical and technical knowledge, daughters must prove that they can work on-the-job. "You must show to your father that you are not just the little beautiful girl, you must learn to be less beautiful ... it is like this if we want to be taken seriously." In particular, Carole was a tomboy, "There was nothing feminine in me," she explained, "and perhaps that helped my father to accept me as a successor." Besides, she was integrated in the family business, and has always been there to help, from a young age. Finally, the fact that Carole left the family business for a while may have also helped, in the sense that her father has been able to realize all that she was able to do.

FAMILY AND NON-FAMILY MEMBERS' RIVALRY

The first challenge that Carole experienced was when the former owner of "Canevas Décor Camping" entered the family business and took what she considered to be "her place." He had a lot more experience than her at that time and was bringing all his knowledge and expertise with him. That was frustrating at the highest level for Carole, who was quite young then. She thought, "Hey, I must not lose my place, so what do I have to do in order to go and get it?" She set as an objective to learn from him and to make hers his experience and expertise. She observed him working and collaborated with him. Finally, she learned a lot from this man while still having fun, as he was working differently from her father.

Carole did not experience any sibling rivalry. Her two sisters were not interested in taking over the family business. They both worked in the family firm for some years. After leaving the business, her middle sister became a professor in Quebec City. The youngest one, after working for one year in the firm, stayed home to raise her children in the Montreal area. When Carole declared her intention to take over the business, her sisters were already gone. Moreover, when Carole bought the business with her partners, the business had been evaluated by external experts and the selling price had been negotiated with her father; this prevented any family disagreement over the deal. At his death, the money that her father had gained from the sale was redistributed between his three daughters.

MULTIPLE IDENTITIES

Carole has been a daughter–successor after three generations of men at the head of the family business. She has also been a woman in a traditionally male-dominated industry as well as a French-Canadian in an English business world. She has always managed to take her place, with an egalitarian perspective on business and society.

Carole has always seen herself as an integral part of the family business. For instance, when she talks about the visit of King George VI to Canada in 1939, she identifies herself as part of the event even if she was not yet born: "We made all kinds of banners, all kinds of canvas for them. I ... I was not there, of course!" When Carole came back to the family business in 1982, with the declared intention to take her father's succession, she managed to position herself fully as a business manager and future successor, disconnecting her identity as a daughter from the workplace. That was the condition for her to come back. "At work, his name was Mister Bellon, I was Carole Bellon. I was not his little girl anymore, and he was not my father anymore. We had really settled a business relationship together. That is really there that this transition took place."

Considering herself as a French-Canadian, she never saw any barrier or difference in dealing with French- or English-Canadians. She worked in English companies, had English friends, and most of their customers were English-Canadian. As she said, "Business is business and we all live the same thing."

SUCCESSION PLANNING

Carole and her father had no formal planning for succession. They considered the family business as too small. With only two family members, it was not difficult to know who would be the successor. Moreover, the succession took place "in a natural way." Carole's father was bringing her when he was meeting the customers, suppliers, or bankers, and he introduced her progressively to them. Gradually, she became the person of reference and managed everything. From her point of view, the process was progressive and easy.

AGE ASYNCHRONY AND OWNERS' WILLINGNESS TO RELINQUISH CONTROL

Carole faced a particular situation where her father and her own expectations and desires were conflicting, due to age-related and gender-related issues. At the time when Carole felt ready to take over the business, her father considered himself too young to relinquish control. And at the time when Carole's father was ready to release the business, Carole had just had two small children and did not want to penalize her family. Finally, she managed to take over the business in partnership with non-family associates, as suggested by her father's accountants. Carole had never thought about this solution before. "I never thought about working with other people than the family. It has always been part of the family."

MANAGERIAL AND PATRIMONIAL TRANSFER

The transfer of the business itself was not a family transmission but a buy-out, as it had been the case before for her father and grandfather. "That was not given to us. We bought the business." So Carole did not "take it from her sisters," who were thus not penalized regarding the business. Selling out rather than handing over the business made things clearer for every family member. Moreover, Carole's sisters never wanted to be part of the business and that made the succession even easier to manage.

WORK–FAMILY INTEGRATION

Carole has had two children and was used to work six days a week in the family business. "I learned to manage my time differently," she explained. Sleeping few hours, she was alternating work and family care during the course of the day, work activities taking place according to the school or kindergarten hours of activity, from early in the morning until late in the evening. She also learned to delegate. It was one of the most difficult things that she had to learn, as her father did not used to and was proud of doing everything in the business. On the contrary, Carole developed her team, which enabled her to have more time for herself and to participate in multiple other activities, such as business networks or committees.

Another challenge was to get her husband to accept that she was working so many hours. What helped was that he was also working long hours out of the city. In 2007, her husband joined her in the family business, as a consultant–employee. At this point, he realized that it was necessary to work so many hours. Learning to work together with her husband was also a challenge in terms of work–family balance. However, there have not been any conflicts or tensions, each of them having their domains of competence and respecting them. With her own children, Carole has learned to separate the business and the family and to pay attention not to talk about the business all the time.

DISCRIMINATION AND STEREOTYPING

From a family perspective, Carole thinks it can be a little bit different for men or women. She faced some criticisms from her entourage when she did not stop working to raise her children full time; never those criticisms would have been done to a man. A lot of her female friends stopped working to raise their children. Carole emphasized how much she liked her work and her independence. "There is a little 'macho' side there. I liked to have to manage *my* business, *my* money. I don't want to wait for my husband to give me my money. I did not feel at ease with that."

The roles of women in society, and in particular of daughters in family businesses, also depend a lot on the generation. While Carole's father was quite open, there was no way for her grandfather to accept a woman as a potential successor. At that time, some girls did work within the family business, but they were expected to marry, to have children, and to raise them. "It was not fashionable to have women in business." Important factors are also the society values and culture. Quebec is described as a very egalitarian society, which is not the case in all parts of the world. "The new generation does not see any difference. We are all together, differences are not important, that does not matter. Our society has evolved a lot."

Carole thus does not perceive any differences between men and women in the new generation. She does not see any difficulties or tensions anymore. She considers that a woman is as influent as a man, even if they may perhaps be different in their behaviors or attitudes. Carole also does not perceive any difficulties related to a "language barrier" between English- and French-Canadian. Finally, she has never made any difference and has always been at ease with anybody, no matter his or her sex, age, ethnic origin, color, religion, or language.

MANAGEMENT STYLE

Carole encountered absolutely no problems with employees and had enough authority, even if she did not have the same tough management style as her father. "That is a big family," she said. She handles and settles conflicts immediately because they can potentially lead to a lack of motivation among employees and result in a decrease in business performance. She never hesitates to take action in difficult situations, to protect the business, even when her decisions could affect her own family relatives or her business partners. For her, "business is business."

One of Carole's biggest challenges was to learn to work with associates. As a woman, she felt that she had to take her place actively toward the three male associates and to put energy into bringing all these people into a common line of conduct, in order to be successful as a business. One of the partners left because of tensions about his high salary expectations. The second left one year later because he wanted to change job. Finally, Carole bought her accountants' shares in 2008, in order to clear the way and prepare the succession for the next generation.

THE NEXT GENERATION

Carole has two children, a 20-year-old son and a 17-year-old daughter, who have both been initiated in the family business from a young age. Her son has already worked part time in the business during holidays and occupied diverse positions in the company. He is currently finishing his studies at the University of Ottawa. Carole has offered him a position with more responsibilities next summer, to begin to learn about the business more seriously and to discover what it is. Her daughter is not interested by the family business for the moment. She wants to become a lawyer, even if she is young and still can change her mind. Meanwhile, Carole has developed a team of people inside the business who are responsible and trained, and who can take over and manage the business if necessary.

Carole intends to plan the succession a lot more than her father did. The company is not a small business anymore and she is willing to provide coaching and guidance to her successor, whoever it should be. If both her children expressed an interest in running the family business, it would not bother her. "I think that they would do a good partnership, both together in the business. I would have nothing against that. If they want, they will enter together. Eventually, one of them will demarcate more strongly. The future will tell us."

Discussion and Conclusions

The case of Carole Bellon, as successor to the head of the Bellon Industries, shows that it is possible for a daughter to become a legitimate successor and to have success as an entrepreneur, by her own merit and her hard work. Since she took over the business, 15 years ago, the company's turnover has quintupled and many new products have been introduced to satisfy new demands, for instance, the smokers' shelter.

Some elements need to be added to this Canadian case study. First, the "language divide" between French-speaking and Anglo-speaking Canadians, that has marked the history of the province of Quebec, is absent because this aspect is not considered as a barrier for Carole Bellon; for her, "business is business." She is French-Canadian but she did her grades in both languages so that she is truly bilingual and able to interact as well in French as in English. Maybe the fact that her great-grandfather emigrated from the then Czechoslovakia helped to develop in the Bellon family an open-minded attitude toward other languages.

Second, the case illustrates what can stem from an egalitarian society which promotes an egalitarian access to education, and gives the same rights to all citizens, notwithstanding their origin, gender, ethnicity, or religion. Here, a qualified woman has been encouraged to take over the family business by men who were convinced that she was legitimate and competent. Caroles' dedication to the family business and hard work proved to all that she was a valuable successor and a real leader. That was made possible in the Quebec society but this is not the case everywhere in the world and was not the case few decades ago.

Third, in the case of Carole, there was no brother to contradict her desire to succeed to her father; so it is impossible to assess if this would have changed something in her father's decision to choose her as his successor. However, as Ibrahim et al. have shown from a survey of 42 Canadian family businesses, some qualities are critical in the selection of an effective successor. "These include the successor's capacity to lead, his or her managerial skills and competencies, and the willingness and commitment of the successor to take over the family business and to assume his or her leadership role" (2004:476). There is no doubt that Carole had the required qualities.

References

Adams, M. 2004. Canadians are not Like Americans. *The Walrus*, April/May, 1(4), 62–71.

Cadieux L., Lorrain J. and Hugron P. 2002. Succession in Women-Owned Family Businesses: A Case Study. *Family Business Review*, 15(1), 17–30.

Carrington, C. 2004. *Small Business Financing Profiles*. SME Financing Data Initiative, Industry Canada, November. Available at: http://www.sme-fdi.gc.ca/eic/site/sme_fdi-prf_pme.nsf/eng/h_01304.html [accessed: 14 July 2010].

Collerette, P. and Aubry, P. 1990. Socio-Economic Evolution of Women Business Owners in Quebec. *Journal of Business Ethics*, 9, 417–422.

Conseil du statut de la femme. 2010. *Portrait des Québécoises en 8 Temps*. Bibliothèque et Archives Nationales du Québec, Gouvernement du Québec.

Hughes, K.D. 2006. Exploring Motivation and Success Among Canadian Women Entrepreneurs. *Journal of Small Business Entrepreneurship*, 19(2), 107–120.

Ibrahim, A.B., Soufani, K., Poutziouris, P. and Lam J. 2004. Qualities of an Effective Successor: The Role of Education and Training. *Education and Training*, 46(8/9), 474–480.

Langlois, S. 1990. L'Évolution Récente des Valeurs dans la Société Québécoise. *L'Action Nationale*, 80(7), 925–937.

PriceWaterhouseCoopers. 2008. *Making a Difference*. PriceWaterhouseCoopers Global, *Family Business Survey*, 2007–2008.

Verheul, I. and Thurik, A.R. 2001. Start-up Capital: Does Gender Matter? *Small Business Economics*, 16(4), 329–345.

Verheul, I., VanStel, A. and Thurik, A.R. 2006. Explaining Female and Male Entrepreneurship at the Country Level. *Entrepreneurship and Regional Development*, 18(2), 151–183.

Zinger, J.T., Lebrasseur, R., Robichaud, Y. and Riverin, N. 2007. Stages of Small Enterprise Development: a Comparison of Canadian Female and Male Entrepreneurs. *Journal of Enterprising Culture*, 15(2), 107–131.

CHAPTER **20**

South Carolina, USA: The Challenge of Father–Daughter Succession in Family Business: A Case Study in South Carolina

TERESA L. SMITH AND JEAN-LUC E. GROSSO

Introduction

Like many small businesses in the US, Mary Ann's Deli Restaurant in Sumter, South Carolina, was started by someone with no experience running his own business, and no experience in the food industry prior to opening what he dreamed would be "a little deli restaurant where people could enjoy good food and friendly service." That dream began in 1987, defied the dire odds of the restaurant business (Boden, 2001) and continues to grow and prosper today despite difficult economic times, under the experienced, loving hand of a daughter who took over when her father died, in order to carry on his dream and honor his memory. Twenty-three years after it opened, this warm, cheery, family restaurant continues to serve hearty, fresh food where "everything—from the soups to the desserts—is made from scratch," to long-time customers who remember a father's good cheer and to new patrons who come because of word-of-mouth recommendations to try the famous chicken salad, pasta, and iced tea. Mary Ann's has succeeded in establishing itself as a tradition for the small-town crowd and fulfills its mission of serving great food, "and a lot of it," at fair prices, while always giving back to the community that made it what it is today.

Mary Ann's Deli provides a useful example of a case which can help to expand the under-researched intersection of gender and family business. Despite the tremendous importance of family businesses and women's leadership in the United States (US) economy, little is known about the unique issues surrounding women in family firms. We help to illuminate this arena by exploring a case of father–daughter succession in the family firm.

Literature Review

FEMALE ENTREPRENEURSHIP IN THE UNITED STATES

Women in the US have been increasingly starting their own businesses over the past ten years (Hackler et al., 2008), but they are still less likely to start a business than a man (Fairlie, 2008). Most female business owners are white, but African-American-owned businesses showed the highest rate of growth between 1997 and 2002 among all minority-owned businesses (Lowery, 2007). The majority of women-owned businesses are in the service sector, followed by the retail sector, but the variety of industries represented by women-owned businesses is increasing. Women are now entering the high-tech, construction, transportation, utilities, and consulting sectors (Hackler et al., 2008). The majority of female entrepreneurs in the US have a high school education with some college, or have college degrees. Both the level of education and the age of a woman are positively related to business ownership for women. Despite their increasing level of business ownership and education, income of female entrepreneurs still lags that of male owners (Ibid.).

FATHER–DAUGHTER SUCCESSION IN THE UNITED STATES

According to many researchers, "Family has been a neglected variable in organizational research," especially in regards to father–daughter succession in family firms (Dyer, 2003). Interest in the dynamics of family business has been increasing in the US in recent years, especially since 90 percent of businesses in the US are family businesses, and since family businesses employ over 60 percent of the workforce in the US (Mangan, 2007). Studies are now beginning to examine factors that influence multigenerational success in family business as well as the difficulties that arise from the succession process in those businesses. A recent report from the US Small Business Administration highlights the problems faced by family businesses today, stating that while 40 percent of US businesses face the issue of transfer of ownership at any given time, "less than one-third of family businesses survive the transition from first to second generation ownership" (Bowman-Upton, 2009). In family businesses, there is a "natural tendency" to push the children into the business, whether or not the children want to be involved. When children do enter the business, there may be rivalry between the children as to who will be in charge. Daughters especially face difficulties breaking out of the role of "daddy's little girl" and into the role of manager or owner of the business (Longenecker, et al., 2009). While there is little specific research on the succession of daughters in their father's businesses, case studies such as this will pave the way for the systematic examination of this critical part of the US economy.

CULTURE INFLUENCES ON FAMILY BUSINESS

Family-owned firms are "among the world's largest and oldest enterprises" (Longenecker et al., 2009). Family businesses have "a special culture" (Welch and Welch, 2009) that makes them different from other types of businesses. There is a closeness that makes them seem more intimate than other businesses and attracts employees and customers curious to experience the sense of belonging, security, and pride that is evident in a well-run family business. The values of the founder of the business become engrained in the culture of the business and in the "family code" for all of those working in the business (Longenecker et al., 2009). In order for the business to survive, that strong culture must be passed on to the next generation; but that same strong culture makes it often more difficult for the successor to continue in the founder's footsteps. One study of more than 400 children of small business owners showed that 80 percent of those not already working in the business had no desire to work in the business or succeed their parents in the business. Even the majority of those who did plan to take over the business intended on working somewhere else before joining the business (Longenecker et al., 2009).

Because of the strong, established culture in a family business, when children do take over the business, change takes longer and must be handled carefully so that it will be accepted by employees and customers. Unfortunately, that change process is usually "about as orderly and predictable as families are" (Welch and Welch, 2009) which makes the succession much harder than in a non-family business. According to Zahra et al. (2008), a strong family culture improves the business's ability to adapt and survive. That same strong sense of culture, however, can lead to resistance to change and eventual stagnation. According to Eddleston (2008), the key to maintaining a strong sense of family as well as adaptability that will allow the business to survive and grow beyond the founder father's time to future generations is the founder's leadership ability to create in the minds and hearts of the family members a clear vision and mission for the business, goals for the future, and an example of commitment to the business that the children and children's children will want to emulate.

The Case Study

BRIEF HISTORY OF THE FIRM

"Mary Ann's Deli Restaurant" was started in 1987 and has been in continuous operation ever since, in the same location, with two of the original employees. The business was started by a retired Air Force officer who was a successful boat salesman after leaving the Air Force. According to his daughter, Donna, "He could sell anything." He loved to cook and had always wanted to open a "little deli" when he retired. He found a good location in a strip mall on the "main drag" of town, negotiated the lease, and started making his dream a reality. He created the menu and worked with his own mother to come up with all of the recipes. He wasn't sure what to name his restaurant, but decided on "Mary Ann's" since his mother and one of his daughters were both named Mary, and his sister's name was Ann. He opened the small restaurant with about 20 tables for lunch and dinner, but quickly realized that he did all of his business at lunch, so changed to offering lunch only, which is the way the restaurant continues to operate. He allowed smoking for one day, couldn't stand it, and has made his restaurant non-smoking ever since. That was quite a bold move in 1987, especially in a small southern town. He had no experience running any business on his own, especially a restaurant, but learned as he went along, always listening to his customers when they told him what they liked as well as what they didn't.

THE SUCCESSION PROCESS

Succession, or the transfer of leadership to the next generation, is a "difficult process" for most family businesses (Bowman-Upton, 2009). Many times, the owner of the business does not want to face the issue of succession, so there is no planning for the future. The succession for this restaurant was like that in many family businesses in that it was not planned nor discussed in any formal way between the father and the daughter. Donna succeeded her father in the restaurant after his death. She had informally "helped him" from the beginning offering advice and answering questions whenever he asked, but had never actually worked for him in the restaurant as a paid employee, preferring to maintain her independence and her own full-time job.

THE NEXT GENERATION ENTREPRENEUR

Donna, the daughter who is now running the business her father started, is the youngest of her parent's four children—three girls and one boy. The children grew up in Sumter, South Carolina, and all continue to live there. The entrepreneurial spirit runs in the family—Donna's older sister runs her own fabric business in the storefront next to Mary Ann's. Donna attended college for one year following high school, but left to start working. Her position involved opening convenience stores and training the new employees. She gained experience with the day-to-day operations of a business and learned things like how to run a cash register, how to order equipment and supplies, how to create invoices, and how to hire and train employees. Her brother is "good with fixing things," so he was and is still often called on to make repairs in the restaurant when something breaks down.

While Donna and her brother did not formally work for their father in the restaurant, Donna's older sister did try it for a time, with "entertaining" results for the customers, but a great deal of conflict with her father. Donna's sister engaged in "spirited" discussions with her father in front of the customers. The customers loved the banter, but the nearly constant bickering between the two interfered with getting the work done and getting the food on the tables. In order to preserve her relationship with her father and her family, Donna's sister left the restaurant, so Donna's father was again on his own running the business. His initial goal was to double his sales in three months. If he met that target, he decided he could survive in the business, and survive he did. Donna believes that the key to the success and longevity of the business is two-fold: 1) great relationships with the customers and truly liking people, and 2) having great employees and treating them with respect, valuing their input, and making them feel like "part of the family."

Cultural Dimensions and their Role in Father–Daughter Succession

This case illustrates several important aspects of the challenges of succession in the family business and of the difficulties that can occur when that succession is not planned. Despite the challenges present, this case also illustrates role of a strong daughter in creating a successful continuation of the business that can help future researchers better understand the importance of the daughter's commitment to her father's vision of the business to carry it forward to the next generation.

Reasons for joining the company

After witnessing her older sister's difficulty working in the restaurant, Donna was reluctant to take a formal role in the business. She was involved from the beginning, helping her father get started with ordering, facilities layout, hiring employees, handling basic accounting and payroll, and "teaching" him what she knew about running a business in the service sector. Donna worked hard in her own field as a divorced mother raising a daughter. When her father's health began failing, Donna began to step in more to help. She began to take on a day-to-day role supervising the employees in the kitchen, ordering, and maintaining the "front," carrying on her father's tradition of warm, friendly service to the numerous regular customers as well as to new ones always coming in. Her father's illness put a strain on the business, on Donna personally, on the family, and financially on the restaurant itself. Of the four children, she was the only one who had the knowledge and personality to handle the business while her father was ill.

Owners' willingness to relinquish control

Donna's father loved his business with all his heart. He worked through his illness, finding strength and joy from seeing his regular customers. Always the optimist, he thought he would be back at work after receiving a kidney transplant, but sadly, did not recover from that. He liked running the business himself and was reluctant to delegate his day-to-day responsibilities to someone else, even as his failing health started to strain the business with mounting debts.

Succession planning

Mary Ann's Deli typifies the situation in many family businesses—there was no succession planning. While research shows that succession planning can greatly assist the transfer process, and in many cases is necessary to the continued operation of the business, most companies do not plan for a takeover and do not have plans in place if illness or sudden tragedy occur. Donna said that her father did not talk to his children about taking over the business, even when he was ill. She believes that her father's reluctance to talk about succession stemmed from his sincere belief that he would be back after his illness and his desire not to place negative thoughts among his family and his customers that he would not be back.

Father–daughter relationship

Donna feels that of all her siblings, she is the most like her father. She is outgoing, loves people, and optimistic about the business, and life in general. Even now, she smiles when speaking about him, and said that she still "wanted to make him proud." She "loves the business as much as he did," and that is evident by her constant enthusiasm when talking about the restaurant. She said how important it is to her to carry on his tradition of giving back to the community, through food donations to charitable events, to free meal coupons to those who look like they need it. Donna says that every morning when she walks into the restaurant, she "feels close to her father, even now."

Identity issues

Donna was not worried about her identity or establishing herself as the person in charge when she took over the restaurant. She credits her confidence to a good self-image, a positive attitude, a willingness to work hard, and a willingness to listen and learn from her employees. She also credits her success in the restaurant over the past nine years since her father died to her determination to continue in her father's footsteps and to her "hard-headedness." She says that she's "too stubborn to quit until she has to."

Sibling/family members' rivalry

When her father died, Donna was the only one of her siblings who actually wanted to step in and take over. Her family did not want to sell the business, but quickly realized that Donna would be the best choice to take over for their father. The siblings are still involved with the restaurant as co-owners, and meet regularly to discuss the business. There are disagreements, but the siblings understand that Donna is in charge and will ultimately make the final decisions about running the business. For instance, even though they constantly complain about the costs, Donna will not budge on her "big portion sizes and quality ingredients" because that's what the restaurant has always been known for and since her father started it that way, she "had to keep it that way."

Non-family members' rivalry

Even though the restaurant is very small, Donna has been able to make it work despite a great deal of competition from the local market. She says that her sales have "increased every year" since she formally took over the business, and are now double the level that they were when her father ran the business. She credits her success to loving what she does, loving people, hard work, and "great employees who aren't afraid of hard work." All of the employees in the restaurant are women, but instead of leading to more rivalry and arguments, Donna thinks it strengthens the business because everyone works as a team.

Managerial transfer

The transfer process for this business involved formal and informal dimensions, but without consciously knowing it, the family followed many tenants for a successful transition by encouraging collaboration among family members, good relations between the successor and the employees, and a continued communication among the family members (Stavrou et al., 2005). Formally, the siblings decided to make themselves equal partners in the business. They also decided to incorporate as an LLC (Limited Liability Corporation) to personally protect and separate themselves from the business. They became the board of directors and divided profits equally. The children did not inherit the business from their father. They had to pay off all the debts and officially buy it in order to continue. There was no formal plan even at that point. The children just decided that they wanted to "keep the business for awhile and try it." That was nine years ago, and Donna is still running the business. Donna receives a salary from the business and acts as the sole manager, handling all aspects of running the business on a daily basis. Informally, nothing changed for Donna when she took over since she was already managing the business by herself. Donna says that she and her siblings sit down each month and review financial reports for the restaurant and talk about what's going well and possible changes they might make in kinds of food to serve, physical layouts, schedules, and so on. Donna says that she is always open to hearing ideas from her siblings, but she is in charge. If she does not think something is a good idea, she will not do it.

BEING A VIABLE SUCCESSOR/INVISIBILITY

Donna feels that one factor that helped her succession into her father's business was that fact that she was known to the employees and customers in the business. Even though she did not formally work for her father, she "was a regular face" to everyone who knew the business. She realized the need to "ease into" her new role as manager/owner of the business, especially when the business was so identified by her father and his large, outgoing presence. She knew she wanted to make changes to "a lot of the ways that things were done" but wisely knew that she had to make those changes gradually and let the long-time employees "be a real part of the changes." The mainstays of the menu have remained the same over the years, but Donna has added her own ideas, from daily specials to newer sandwich options to keep up with changing customer tastes and preferences. As she speaks about the menu, it is clear that she knows every detail about her restaurant and is passionate about everything there, from changing the decor to make it "bright and cheery" to rearranging the cook and prep area in the back so that the work would flow quicker and more smoothly. She knows her customers by name, knows what they like to eat, and feels a real responsibility to make her restaurant stand on taste, looks, cleanliness, and quality. She says that she "wants quality, even if it costs more" and "won't skimp" on what she does. If she likes it, her customers will like it too.

Work–family conflict

Donna is a single mother, raising a teenage daughter. Her daughter has "grown up with the business" and seen her mother working there "as long as she can remember." Donna says that her divorce many years ago was not due to a conflict with her running the business. Donna works a long day in the restaurant but is able to be home with her daughter in the evenings. She does not like to leave the business though, and only takes one week vacation away from the restaurant every year. She is now starting to think about cutting back some and allowing her employees to manage the restaurant when she is gone, not because she necessarily wants to, but because chronic health issues are forcing her to slow down somewhat. She worries about the future of the restaurant since her daughter "doesn't want" the business, and she worries about her own ability to let go since she "does everything" now and knows that "everyone depends" on her.

Discrimination and stereotyping

Despite the fact that she is a woman in a small southern town, Donna says that she never felt any sense of discrimination or stereotyping from her employees or customers. She says that it was important for her to establish herself as the person in charge very early when she took over, to be firm but fair with people, and to treat people with respect in all of her business dealings. She thinks that the customers still see her father when they come in and talk to her, and that makes her very proud to be continuing his legacy. She says that she will continue to work in the restaurant until she "can't do it anymore," because she truly has a passion for what she does.

Discussion and Conclusions

While the case of Mary Ann's Deli restaurant is quite interesting and highlights many best practices in long-term management of a small, family-owned business, it has the limitation of being just one case among the thousands of small businesses in South Carolina and millions in the US. As such, it is not possible to generalize findings based on one family's experience. What it is possible to garner from this case are suggestions for future research directions. Future studies could focus on the factors that help family businesses like Mary Ann's Deli defy the formidable odds against successful transition from one generation to the next, specifically: 1) what management, leadership and interpersonal skills and abilities must the daughter possess in order to orchestrate a successful takeover of the family business; 2) what role does sibling support for the daughter play in the succession; 3) how can the daughter garner support from the stakeholders in the firm—the customers, the suppliers, the community, to foster a successful takeover; 4) does the creation of a formal succession plan help the succession process when a daughter takes over the business; and 5) what motivates a daughter to take on the challenge of succeeding her father or mother in a business and what motivates her to continue in the business despite the difficulties the business may cause in her personal and professional life.

This case exemplifies the research findings of an overall lack of succession planning in family business and the challenges that lack of planning can bring to the family. As this case illustrates, the success of continuing a family business to the next generation even without formal succession planning depends on the strong culture of charismatic leadership begun by the founder, and the willingness of the daughter–successor to take what she learned from her father and retain the good, but also adapt to new challenges and situations. Donna has continued in her father's footsteps to make her restaurant a place that is "friendly, personable, and a place to see each other in good times or bad, where people can leave feeling happy, not hungry!"

References

Boden, R.J. 2001. *Analyses of Business Dissolution by Demographic Category of Business Ownership*. Washington: US Small Business Administration Office of Advocacy Research Summary.

Bowman-Upton, N. 2009. *Transferring Management in the Family-Owned Business*. Washington: US Small Business Administration Office of Entrepreneurship Education.

Dyer, W.G. Jr. 2003. The Family: The Missing Variable in Organizational Research. *Entrepreneurship, Theory & Practice*, 27(4), 401–416.

Eddleston, K.A. 2008. Commentary: The Prequel to Family Firm Culture and Stewardship: The Leadership Perspective of the Founder. *Entrepreneurship, Theory & Practice*, 32(6), 1055–1062.

Fairlie, R.W. 2008. *Estimating the Contribution of Immigrant Business Owners to the US Economy*. Washington: US Small Business Administration Office of Advocacy Research Summary.

Hackler, D., Harpel, E. and Mayer, H. 2008. *Human Capital and Women's Business Ownership.* Washington: US Small Business Administration Office of Advocacy Research Summary.

Longenecker, J.G., Petty, J.W., Palich, L.E. and Moore, C.W. 2009. *Small Business Management: Launching and Growing Entrepreneurial Ventures* (15th Edition). Mason: South-Western Cengage Learning.

Lowery, Y. 2007. *Minorities in Business: A Demographic Review of Minority Business Ownership.* Washington: US Small Business Administration Office of Advocacy Research Summary.

Mangan, K. 2007. Look Who's Minding the Store. *The Chronicle of Higher Education,* 53(35), A19.

Stavrou, E.T., Kleanthous, T. and Anastasiou, T. 2005. Leadership Personality and Firm Culture During Hereditary Transitions in Family Firms: Model Development and Empirical Investigation. *Journal of Small Business Management,* 43(2), 187–207.

Welch, J. and Welch, S. 2009. Transforming the Family Business. *BusinessWeek,* May 13. Available at: http://www.businessweek.com/magazine/content/09_21/b4132000967749.htm [accessed: 15 July 2010].

Zahra, S.A., Hayton, J.C., Neubaum, D.O., Dibrell, C. and Craig, J. 2008. Culture of Family Commitment and Strategic Flexibility: The Moderating Effect of Stewardship. *Entrepreneurship, Theory & Practice,* 32(6), 1035–1055.

CHAPTER 21

Washington, USA: It's a Sweet Life: A Daughter Successfully Manages an Immigrant Family Business

MEENAKSHI RISHI AND DAPHNE HALKIAS

Introduction

ETHNIC IDENTITY ISSUES FOR IMMIGRANT FAMILY BUSINESSES IN THE UNITED STATES

The majority of studies and rhetoric on immigrant entrepreneurship by and large overlook the phenomenon's gendered character, which in itself produces a one-sided perception of the socio-economic processes at play in this field of research. Although gender is highlighted as an issue for further research in many studies, it does not preclude simultaneous investigation into other differentiating issues in the life of female immigrant entrepreneurs such as ethnicity, class, generation, family interrelationships, motivations behind becoming self-employed, the strategy applied in their approach to entrepreneurship, being part of the family business and how these factors relate to personal identity construction (Lund Thomsen, 2006; Halkias and Caracatsanis, 2011).

Ethnic identity can be understood as a part of self-concept that consciously anchors an individual to a particular ethnic group. Central to this identity is a sense of belonging as well as a commitment to the group's values, beliefs, conventions, and customs (Phinney, 1990). Uba (1994) contends that maintenance of traditional culture by a minority group and adoption of a stable ethnic identity is integrally linked. However, the strength of commitment to this identity may differ from person to person according to two factors: the degree to which one is devoted to various aspects of the natal culture and the degree to which one is identified with the dominant group (Sue and Sue, 1990; Uba, 1994; Berry, 1997).

The Sikhs as a Cultural Group in America

The traditions of Indian immigrants in the United States of America (USA) are an affirmation of their ethnic identity, which is a critical psychological aspect of the minority individual in society (Dasgupta, 1998). Ethnic identity not only sheds light on attitudes and behaviors of the post-1965 Asian Indian immigrant community in the US, but also explains intragroup variations. The Asian Indian community in the US is an ethnically diverse one, with subgroups that follow distinct customs and religious beliefs. Of all the Asian Indian religious communities, the Sikhs are the oldest, originating from the Indian state of Punjabi, and tend to be the best organized in terms of religious activity.

Sikhism is a monistic religion founded in fifteenth-century Punjab on the teachings of Guru Nanak Dev and ten successive Sikh Gurus. Sikhism teaches its followers to embrace compassion, truth, contentment, humility, and love. In addition, it is every Sikh's duty to control and subdue lust, anger, greed, attachment, and ego. Sikhism unequivocally recognizes equality for all human beings and specifically for both men and women. Consequently, Sikhism advocates active and equal participation in congregation, academics, healthcare, and military among other aspects of society. Female subordination, including practicing rituals that imply dependence, is shunned within Sikhism (Mann, 2004).

Cultural Values Guiding the Daughters of Indian-American Family Business

Census data show that 81.8 percent of Indian immigrants arrived in the US after 1980. They received no special treatment or support and faced the same discrimination and hardship that any immigrant group does. Yet, they learned to thrive in American society. In a 2006 *BusinessWeek* article, Vivek Wadhwa compiled a list of Indian cultural values to illustrate the successful marrying of Indian-American entrepreneurial success and Indian cultural values: education, upbringing, hard work, determination to overcome obstacles, an entrepreneurial spirit, recognizing diversity, humility, family support/values, careful financial management, and forming and leveraging networks.

Scholars claim that Asian Indian immigrants have transplanted old-world gender ideologies and clearly dichotomized gender roles in their adopted country of residence (Kar et al., 1995, 1996; Dasgupta, 1998). In her study of immigrants and their children, Agarwal states that although "several [first generation] women said their immigration to the United States brought them independence and liberation from the institutional repression of women in India ... the second generation Indian woman feels that old-world gender roles are still rigidly being upheld for her" (1991:52). This phenomenon can perhaps be explained by examining the gender-specific role that daughters of immigrants are given in the preservation of Indian ethnic/cultural identity.

Despite such findings regarding the egalitarian gender beliefs among adult immigrant daughters, many second generation women tend to complain about the restrictive gender role prescriptions imposed on them (Dasgupta, 1998). Mani (1992) claims that as the keepers of South Asian culture and heritage in the US, second generation daughters are monitored more strictly than those of sons. Fears of cultural obliteration by "Americanization" and exogamy have played a large role in imposing such constructions on the female gender role. This gender imbalance expectation is coming to a head as the second generation Asian Indian daughters have matured, received their education, and entered the market, either through professions or as entrepreneurs in Indian family businesses.

In-depth research on father–daughter succession in Indian family businesses in the US has, until now, eluded scholarly investigation. One Indian daughter's eloquent voice has been heard on the delicate balance of culture and business success in an interview given to Dr Michael Useem of the Wharton School at the University of Pennsylvania by Indra Nooyi, PepsiCo CEO. Useem asked Nooyi how she would define success among Indian-American women entrepreneurs and how this spirit of entrepreneurship is supported by Indian cultural values. Nooyi maintained that, in spite of her academic achievements and business acumen, her values remained profoundly personal and cultural, keeping family as the nucleus of her life. Even as CEO of one of America's biggest enterprises, she still called her mother in India twice a day. "At the end of the day," said Nooyi "don't forget that you're a person, don't forget you're a mother, don't forget you're a wife, don't forget you're a daughter ... and what you're left with is family, friends, and faith" (Useem, 2008).

The above has highlighted some ethnic/cultural issues surrounding Indian family businesses in the US and has also noted the paucity of studies in the father–daughter succession theme for such businesses. The following case study is our attempt to contribute to the literature. The case illustrates the drive, determination, and perseverance of an unusual woman who is dealing with the complexities involved in merging a formal MBA education within a family business that was started by her immigrant parents and operates in a traditional ethnic neighborhood.

Case Study: An Immigrant Entrepreneurial Family Business in the US

"Punjab Sweets" is a family-owned Vegetarian Indian Café in Kent, Washington, that has been in operation since 2001. In its early years, Punjab Sweets was a small bakery/snack shop that prided itself on selling fresh and appetizing Indian snacks and desserts. This family business was the original brain child of Iqbal Dha, Gurmit Dha, and Jasbir Rai. Iqbal and her husband Gurmit Dha immigrated to the US in 1980. Iqbal was a skilled cook and wanted to share her passion and excitement for experimenting with food and creating new recipes with the community. She initially catered small events but began to dream big as people complimented her on her culinary skills. In 2001, Iqbal Dha and Gurmit Dha founded Punjab Sweets in a joint effort with Iqbal's brother, Jasbir Rai.

In 2006, Harpreet Gill, the daughter of Iqbal and Gurmit, became co-owner of the family business and since then Punjab Sweets has come a long way from its small, dusty beginnings. Harpreet has used her considerable artistic talents to completely redesign the restaurant. The menu has been expanded to accommodate Vegan preferences and "eggless" cakes that appeal to the large Indian immigrant community. Punjab Sweets has a Facebook page and a loyal fan following. It receives glowing reviews in the local press and boasts a growing clientele of customers. *Seattle Weekly*, a widely-read source of information on restaurants in Seattle, featured Punjab Sweets on their 2006 Dining Guide cover and a 2007 review in the *Seattle Magazine* called the homemade fare at Punjab Sweets "hard to resist." Under the daughter–successor's guidance, it is clear that the restaurant has indeed "arrived."

Harpreet's own entry into the family business was as dramatic as the success of *Punjab* Sweets has been. In 2004, while helping her parents manage Punjab Sweets, Harpreet decided to study for an MBA. Her original plan was to work part time at the business, get her degree, and then seek a career as a business consultant. Her life changed with the cover story on Punjab Sweets that was featured in *Seattle Weekly*. She interpreted this as a sign from God and decided to stay in the family business and help it grow.

Harpreet's transition from worker/helper to family business co-owner was gradual; in her own words: "The lines were muddled at first, but eventually and over time the decisions, trust, and facets of running the business were my responsibility." The smooth path of the transition process was enabled by the fact that Harpreet's parents leave for India every year for several months and this has required them to handover large chunks of responsibility to Harpreet. Today, Harpreet is very comfortable in her new role and manages the overall operations of the company. She handles marketing, the presentation of the dishes, and maintains regular contact with distributors and several local restaurants that Punjab Sweets caters to. Harpreet works as the cashier, serves guests, and spends up to 80 hours a week working for her business. Harpreet thinks it's her MBA that challenged her to be a leader and constantly adapt to changing circumstances. As she comments in Seattle University's alumni magazine, "It is a blessing to be able to come into work and not know exactly what is to be expected."

Harpreet's deft handling of the business has certainly taken a load of responsibility off her father's shoulders and enabled her mother to retire. Harpreet beams when her father comes into the restaurant to ask her opinion. "My dad's proud of me—little things I do matter to him a great deal."

The success enjoyed by Punjab Sweets has spawned the opening of a second restaurant on the Eastside of Seattle. This new restaurant, called "Preet's" is managed by Harpreet's brother, Manpreet Dha. While Harpreet's parents wanted the ownership of Preet's to be split equally between the two siblings, Harpreet declined. She wanted to concentrate on running Punjab Sweets and, as she states, "I didn't want to lose a relationship with my brother over money and ownership." Family and relationships are very important to Harpreet and she is content helping her brother out occasionally and without acrimony over finances and responsibilities. She feels it is important to model harmonious family relationships to her daughter, Jasneet, who is 10 years old and at "an impressionable age."

BUT, WHERE'S THE HUSBAND?

Dunemann and Barett note that, "Family values and other social considerations have a demonstrable influence over the conduct of family business" (2004:24). Harpreet's case is illustrative. While some may view her as an immigrant success story, people in her own community look down upon her choice of occupation. "The cultural mindset of Indians is very narrow and they do not consider serving customers in a restaurant as an appropriate occupation for someone with an MBA," said Harpreet. For Indians in general, and in particular Punjabis who hail from villages in North India, having an office and a secretary is the mark of success and picking up someone's dirty dishes after a meal is considered almost a menial task. Harpreet has tried to stand up for herself but it does not help that she is also a divorced single mother. People in the community still ask her mother when she will get remarried!

Traditional cultural values also permeate Harpreet's relationships with her parents. While her parents talked over the steps of running the business with her, they left some responsibilities unclear. This frustrated Harpreet in the beginning because she did not want to assume that she was "completely in charge" and question her parents' authority. In the Indian culture, the male is the head of the household and often makes decisions on behalf of the family. As Harpreet puts it: "Sometimes my dad would make a decision and not inform anyone as he thought it was his decision to make." Or, Harpreet's father would not give her the contact numbers of the suppliers leaving Harpreet aggravated and annoyed at his lack of trust. However, Harpreet's father soon had to relent on this score as his annual trips to India necessitated the sharing of information with Harpreet.

Harpreet has had to encounter cultural barriers and power distance issues at the supplier level too. As most of her Indian distributors are known to her family and several years older than her, Harpreet has to call them "uncle" because, "In our culture we have to call anybody older than us uncle or auntie." However, this cultural upbringing and respect for elders also sets the stage for cultural power distance. Harpreet gets the impression that her Indian distributors don't like to deal with a woman in charge and that conversations often seem to be going on at different wavelengths. It is at such moments that Harpreet has to solicit her father's help and experience in dealing with suppliers and distributors. She does not mind asking for assistance as she sees the business as a family business that is predicated on cultural values and interpersonal relationships.

The complexities of Indian management culture are also magnified when it comes to employee–employer relationships. As Harpreet notes, "My textbooks may talk about keeping my employees at a distance; but my culture renders this impossible." Punjab Sweets has ten employees, all women, who live in the surrounding communities. Some of her employees do not have reliable modes of transportation so Harpreet's family has to pick up and drop off the ladies at home. While this may seem awkward to Harpreet, she recognizes that her business is not a textbook business and that treating her employees with the respect she reserves for her own family members imbues them with a sense of pride in working for her. Hugs are commonplace in the kitchens of Punjab Sweets and Harpreet's mother visits the employees' families in India whenever she can.

VISION AND STRATEGY

While it is tough to operate a family business, Harpreet would have it no other way. She is interested in taking Punjab Sweets to a whole new plane of operations. Harpreet hopes to market her store's salted vegan snacks, which are currently available online (www.punjabsweetsonline.com). She has recently redesigned the snack's labels and envisions the healthy snacks being sold at local health food stores.

Harpreet also feels frustrated in her present location—a tiny ethnic enclave in the community of Kent that is a good half an hour's drive from downtown Seattle. She says that she is well-accustomed to the "penny-pinching immigrant mindset," and would like to deal with a younger, hipper, more business-like crowd that is closer to her in age and tastes. Her vision involves moving the restaurant out of its strip mall location to a downtown Seattle address. As a matter of fact, several of her clientele have been urging her to do so for a long time. While her parents do not object to this plan, Harpreet does not think she is in a financial position to make the transition. Plus, she does gain a lot from living in the tiny enclave of Kent. Her mom is available to take care of her daughter and her daughter is able to waltz into the restaurant and "help out" the staff on several occasions. Moving further away from such a support network is not easy for anyone—least of all a single mother/entrepreneur like Harpreet.

The community is clearly important to Harpreet and despite the hectic demands on her time, she still manages to do good in the community. On a monthly basis, Punjab Sweets donates food and clothing to the Union Gospel Mission and Harpreet provides gift certificates for auctions and school fundraisers. Harpreet serves as an ambassador with the Kent Chamber of Commerce and is an active volunteer for Chaya, an organization committed to raising awareness about domestic violence issues in South Asia.

Harpreet is not sure of a plan of succession. She does not know if her daughter would like to follow in her footsteps. Meanwhile, Harpreet has come to realize that her management skills are a hodge-podge of her cultural values combining respect for her parents as well as a top-notch management education. While her parents may disagree on the "right" way of doing things sometimes, there is no debate on the core principle behind the daily operations of Punjab Sweets: Harpreet's parents and Harpreet are in total agreement that, "each and every person that steps through our door should feel as if they are very special and the guest of honor."

References

Agarwal, P. 1991. *Passage from India: Post 1965 Indian Immigrants and Their Children; Conflicts, Concerns, and Solutions*. Palos Verdes: Yuvati Publications.

Berry, J.W. 1997. Immigration, Acculturation, and Adaptation. *Applied Psychology: An International Review*, 46(1), 5–68.

Dasgupta, D.S. 1998. Gender Roles and Cultural Continuity in the Asian Indian Immigrant Community in the US. *Sex Roles*, 38(11/12), 953–974.

Dunemann, M. and Barett, R. 2004. *Family Business and Succession Planning—A Review of the Literature*. Research paper. Berwick: Monash University, Family and Small Business Research Unit.

Halkias, D. and Caracatsanis, S.M. 2011. The Evolution of Researching Female Immigrant Entrepreneurship: A Commentary in *Female Immigrant Entrepreneurs: The Economic and Social Impact of a Global Phenomenon* (pp. 3–7), edited by D. Halkias, P. Thurman, N. Harkiolakis and S.M. Caracatsanis. Farnham: Gower.

Kar, S.B., Cambell, K., Jimenez, A. and Gupta, S.R. 1995/1996. Invisible Americans: Indo-American Quality of Life. *Amerasia Journal*, 21(3), 25–52.

Lund Thomsen, T. 2006. *Self-employment Activities Concerning Women and Minorities: Their Success and Failure in Relation to Social Citizenship Policies*, PhD Defence, March 3. Available at: kdb2.portal.aau.dk/kdb2literature/download?cid=240441&litid=272122 [accessed: 17 September 2010].

Mani, L. 1992. Gender, Class, and Cultural Conflict: Indu Krishnan's Knowing her Place. *South Asian Magazine for Reflection and Action* , 11–14.

Mann, G.S. 2004. *Sikhism*. New York: Prentice Hall.

Phinney, J.S. 1990. Ethnic Identity in Adolescents and Adults: Review of Research. *Psychological Bulletin*, 108(3), 499–514.

Sue, D.W. and Sue, D. 1990. *Counseling the Culturally Different: Theory & Practice* (2nd Edition). New York: John Wiley & Sons.

Uba, L. 1994. *Asian Americans: Personality Patterns, Identity, and Mental Health.* New York: The Guilford Press.

Useem, M. 2008. *America's Best Leaders: Indra Nooyi, PepsiCo CEO.* US News & World Report [online, 19 November] Available at: http://politics.usnews.com/news/best-leaders/articles/2008/11/19/americas-best-leaders-indra-nooyi-pepsico-ceo.html [accessed: 7 July 2010].

CHAPTER 22 West Virginia, USA: Father–Daughter Succession in a West Virginia Family Business

LEANN MISCHEL AND CINDY IANNARELLI

Introduction

The family business setting dates back centuries but only relatively recently has it been studied by researchers as an important component of current world economy (Lank and Thomassen, 1991; Ward, 1987). Family businesses have been described by Davis and Stern (1980) as exceptional entities due to their concern for the long run over generations, a commitment to quality which stands behind the family name, and their humanity in the workplace where there is more care and concern for employees. While family businesses around the world have been studied, there has been scant research on rural family businesses and in particular few studies have been done on family businesses in mountain regions such as the Appalachia region located in West Virginia in the United States and, specifically, in father–daughter successions in family business.

Literature Review: The Culture of Appalachia and Economic Development

Literature that has touched on issues of how to improve income, living conditions, and human welfare in the southern mountain region of the United States of America (USA), assumes that a significant relationship exists between the culture of those who live in Appalachia and the prospects for the region's economic development. In fact, assumptions regarding the distinct character of the Appalachian culture, despite many Americans not being favorable to the idea of a Rocky Mountain or Adirondack culture, actually contribute to the notion that Appalachia is indeed a separate region with a unique culture (Lewis and Billings, 1997).

A set of powerful beliefs exists in the American cognitive map about Appalachian culture and its presumed impoverished economic development. These assumptions include such concepts as isolationism, homogeneity, familism, and fundamentalism.

These and a variety of corollary concepts grew out of a popular mythology which came to be accepted and then researched by professionals whose works were influential during the 1960s and 1970s and still influence economic theory and policy analysis today in the region. The validity of these beliefs, many of which became stereotypes, were challenged in Appalachia with the rise of social activism in the 1970s. Scholarly work from 1970 to 1995 significantly deepened the understanding of the diversity presented by Appalachia's geography, history, cultural resources, forms of social and political participation, and its relationship with the national and global markets (Lewis and Billings, 1997).

THE CHANGING STEREOTYPES OF TRADITIONAL APPALACHIA CULTURE

On account of its "removed" geographical setting, some 30 years ago researchers assumed that rural Appalachia was previously a self-directed subculture essentially disconnected from mainstream America. Although traditional values such as "traditionalism, individualism, familism, and fundamentalism" once amply served rural Appalachia's isolated areas, they came to be considered no longer appropriate for modern-day living—the realities of which gradually spread across the region through urbanization and industrialization (Billings and Lewis, 1997).

The more traditional Appalachians had difficulties adjusting to the demands of change as long-established values started to wane in the shadow of economic development. The latter called for social and economic flexibility, a shift in emphasis to achievement, interdependency rather than individualism, and all-encompassing attention to organization rather than personalism. The region's traditional values were not aligned with the pace of progress in America; rather they were regarded as being shielded from change due not only to location but also a "psychological isolationism" that allowed for withdrawal into the "protective space of a 'culture of poverty'" (Billings and Lewis, 1997).

ENTREPRENEURSHIP AND ECONOMIC GROWTH IN APPALACHIA

Susan E. Keefe at the Department of Anthropology at Appalachian State University has compiled case studies collected by seasoned professionals to examine the culture of rural Appalachia and show how the region has worked against old stereotypes of poverty through social change, leadership, and better decision making. The scholars highlight the need for examination of cultural identity, community, and sustainability initiatives to promote citizen participation in the economic and social growth of Appalachia. These community-based case studies documents recent community rebuilding projects that have focused on economic development, cultural styles of political action, and "better connecting" schools (Keefe, 2009).

In a recent research study at the University of West Virginia (located in Morgantown, West Virginia, the location of the family business presented in this chapter) Mojica et al. (2009), determined the relationship between entrepreneurship and economic growth in the counties of West Virginia. This was accomplished by including entrepreneurship variables constructed from proprietorship and firm birth data into endogenous growth models. The model utilized measures of economic growth as endogenous variables including population growth, employment growth, and per capita income growth estimated individually. In addition to entrepreneurship, the model included other factors that are traditionally linked to economic growth (Mojica et al., 2009).

Results point to entrepreneurial activity contributing positively to economic growth, with counties that had more proprietors and business start-ups exhibiting higher levels of population growth. In addition, increased instances of proprietorship and higher employee numbers in businesses indicated a positive impact on growth of employment. The results also point to increased levels of entrepreneurship being positively related to positive economic growth in two relevant areas as measured by the study. The research highlights how significant it is to have an understanding of the role of entrepreneurship in analyzing determinants of economic growth and especially in areas that are tirelessly looking for improved strategies of spurring on economic development (Mojica et al., 2009).

This chapter outlines a father–daughter succession case in this unique American setting—the Appalachian Mountains of West Virginia. West Virginia offers an opportunity to examine family businesses embedded in the Appalachian culture—one where much of the popular and scholarly literature contend that deficiencies have contributed to, or reinforced, economic poverty and backwardness (Lewis and Billings, 1997). These ideals are now being challenged and this case offers evidence of reversal.

Brief History of the Firm

Since so few family businesses succeed to the next generation, succession planning is critical. In this chapter we will outline a father–daughter succession case, "MPE Rentals." MPE Rentals (located in Morgantown, West Virginia, USA) is a first and second generation family business. The father, Argyle, started the business in 1989. His daughter, Heather, has been spending time in the company since she was just eight days old. Over the years, she has learned the ins and outs of the business and is currently working toward taking over the company. MPE Rentals is now a full service rental store serving contractors, homeowners, and businesses. The company offers lift rentals, equipment rentals, events rentals (general event items, fun foods, party suppliers, costumes, games, tents, and accessories), parts, and new or used equipment sales.

MPE Rentals evolved in 1989, but Argyle, who started the company, did not begin his career in equipment rental. In 1963, when Argyle was in high school, his father relocated to West Virginia to find work in the coal mines. During this time, Argyle started working on cars to make additional money. While he was just in his 20s, he began sharing a property with a local electrician. They worked together for three years with Argyle fixing automobiles and learning the electrical business. Those skill sets eventually led to him fixing equipment for business owners. He began to purchase, resell, and rent equipment. Over time, he added on more equipment and purchased more property. When he outgrew his business location, he would build on to it. Eventually, he constructed several buildings including a shopping plaza, a mini warehouse, and some additional property behind where they are currently located.

The company today boasts dozens of employees and several departments; Lift, Equipment and Event rentals, Parts and Service, Equipment Sales and Storage. Heather, Argyle's daughter, is the vice president (VP) of MPE. She manages the operations and administrative sides of the company. Argyle likes to work with his hands and controls the heavy equipment and maintenance. Argyle's wife manages the party and event rental and takes care of payroll. Gary, Heather's husband, works on all the company's equipment and works in all departments. Even Heather's twins (a son and daughter, now 11 years old) work in the business during the summer.

The Succession Process

When Heather was very young, she was often brought to her parents' or aunt's workplace. She was encouraged to use her people skills to get along with employees and customers. She was often given tasks, such as copying, stapling, or bookkeeping, which would eventually enhance customer service. Since she was able to observe the effects of her actions on a day-to-day basis, she quickly learned solid people skills, and had far more business exposure and hands-on experience than her peers. Being in the business was so natural for her that when she was in junior high and high school, she preferred to spend her spare time in the office, learning and making money, rather than with friends.

The succession process for MPE Rentals is still in the planning phase. Argyle has recently hired professionals to work on a five-year succession plan. He wants to make sure that his future vision for the business stays intact. He doesn't want his business to be sold, and would like the employees to eventually have some ownership.

While Argyle has two children, a son and a daughter, it is the daughter who will be taking over the business. Since Argyle and his son have different philosophies about how the company should be run, Argyle set his son up in a separate, sign-making business. Therefore, the son has no part of MPE Rentals. As the current VP and daughter of Argyle, Heather knows the business inside and out. It has been known for a long time that Heather will take over the business. Therefore, accommodations have been made for that transfer to occur. About ten years ago, Heather set up a separate company called GH Enterprises. It is that company that continues to buy equipment to be rented. As equipment owned by MPE breaks or becomes outdated, GH replaces it. Over time, most or all of the equipment will eventually be owned by GH Enterprises and Heather and her husband will have full ownership of the company.

The Entrepreneur

When MPE Rentals first began, Heather's mother would carry out the financial and administrative activities. Even as early as just a couple weeks old, Heather was already being exposed to what went on in the company. Instead of paying a babysitter, Heather's mother would bring her into the office and work with Heather by her side. As Heather got older, she was given age-appropriate business tasks to accomplish. While growing up, Heather also spent time with her aunt, who owned a copy store. Heather was constantly being exposed to women in business, to business activities, and to adult business conversation. During junior high and high school, instead of going to play with her friends, Heather would spend time in the business making money. As she got older, she was given more significant tasks to perform so she could learn the inner workings of the company.

Heather's working relationship with her father has always been positive. When an older brother is absent from the business, the daughter has a greater succession opportunity (Iannarelli, 1992). Heather and Argyle clearly recognize each other's strengths and weaknesses and are able to work things out when each is in need. There are some employees who Argyle will get along with better, and some who will get along better with Heather. These personality differences allow each of them to see more sides of their employees. While Argyle's relationship with a particular employee may expose him to very positive aspects of their personality, Heather may be able to see other parts of the person's work ethic. Argyle's and Heather's views, together, give them a more balanced picture of what is actually going on in the company.

Argyle and Heather continue to work together to better the company. They have both been going to conferences and retreats that will help and prepare them for the next generation to continue the company. This doesn't mean just Heather, but also her children. Argyle continues to make the company better by searching for the missing components; reviewing the competition, learning about the needs of their current clients and, in some cases, adding on new equipment and services. Most importantly, they continue to study how and in which direction to grow the business.

While gender discrimination has not been an issue for Heather, gender stereotyping has. The business is a fairly male-dominated one, and as such, many of her customers expect to see a man behind the sales desk. When they approach and see a young woman, instead, some have treated her as if she didn't know anything about the business products. This never bothered her though. Heather stated that she would just let the customer speak to someone else. Her reaction is probably influenced by the fact that she was never treated any different in the business because of her gender. Both of her parents exposed her to as much of the business as possible without any regard to whether she was a man or a woman.

Heather's experiences growing up with MPE Rentals have developed her into a natural family business successor. She was often given opportunities to work with people, handle money, and, later, exhibit leadership skills. She had business exposure since she was just days old, and age-appropriate, hands-on experience as she grew older. Eventually, she made her formal entry into a career with MPE and was given more formal leadership opportunities. Her mother and father consistently provided her with continuity in the business and presented her with business problems and solutions—often over the dinner table. While growing up, Heather was also exposed to other entrepreneurs, including her aunt who ran a copy store. Once Heather formally entered into the business, Argyle made sure she had already created the appropriate networks of advisors and resources as a foundation upon which Heather could build her own entrepreneurial success.

Discussion and Conclusions

Leaders have been studied for decades (Bennis, 1985; Gardner, 1990; Kouzes and Posner, 1984). However, the socialization process of children as they become leaders in a family business setting is only just becoming a target of interest in entrepreneurial research. Children of entrepreneurs learn throughout their lifetimes as participant observers of their parent entrepreneurs, with varying degrees of knowledge transferred to them. This accumulation of knowledge may be learned vicariously such as over the dinner table or at family gatherings, or though actual experiences at the business. When children choose to work in the family business, to work for someone else, or to operate their own business, they draw from this well of accumulated knowledge to guide their choices and leadership styles. It is believed that children who grow up in a family business environment are more clearly provided with steps to encourage learning. As a result, it is posited that these children are more likely to have positive attitudes toward entrepreneurship, are more likely to go into a family business as adults, and are more likely to become more successful entrepreneurs or leaders (Iannarelli et al., 2005).

When daughters take over a business a different set of challenges are faced. The daughter may be entering a male-dominated industry that is difficult for a woman to penetrate. She may be confronted with gender discrimination or stereotyping, suggesting that she take on more female-oriented tasks. In one example, a father who owns a construction company into which a daughter had expressed an interest in entering, was heard saying "I'm scared to bring her into the company. I know she's qualified, but I just can't see my Dotty leading and giving orders. She's a good girl, and I know that no one in this business will listen to her" (Astrachan and Whiteside, 1990:47).

Quite often, it is the personal relationship between the father and daughter that is the most difficult to manage in a work setting. Boundaries must be set between personal and business issues. If disagreements occur, they must be worked out in a professional way. Some other major concerns that are important to consider when transferring the reins from father to daughter include ensuring that the daughter will continue the business at the same level that the father did, ensuring that the relationships with children who choose not to enter the family business remain intact, do not alienate employees when the daughter is promoted, and finally, learning when to have your way, when to let the daughter have her way, and when to keep fighting for an issue (Munn, 2009).

The family business, MPE Rentals, provides an interesting father–daughter succession example. While Heather and Argyle don't agree on everything, they work very well together. For instance, while Argyle would like to see some kind of stock sharing for employees in the future, Heather is not so convinced that is the right thing to do. However, for issues like stock sharing that do not immediately impact the company, she is willing to defer to her father. She knows that when she takes over, the major decisions will be hers to make.

Quite often, women face certain challenges when growing up in a family business, including gender discrimination and stereotyping. Research on women in family businesses often describe struggles women have with their fathers, with their brothers, with their mates, and particularly with themselves. These struggles center on their roles and identity within the family business. Females face a major obstacle right from the start in family business because fathers typically consider sons and not daughters to be the successors and the process of preparing daughters has been largely ignored (Dumas, 1990; Rosenblatt et al., 1985). Salganicoff (1990) reports that of nearly 100 women who attended family business workshops at The Wharton School of Business over a three-year period, only 27 percent planned to enter the family business and only 22 percent studied business in college.

Heather's situation is clearly different from those just described. She has been socialized into the business since she was a baby. While her brother may have received similar treatment, the differences in opinion he has had with Argyle have prevented him from entering the family business. In some families, the daughter may not even be considered a successor, especially in a male-dominated business. It is refreshing to see that, in MPE Rentals, Heather was never treated any different because she is a woman. She was socialized into the business just as anyone else would have been. She was taught all the aspects of the company and allowed to choose her expertise as her abilities evolved.

Limitations and Future Research

With an increasing trend of family enterprise management being passed on from one generation to another, there is a very real need for policymakers to ensure the ongoing support of entrepreneurial activity and thereby employee retention, attracting individuals to reside in Appalachian communities, and to step up the creation of new employment opportunities. This points to the need for programs that will assist entrepreneurs in growing their income; efforts in this area may include entrepreneur training and better access to capital loans. As communities in Appalachia seek out new strategies aimed at economic development there is now more than ever a pressing need to encourage start-ups and the building of healthy businesses practices.

Research tells us that personality measures have failed to be convincing predictors of entrepreneurial behavior. Although personality traits have been found to distinguish between entrepreneurs and other managers, these relationships have lacked predictive validity (Shaver and Scott, 1991). Studies investigating the role of personality traits in entrepreneurship have been inconclusive suggesting that we should focus more on variables that are more malleable—the life experiences that affect one's later cognitive maps as they relate to entrepreneurship—and especially those built through entrepreneurship education. The family business is an ongoing educational experience that children are exposed to from a very young age.

Future research on family business and issues of succession in the Appalachia region should focus on two factors, entrepreneurial education and community economic and sustainable development to promote family enterprise activities. Firstly, developmental research should longitudinally measure variables of entrepreneurship education in children of various ages. The goal of such studies is a child's exposure to the family business and to examine how their cognitions of entrepreneurship evolve. Ideally, longitudinal studies could track the same children over time and look at their entrepreneurial choices as adults (Iannarelli et al., 2006). Finally, it would be interesting to examine whether sons and daughters are exposed to different aspects of the model throughout their growth. Secondly, empirical evidence shows the need for policymakers to design the necessary programs to assist young entrepreneurs by creating a business environment where barriers for startup firms are controlled and where young entrepreneurship and firm growth is encouraged. Along with youth entrepreneurship, family business research issues such as succession should also focus on examining gender-based variables.

References

Astrachan, J.H. and Whiteside, M. 1990. She'll Always be my Little Sister. *Nation's Business*, 78(8), 47.

Bennis, B. 1985. On *Becoming a Leader.* Boston: Addison-Wesley Publishing.

Davis, P. and Stern, D. 1980. Adaptation, Survival and Growth of the Gamily business: An Integrated Systems Perspective. *Family Business Review*, 1(1), 66–86.

Dumas, C. 1990. Preparing the New CEO: Managing the Father–Daughter Succession Process in Family Business. *Family Business Review*, III(2), 169–183.

Gardner, J. 1990. *On Leadership*. New York: The Free Press.

Iannarelli, C. 1992. *The Socialization of Leaders in Family Business: A Study of Gender*, Unpublished dissertation.

Iannarelli, D., Iannarelli, C. and Mischel, L. 2006. Widows at the Helm of the Family Business: Organizational Performance Following Death of a Spouse. *Business Journal for Entrepreneurs*, 1.

Keefe, S.E. 2009. *Participatory Development in Appalachia; Cultural Identity, Community, and Sustainability.* Tennessee: University of Tennessee Press.

Kouzes, J. and Posner, B. 1984. *The Leadership Challenge*. San Francisco: Jossey-Bass.

Lank, A. and Thomassen, A. 1991. Introducing the Family Business Network. *Family Business Review*, IV(2), 225–231.

Lewis, R. and Billings, D. 1997. Appalachian Culture and Economic Development. *Journal of Appalachian Studies*, 3(1), 43–69.

Mojica, M.N, Gebremedhin, T.G. and Schaeffer, P.V. 2009. An Empirical Analysis of the Link between Entrepreneurship and Economic Growth in West Virginia. *IUP Journal of Entrepreneurship Development*, 6(3–4), 39–53.

Munn, K. 2009. Succession Planning in Family Businesses: Families Must Manage Conflict in Transferring Ownership. *The Lawyers Weekly*, September 19.

Rosenblatt, P., Mik, L., Anderson, R. and Johnson, P. 1985. *The Family in Business*. San Francisco: Jossey Bass.

Salganicoff, M. 1990. Women in Family Business: Challenges and Opportunities. *Family Business Review*, III(2), 135–139.

Shaver K. and Scott, L. 1991. The Psychology of New Venture Creation. *Entrepreneurship Theory & Practice*, 16(2), 23–45.

Ward, J. 1987. *Keeping the Family Business Healthy*. San Francisco: Jossey Bass.

The authors wish to thank the contributions of the following colleagues to the development of this chapter: Profs. Miroslav Pivoda and Joe Aniello, and graduate assistant Kandi Conda.

PART VI South America

CHAPTER 23 Brazil: The Course of Father–Daughter Succession in a Brazilian Family Business

CELINA SMITH AND ROSAMOND TOMPKINS

While little is known about father–daughter succession around the globe, even less is understood about its impact on family life. What happens, for example, when more than one daughter considers herself the rightful heir to succession, when a father views a daughter as a potential rival, when family life and business become intertwined, or when such businesses are highly dominated by a strong controlling father–owner? In this chapter, we shine a light on such hidden issues to reveal a process fraught with rivalries, tensions, and pressures that can threaten to disrupt the very fabric of family life itself. We focus on the case of a potential father–daughter succession in a highly industrial male-dominated sector in Brazil to understand how such issues are played out.

Introduction and Literature Review

The Brazilian landscape is dotted with family-owned businesses. Until the 1960s, the formation of these businesses followed along strong ethnic lines and were in concert with waves of immigration that flowed into the country (Mello, 2006). For women, the development of family-owned firms coincided with a truncated role, they were subordinate to men at home, and largely unable to take up outside employment without their husband's approval (Jones, 2000; Olivas-Lujan et al., 2009). Today, family-owned businesses dominate; some 70 percent of the largest companies and almost all small and medium-size businesses are family controlled (Mello, 2006; Viegas, 2006). Most of these are in the hands of the second generation of family members, however 20 centennial companies are in their fourth and fifth generation of family ownership (Mello, 2000). Together, they account for 10 percent of agribusiness, 30 percent of industry, 60 percent of services, and employ 78 percent of the labor force (Mello, 2006).

Female involvement in the wider economy has also made an impressive impact. In 2007, female entrepreneurship in Brazil was ranked as the tenth most active in the world (Xeyla, 2007). By 2003 their participation in the labor market rose to 46 percent, and they have now overtaken men in their completion rates of university degrees. However, these statistics mask a more complex fate for women in wider Brazilian society. Despite these achievements, their contributions are not always rewarded with salaries commensurate with men or with the attainment of leadership positions. In the private sector, women hold 21 percent of management positions (Santos, 2006) and represent just 21 percent of the legal profession. Even these small gains however are not enjoyed by women across the board; rather they are "often confined to women of the upper classes" (World Trade Press, undated). Women in family-owned firms fare little better as they are largely subordinate to their male counterparts (Barbieri, 1997; Curimbaba, 2002; Durand, 1984). Overall, there is insufficient research on the fate of female successors once they are in family businesses, and what happens when there is more than one daughter in contention for succession. Further, under what circumstances sons are passed over for daughters, and how daughters can manage future success in light of domineering father–owners remains unclear. This chapter addresses these issues in the following sections.

Family Ownership, National Culture and Legal Status

Brazil can be viewed as a land of contrasts. Colonized by the Portuguese in the fifteenth century, it is today ethnically diverse, yet "contemporary Brazilians ... share a common culture" (EveryCulture.com, 2010). In general, there is a respect in Brazilian society for the hierarchy embedded in social relationships with family as the center of identity and loyalty (The Economist, 2008).

As major providers of employment in the country, family business owners have historically viewed their role as protector both of their own families and their employees. This lingering paternalism (Mello, 2006; Rodrigues, 1991), also reflected in the wider society surrounding them, resulted in slow developments in women's legal status. While the right to vote was acquired in 1932, other legal rights for women have lagged behind; for example it was not until the passage of the Brazilian Federal Constitution of 1988 that married women were given equal status to their husbands.

Father–Daughter Succession in Family-owned Businesses

There is little documentation of daughters succeeding fathers in Brazil's family firms among English sources. Some of what is known is anecdotal, for example, in 1977 the head of the Matarazzo family died, skipping over four sons to choose his youngest child and only daughter as the controlling owner (Vidigal, 1990). An early study of family-controlled Brazilian textile companies (Durand, 1984) found neither daughters, daughters-in-law, nor wives held managerial positions in their family companies unless there were no sons, including sons-in-law, to fill them. Durand noted the trend to only include women if the business targeted a female clientele, such as the fashion industry, where their participation might be a business asset.

A more recent study of daughters' participation in family firms (Curimbaba, 2002) chronicles the experience of 12 female family heiresses in three Brazilian states. Again, women's opportunities as successors seemed largely determined by the presence of males within the immediate and extended family, that is, the more men, the less opportunity for women.

Brazilian family businesses are influenced by a national culture that respects traditional notions of hierarchy, including paternalistic caretaking, a preference for male successors, and respect for the "exalted" role of women as the center of the home. But women's expanded participation in the body politic through university degrees, entrepreneurial ventures, and professional pursuits is pushing this traditional view in new directions. As the number of households headed by women has increased, so too has their need for incorporation as mainstream economic contributors. According to the 2004 Global Entrepreneurship Monitor, women run some 46 percent of small manufacturing and retail establishments (World Trade Press, undated). In the following sections we present the case of one potential daughter–successor who has come face-to-face with the country's culture, traditions, and dominating father–owner in a historically male-dominated industry.

The Case Study

THE FAMILY BUSINESS

Starting out with few resources, the father–owner in this case study has built a successful near billion dollar operation in industrial operations, one of the biggest in its field in the country. The business was started in the 1950s by an ambitious and impoverished young man, with investment support from his father in a region close to the capital Sao Paolo. The business initially was split 50:50 between the two men but when the father passed away, a majority of the shares passed to the son and initial founder. A further turning point came when the company bought a neighboring industrial plant in 1965, extending the businesses focus from one purely based on its core operation to the development of further spin-off products.

Today the company owns three plants in Brazil, has interests in North America, and employs more than 2,000 people including many of the founder's extended family. From its relatively simple beginnings the business has evolved into a complex, highly sophisticated, industrialized operation, outgrowing the initial skills of its founder. However, these skills have been supplemented over the years by a professional management team.

At the helm of this vast and growing industrial empire is a father–owner who has maintained a pervasive influence on his business for more than 60 years. His continuing influence on the company, despite the existence of other shareholders, is testament to a powerful and dominating personality. As one daughter puts it: "My father was always controller of everything ... the president ... he is the kind of personality that ... he's very dominant ... he's the big boss and is not very interested in losing power in the company."

This dominating control of the business has had a significant impact on many aspects of the family's own development and involvement in the business.

SUCCESSION CONTENDERS

One marriage and four children later, the founding owner–father has reached 87 years of age, and the issue of succession has become a hot family topic. First in line, as she sees it, is his second eldest daughter Marina, whom we have renamed to preserve the family's anonymity. Marina is the second of three daughters, all of whom are older than the only son. The youngest daughter passed away leaving the two eldest daughters in line for succession. Marina, now 55 years old and a member of the board is the key focus of this study.

Marina has worked in her father's company for most of her working life. She believes that she was her father's first choice for succession, as she says: "My father said 'she's going to be my successor', this was the initial plan." One reason for this is that she seemed to excel early, rising to the top of her class in school. This led to a degree in chemical engineering and a business education in two of the best schools in Sao Paulo, as she notes: "I went to study business ... in a very important school, one of the best business schools in Sao Paulo, which is why I think he wanted me to be his successor." This was to prove invaluable to her father's business. To underline the idea that despite being the second born child that she was indeed earmarked for succession in a way her siblings were not, Marina notes her siblings were allowed to follow their own careers and aspirations:

> *My sister, who's one year older than me, was not brought to the business at first as she followed another career path and had different plans ... she decided to go into physics, then got married, went to work in the business, but I think she was not the elected [one] because she had her own plans, and I had accepted the job in the family business because we are a family with three girls and one boy, and my brother is 5 years younger than me ... so I was elected ... or at least accepted the challenge.*

The reference to her brother being the youngest indicates that this was a special family position that absolved him from the duties of succession, although it seems this went too far:

> *Since my sister and I were older, we were very responsible, went to the university very young, and could answer to the demands of the family business in a certain way. My brother and younger sister were educated in a different way, they were not demanded of as we were. They had everything that they wanted, it was a problem. In fact my brother never found a job in his life, to be honest, he was spoiled.*

It appears that Marina's brother has not been targeted or groomed for succession. He seems to have been passed over and liberated from the constraints of succession. This is at odds with research in Brazil and in the wider literature that indicates primogeniture is the norm in family firms (Durand, 1984; Haberman and Danes, 2007; Hollander and Bukowitz, 1990; Keating and Little, 1997). Marina provides an additional explanation, she believes that the age gap of five and seven years between her brother and his two sisters, coupled with the fact that there were more daughters than sons making this a predominantly female household, was the decisive factor. As she says, "He was a minority in this family."

Today many highly educated women are taking their place in the wider Brazilian economy. The daughters in Marina's family themselves received a very good education; further, the family's increasing wealth may have meant that they did not have to stay at home to sustain the family. Finally, family businesses may be a good environment for women as it allows them flexibility in having and maintaining their own families. Marina alludes to this point when she states:

It's easier to be in the family business, I think for me it was important, because I had to be next to my son, to be flexible with my time with my son and the business, I never stopped work to be at home to have babies and so on.

In these excerpts, Marina places emphasis on earning the right to be first in line, and on the importance of duty. This infers that she herself had to make a sacrifice by not following her own professional ambitions. Instead she entered engineering, a typically male-dominated degree because, as she says, "My father wanted me to go." It appears that, for Marina, succession was very much a last option in the absence of opportunities allowing her to pursue her own ambitions. Her sister, it would seem, was not groomed for succession and did not enter the company until much later.

However, Marina's initial selection as first in line for succession appears to have changed. Following a quarrel with her father about the way the business was run. Marina left the company for the United States (US) where she completed a master's degree, this time in a social science. Two years later she returned to the fold when her father invited her back and made key concessions, agreeing to a new company structure. This has involved creating a holding company, clearing out some of the family members from the staff, and creating new internal structures.

When I came I decided to change things; in fact my ideas after the master's were important, because my father accepted the ideas, it was my contribution to the business. We created the board with shareholders, the family office, the two holding companies, and on the other hand we started the succession as a process, not as a single act, creating a corporate level.

This initial success, however, was to store future problems in relation to succession for Marina.

FAMILY PLANNING: SUCCESSION

With an ageing father–owner, numerous attempts have been made at planning for succession; most of which have been resisted. Despite advancing age, Marina's father has thwarted attempts for him to cede control to another family member.

When we started to try to do a succession plan, he could follow the first steps, but the last step, that is to create a structure that would rather place him in the board position and a little bit less in the business it wasn't a situation that fit to him, because he's an entrepreneur, and wants to be in the business.

Marina, however, has tried to get around this by using shareholders' power in the family holding company, of which she is an 11 percent shareholder, with a view to, as she says, "create a structure for succession." Combined with the voting power of other family shareholders she has been able to effect some change. Other authors have noted the practice of using outsiders as a bridge to succession (Rawls, 2004). Her father's continuing resistance to succession planning has led to Marina's conclusion that it won't happen "while he is still alive." However, if they do not plan ahead, this could engender great turbulence for the family and the business. Following a return to the business, Marina has taken a leading role in trying to facilitate some succession planning: "I think it's my position in the board to convince the president to change." She has felt more confident and emboldened in this process following her return in contrast with other family members who have felt less able to challenge her father.

BATTLES FOR SUCCESSION

Notwithstanding attempts to plan ahead, the two key candidates in line for succession are Marina and her elder sister Ana, also now a board member. While Ana had previously shown little interest in the family business, all that has changed, she is now very much in contention:

> *There are only two persons that can be successors for president of the board in this company, me and my sister. My father said that I would be the one to succeed ... at the beginning she claimed that she didn't want to be the president of the board but that she wanted to be the first position in one company, and then we started to have problems.*

As a short-term solution the family has started to develop a strategic plan which would see the sisters rotating between different positions within the business, and sharing future responsibilities. Marina recognizes that her sister has an important contribution to make to the business and is keen to find an arrangement that keeps them both happy:

> *We decided to share the areas, my sister is responsible for markets and product development, and I'm responsible for all the finance and legal issues, but we have to share these positions every two years if we want. If we don't want we can continue as we are. It's a good solution for a succession to be shared with two people that are in the same level of responsibility, same number of shares, we are comfortable with this position.*

While this has served as a temporary solution, Marina believes that the only way to avoid divisive conflict in the future as to who should succeed their father, is for both daughters to be passed over in favor of a third outside party appointed as CEO, at least initially.

> *... the first member of the board in the years following my father's passing away, I don't think should be anyone of us. We have an external board member since 2003, and we need someone that comes from outside to give weight to the board and the meetings. I don't think it's easy to give succession following my father's strong personality, and it would be too much conflict to take over such a position, which is why I don't want to take over this position.*

This strategy is in keeping with suggestions that a succession bridge may be an effective way forward (Rawls, 2004). Ironically, it now seems that the time for succession for these two sisters may have passed. Marina concedes it may be "too late," adding, "... this succession would have to have happened ten years ago. He would have to be in this position when we first started working with external members in 1995, which is when my father and I had the quarrel."

FATHER–DAUGHTER RIVALRY

The father–owner in this case appears to have played a key role in the turmoil that has resulted in the delay and lack of certainty that has surrounded succession. His dominating and controlling personality has had a profound influence on the current state of affairs, by his unwillingness to cede control to other family members (Barach and Ganitsky, 1995; Lansberg, 1988).

However, an additional explanation may lie not only in his desire to retain control but also in his perception of his daughter Marina as a rival. In educating and grooming his daughter it appears that the father–owner may have contributed to the development of an independent professional with strong and different ideas to his own. Coupled with his own lack of education, the father may have a sense of insecurity in relation to his own daughters. Marina goes as far as to suggest he is threatened:

> *... when the situation was showing that I was prepared, that I had good ideas, that I had leadership for the company, he was afraid of this, in fact he was very jealous, and sometimes we had to deal with my father with a lot of care, because if he turned out to be not taken in consideration as the most important idea, the most important person, the best, it would be very difficult ... although he had good ideas, he was not the only one.*

She is also one of few people who it seems has been strong enough and prepared to stand up to him. "He is very hard, very difficult to open to other opinions, but I learnt to deal with him, and I am not frightened with him going against a project." This may have contributed to Marina's breach with her father and subsequent departure from the company, which may have been a key turning point in their relationship. To heal the rift and encourage her return, Marina's father made significant concessions, but all talk of her becoming a successor seems to have faded after this point. This may be because he realized that his daughter had ideas of her own and was willing to fight to achieve them.

FAMILY VERSUS BUSINESS

The impact of the business on this family has been far reaching. It has encroached on family life, blurring the boundaries between work and home. In fact the business has so dominated family life that the family can barely relate to each other in its absence. Marina herself says "the family side suffers," and recalls that prior attempts by her mother to separate the two have largely failed: "My mother doesn't want us to talk about business with my father when we meet for dinner. So we didn't have anything to talk about, what keep us together was the business! So we don't have dinners!"

Even for the two sisters, forging a relationship outside the business has been difficult. When they meet socially, business tends to intrude, so in order to mitigate this and reduce the potential for conflict Marina tries to "restrain contact" and adds:

> *I have to be very careful with the situation, because she tries to pressure me sometimes, the personal relationships suffer a lot I think ... I prefer not to talk too much about the business when [we] meet outside the company ... nevertheless we have a good friendship in general since we suffer together the same difficulties.*

The daughters' relationship with their mother also has been tested as a result of the family business. It seems that with no direct role to play in the business, the mother has suffered some marginalization and alienation, and in turn appears to place very little value on the work that her daughters do inside the company. The following excerpt from Marina emphasizes this:

> *... my mother doesn't give value to me and my sister, she's always competing for attention, for ideas with my father, and she tries to devaluate what we do ... once she went to our offices in Sao Paulo, and she arrived there, and said "Oh, but you work in fact!," she thought that we were in a decorative position, and because we have a flexible agenda, people think we don't work! When we have a position like this in a firm, the recognition from outside is very difficult, even from inside, my mother never recognizes anything, she can't recognize. I don't wait for recognition anymore. But I think that our family union is not good.*

Born in a more traditional era, Marina's mother has witnessed dramatic changes in notions about family life. This clash between the old and the new manifests itself nowhere more clearly than when she decides to visit the offices:

> *My mother used to come to the holding offices in the afternoon trying to bring cakes to our secretaries, to disturb the job, to interrupt the meetings with ten people! My sister once had a very important meeting with people from the US, and said "I don't know what to do if my mother arrives in the middle of the meeting!" and I said that "if she comes and opens the door you have to say that the meeting is interrupted for five minutes, let's take a coffee, and take my mother away!"*

These incidents reveal a mother who may have been marginalized in relation to the business and who now seeks to carve out a role for herself; such behavior has also been noted by Dumas (1992). However, there may be another explanation for this behavior. As Marina's mother has a 20 percent holding in the business it is possible that her actions are instead an expression of owner power. This point is made by Marina who explains that her mother may feel that this power supersedes "professionalism" and gives her "the right to interrupt" day-to-day business proceedings.

Despite this interpretation, there are indications that Marina's mother has been sidelined by her husband in favor of his business. One result of this is that Marina believes she may now view her two daughters as potential rivals for his affections. She suggests that this may explain why her mother may have been less supportive of them as potential successors than she may have been of her son, as she states:

> *The competition is much more with her and her ability, her importance to my father and to the family. It's because we are daughters, this I am absolutely sure. Maybe my mother would give support, energy, and everything to the son.*

Such family pressures have taken their toll leaving it in a "dysfunctional" state. Consequently, Marina has paid a high emotional price needing psychoanalytical support to cope with the pressures of being part of a family-business family and for having to forsake her own personal and professional aspirations to support the firm.

> *I wasn't prepared, because I needed a lot of psychoanalysis to deal with the situation with the conflicts, with the idea of not doing my own project, my own desires.*

Discussion and Conclusion

It is clear from the data in this case that two forces have combined to shape the lives and the succession outcomes for this family—the paternalism of a bygone age (Rodrigues, 1991; Mello, 2006) and respect for family hierarchy. These manifest themselves in an overarching and dominating father–owner, and a strong sense of duty and obligation. Together, they conspire to shape the actions of the two daughters potentially in line for succession. Despite a changing and more liberal wider society, these two forces continue to maintain a grip at the family level and highlight the tensions that can exist when different generations in the same family are exposed to different values and opportunities for education. Marina's experience is consistent with research that indicates founding entrepreneurs are reluctant to let go of their business (Barach and Ganitsky, 1995; Lansberg, 1988). This reluctance is described as the "single most cited obstacle to effective succession" (Le Breton-Miller et al., 2004).

While their opportunities for advancement may be tied up with the demands of key familial male figures (Curimbaba, 2002), there are indications in this case that women can act to reshape existing norms as when Marina left the business only to rejoin under new terms creating a new business structure.

Implications, Limitations, and Future Research

The implications of this research are that emphasis in family-owned businesses should be placed on grooming a successor and planning for transition. Our contribution to the father–daughter succession literature is in highlighting how deeply tensions within families can run when women are in line for succession, how a dominating father–owner can continue to shape succession to the detriment of daughters even after control is ceded, and how a desire to maintain family harmony can lead to deep personal and professional sacrifices for potential daughter–successors.

While our work makes clear contributions there are limitations, chief among these are its methodology focusing on one case. However, as this study is aimed at developing theory in a new and contemporary area, one case can provide a suitable framework for this research (Yin, 1994). We suggest future work could focus on understanding how succession is resolved when there is more than one daughter contender, and on the role and effectiveness of succession bridges, and how daughters can deal with dominating father–owners.

References

Barach, J.A. and Ganitsky, J.B. 1995. Successful Succession in Family Business. *Family Business Review*, 8(2), 131–155.

Barbieri, E. 1997. *A Batalha das Herdeiras na Empresa Familiar*. Porto Alegre Brazil: Sagra-D.C. Luzzatto.

Curimbaba, F. 2002. The Dynamics of Women's Roles as Family Business Managers. *Family Business Review*, 15(3), 239–252.

Dumas, C. 1992. Integrating the Daughter into Family Business Management. *Entrepreneurship, Theory & Practice* (Summer), 41–55.

Durand, J.C.G. 1984. Acesso a Propriedade, Familia e Heranca (Formacao e Reproducao da Pequena Burguesia Textil em Sao Paulo). *Revista de Administracao de Empresas*, 24(4), 107–112.

EveryCulture.com. 2010. *Brazil*. Advameg, Inc. Available at: http://www.everyculture.com/Bo-Co/Brazil [accessed: 13 July 2010].

Haberman, H. and Danes, S.M. 2007. Father–Daughter and Father–Son Family Business Management Transfer Comparison: Family FIRO Model Application. *Family Business Review*, 20(2), 163–184.

Hollander, B.S. and Bukowitz, W.R. 1990. Women, Family Culture and Family Business. *Family Business Review*, 3(2), 139–151.

Jones, K. 2000. Psychodynamics, Gender, and Reactionary Entrepreneurship in Metropolitan Sao Paulo, Brazil. *Women in Management Review*, 15(4), 207–220.

Keating, N.C. and Little, H.M. 1997. Choosing the Successor in New Zealand Family Farms. *Family Business Review*, 10(2), 157–171.

Lansberg, I.E.P. 1988. The Succession Conspiracy. *Family Business Review*, 1(2), 119–143.

Lansberg, I.E.P. 1991. Understanding and Working with Leading Family Businesses in Latin America. *Family Business Review*, 4(2), 127–147.

Le Breton Miller, I., Miller, D. and Steier, L.P. 2004, Toward an Integrative Model of Effective Family Owned Business Succession. *Entrepreneurship, Theory & Practice*, 28(4), 305–328.

Mello, D.N.D. 2000. *An Abridged History of Family Business in Brazil*. Available at: http://www.empresafamiliar.org.br/artigos/an_abridged_history.htm [accessed: 29 April 2010].

Mello, D.N.D. 2006. Brazil, in *Handbook of Family Businesses and Family Business Consultation: A Global Perspective* (pp. 115–132), edited by F.W. Kaslow. Binghamton: The Haworth Press, Inc.

Olivas-Lujan, M.R., Monserrat, S.I., Ruiz-Gutierrez, J.A., Greenwood, R.A., Gomez, S.M., Murphy, J. and Santos, N.M. 2009. Values and Attitudes Towards Women in Argentina, Brazil, Colombia, and Mexico. *Employee Relations*, 31(3), 227–244.

Rawls, L.H. 2004. *The Succession Bridge*. Fairfield: The Family Business Resource Center.

Rodrigues, A.M. 1991. Padroes Afetivos na Familia e Empresa Familiar. *Revista de Administracao de Empresas RAE/FGV*, 31(4), 35–48.

Santos, N.M. 2006. Successful Women: A Vision of Brazil, in *Successful Professional Women of the Americas: From Polar Winds to Tropical Breezes* (pp. 183–194), edited by B.J. Punnett, J.A. Duffy, S. Fox, A. Gregory, T.R. Lituchy, S.I. Monserrat, M.R. Olivas-Lujan and N.M.B.F. Santos. Cheltenham: Edward Elgar.

The Economist. 2008. The Americas: Betting the Fazenda; Entrepreneurs in Brazil. *The Economist*, 386, 68.

Vidigal. 1990. *Family Business in Brazil*. Available at: http://www.acvidigal.com.br/English/engacv/articles/engart6.htm [accessed: 29 April 2010].

Viegas, L. 2006. Brazil: Corporate Governance—Challenges and Opportunities, in *Corporate Governance of Non-listed Companies in Emerging Markets* (pp. 133–137). Paris: OECD Publishing.

World Trade Press. (undated). *Women in Culture, Business, and Travel: Brazil (1993—2008)*. World Trade Press. Available at: http://www.WorldTradePress.com [accessed: 29 April 2010].

Xeyla, R. 2007. Brazil Women Beat French and Swedish Colleagues in Entrepreneurship. *BrazzilMag.com*. Available at: http://www.brazzilmag.com/component/content/article/47/8174-brazil-women-beat-french-and-swedish-colleagues-in-entrepreneurship.html [accessed: 19 July 2010].

Yin, R.K. 2003. *Case Study Research* (3rd Edition). Thousand Oaks, Sage Publications.

CHAPTER 24 Brazil: The Challenge of Female Successors in a Brazilian Family Business: A Case Study

HILKA VIER MACHADO

Introduction

Family-controlled companies are the main source of private property in several industrial sectors in Latin America (Gersick et al., 2006). According to the International Family Enterprise Research Academy (2003), family companies in Brazil comprised more than 90 percent of private companies and produced 65 percent of the gross national product in 2003. For the first time, according to data published in the 2009 Global Entrepreneurship report (Brazilian Institute for Quality and Productivity, 2010), there are currently more female (53.4 percent) than male (46.6 percent) entrepreneurs starting companies through opportunity.[1]

Researchers have placed less emphasis on studies related to female entrepreneurs. Increasing the recognition of female participation in business is one of the priorities of the Ministry of Women's Affairs, established in 2003. Its key objectives are the promotion of women's role in the economy and supporting their financial autonomy through entrepreneurship, and developing policies to facilitate this (Ministry of Women's Affairs, 2008). Nevertheless, women's participation in business is barely acknowledged in established firms, especially in relation to female succession in family business. Evidence suggests that some family companies have had to shut down because their female members were not prepared as successors, however scant research has been carried out in this area.

This chapter focuses on the case of a father–daughter succession in Brazil to shed more light on what is a relatively hidden and under-researched phenomenon in this country.

1 The Global Entrepreneurship Report classifies entrepreneurs into two groups: those who become entrepreneurs by necessity—when they do not have any other employment option, and those who become entrepreneurs by opportunity—when they start a business because they perceive an opportunity and they want to take advantage of it.

Literature Review

Although succession in family business is a well-researched area, scarcely any investigation has been conducted on the needs of women in this process. In general, the choice of successor in Brazilian family companies is considered to be "a male issue" (Rodrigues, 1991:37). Further, there is evidence to indicate that many women may be excluded from succession opportunities in parts of Brazil, and that this may have a regional dimension.

Studies on southern Brazil investigated the visibility of women in rural family companies and showed that succession is still the privilege of male heirs (Deere and León, 2002; Morganti and Barbieri, 1997; Spanevello, 2008). In the central region of Brazil, Macedo et al. (2004) contend that women have been excluded from family business succession processes, while in São Paulo there are suggestions that Brazilian families of Italian origin have the "habit of not allowing daughters to become partners in their companies" (Vidigal, 2000:68). Low visibility and autonomy have also been reported in cases of daughter succession in urban companies (Machado, 2008).Women are also frequently prevented from inheriting land, and while they may receive some compensation, generally financial, usually this is not equivalent in value with that received by their male counterparts.

Although little is known about daughter–successors, Curinmbaba (2002:247) suggests that there are three types of female successors in Brazilian companies, namely, "the professionals," "the invisibles," and "the anchors." The first type interacts professionally, distinguishes the company from the family and constantly seeks merit and competence. The "invisible" females come from families with a large number of male descendants and are unprepared for succession. As a result, they enter and leave the company when they wish, without any great commitment. The "anchor" females come from families with a predominant number of women who are essential for the continuation of the business. They usually go through some form of preparation, which assures them autonomy and responsibility. In the following case study, based on a study of father–daughter succession in a company featuring male and female successors, the aim is to understand how women fare when they compete with male heirs.

The Case Study

In the current study the name of the company has been changed to "Roma" to protect its identity and the names of key interviewees. Roma was selected for the current research for three reasons: 1) the company achieved significant growth during its 50 years of establishment and holds a leading position in its sector within the Brazilian market; 2) the company was going through a succession process involving both male and female successors; 3) it operates in a sector in which males are traditionally predominant.

The business, established in the 1960s, specializes in the electrical sector, with special emphasis on telephone infrastructure (equipment and materials that make up telephone systems). It is a large enterprise employing approximately 1,100 people and manufacturing more than 3,000 different products. It has production plants in several states (Paraná, São Paulo, Mato Grosso do Sul, and Rio de Janeiro), commercial representatives throughout the country, and exports its products to Africa, India, and the Middle East. In addition to achieving awards for the quality of its products, the company has received national awards for social responsibility and for its good working conditions.

THE ENTREPRENEURS

The company at the center of this study was established by two brothers; Marcos was 20 years old and his brother Bruno was ten. Despite Bruno's young age, Marcos explains that Bruno nevertheless was a valuable contribution, as he recalls: "He was 10 years old and could help me. He did the electrical work, mounted the hydro ... hydraulics ... those things. Then we began a small company. It was run in a simple kitchen; we had a 4 by 6 meter space." Today, Marcos is credited with the entrepreneurial and business vision, while Bruno, his younger brother, has acquired the managerial abilities. The friendship between the two brothers and their complementary competences have led to five successful decades in business. However, this success is in stark contrast to the limited resources with which they first started the venture, according to Marcos:

> *We had a small office. We built a telephone, which at that time was a rarity, and began to manufacture little things. And, in just a short time—in two or three years—we had a few assets, which allowed us to buy things. I bought a small house, since I was living in a rented one, and he lived in our mother's house. And we began to support our mother. When Bruno was 18 years old, we had enough money to buy a house for him too.*

This excerpt indicates that the relationship between company and family was both close and strong, with the company also playing a role in helping to support the brothers' extended family. A sense of family was further strengthened when Bruno married the niece of Marcos's wife and became in effect both brother and nephew-in-law to Marcos. As the company consolidated, the wives, who were both seamstresses, gave up working, and the social life of the two families' became further integrated as birthdays and other events were celebrated on company's premises.

THE SUCCESSION PROCESS

When the founder–brothers decided to retire at the ages of 77 and 67 in 2008, a succession process was planned with the support of an external consultant. Each of the two founders chose two successors from among their children. As they had only one son each, they were considered "natural" candidates for succession, a phenomenon also noted by St-Cyr and Inoussa (2000:6). Nevertheless, in this case, two daughters, one from each family, were also considered potential candidates by the joint father–owners.

After agreement on the successor shortlist, a plan covering activities such as courses, seminars, and visits to other companies, was begun to prepare each candidate. According to Dyck et al. (2002), it is important to decide when the process will begin, how long it will take, and how the baton will be passed on. In this case, a shared vision of the transition (Le Breton-Miller et al., 2004) has developed between the founders, who have not yet permanently retired. They continue to be involved in key areas of the process, for example they transformed factory units into a holding company, and have sought to centralize decision-making processes by creating an administrative council made up of themselves and their potential successors.

HIERARCHICAL POSITIONS WITHIN THE COMPANY

As part of the succession process, the male successors were assigned positions respectively as directors of finance and production, while the females were assigned roles below this level, as managers. Laura, Marcos's daughter, originally the HR manager, was transferred to social projects and institutional marketing management by the founders, even though her interests lay in another area. A similar story was narrated by Laura's cousin and Bruno's daughter, Louise, who began as the financial manager but later became HR manager, as she explains this was not an area that she would have chosen for herself:

> *I really like the area of personnel development, which is an area where I ended up developing many things. But an area that I would have really liked to work in was the exports area—to have contact with other clients, visit other countries, and get to know other cultures.*

Louise's comments also show the lack of choice the women had in deciding where they would work in the company, she further notes: "Here we do not get much choice; you accept the opportunities as they present themselves." Both Laura and Louise have degrees in Business Administration and have also done postgraduate studies in this area. However, in spite of their competence, Louise believed that career outcomes were different for the potential male successors, as she says, "For the males, careers were much faster," even though, in the case of Laura, her brother was younger and less experienced in business administration.

The challenges faced by the female successors were not restricted to their lack of choice about managerial areas of responsibility. Another issue was the lack of free time due to their intense workload. Laura remarks:

> *Today, for me, the demands on us are much greater than for a regular employee ... so I ended up overloading myself. I am covering almost four areas, and currently the area that is most difficult for me is really the area of personnel development and work safety, because I work under a lot of stress the whole time.*

Further, what free time there is can be interrupted by the demands of work at any time, as Laura further commented:

> *I don't have weekends off; they call me at any time on my mobile phone. If there is an accident I have to drop whatever I am doing. So this is very stressful. I am on call 24 hours a day, because there are 1,100 people, so there is a big risk of accidents.*

VISIBILITY OF FEMALE SUCCESSORS

External visibility, along with internal and external credibility, is an important aspect of the succession process (Cadieux et al., 2000; Lee et al., 2000). In the present case, however, the founders seemed to regard this as a low priority for female successors, whose visibility is restricted to the firm's internal environment. Unlike their male successors, who are members of an association for successors of family companies, they do not participate in external networks. Furthermore, they do not take part in client or supplier negotiations since such activities are handled by the directors. For Laura, this is yet another area where her choice has been restricted, as she says, if "I had to choose, I would work in the export area." By not having exposure outside the company the female successors are less able to develop their networks or to develop key skills that could enhance the chances of successful succession.

The chance to raise their external and internal visibility was further hampered by family commitments; this was especially the case once they had children as they required additional attention when they were young. Family life also impacted upon the execution of their managerial duties, Louise, for example, recounts some of the difficulties: "I went through a period of not being able to go on trips very much, because I was going through a period of separation, with small children, and my personal life interfered a bit." Even though they are successors, no concessions are made to family life and there is no flexibility in their working hours. As a consequence this is more likely to lead to disadvantage for female successors with families in relation to their male counterparts.

In addition to conflicts between work and family life, the female successors also had to cope with the effects of having dual roles in the same company. These dual roles made it difficult for the women not only to establish their professional identities but also to manage the limits of each role. Laura explains, for example, that she occupied positions of both manager at a supervisory position, and administrative advisor at an executive position. The latter implied a strategic and decision-making role, which created tensions in interpreting her role:

> *Actually, I wear two badges. I am a manager, which is one specific position, and I also hold a position on the Administrative Council. So, in the HR department I need to make strategic decisions, but as a successor I can also participate in any meeting ... and they also interpret my position differently, depending on the meeting I am in. There are times when you do not agree and want to stand as a successor, but it cannot be done. Your vote does not have any weight. You have to know which badge you are wearing at that moment.*

As a manager there are restrictions on the amount of decision-making power that Laura may wield, but when acting as an advisor at executive level, she has a much greater say. These differences can make it difficult for successors to reconcile their role in a company and their professional identities (Dubar, 1996).

THE RELATIONSHIP BETWEEN THE FOUNDERS AND THEIR FEMALE SUCCESSORS

Notwithstanding the day-to-day difficulties of doing their jobs, the women have a good relationship with their father–owners based on mutual respect. In a study centered on the preparation of female successors and their relationships with female predecessors, Campbell (2002) noted the existence of amicable relationships, marked by mutual respect and interdependence. This case highlights that this is also possible in relationships between father–owners and daughter–successors, Laura provides an insight into this when she says: "My father has always been a really great mentor ... I consider my father my idol; I think he is great. He is very intelligent, a super businessman." While good relationships are important in succession processes, especially those based on trust and mutual respect (Janjuha-Jivraj and Woods, 2002), it is also important for father–owners to recognize the managerial potential of their daughters.

Conclusions

In a study on family companies in southern Brazil, Scheffer (1985) identified the following possible difficulties in succession processes: the successor's lack of preparation, the negative influence of the family in business (conflicts, rivalries, and so on), the predecessor's reluctance to leave their company and successors' lack of interest in the family business. Since these issues were not encountered in this study, on the face of it the succession process in this case appears to be smooth. However, careful examination reveals an undercurrent of resentment, repressed potential, and limited opportunities for the female successors here.

Analysis shows that female successors were, and are, being prepared for succession, but that the "glass ceiling" phenomenon is evident in various ways within the company. Its first manifestation is the female successors' lack of choice as to which area of the company they could work in, with both being transferred to junior positions which they did not select. The second is related to their lower positions as managers in the company hierarchy whereas their male counterparts became directors. Thirdly, the positions to which they were designated gave them some internal but no external visibility, in contrast with their male successors. This was further compounded by their exclusion from opportunities to participate in external networks.

Other difficulties were also faced by the female successors, such as negotiating a balance between work and family commitments, little flexibility in their working hours, and difficulties in developing a career plan. This is in contrast to findings by Cromie and Sullivan (1999) who report that women's conflicts between work and family are usually less serious in family organizations.

Inequalities relating to the roles played by the female successors in contrast with the male successors are evident, suggesting that the belief still exists that women should play different and unequal roles where men are also involved. These attitudes can make it difficult for women to progress and become fully fledged successors unless they are brought out into the open and discussed by both father–owners and their potential daughter–successors.

Limitations

Finally, it is worth noting that there are two main limitations in this study. First, it only presents a cross-sectional view of the company and its succession process, while a more longitudinal approach would result in further valuable information. Second, as it is a single case there are limits to its generalization. Nevertheless, the findings of this case study indicate the need for further research on succession processes and for this to be set within social and cultural contexts.

References

Brazilian Institute for Quality and Productivity. 2010. *Empreendedorismo no Brasil 2009. Relatório Executivo*, p. 22. Available at: http://www.ibpq.org.br/empreendedorismo/home/ [accessed: 12 May 2010].

Cadieux. L. Lorrain, J. and Hugron, P. 2000. *La Succession dans les Entreprises Familiales: Une Étude de cas Exploratoire Faite Auprès de Quatre PME Manufacturieères Fondées et Dirigées par des Femmes.* Actes du Congrès V Congrès International Francophone sur la PME CIFPME, Lille.

Campbell, K.L. 2002. *Theorizing Matrilineal Business Enterprises to Add Mother/Daughter Business to the Entrepreneurial Mix.* Proceedings of the ICSB 47th World Conference, Puerto Rico: ICSB.

Cromie, S. and Sullivan, S.O. 1999. Women as Managers in Family Firms. *Women in Management Review*, 14(3), 76–88.

Curimbaba, F. 2002. The Dynamics of Women's Roles as Family Business Managers. *Family Business Review*, 15(3), 239–252.

Deere, C.D. and León, M. 2002. *O Empoderamento da Mulher—Direitos à Terra e Direitos de Propriedade na América Latina.* Porto Algere: Editora da Universidade Federal do Rio Grande do Sul.

Dubar, C. 1996. *La Socialization: Construction des Identités Sociales et Professionnelles*, 2nd Edition. Paris: Armand Colin.

Dyck, B., Mauws, M., Starke, F.A. and Misschke, A. 2002. Passing the Baton. The Importance of Sequence, Timing, Technique, and Communication in Executive Succession. *Journal of Business Venturing*, 17(2), 143–162.

Gersick, K.E., Davis, J.A, Hampton, M.M. and Lansberg, I. 2006. *De Geração para Geração: Ciclos de Vida das Empresas Familiares.* Rio de Janeiro: Elsevier.

International Family Enterprise Research Academy. 2003. Family Businesses Dominate. *Family Business Review*, 16(4), 235–240.

Janjuha-Jivraj, S. and Woods, A. 2002. Succession Issues within Asian family firms. *International Small Business Journal*, 20(1), 77–94.

Le Breton-Miller, I., Miller, D., Steier, L.P. 2004. Toward an Integrative Model of Effective FOB Succession. *Entrepreneurship Theory and Practice*, 28(4), 305–328.

Lee, K., Lin, W.S. and Lin, G.H. 2000. *Succession and Survival of Family Businesses.* Proceedings of the 45th ICSB. Brisbane.

Macedo, K., Caixta, C., Moura, M.S. and Gimenex, D. 2004. O Processo Sucessório em Organizações Familiares e a Exclusão da Mulher. *Psicologia & Sociedade*, 16(3), 69–81.

Machado, H.V. 2008. A Integração de Sucessoras em Indústrias Brasileiras, in *Organizações Familiares um Mosaico Brasileiro* (pp. 181–207), edited by A.P. Carrieri, L.A.S. Saraiva and D. Grzybovski. Passo Fundo: Editora da Universidade de Passo Fundo.

Ministry of Women's Affairs. 2008. *II Plano Nacional de Políticas para as Mulheres.* Brasília: Presidência da República.

Morganti, E. and Barbieri, B. 1997. *A Batalha das Herdeiras na Empresa Familiar.* S Porto Alegre: agra-P.C. Luzatto Editores.

Rodrigues, A.M. 1991. Padrões Afetivos na Família e Empresa Familiar. *Revista de Administração de Empresas*, 31(4), 36–48.

Scheffer, A.B. 1985. Fatores Dificultadores e Facilitadores ao Processo de Sucessão Familiar. *Revista de Administração*, 30(3), 80–90.

Spanevello, R.M. 2008. *A Situação das Filhas na Transmissão do Patrimônio na Agricultura Familiar.* Proceedings Fazendo Gênero 8, Florianópolis, 25–28 August, 1–7.

St-Cyr, L. and Inoussa, R. 2000. *La Planification de La Relève dans les PME.* Actes du 5ème Congrès International Francophone sur la PME, 5, 26–27 October, Lille.

Vidigal, A.C. 2000. A Sobrevivência da Empresa Familiar no Brasil. *Revista de Administração*, 35(2), 66–71.

CHAPTER 25

Colombia: Father–Daughter Succession Issues in the Colombian Family Business Context

MELQUICEDEC LOZANO, KATHY KESSLER OVERBEKE AND KEANON J. ALDERSON

Introduction

Colombia ranks as the third most populous country in Latin America following Brazil and Mexico, with 46.7 million people (Worldbank, 2009). The population is relatively young; the median age in 2006 was estimated at 26.3 years. Approximately 95 percent of *Colombianos* are Roman Catholic and the Church exerts a strong influence on both society and family (Country Profile, 2007).

As a collectivist society, families are the centerpiece of Colombian culture. Extended families are large and intertwined through participation in various businesses, social activities, and politics. Colombian culture is also characterized by an economic and cultural hierarchy. The ruling upper class constitutes approximately 5 percent of the Colombian population and owns 90 percent of the property and the majority of large businesses. The middle class represents approximately 20 percent of the population followed by the large lower classes, including poor and indigent (Datamonitor, 2009). Colombia provides a rich landscape in which to examine unique family business and gender issues through a case study of father–daughter succession.

The Colombian Business and Family Business Environment

In the last two decades the population has migrated from rural to urban areas as a result of high levels of violence and a decline in agriculture caused by deforestation. Colombia is the fifth largest economy in Latin America, exhibiting an average growth rate of 3.7 percent. Unemployment is high, at just under 14 percent (Datamonitor, 2009). Micro, small, and medium-sized businesses account for 91.7 percent of all businesses and employ 46.5 percent of the working population (Fernández, 2005). Family-owned or controlled firms constitute 70 percent of Colombian companies and range from small businesses to large *groupos (*Berdugo and Cáceres, 2010; Dávila L. de Guevara, 2003).

Groupos are large, primarily family controlled, interrelated businesses that dominate certain Colombian industries (Gutiérrez et al., 2008; Lansberg and Perrow, 2004). They control industries such as beer and soft drinks, cement, cut-flower, and retailing industries (Gutiérrez, et al., 2008).

Role of Women in Colombia

Women's roles in Colombia have changed dramatically in the last 25 years and women are now prevalent in businesses, education, and politics (Schwindt-Bayer, 2006; Ogliastri, 2007). Ogliastri notes, "Colombian managers describe a culture where gender equality is now the norm" (2007:698). The wage gender gap is the lowest in Latin America (Angel-Urdinola and Wodon, 2006), and 29 percent of all management positions are occupied by women—the highest rate in Latin America (Maxfield, 2005).

Women in higher social classes are well educated and often work in the family foundation, charitable organizations, or politics (Hanratty and Meditz, 1988; Lansberg and Perrow, 2004). The increasing importance of women in politics is demonstrated by the fact that half of the Colombian cabinet was female in 2003 (Schwindt-Bayer, 2006). Recent research also indicates that the elevation of women's status has been accompanied by an erosion of the machismo culture. According to a study of 120 Latin American senior-level business women including Colombians, men are now becoming more paternalistic (Maxfield, 2005).

Yet despite some advances in gender parity, Colombia continues to be a male-dominated society. Fathers are the family's primary economic provider and primogeniture is common (Schwindt-Bayer, 2006). In Maxfield's study, women felt they needed to work two to three times harder than their male counterparts in order to be noticed. Continued subordination of Colombian women is also apparent as 62.22 percent of lower paid, informally employed workers and 86.36 percent of self-employed workers are women. Furthermore, the rate of unemployment is higher for women at 16.79 percent versus 12 percent for men (Fernández, 2005).

Overall, gender parity has increased in Colombia but men continue to hold more status. Furthermore, gender egalitarianism is often subject to class, and employment opportunities are influenced by family ties, status, income, power, success, age, and skin color (Ogliastri, 2007).

Family Business Succession in Colombia

While there is a dearth of literature on father–daughter succession practices in Colombia, there are a few studies examining the unique needs and processes of Colombian family firms. Succession studies have revealed that in large and some medium-sized family businesses, Colombian firms utilize outside professional management (Martinez, 2001). One study showed that only 39 percent of family-owned firms were managed by family members, including families where some members are trained as professional managers (Martinez-López, 2008).

Gómez-Betancourt et al. (2007) analyzed six large Colombian family firms and identified four factors that influence the succession mechanism: security, property distribution, experience, and culture. Security may be a relatively unique factor compared with other countries, as Colombia has experienced considerable violence, terrorism, and kidnapping. Thus, the founder's concern for the safety of his family is a deciding factor to sell the business, use intergenerational succession, or hire professional management.

The Case Study

HISTORY OF THE FIRM

"Diversipartes" was founded in the city of Cali, Colombia, in 1976. It is a large company that exports to 14 countries monthly and employs 700 workers. The company currently consists of two manufacturing facilities—one with 16,000 square meters and the other with 18,000 square meters—where they manufacture over 5,000 products for the home, office, and transportation vehicles. Automotive parts are their principal product including wheels, bearings, and headlights for motorcycles, trucks, and buses. The company also owns an office in Bogotá, the capital of Colombia, which employs approximately 20 people and provides service to the central part of the country.

The founder of the firm, Roger, received a civil engineering degree in Colombia and later attended school in the United States. Subsequently, he managed a propane and aviation fuel company and a fertilizer factory. He learned how to turn around businesses in bankruptcy before returning home to work for the city government of Cali. He was then offered a job as manager of a fish company where he worked for a few years before taking a management position with a wood mill employing 1,500 workers. He continually saved money and when he identified an opportunity to start his own business, he created Diversipartes, S.A.

THE FAMILY

Roger is married to Esther and they have three children: Monica, 56 years old, Sara, 52 years old, and the only male child, Robinson, 49 years old. Roger and Esther represented two different role models to their children. Roger was an assiduous business and community leader and Esther was a tireless housewife. The children were raised in a middle class environment and attended bilingual schools, but they had very different interests. The oldest, Monica, identified more with her mother. When she was young she enjoyed playing with dolls and she was always a dedicated student in school. Contrastingly, Sara disliked playing with dolls and other stereotypical "feminine" activities, did not like school, but exhibited good leadership skills. She identified more with her father and because of her rebellious nature, had a contentious relationship with her mother. Robinson, who was in elementary school when Monica left for college, had little in common with his older sisters. He lacked initiative or interest in any particular subject or activity and the sisters felt that he was favored by the mother.

THE FIRST SUCCESSION PROCESS

Roger always considered his only son, Robinson, to be the future leader of the business. Sara recalls her father saying that he wanted a son with his same temperament to inherit the company management. Roger was very strict, but was a frank and respectful manager. He hated excuses and never hesitated to fire someone for lying, stealing, or inefficiency. Yet, he also believed it important to be sensitive to the problems of his workers, from machine operators to top management.

When Robinson entered the family business as the expected next leader of the firm it quickly became clear that he did not share his father's disposition or work ethic. Robinson worked as he pleased, consuming company resources to tinker with his own product line, and flaunted his authority among employees. His father enabled this behavior by placing few demands on him and, when confronted with his son's destructive behavior, Roger would say, "Have patience, have patience, he will grow up."

Robinson's capricious behavior peaked at a conference that he attended with Sara. As Monica was a professor where the conference was being held, she also attended the conference. While the sisters attended all the conference meetings, Robinson stayed in bed almost half the time. Consequently, Sara prevailed upon Monica to help the family business. Sara was already working in the business and Monica, separated from her husband, had been living in Bogotá with her children. After witnessing their brother's irresponsible behavior, Monica agreed to join the company and at the age of 46 she helped found and direct a quality control department based in Bogotá.

THE DAUGHTER AS A SUCCESSOR

As a child, Sara would ask to go with her father when he visited his factories at night. Roger was rarely home and Sara saw this as an opportunity to spend time with him. They would walk through the plant, side-by-side, with Roger answering young Sara's many and enthusiastic questions. Inadvertently, these visits engendered Sara's love for business as she developed a relationship with her father in the context of his work environment.

The confluence of Sarah's love and admiration for her father and her interest in the family business is exemplified by her recollection of her father's attitude toward his business. She reminisces that when she and her siblings would ask him, "Why don't you have a country house?" he would respond, "What we have is a factory. Someone who has a house in the country diverts resources and I do not raise cattle nor am I a farmer. I have been a factory owner and I will remain a factory owner." Sara was imbued in her father's spirit and pride.

Sara's interest in her family's business was further enhanced by dinner conversations addressing business and politics, and observations of her father as a civic leader. The fact that many community members sought her father's advice and support augmented Sara's admiration for her father and the respect he derived from his leadership skills. Roger was able to solve problems, answer questions, and supervise projects. He had the ability to personally guarantee that projects were completed and was esteemed as a contributor to the community's beauty and development.

Sara's perceptions of her father as a businessman and the closeness she felt toward him generated a passion to lead her family's business. The relationship she developed with her father during her youth also foreshadowed father–daughter interactions as a successor. Roger would answer young Sara's many and enthusiastic questions as they walked side-by-side through the plant; yet, he was outwardly indifferent. Sara accepted her father's indifference, perceiving it to be the norm among fathers and daughters. Most importantly, she did not interpret his insensitivity as a reflection of his love, or lack thereof. She believed that they communicated through empathy, having a sort of unspoken understanding of each other. Sara maintained this interpretation of her relationship with her father and it helped support her through many father–daughter conflicts experienced while trying to lead the company toward prosperity.

With her passion ignited, Sara's love for business grew with her age and her earnest in learning about business was irrepressible. When she was young and her father worked for a fishing company, she would go deep sea fishing with the employees and learn how to fish, filet, and create products from fish. When her father managed lumber businesses in Cali, she learned how to transport wood, process it, and operate the machinery. In all the factories she visited, she would become familiar with processes, raw materials, specifications, and transformations. She enjoyed listening to conversations about the smells, glues, humidity, colors, packaging, temperatures, problems, and decisions.

When Sara reached college age, she continued to pursue her interest in business by studying industrial engineering and collaborating with classmates to write a thesis on her father's factories. Immediately following graduation she entered a six-month practicum with Colgate-Palmolive. Having completed rigorous training, Sara joined Diversipartes, S.A. with an indefinite work contract. From this point, Sara's dream to be a next generation leader of the family business was encumbered by the fact that she was a woman. The next few years were spent struggling to convince her father that women are equal to men in their ability to run a successful business. Roger did not approve of Sara's return to Diversipartes, S.A. and assumed that she would not last long in the factories. He tried to undermine her efforts, would not assign her to any specific job, and openly favored male supervisors.

Sara responded by immersing herself in all aspects of the business. She learned how to do the most menial jobs and developed top management skills. She began to make meaningful contributions to the company. For example, when she thought she had a comprehensive understanding of the industrial engineering department, she began to generate efficiency reports in a factory that was very disorganized. She also applied the knowledge she gained from her apprenticeship with Colgate-Palmolive to dramatically improve production in the firm. Eventually, Roger recognized the improvements in his factory but did not credit Sara with the results. Rather, he attributed these achievements to himself. Initially, Sara was bothered by this but learned to disregard these behaviors.

During the next five years, Sara persisted in learning about the company and finding ways to improve production. She reorganized everything related to time, reports, the product sheets, and machinery. The workers noticed that "the owner's daughter" was making very important contributions to the functioning of the company. They began to respect her authority and she was able to coordinate production meetings and lead her own initiatives.

In addition to working in the factory and learning how to work among the laborers without fear or intimidation, Sara dedicated many hours to studying in Roger's library. She specialized in technical journals in plastics and technology and attended seminars in this field. This learning agenda enabled her to converse with mechanics and plastics supervisors. She was able to partake in meetings, implement changes, and deliver effective results.

Sara's father finally realized his daughter was becoming a leader in his company. He saw her assuming responsibilities that he perceived to be outside the female domain. To him, this was unacceptable. He had his own criteria for men and women and his daughter's actions did not conform. His treatment of Sara became even more difficult as he discouraged her due to her gender and simultaneously held her to higher standards as the boss's daughter. For example, the daily work schedule began at 7:00 am in the morning. One morning Sara arrived at 7:10 am and Roger scolded:

> *You are arriving too late and making a bad example. The example begins with you, as does the discipline. If the boss arrives late, his people arrive late; if the boss smokes, the employees around him smoke. Discipline starts at the top and the organization adjusts itself to those standards of conduct of the boss.*

Sara reacted by separating the boss from her father because she knew she had to see him at home after working in the factory. She was infinitely patient with him, deciding to try to understand him rather than argue. In her mind, she was in the business for the long term and felt she had a "calling" to be the successor.

The discouraging momentum changed on two occasions, both in response to Sara's leaving the company. When she was 38 years old she was kidnapped and held for six months. This tragedy unified the family and her absence was deeply felt. Sara believes this event helped her family to recognize all her special contributions to the business and family.

After being in the family business for 12 years, Sara left to work on a train transportation project in the city. Three years later she returned to the company and Roger was more disposed to utilize her skills. He shared more information with her and slowly began to assign projects. Without saying anything, he began to turn over control. With his support, Sara began to simplify projects, reduce costs, and introduce new technology. She computerized the plant so that information regarding products, orders, invoices, and other information may be easily accessed, and trained family members and employees to use these new systems. She typically consulted with her father and considered his advice before making changes and together they built new product lines such as traffic lights and stadium seats.

The vicissitudes of Roger and Sara's relationship continued. However, they developed an understanding similar to the empathetic relationship they enjoyed when Sara was a child. When Sara and her father were distanced by disagreements, there was an unspoken respect that allowed them to renew a harmonious relationship. As a result, Roger became more tranquil. His age, and knowing that he may rely primarily on Sara, allowed him to be more relaxed and engage in other activities such as teaching. He is still very disciplined and obsesses over his products, but he is not as antagonistic as before, allowing Sarah to take over control of the firm.

THE PRESENT AND FUTURE OF THE COMPANY

Currently, Roger has divested himself of all his stock in the business. Sara and her siblings own 90 percent of the stock, divided into equal shares, and their mother owns the remaining 10 percent. Sara is the manager of Diversipartes, S.A. and is on the board of directors and Monica manages the office in Bogotá.

Discussions are already taking place regarding the next generation. Sara's daughter, Clotilde, began a training process to become a leader of the company, working as a line supervisor and in other factory positions. She became discouraged by the fact that her grandfather refused to pay her a comparable salary to the men in the same positions and left the company. Today, she manages a small factory owned by her mother and aunt, separate from Roger's business. In contrast, Monica's son is expected to help Sara manage the company after graduation from college.

The family is only considering outside professional management for positions lower in ranking than CEO. It is important to the family to maintain ownership and leadership of the company.

Discussion and Conclusions

The case of Diversipartes, S.A. exemplifies the strength of the family in Colombia as well as tension between old and new gender norms. It offers a unique look at how agency, or the ability to "intentionally make things happen by one's actions" (Bandura, 2001), may be a counter-measure to traditional gender biases. Moreover, this case suggests that trust may evolve from agency and an acceptance of modern gender norms. Sara's persistent agentic behaviors and her father's acceptance of her abilities ultimately allowed Roger to trust her to take over many of his responsibilities. Finally, this case supports the idea that fathers and sons may be more likely to have a corrosive, competitive relationship in the family business, than fathers and daughters.

There are several incidences where family support is salient. Sara was rescued from the kidnappers by her family and received help so that she could resume a normal life. Monica left her teaching position to help the family business and built a strong relationship with her sister. Robinson continues to own stock in the family business even though he was not able to manage the business. Importantly, Sara's mother took care of Sara's children so that Sara could work outside the home.

This story suggests that gender parity in Colombia is still emerging. Sara's rise to top management resulted from her persistent agentic behaviors in spite of strong cultural gender biases, rather than a planned succession. Although Sara exhibited the most interest in the family business, she was not invited, expected, or encouraged to become a successor. In fact, she appeared to hit the glass ceiling immediately upon entrance into the business. As she doggedly pursued her dream of helping her family's companies grow, her father responded by assuming the credit and denigrating her efforts. Gender role orientation, or beliefs about the proper roles for men and women (Judge and Livingston, 2008) seem to have contributed to Roger's response as Sara noted that he had his own views on how men and women should behave.

Sara's rise to succession would not have been achieved without agency or proactivity. She created her own learning agenda and followed it despite her father's chiding and interference. Her business acumen was augmented by both a love and admiration for her father and her own assertiveness in asking questions and learning alongside the workers. She decided to study engineering and continued even after her children were born and she pursued leadership in an industry where female leaders are typically "taboo" (Curimbaba, 2002). All these actions demonstrate a willingness and ability to intentionally make things happen.

Agency led to trust as Sara persisted in demonstrating her abilities and her father finally accepted his daughter's business and leadership skills. The family as a whole appears to have benefitted from this transformation as Roger is currently more relaxed as result of his trust in his daughter's competency and confidence in the continuity of his business. The business has benefitted as indicated by growth in recent years. In 2007, when Colombia was experiencing a strong economy, Diversipartes, S.A. grew by 37 percent under the combined leadership of Roger and Sara.

Finally, Roger and Robinson were not able to coexist in the company. Sara notes that Robinson saw his father as a competitor more than a partner. Previous studies have suggested that father–daughter teams are sometimes more effective because there is less rivalry than found in father–son teams (Dumas, 1989; Jiménez, 2009).

Limitations and Future Research Directions

Sara and her father were the only family members interviewed for this study. Other family members may provide different insights and explanations. This is noted as a limitation.

This study suggests at least two future areas of research. First, Roger was more accepting of Sara as a skilled business leader after she returned from working with the Transportation Department. Family business literature is inconclusive in determining a causal relationship between an offspring working outside the family business for a few years and success in the family business (Astrachan, 2009). Perhaps Roger was influenced by Sara's work in another company, but there may have been other factors. This is an area for exploration.

Secondly, an area of research that may be more unique to Colombia relates to the need to have support from government and a culture that still largely adheres to traditional gender norms. For example, will Sara and her family's political and social influence decline upon Roger's death? Will Diversipartes, S.A. have the same protections? More women are entering politics in Colombia. Known as "Supermadres" (supermoms), these women see political involvement as an extension of their motherly duties and introduce bills and legislation that protect women and children (Chaney, 1979). Will they also have the interest and power to represent business women and promote their issues?

References

Angel-Urdinola, D. and Wodon, Q. 2006. The Gender Wage Gap and Poverty in Colombia. *Labour: Review of Labour Economics & Industrial Relations*, 20(4), 721–739.

Astrachan, J.H. 2009. Using and Abusing Family Business Research. *Family Business*, 20(4), 40–43.

Bandura, A. 2001. Social Cognitive Theory: An Agentic Perspective. *Annual Review of Psychology*, 52, 1–26.

Berdugo, E., and Cáceres, L.S. 2010. Aproximación al Estado de la Investigación en Empresas de Familia en Colombia: 1989–2009. *Gestión & Sociedad*, 2(2), 39–60.

Chaney, E.M. 1979. *Supermadre: Women in Politics in Latin America*. Austin: University of Texas Press.

Curimbaba, F. 2002. The Dynamics of Women's Roles as Family Business Managers. *The Family Business Review*, 25(1), 239–252.

Datamonitor. 2009. *Colombia: Country Analysis Report*—In Depth PESTLE Insights.

Dávila, L. de Guevara, C. (compilador) 2003. *Empresas y Empresarios en la Historia de Colombia. Siglos XIX–XX: Una Colección de Estudios Recientes (Firms and Entrepreneurs in the history of Colombia in the Nineteenth and Twentieth Centuries: A Collection of Recent Studies)*. 2 vols. Bogotá: Editorial Norma S. A and Ediciones Uniandes.

Dumas, C. 1989. Understanding of Father–Daughter and Father–Son Dyads in Family-Owned Businesses. *Family Business Review*, 2, 31–46.

Fernández, H.V. 2005. Employment and Quality of Work in Colombia. *Escuela Nacional Sindical*. Available at: http://www.gpn.org [accessed: 10 April 2010].

Gómez-Betancourt, G., Lopez Vergara, M.P. and Betancourt Ramirez, J.B. 2007. Factors that Influence the Selection of an Ownership Succession Mechanism in Colombian Family Businesses. *Cuadernos de administración*, 21(37), 269–292.

Gutiérrez, L.H., Pombo, C. and Taborda, R. 2008. Ownership and Control in Colombian Corporations. *The Quarterly review of Economics and Finance*, 48(1), 2–47.

Hanratty, D.M. and Meditz, S.W. (Eds). *Colombia: A Country Study*. Washington: GPO for the Library of Congress, 1988. Available at: http://countrystudies.us/colombia/ [accessed: 31 March 2010].

Jiménez, R.M. 2009. Research on Women in Family Firms: Current Status and Future Directions. *Family Business Review*, 22(1), 53–64.

Judge, T.A. and Livingston, B.A. 2008. Is the Gap More than Gender? A Longitudinal Analysis of Gender, Gender Role Orientation, and Earning. *Journal of Applied Social Psychology*, 93(5), 994–1012.

Lansberg, I. and Perrow, E. 2004. Understanding and Working with Leading Family Businesses in Latin America. *Family Business Review*, 14(2), 127–147.

Martinez, C.L. (2001). *Modern Management Thought and Theories: Evidence from the Evolution of a Colombian Corporation*. Revista Universidad EAFIT, 122 Abril–Mayo, 39–45.

Martinez-López, C. 2008. Myths about Family Firms: An Exploratory Study of Native Family-Owned Firms in Colombia. *Review of Business Research*, 8(3), 125–130.

Maxfield, S. 2005. *Women on the Verge: Corporate Power in Latin America*. Report on the Women's Leadership Conference of the Americas. Produced in collaboration with Simmons School of Management. Available at: http://www.simmons.edu/som/docs/centers/WomenontheVerge.pdf [accessed: 12 April 2010].

Ogliastri, E. 2007. *Columbia: The Human Relations Side of Enterprise in Culture and Leadership around the World: The GLOBE Book of In-depth Studies of 25 Societies*, edited by J.S. Chhokar, F.C. Brodbeck and R.J. House. New York: Lawrence Erlbaum Associates.

Schwindt-Bayer, L. 2006. Still Supermadres? Gender and the Policy Priorities of Latin American Legislators. *American Journal of Political Science*, 50(3), 570–585.

Worldbank. 2009. *Colombia—Brief Quick Facts*. Available at: http://web.worldbank.org [accessed: 31 March 2010].

CHAPTER 26

Peru: From Father to Daughter: A Case Study of Family Business Succession in Peru

MARINA NIFOROS AND PENELOPE ROBOTIS

The Peruvian Culture and its Influence on Family Business

Around the world, family businesses constitute a dominant form of business organization that contributes significantly to economic growth (FBN, 2008). In developing countries, family businesses emerge to address basic needs or unexplored market opportunities in a given social context, thus allowing for entrepreneurial activity to emerge (Baker et al., 2005). Family businesses remain the prevalent type of business organization in Peru, a collectivist society that embraces values that serve group interests, safeguard family security, and support social relationships (Shimizu, 2006; Lenartowicz and Johnson, 2003). Although culture is a complex and dynamic concept that defines social values, norms, and gender roles, it is also shaped by political and historical events that lead to modification of existing values, social roles, and conditions (Cheung and Halpern, 2010).

The internal conflicts that Peru experienced in the late 1980s and early 1990s led to disintegration of family economies and communities. The socio-economic and political events redefined the existing social roles of women by expanding their freedom, and challenging the rigid patriarchal values once prescribed by the Catholic and agricultural traditions. Women were challenged to take on non-traditional roles and learn new ways to generate income and sustain a living. The existing social circumstances presented both an opportunity for evaluation and exploitation of entrepreneurial ventures for these women in order to modify their living conditions (Baker et al., 2005; Celle de Bowman, 2000).

The liberal reforms and privatization of state enterprises in the 1990s resulted in high unemployment that affected mostly young middle class professionals and technocrats, who searched for employment in small-scale industries and the trade sector (Celle de Bowman, 2000). Today, micro and small enterprises comprise 98 percent of the entrepreneurial sector in Peru, contributing to 42.1 percent of the country's gross domestic product (GDP) and 88 percent of private employment. Programs implemented by the Government of Peru aim to sustain the economic growth of these enterprises that often evolve into small family enterprises (Weeks and Seiler, 2001; Thunderbird School of Global Management, 2009).

Female Entrepreneurship in the Peruvian Context

Female entrepreneurship is a key contributor to economic growth in Latin America and the Caribbean (Jalbert, 2000). According to the findings of the Global Entrepreneurship Monitor (Allen et al., 2008), Peru, along with Japan, were the only two countries where women were more active than males in starting a business. In Peru, entrepreneurial activity is significantly higher compared to other low-income countries including Latin America.

Given that women's entrepreneurial activity has a stronger impact on GDP than economic activity in general, policymakers are implementing measures to stimulate the rate of entrepreneurial activity (Weeks and Seiler, 2001). Government-sponsored programs aim to address some of the obstacles entrepreneurs encounter in the areas of technology, education, and training. Women's business associations play a vital role in addressing key issues, such as access to capital, markets, and networks (Jalbert, 2000; Weeks and Seiler, 2001).

Women are more active in starting their own enterprises and leading small-scale enterprises, both in traditionally female markets and in male-dominated markets (Celle de Bowman, 2000). While the social role expectations of Peruvian women as mothers and wives often conflict with their entrepreneurial role, their commitment and determination empowers them to overcome the existing gender role inequalities embedded in the Peruvian culture. Consistent with findings of cross-cultural studies on women's leadership (Cheung and Halpern, 2010), Peruvian women entrepreneurs are challenging the rigid gender stereotypes by embracing their multiple roles with growing confidence as they utilize strategies to combine their work–family roles (Jalbert, 2000). A study of small-scale female industrialists in Peru reported that women exhibit low optimism and self-confidence, as well as an increased fear of failure compared to males when engaging in entrepreneurial activities. Other studies, however, indicate that, driven by their need to be independent, economically self-sufficient, and attain personal fulfillment, women feel empowered and liberated through their business endeavors (Celle de Bowman, 2000).

Father–Daughter Succession in the Peruvian Context

Family businesses that retain both management and ownership are still by large the dominant type of business enterprise in Peru (Shimizu, 2006), making succession vital to the survival of the business (Vera and Dean 2005; Stavrou et al., 2005). Studies on family business succession issues indicate that only 30 percent of family businesses survive the first to second generation transition and less than 10 percent survive the third generation (Stavrou et al., 2005; Le Breton-Miller et al., 2004).

Succession encompasses both actions and organizational mechanisms to secure the successful transition of management and ownership to the next generation (Stavrou et al., 2005). Variables contingent to successful transitions include shared values between successor and incumbent, a positive parent–child relationship, ability of the founder to convey values crucial to the future success of the business, and a collaborative value system that integrates family and business values (Cole, 1997; Alvarez and Sintas, 2003). Successful succession of family firms is not a single event but a process subject to the challenges of a dynamic and evolving business environment (Alvarez and Sintas, 2003; Le Breton-Miller et al., 2004). Peru's adoption of neoliberal policies and liberalization of foreign exchange controls and foreign trade present a challenge to the future survival of family businesses in Peru.

The successful integration of offspring into family-owned businesses is crucial for assuring the continued survival of such firms (Dumas, 1992; Vera and Dean, 2005). Studies on family business succession report that influential factors in choosing a successor include primogeniture, followed by skills, experience in the business, previous work experience outside the family firm, and compliance with the requirements established by the family (Azucena et al., 2009; Dumas, 1992). Daughters are not preferred successors, they rather join the family firm when there is a life cycle or organizational crisis and usually in low rank positions, which may explain why they extend themselves to attain visibility in the company (Vera and Dean, 2005; Dumas, 1992). Despite the significant contribution of family businesses in the Peruvian economy and evolving entrepreneurial role of women in Peru, hardly any information exists in the literature regarding the role of daughters in the succession of family business in Peru.

The Case Study

BRIEF HISTORY OF THE FIRM

The family business we are examining is the outgrowth of a third generation family business, yet at the same time it can be considered as a first generation/entrepreneur-owned. This duality lies in the particular history of the family business, which has been through many turbulent restructurings and divisions among the family members. In its current formation, it can be considered the brainchild of the current owner and father of our subject and potential successor.

The original venture started in 1911 with the grandfather of the current owner and CEO (Edgardo)—a small drugstore that in one generation grew into a healthcare and pharmaceutical national giant. The founder's decision to (informally) divide the business branches among his six children led quickly to serious operational problems, as there was no oversight or process for resolving strategic issues. The situation deteriorated with the entry of the third generation into management and the rivalry that ensued. The two brothers/acting CEOs were involved in a damaging lawsuit, which all but destroyed the business. In the 1970s, a left-wing military coup overthrew the Government and started nationalizing businesses. The company was once again divided. Edgardo, father of our subject, retained the direct sales commercial part of the business (based on the Avon American model), worthless after years of hyperinflation and political instability, and turned it into a regional powerhouse of direct sales cosmetics. Today, the company reports over USD 700 million in annual sales and is present in 15 countries in Latin America, with plans to enter the United States (US) market this year. It has over 5,000 employees and gives over 500,000 women in Latin America the opportunity to have their own enterprise. The company has created a Foundation, dedicated to the education of underprivileged girls and women in Latin America.

THE FIRM, THE SUCCESSION PROCESS, AND THE ENTREPRENEUR

The succession process has not yet taken place in this case. The father of our subject is still the owner and CEO of the family business and in control of the major strategic decisions concerning the enterprise. The family has taken, though, several steps to put in place processes and structures (family council meetings, a constitution, and so on) that will allow the family to address issues on the evolution of the business and ownership in a more neutral and systematic way. Their primary objective is to keep the family together and avoid the conflicts that tore them apart in the past. They have worked over the years with external consultants to help them in the process. The family does not exclude the possibility of professional outside management either in collaboration with the family members or as a transition solution.

> *My dad would love for one of us to take over, but none of us feels ready. I am trying to learn as much as I can on the business, earn my stripes and my way in the family business ... he is clear that if we are not ready then there is going to be a professional management.*

Carolina is the youngest of three siblings, two girls and one boy. All three have professional qualifications and were educated abroad. After some years of alternative career paths and experiences outside the family business and the country, all three are finally working for the family business. Carolina is the one with the highest exposure in the business and the longest tenure (almost seven years) and has had a series of stretch assignments that have solidified her working relationship with her father.

OWNER'S WILLINGNESS TO RELINQUISH CONTROL

At 65, the owner is still the sole owner and very much in control of the family firm, with no signs of relinquishing control in the next few years. He has worked very hard in the business for 43 years. The daughter does indicate though that he has realized he will have to start slowing down and spend time with his family.

THE RELATIONSHIP WITH THE FATHER AND FOUNDER

Carolina has an excellent overall personal and working relationship with her father and, by her own assessment, they are very similar in character and leadership styles. With his support, she has introduced a good number of difficult reforms and restructurings in the business. "He is my best friend, every morning we have coffee together before the day starts and then go home to have lunch together. Our fights never last, we have a rule that cannot be mad with each other for more than an hour."

RELATIONSHIP WITH THE SIBLINGS

Our subject assesses that her relationship with her siblings is a well-balanced one. The mother, on the other hand, was seldom mentioned in the interviews. Carolina senses more competition and rivalry with her older sister, with whom she recognizes having similar character traits, being strong-minded and ambitious. The older brother she considers more of an ally. He seems to have drifted back to business more as a de facto rather than a purposeful decision, after changing many professional paths. The older sister had taken a step back from professional life, after an initial couple of years working for the company, to raise a family of four children. She has recently joined the business again and is assuming a more assertive role.

THE ENTREPRENEUR: REASONS FOR JOINING THE COMPANY

Carolina did not want to enter the family business. She left to study in the US and then worked on unrelated small jobs. "I was a hippie after college and against my dad for selling cosmetics to poor women, a 'dirty capitalist'." She was convinced to join when she saw that the family business could be a great vehicle for social change, that she could "do good while doing business." "Why did I join the business? My Dad convinced me to come back. I finally fell in love with the whole business model. I had dreams of working in development and changing the world for the poor."

She is now also president of the company's Foundation that is giving out scholarships and helping women's training and empowerment in the region.

AGE ASYNCHRONY

In the current state of affairs, the person who seems the most likely to succeed the owner and CEO is Carolina, the youngest of the three siblings. Contrary to an assumption that primogeniture constitutes a competitive advantage in the selection and grooming of the next generation of leaders in family firms, Carolina was the one with the most developmental opportunities within the firm and has exercised the most influence over her father concerning the future direction and strategy of the firm.

FATHER–DAUGHTER RELATIONSHIP—GROWING PAINS

The father is a dominant figure in the family business and a powerful role model for the daughter, both in terms of leadership style and in his thirst for continued learning and development. She describes admiringly his accomplishments and his relationship with his employees ("charismatic, low profile"). "I admire him so much and I want to imitate him ... he is keen to learn new things, seek always the best advice, wanting to improve himself and move forward ..." Carolina, in turn, strongly influences her father, bringing in new ideas on how to improve the business operations and to reposition its mission and value system. This has not always coincided with the founder's vision and traditional values and Carolina had to resort to extensive internal lobbying to get her ideas through.

> *He needed a lot of convincing, right now he is fully behind the project. It's been good ... it allowed us though to talk a lot about what each of us wanted ... we had fighting [spells] but it was good fighting, we had a lot of serious talks ... he is my best friend, every morning we have coffee together. I have never been scared of him, I think less than my siblings.*

IDENTITY AND LEADERSHIP STYLE: A PROCESS OF RECONCILIATION

Carolina faced an important dilemma in returning to Peru to work for the family firm and had to resolve a conflict with her own value system. Eventually, she was convinced that she could be more effective in promoting economic and social development through her own family firm than she could by working anywhere else. Once the decision was taken, she worked hard to tailor the business around her own vision and aspirations. She has been instrumental in launching and managing the family Foundation and she has orchestrated highly visible strategic partnerships with multilateral institutions such as the World Bank and the UN, profiling their business model as one promoting women's economic empowerment in the region.

> *Since I came back in 2007, I have a vision of what I want this company to look like. We have 700,000 women working for us. This is a great opportunity to change the region and empower women. I want our company to set an example of doing good and doing business.*

The second conflict occurred when Carolina came back with an MBA from Kellogg and full of new ideas on modernizing the business. She experienced a culture shock with the company's norms that made her question her decision to return. "The culture was very hierarchical, power-oriented, people were very much into status and titles. It made me very uncomfortable; here was my own family's business and it was not a place where I could see myself working in." Human talent was in shortage and not up to the ambitions of the company.

> *The CFO and the VP of Marketing were people who had risen with (father) when he started the business but who no longer had the qualifications to do the job, did not even speak English ... we needed a strategy to bring in and retain talent, if we were to keep on growing.*

This she resolved by putting through a major restructuring of the organization. "We fired a lot of people as part of the restructuring. Now the culture has changed dramatically and we are attracting very high-level people."

Carolina has been ambivalent about her own desire to succeed her father in family business, but is steadily gaining in confidence and conviction, finding her own leadership style and voice.

> *I have gone back and forth. In the beginning I was scared, his shoes too big to fill. Now I am realizing I could do it my own way and with my own leadership style—I could fill his shoes but wearing my own ... just walking in ... [my father's] own footsteps was not enough for me, it was not challenging enough. He has been a successful entrepreneur, but so am I. I am also an entrepreneur and I need to do things they I see them, I like to have my own accomplishments and not just step on secure ground. I have my vision of where I wanted to go ...*

Sibling/Family Members' Rivalry: Managing the Potential Fallout

The family's history of bitter sibling rivalry has marked Carolina very deeply. To a great extent the ambivalence toward succession seems to stem mostly from the possibility of internal conflict rather than any fear of power and responsibility.

> *Now that my sister in back in the family business, tensions started appearing ... we are both competitive and with a business background ... we know we have to manage the family in a business-like manner. We hired consultants that facilitate meetings every three months, we have a long way to go, but we are really talking about the issues. We are advancing and taking positive steps.*

NON-FAMILY MEMBERS: RIVALS AND ALLIES

Professional management from the business has served both as a source of mentorship as well as resistance to the operational changes Carolina has put through. In the reorganization process that Carolina implemented, which led to significant turnover of people, Carolina enlisted the help of internal sponsors/mentors to build political support for her plans and to overcome the traditional paternalistic culture and her father's objections. "My father would never fire people. This insolent little girl asks me to let go people who have been there from the beginning! It was really hard for my dad to accept."

MANAGERIAL AND PATRIMONIAL TRANSFER: BEING A VIABLE SUCCESSOR/INVISIBILITY

There are few arguments to question the viability of Carolina as the favorite contender to take over the family business. She has acquired the formal professional qualifications (studies in renowned US institutions and an MBA), has gained experience externally in the industry, and has worked through almost all the critical functions of the family business, as brand manager, then marketing director, and then restructuring the human resource and finance functions. Successively she has led important strategic projects (with external consultants and internal mentors) to restructure the business and its corporate identity. She has modernized internal functions, attracted new professional talent, dealt with the difficult issues of transitioning from a paternalistic family business culture to a corporate one and is now reengineering the brand around issues of social responsibility and women's economic empowerment. She has been highly visible internationally, acting as ambassador for the firm in global partnerships. In this process, her father has been highly supportive and, even when resistant to change, has allowed her the stretch space to move forward. Invisibility is certainly not an issue in this case.

Gender Gap or Generational Gap?

If any discrimination were evident to Carolina, it has been related more to generational gap than to gender attributions, at least within the context of the family business. She perceives that her age has been a major obstacle in overcoming internal resistance and gain credibility for her ideas.

Not just about gender, it is more about age. When a young person arrives, man or woman, it is very difficult. The leadership in a family business is there for very long time, with no frequent transitions. The culture is entrenched. Having a young person take over is not easy for the older members of the firm. Being a woman is even harder because we lead differently, we are more team-oriented, but the harder is the generation change. They say: It's worked for many years why change? For my dad it was hard as well, seeing my involvement in the social responsibility project, he did not understand it. He was focused on "sell, sell, sell." Now he understands and is on my side. But not many are so open-minded.

THE "GLASS CEILING" ISSUE

Carolina did not find that a glass ceiling was an obstacle in her efforts to integrate the family firm so far. She attributes this partially to the nature of the business itself, where most employees and customers are women, and to her father being progressive and open-minded. "My dad was educated in the US and had seen the competition, Avon, being run by a woman. He was never a 'machista' dad and made sure he treated the three of us [siblings] the same way, giving the same educational opportunities."

Yet, she stresses that there is a strong "machista" culture in Latin America. Local culture requires that women stay at home, particularly when they have children.

In the business arena in LA, I have sensed it is a problem for my peers, when I represent my father in conferences. Outside of our company I see a resistance in taking me seriously. Out of the five most important family businesses in Peru, no woman is in charge. We are the only one. It has to do with my dad being so open-minded. I have friends whose parents would never let them study abroad. We were encouraged to go out and study.

WORK–FAMILY CONFLICT AND THE LACK OF POSITIVE ROLE MODELS

The restriction comes from the fact that you are the wife and the mother and the burden for everything is on you. The choice at the individual level is where it is played. Right now I do not have kids, I have the time, but when I have a family I know it would be very difficult. I have seen it was difficult for my sister.

She also underlines how scarce positive women leadership role models are in Latin America, at least the ones younger professional women can identify with.

A woman role model is very rare in Latin America. For women that are older than us, it was hard, so they have become very aggressive and they have a problem in "being themselves, not being guys." They seem not to have balance in their lives.

Discussion and Conclusions

While our findings from the Peru case study substantiate certain lessons emerging from existing literature, they challenge two main themes, namely the primogeniture advantage and the gender stereotyping and invisibility issues impacting the succession process. Although a successor is still not officially assigned in our case, our female entrepreneur seems the likeliest candidate. Although gender is signaled out as a societal constraint in conducting business in the Peruvian context at large, our subject has not found this to be an inhibiting factor in the context of the family business and signals generational transition issues as far more important. Neither does primogeniture seem to have a decisive favorable impact in the choice of successor, our subject being the youngest child and successor (favored over a first-born son).

The daughter in our case conforms to the literature's assessment of Peruvian women as becoming increasingly assertive and confident. Her aspirations do not seem to be compromised by considerations of inadequacy or invisibility, although there are lingering doubts about the possibility of combining their multiple roles as family caregivers and business leaders. As the literature indicates, the critical factors for her selection are a strong parent–child relationship, strong educational qualifications, and an extensive business experience both within and outside the family enterprise. Also, the entrepreneur's commitment to social issues conforms with the collectivist cultural traits and paternalistic culture attributed to Peru, although structured and modernized in the context of corporate social responsibility.

Limitations and Future Research Directions

A single case study on one family business does not constitute conclusive evidence of a shift in cultural perceptions of the role of women in family business nor of the critical factors impacting father–daughter succession issues in Peru. Our subject, when prompted, hinted that their family constituted an exception, in terms of the kind of freedom and equal opportunities both male and female children have received from their father. This case study is also based exclusively on interviews conducted with the daughter–successor. We were not able to obtain the feedback of other family members (father/siblings) that could have enriched our analysis and provided an additional perspective.

A more in-depth analysis needs to be conducted across the region to identify new emerging trends. There is very limited research documenting in general the role of women in family business in Latin America, and even less in Peru. Additional case studies and regional surveys could shed more light in this area, where female entrepreneurial activity as whole seems to be higher than in other regions and yet their activity within the family firm (the most prevalent form of private sector enterprise in the region) remains largely unexplored.

References

Allen, I.E., Elam, A., Langowitz, N. and Dean, M. 2008. 2007 *Report on Women and Entrepreneurship*. Global Entrepreneurship Monitor. Available at: http://www.gemconsortium.org/download.asp?fid=681 [accessed: 24 August 2010].

Alvarez, E.G and Sintas, J.L. 2003. *Coherence Between Values and Successor Socialization: Facilitating Family Business Continuity*. Barcelona: IESE Business School University of Navarra.

Azucena V., Idoia, I. and Covadogna, A.E. 2009. *Gender Influence on the Succession Planning in Family Owned Businesses*. WP [No 512] July University of the Basque Country, Spain (part of a larger research project financed by EMAKUNDE—Basque Institute for Women and FESIDE).

Baker, T., Gedajlovic, E. and Lubatkin, M. 2005. A Framework for Comparing Entrepreneurs Processes Across Nations. *Journal of International Business Studies*, 36(5), 492–504.

Celle de Bowman, O. 2000. Peruvian Female Industrialists and the Globalization Project: Deindustrialization and Women's Independence. *Gender and Society*, 14(4), 540–559.

Cheung, F.M., and Halpern, D.F. 2010. Women at the Top: Powerful Leaders Define Success as Work + Family in a Culture of Gender. *American Psychologist*, 65(3), 182–193.

Cole, P.M. 1997. Women in Family Business. *Family Business Review*, 10(4), 353–371.

Dumas, C. 1992. Integrating the Daughter into Family Business Management. *Entrepreneurship Theory and Practice* (Summer), 41–55.

Family Business Network (FBN). 2008. *Family Business International Monitor 2008*. Family Business Network International. Available at: http://www.fbn-i.org/fbn/web.nsf/doclu/AA3786AA36C250F9872575210070073E/$FILE/Monitor2008.pdf [accessed: 24 August 2010].

Jalbert, E.S. 2000. Women Entrepreneurs in the Global Economy. Available at: http://www.cipe.org/programs/women/pdf/jalbert.pdf [accessed: 24 August 2010].

Le Breton-Miller I., Miller, D. and Steier, L.P. 2004. Toward an Integrative Model of Effective FOB Succession. *Entrepreneurship Theory and Practice* (Summer), 305–328.

Lenartowicz, T. and Johnson, J.P. 2003. Cross-national Assessment of the Values of Latin America Managers: Contrasting Hues or Shades of Grey. *Journal of International Business Studies*, 34(3), 266–281.

Shimizu, T. 2006. *Executive Managers in Peru's Family Business*. Institute of Developing Economies, Discussion Paper [59], April. Available at: http://www.ide.go.jp/English/publish/Download/Dr/pdf/059.pdf [accessed: 10 May 2010].

Stavrou, E.T., Kleanthous, T. and Anastasiou, T. 2005. Leadership Personality and Firm Culture during Hereditary Transitions in Family Firms: Model Development and Empirical Investigation. *Journal of Small Business Management*, 43(2), 187–206.

Thunderbird School of Global Management. 2009. *Global Partners to Educate Women Entrepreneurs in Peru*. Thunderbird for Good, Thunderbird School of Global Management. Available at: http://knowledgenetwork.thunderbird.edu/thunderbirdforgood/2009/09/28/peru/ [accessed: 10 May 2010].

Vera, C.V. and Dean, M.A. 2005. An Examination of the Challenges Daughters Face in Family Business Succession. *Family Business Review*, XVIII(4), 321–345.

Weeks J.R. and Seiler, D. 2001. *Women's Entrepreneurship in Latin America: An Exploration of Current Knowledge*. Inter-American Development Bank, Washington, DC. Sustainable Development Department, Technical Papers Series. Available at: http://www.idisc.net/en/Article.38804.html [accessed: 10 May 2010].

Advice to Other Successors

You have to believe that the more you are able to find your own style and identity, the more comfortable you will be, you do not have to prove anything to anyone, just because you are a woman. One style does not have to be better than the other. This is what has worked for me. Realize your own style and capabilities, people feel that and realize it's real. You do not wear a mask for anyone. Education is crucial, go abroad, get exposure internationally, work outside the family, earn your stripes and prove your capabilities that will earn your credibility within the family business.

(Carolina)

PART VII Oceania

CHAPTER 27 Australia: The Challenge of Father–Daughter Succession in Family Business: A Case Study from the Land Down Under

MARY BARRETT AND KEN MOORES

Introduction

This chapter examines the case of an Australian woman, Roz, who succeeded her father as the CEO of a large fourth generation family business, "Hawkins Family Group," in the traditionally male-dominated transport industry. The case is described in three phases. First, we outline Australian culture and how it influences business life, including the position of women in the Australian workforce especially as managers and entrepreneurs. We then describe the history of the Hawkins Family Group and how Roz eventually came to lead it. Finally, we return to aspects of Australian values and culture and other literature to draw conclusions about the case. The chapter ends with a discussion of limitations and suggestions for further research.

Australian Culture and Values

The well-known theorist of international workplace culture, Geert Hofstede, places Australia high on the dimension of Individuality, or the extent to which people are expected to look after themselves and their own families as opposed to being integrated into groups. Australia is almost as strongly Individualist (IDV) as the United States of America (USA), the highest-ranking country on this dimension. Accordingly, Australians expect to do things independently rather than seek much help from others, and they strongly value privacy. Australia also scores high on Masculinity (MAS). Both men and women in Australia are assertive and competitive, though women are typically less so than men. In contrast, Australia ranks lower on Hofstede's Uncertainty Avoidance (UAI) scale. Australians are fairly tolerant of opinions different from what they are used to; they try to have as few rules as possible, and on the philosophical and religious level they are relativist and allow many currents to flow side by side. People in Australia are more phlegmatic and contemplative than in countries with more Uncertainty Avoidance, and tend not to express emotions. Australians see themselves as relaxed and "laid-back." Australia also ranks low on Power Distance (PDI). This is reflected in the pride Australians take in their "mateship" with others, that is, their belief in equality. Australians believe in a "fair go," that is, they think everyone should have a reasonable possibility of finding and exercising opportunities. Finally, Australians tend not to take a long-term perspective, as indicated by Australia's low score on the Long Term Orientation (LTO) dimension. These results are summarized in Figure 27.1.

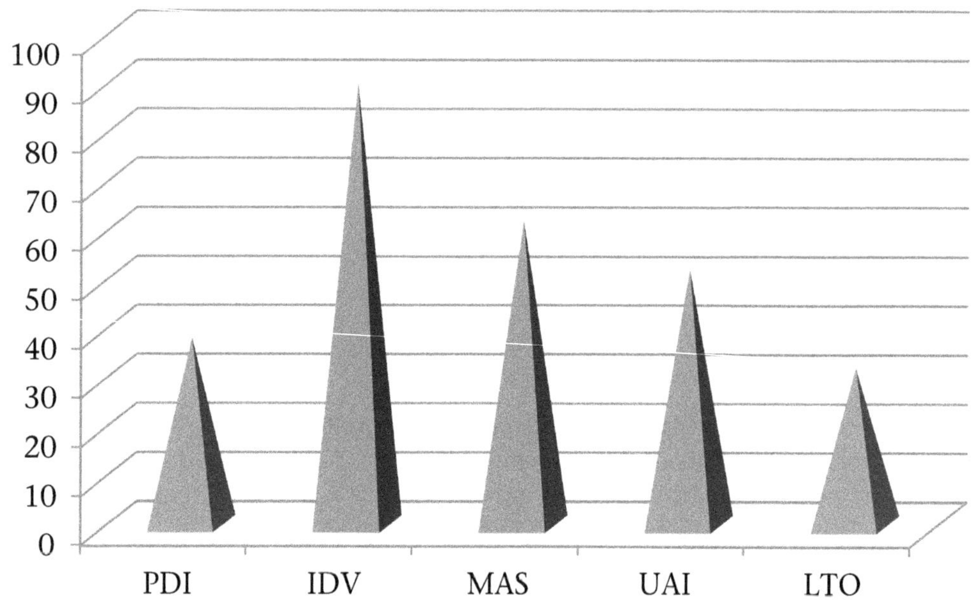

Figure 27.1 Australia's ratings on Hofstede's cultural dimensions
Source: ITIM International (2010)

The predominant religion in Australia is Christianity (50 percent), defined as the practice of Christian religions other than Catholicism. Australia's high IDV index correlates well with other Christian-based cultures.

Women and Minority Groups in the Australian Workplace

Since the colonization of Australia in 1788, and especially since the end of the Second World War, there have been many waves of migration to Australia. As a result of these trends, people with diverse ethnic backgrounds now make up more than 25 percent of the total Australian workforce, making Australia's one of the most culturally and ethnically diverse workforces in the world (DFAT, 2010). Since Federation in 1901, the Government has progressively moved away from its original White Australia policy, which sought to promote a homogeneous society based on European culture. Since the 1970s, the percentage of women in the workforce, which had declined after the end of the Second World War, has also rapidly increased. Successive federal governments have introduced legislation to promote anti-discrimination, equal employment opportunities and multiculturalism requiring firms to recruit, hire, and promote women and members of minority groups. Nevertheless, research shows that few Australian companies actively practice "diversity management," that is, try to help women and employees of diverse backgrounds to realize their full potential at work. In addition, women are still under-represented at senior levels in Australian organizations, especially in the private sector.

Australian Women as Business Owners and Entrepreneurs

We know from Global Entrepreneurship Monitor (GEM) studies (Minniti et al., 2005; Allen et al., 2007; Allen et al., 2008) that over the last three decades Australian women have been starting their own firms in increasing numbers. Nevertheless, their overall entrepreneurial activity does not exceed that of men. Their motivations for going into business are also similar to those of women in developed countries elsewhere. Most Australian women, like most men, start firms because they perceive a business opportunity rather than because they have no other way to make a living. Nevertheless, more Australian women than Australian men are "necessity" entrepreneurs. The glass ceiling still seems to hold sway in Australia where women have made slow progress in attaining positions on company boards, or CEO or other "C-suite" positions. Women hold around 36 percent of senior executive positions in the public service but only around 12 percent of management jobs in the private sector (EOWA, 2008). Some researchers argue that the glass ceiling is actually a source of new female entrepreneurs in Australia, because women feel they must start their own firms if they want to get to the top. Despite this, major Australian organizations such as Telstra sponsor awards for individual business women, and the popular business press regularly features articles on individual women entrepreneurs, often with a mantra-like insistence that glass ceilings do not exist or are simply there to be broken.

Implications for Women Leaders in Family Firms

The implications of these cultural and demographic issues for women in Australian family businesses are mixed. On the one hand, Australian's high scores for Individualism and Masculinity are conducive to entrepreneurship on the part of both women and men. Australians respect people who are prepared to "have a go," that is, make something of themselves using their own wits and resources. The value of the "fair go" ostensibly includes the right of women to make their own path in life, independently of men. In June 2010 the appointment of Australia's first Prime Minister, Julia Gillard, was widely welcomed, with many commenting that it indicates women in Australia can reach the highest jobs in the land.

On the other hand, the value Australians place on equality has also been said to mean they resent people who do *too* well in life. The "tall poppy syndrome," that is, the desire to bring conspicuously successful people back to the same level as others, is said to be strong in Australia. Australians value their privacy and take a stoic, masculine approach to life's problems. This means that family business owners, especially men, may be unwilling to seek advice or to form family business boards or establish other formal governance mechanisms. In addition, Australians' enjoyment of a good time and their refusal to take life too seriously may lead to a neglect of business necessities. Finally, Australians' strong scores for Masculinity mean they are sometimes ambivalent about women stepping out of traditional roles or usurping men in positions of power. While Julia Gillard is now Prime Minister, such appointments remain exceptional.

We continue to explore these contrasts and contradictions in Australian society as we consider the Hawkins Family Group case.

The Case Study

BRIEF HISTORY OF THE BUSINESS

In 1921, Bartholomew and Rosina Hawkins established a service station in Ipswich, Queensland. The business quickly evolved beyond the service station and Hawkins Transport became the first transport company to compete with the railway. It was able to run more efficiently than the railway, but regulations restricted freight carriers from undercutting the railway's charges. Consequently, Hawkins Transport enjoyed substantial profit margins and was highly successful. Despite this, its position deteriorated and it almost failed to survive beyond the second generation. The founders' son, Harold, who was known for enjoying good times rather than growing the firm, sold off the service station and struggled to maintain the financial position of the transport business. His premature death resulted in his son, Neville, taking over the family business in 1952 when he was 19 years old.

Neville was committed to turning the business around. Hard work by him and his family saw the business restored to its former profitable state. Complete reinvestment back into the business enabled Hawkins Transport to grow and commence interstate haulage. In 1971, Hawkins Transport began ferrying passengers and supplies to Moreton Island; this operation also involved the family running the Kooringal General Store. Further growth opportunities presented themselves. In 1990, Hawkins Transport bought a transport company based in Tully in North Queensland's banana growing precinct. Hawkins Family Group soon became involved in growing bananas and Brick Creek Banana Farm has since grown to boast 150 acres of Cavendish bananas under plant. In 2005, Hawkins Family Group established Hawkins Fuels, a retail outlet serving the needs of truck drivers. In August 2007, another service was added to the Group with the opening of Port Wash, a truck, four-wheel drive, and car washing facility.

Currently, Hawkins Family Group consists of a range of diversified business, all with a link back to the family's transport origins. The organization employs over 200 people, including members of the third, fourth and fifth generations. Hawkins Road Transport is the largest privately-owned transport company operating in North Queensland with a network of depots in Brisbane, Townsville, Mackay, Tully, and the Burdekin delta.

The company owns a fleet of trucks and specializes in transporting fresh produce from North Queensland to Brisbane. Hawkins Road Transport also has a fuel and bulk liquid division and is a Shell and Caltex approved carrier. The Moreton Island operations have continued to expand from the humble beginnings of a 34-foot vessel to a 58 meter long, 16 meter wide, fast catamaran that can carry 52 four-wheel drive vehicles and 400 passengers. It is also used for evening river cruises for corporate and private events. The Kooringal store business now includes adventure day trips, four-wheel drive tours, and catered beach events.

Over the years, all four members of the fourth generation, John, Anne, Kerry, and Roz have worked in the business. John, Neville and Shirley's only son took over the transport business and opened the Townsville depot. Neville, and indeed everyone in the family, expected John to run the business once Neville retired. But John eventually left the business and now pursues his own business interests in the US. In the next section we use Roz's story to explain how the three daughters, Anne, Kerry, and Roz, bought the business, and now manage it with Roz as the appointed CEO.

ROZ HAWKINS'S STORY

As a child and a teenager, Roz Hawkins never expected to have a major role in the family firm. At school she studied music, geography, and history, not business-related subjects. Despite being enrolled in a prestigious private girls' school in Brisbane, she was restless and left before her final year, planning to start serious studies in music and to complete high school part time. However, nothing turned out as she thought it would:

> *I think the first day that I went to the Conservatorium I knew that I didn't belong there. I was totally out of place. I did actually manage to almost complete my first year of Hubbards [the college where she planned to finish her high school subjects]. But come to the end of that time before exams I thought, "I don't really want to do these exams." And out of the blue—I don't even know why I said it—I said to my Mum, "Can I come work for you instead?" It was probably a little bit about not wanting to finish my exams, but I don't really know why I said it. Deep down I must have wanted to do it.*

On a superficial level there was every reason for Roz not to want to work in the family firm. As a teenager Roz complained that the work was terrible and that she was treated like a slave—"typical teenager talk," she says now. Moreover, when she began working full time in the firm, not only did she work hard but she had to defer to her brother:

> *I was nearly 18 at that stage so it was my first job. It wasn't easy. I used to have to vacuum the boat, clean all the chairs, do all the ironing, answer the phone, then I had to receive freight on the forklift and basically do what my brother told me to do.*

Nevertheless there were early signs that Roz had potential for business leadership. While she and her brother and sisters had all worked in the family firm outside school time, Roz's early involvement had shown a disciplined approach which marked her as different from her siblings. She had been the only one of them to get paid for what she did—because she presented her parents with a formal invoice for the work done: "I did get paid when I worked. Not much, but I did get paid if I submitted a bill. The others would never get paid because they never bothered to submit the bill. So it wasn't that you just got paid anyway."

The tasks Roz had to do gradually improved; for example she got to see the accounts, although for a long time they remained her father's responsibility. Despite the business growing and becoming more complex, she received little, if any, guidance from her brother about day-to-day matters. So she began making her own decisions almost from the outset:

> *We had two businesses still at that stage. We'd started running the ferry business. We had the vehicular ferry and we had about five or six trucks. We had four phones on the desk—one was the transport phone and the other three were the Moreton Island Ferry phones. There was invoicing to do and I would take calls from customers for the transport as well ... basically he [her brother, John] was a guy who was very hands-on, he was always in the workshop and you were never able to get him into the office, so I started making decisions because I was sick of running and getting him.*

This echoed the independence Roz had already experienced in childhood. Her parents had always traveled a lot for the business, and as a result Roz had spent a lot of time on her own or with her older sisters. This meant she was comfortable about making her own decisions once she formally entered the firm.

> *Mum and Dad were off to the island every day. They would drive the ferry and deliver the freight. They'd go over Tuesday and they wouldn't come back until Thursday so they'd be on the island for three days ... I was much younger than my siblings so by the time I was 12, Kerry was 19, so Mum and Dad had virtually moved out of home by then.*

Roz settled into an office manager role that became more demanding as the business grew. She also became more and more independent of the males in her family. At the same time, her brother John and her father began to argue, and their disputes spread to other members of the family:

> *Dad and John would dispute every day. Every day there would a fight. Sometimes Mum would get involved and if she took John's side then there'd be an even bigger fight. There were fireworks all the time. I don't think it was really all one person's fault. There were definitely two sides to the story. Sometimes Dad would treat John quite unfairly ... I think Dad was threatened by him. He didn't want to let go, but also John didn't manage very well and Dad could see that.*

John was by then in his early 30s. Neville had always assumed John would succeed him, despite his growing lack of confidence in John's ability to run the firm. According to Roz, Neville had never really planned or even discussed the succession. John began to spend even more time away from the firm because of the continual conflicts and because Roz's capable presence allowed him to be absent. The result was that Roz increasingly sorted out the firm's problems and improved its systems. By grappling with the accounts, she also came to understand the firm's financial position better. This eventually led her to question her involvement in the business and even its viability. However, it took some time before she understood the business well enough to do this:

It took me a long time to learn all of this [financial] stuff that I actually would have learnt if I'd done a university degree or something like that. It's only when I started learning about profit and loss statements and balance sheets and how to do them that I started thinking to myself, "This is a really terrible business."

Conflicts increased between Roz and John, John and his parents, and eventually between Neville and Shirley. This and Roz's growing dissatisfaction brought matters to a head:

I remember it was in the backyard. Dad was on the forklift and I went to see him late one afternoon—I was going home. I was still on about wages actually. By this time I had this reputation in the transport business—people were saying to me "You do a great job," whatever, and I thought to myself I can actually go and get a real job outside this business and get twice as much money. We weren't paying dividends. So what am I doing here?

John finally left the firm for good and went to the US. After this Neville began to mentor Roz—though only when she asked questions—and to regard her as his successor. After long and painful negotiations, Roz and her sisters bought out their parents' share in the business. At her father's insistence, Roz has a controlling interest. Roz has since embarked on comprehensive plans to improve the firm's governance structures, continue its growth, and develop the potential of members of the fifth generation to enter the firm. She is completing an MBA in family business studies to professionalize the firm even further.

Discussion

Roz's story partly challenges and partly confirms previous research. Moores and Barrett (2002) found that learning the family business requires four "Ls" or learning phases. L1, "learning business," means learning personal disciplines such as self-reliance and self-control, and how to be accountable to someone else for results. These skills are normally learned early in life, but L1 also normally requires leaving the family business. L2, learning *our* business, means learning the special qualities of the family business. L3, learning to *lead* our business, means gaining a "helicopter view" of the firm and its needs. It typically involves professionalizing the firm but also requires the leader to retain the informality that helps the firm make quick decisions. L4, *letting go* of our business, means achieving a good succession for both the successor and the person letting go.

In contrast with the conventional L1 to L4 learning sequence, Roz never left the family firm to work elsewhere. Of the three daughters who now share ownership, only one, Anne, gained any work experience outside the firm. John, the heir apparent, did gain such experience, but ultimately left the firm. His style of leadership, which focused on operational rather than strategic matters, turned out not to be the right fit for the organization. Even more unusually, Roz's lack of outside experience is not hampering her credibility, even in the transport industry, where women rarely reach senior levels.

Roz's succession was helped by her role as an "anchor" in the family firm. Anchors, according to Curimbaba (2002), are women who are always there, providing low-key but indispensible functions. This, combined with her entrepreneurial qualities (Roz designed the plans for the upgraded catamaran for Moreton Island Ferries), her closeness to customers, and her sheer dedication have qualified her for leadership. In the Hawkins

Family Group, men from earlier generations had sometimes acted like Curimbaba's "Invisibles," using the firm's resources to have a good time. When Roz looked back to her mother, Shirley, and her grandmother, Rosina, she would have seen strong, committed, optimistic women rather than "Invisibles."

Even in Australia, which has a strong tradition of assertive, competitive women, it is unusual that a daughter should "win out" over a son for the CEO position. However, in bringing up their children, Neville and Shirley always regarded gender as irrelevant, expecting their daughters to do as much for the business as John. Yet when Roz entered the business she was expected to defer to her older brother, and everyone regarded him as the natural successor. In line with a traditional Australian reluctance to discuss emotional issues, Neville never talked about the succession in advance. However, it gradually became clear that Roz's and not John's approach to firm management was what the firm needed. The handover to Roz also happened following a rift between her parents, and it was carried out against her mother's wishes. So not only was Roz's father reluctant to relinquish power, but Roz's mother felt deprived of the rewards she had hoped for. Because of all the conflicts, Roz's succession to the CEO role may present itself as the victory of a daughter over other family members. Yet Roz's leadership qualities suggest that "stewardship" rather than a particular person won out.

Conclusions, Limitations, and Future Research Directions

Roz's case illustrates typical succession issues confronting women in Australian family firms. Her family circumstances and upbringing are not unusual and her succession reflects Australia's only gradually changing approach to gender issues. The firm's transport origins typify "male" pioneering culture in Australia. Australians like to think about the early pioneers opening up remote parts of the country, but in so doing few invoke women's presence let alone their contribution. Even now the building in the Port of Brisbane where the firm is headquartered reflects a male world: it is basic, devoid of luxury fittings or fripperies. Like the name of the pop group "Men at Work" whose songs include "The Land Down-Under," a tongue-in-cheek celebration of Australian values, work life in Australia does not easily adapt itself to women's needs. Future research could investigate the extent to which, in the context of a family firm, women overcome barriers to leadership and entrepreneurship within male-oriented industries.

Roz's attention to future planning, governance, and her emphasis on the values of stewardship and family, confirm Barrett and Moores' (2009) finding that women lead their family firms in much the same way as men. Future research should delve into whether there are special obstacles that women leaders in family firms face when attempting to lead their family firms in the same way as men, and how family firms can transcend the idea that "managers are male." Another research question arises from women's non-strategic path to the top of their family firms. Barrett and Moores' (2009) study found this prevented many family business women from achieving self-confidence and legitimacy. How such obstacles might be overcome, and whether a non-strategic path to the top may actually present some advantages, are other important questions.

From these questions, it is evident that looking into the experiences of one female family business leader promises lessons not just for family business women but for women entrepreneurs and leaders in general.

References

Allen, E.I., Langowitz, N. and Minniti, M. 2007. *GEM 2006 Report on Women and Entrepreneurship*. Global Entrepreneurship Monitor (GEM). Available at: http://www.gemconsortium.org/download.asp?fid=580 [accessed: 15 July 2010].

Allen, E.I., Elam, A., Langowitz, N. and Dean, M. 2008. *GEM Global 2007 Report on Women and Entrepreneurship*. Global Entrepreneurship Monitor (GEM). Available at: http://www.gemconsortium.org/document.aspx?id=681 [accessed: 15 July 2010].

Barrett, M.A. and Moores, K. 2009. *Women Leaders in Family Business: Daughters on the Stage*. Cheltenham and Northampton: Edward Elgar.

Curimbaba, F. 2002. The Dynamics of Women's Roles as Family Business Managers. *Family Business Review*, 15(3), 239–252.

Department of Foreign Affairs and Trade (DFAT). 2010. *Australia: A Culturally Diverse Society*. Available at: http://222.dfat.gov.au [accessed: 5 July 2010].

Equal Opportunity in the Workplace Australia (EOWA). 2008. *2008 EOWA Australian Census of Women in Leadership*. Available at: http://www.eowa.gov.au/Australian_Women_In_Leadership_Census/2008_Australian_Women_In_Leadership_Census.asp [accessed: 5 July 2010].

ITIM International. 2010 *Australia—Australian Geert Hofstede Cultural Dimensions Explained*. Available at http://www.geert-hofstede.com/hofstede_australia.shtml [accessed: 15 May 2010].

Minniti, M., Arenius, P. and Langowitz, N. 2005. GEM 2004 Report on Women and Entrepreneurship. *Global Entrepreneurship Monitor* (GEM). Available at: http://www.gemconsortium.org/document.aspx?id=419 [accessed: 5 July 2010].

Moores, K. and Barrett, M.A. 2002. Learning Family Business: Paradoxes and Pathways. London: Ashgate (Routledge).

Telstra Business Women's Awards. About the Telstra Business Women's Awards. Available at: http://www.telstrabusinesswomensawards.com/about-help-13.aspx [accessed: 5 July 2010].

CHAPTER 28 New Zealand: The Daughter Takes Over a Residential Home Building Family Business: A Case Study from Aotearoa New Zealand

FRANCO VACCARINO

Introduction

Aotearoa New Zealand is a small country with around 4 million people situated at the bottom of the globe with "unique difficulties associated with its size and isolation in competing in the global marketplace and in the processes of internationalization" (McGregor and Tweed, 2000:41). Family-owned businesses and small/medium enterprises contribute extensively to its economy.

The fact that New Zealand has had two female Prime Ministers, Jenny Shipley (1997–1999) and Helen Clark (1999–2008), has assisted in highlighting how successful women can be in leadership positions. However, McGregor and Tweed point to research at the start of the new millennium which showed that "the private sector in New Zealand is more conservative about women in the executive suite and that elevating women within managerial ranks remains a fundamental challenge for corporations in the new millennium" (2000:41).

Despite the fact that both women and family businesses play an important role in the New Zealand economy, there is relatively little in the literature exploring their role together. This chapter meets this gap by looking at father–daughter succession in New Zealand family firms. In the following sections, we provide an overview of family business and women leadership in general with a particular focuses on the business situation in Aotearoa New Zealand. We then explore findings from our own study through the case of a director who took over her father's residential home building business. Implications for future research and practice are then examined in the conclusion.

Literature Review

In order to provide a context of the business scenario in New Zealand, Smyrnios and Dana point out that "family and privately owned businesses represent an important section of the New Zealand economy" (2007:2). Massey et al. add that New Zealand:

> *... is a country in which small and medium sized enterprises (SMEs) dominate the business population. There are approximately 370,000 "economically significant enterprises" in New Zealand (that is, those that are registered for Goods and Services Tax (GST) and/or employ two or more staff) and only around 700 of them are large private sector firms; the rest are either SMEs or they belong to the public sector such as hospitals and/or government departments.*
>
> *(2006:17)*

In the 1990s, Roger Maxwell, the then Minister of Business Development in New Zealand, said that, "Historically, women have had a low participation rate in business, however, they have often played a major role behind the scenes" (in Gray, 1993, Foreword). As in many other parts of the world, many New Zealand women still do "work behind the scenes in family businesses often performing roles traditionally undertaken by women, such as bookkeeping and assisting paid employees of the business" (Ministry of Women's Affairs and Ministry of Economic Development, 2008:10).

In the late 1980s in New Zealand, Bollard (1988) mentions that female family members were "in support roles, helping out in family firms or assisting their husbands in new businesses." Ten years later, a report by the Ministry of Women's Affairs (1998) in New Zealand highlighted the crucial role rural women play in their family's farm, and how they help with seasonal work and provide back-up support on the farm. Martinez Jimenez states that traditionally, in family firms, women have played "many subtle roles: spouse, parent, in-law, family leader. These roles are related to the family rather than to the business sphere" (2009:53). Francis echoes this and says that "daughters, wives, and daughters-in-law often are viewed by a family as "helpers" in their business. They may cover when a receptionist is sick, work during the peak season, or assist on a special but temporary project" (1999:3).

However, McGregor and Tweed argue that "New Zealand has been falsely comforting itself that it is uniquely progressive in terms of women's equality" (2000:40) because "New Zealand can justly claim to be the first self-governing nation to grant the vote to all adult women" (Elections New Zealand, 2010:20) in 1893. In their report, Massey and Lewis add that "despite many indicators that suggest women in New Zealand society enjoy a level of equality that surpasses many of our neighbours and trading partners, there is still evidence that points to continuing disparity between men and women at an economic level" (2003:5).

The World Economic Forum introduced the Global Gender Gap Index in 2006 which provides "a comprehensive framework for benchmarking global gender gaps" and "reveals those countries that are role models in dividing resources equitably between women and men, regardless of their level of resources" (Hausmann et al., 2009:*v*). This Index examines the gap between men and women in four groups: economic participation and opportunity, educational attainment, political empowerment, and health and survival. Of the 134 countries included in the 2009 Global Gender Gap Index, New Zealand ranked fifth (the countries in the first to fourth positions being Iceland, Finland, Norway, and

Sweden). Hausmann et al. state that, "New Zealand retains its privileged position in the rankings while showing an absolute increase in scores for economic participation (7) and political empowerment (7)" (2009:20).

Nonetheless, women are playing a more prominent role in the business world, particularly in the SME landscape. In terms of women in enterprise, "New Zealand women are less likely to be self-employed than men, however self-employment of women has increased and the gap between male and female rates of self-employment is gradually reducing. In 2006, women made up 36 percent of self-employed people" (Ministry of Women's Affairs and Ministry of Economic Development, 2008:6). The New Zealand Ministry of Women's Affairs and Ministry of Economic Development report states that, "Many New Zealand women consider self-employment as a way of improving work–life balance" (2008:23). However, in their research, Kirkwood and Mackie (2004) found that women often have to work into the night so they can also maintain their family responsibilities, so they tend to "add" their business role to their existing roles within the family.

McGregor and Tweed suggest that the remarkable explosion of women's participation in small business ownership in New Zealand is part of a worldwide phenomenon. It follows international trends in other western developed nations such as rising education levels for women, increasing female labor force participation through new entry jobs, re-entry, and part-time work (2000:40).

In research conducted in the New Zealand BusinesSMEasure project, in which owners preparing for succession were interviewed, Battisti highlights findings which show that, "58 percent of the owners indicated that they plan to sell their firm, 36 percent plan to pass their firm on and 7 percent are intending to wind the firm down and close it" (2008:11). These findings are in line with research conducted by Smyrnios and Dana in which they found that, "only 24 percent of NZ family business owners have a policy of definitely remaining family owned" (2007:3). Smyrnios and Dana also found that in New Zealand "more sons are involved in the day-to-day running of family firms (32 percent) compared to daughters (6 percent)" and it would "appear that sons (60 percent) are much more likely than daughters (11 percent) to take over the helm from the current CEO" (2007:25). In another research study on small businesses conducted in New Zealand, Lord et al. (2003) found that the majority of family businesses were founded by either one or two family members, and that founding families were still involved in most of the businesses. In 25 percent of cases, children were working in the family business.

This research shows that both family businesses and women have an important role in the New Zealand economy, but there is still little known about the unique role which they play in the family firm context. We discuss an example of a successful father–daughter succession and present learnings to contribute to this knowledge gap.

Case Study and Discussion

HISTORY OF THE FAMILY BUSINESS

Bob and Desma Isles started a residential home building business in 1973. Over the years the company they founded gained a proven and respected track record within the area for quality residential housing. Part of this track record involves the business being awarded a number of prestigious awards.

Tarsha, the director of the business, said that her father built up the business where he had around thirty staff members, but as he got older the numbers decreased. When he was about to retire, Tarsha's brother, who was in a completely different field, decided that he would do an apprenticeship. Tarsha was looking at getting back into the work force after she had had her children and she did not want to go back to her first profession. Thus, in 2004 Tarsha took over the business as the director, and her brother Cameron manages the various projects.

THE DAUGHTER–SUCCESSOR

Tarsha trained and qualified as a clinical veterinarian and did not think of entering the family business. It was only when her father had mentioned that he would like to retire from the business that Tarsha considered the option of joining the family business. This situation is different from other daughters who take over a family business in which they may have been involved from a very young age; for Tarsha, this was a change of career. She did not have a specified time period before joining the family business, which Dumas refers to as an "an initiation stage" which "begins in early childhood and lasts until the woman decides to start working in the firm. During all this time, the daughter internalizes the family and business values, becomes familiar with how things are done in the firm, and becomes steadily more committed to the firm. At the same time, she begins to acquire technical, interpersonal, and managerial skills and knowledge" (Martinez Jimenez, 2009:58). Without this initial stage, it has certainly been a lot more difficult for Tarsha to take over the family business, but with the support she has received, and her willingness to learn, she has become very successful.

CHANGEOVER AND SUCCESSION PROCESS

Tarsha trained as a clinical veterinarian and her brother went into computing when he finished university, so their father never thought Tarsha would take over as director of the family business. Fitzgerald highlights that "succession is not an event, it is a deliberate long-term process determining the continuity of the family business from one generation to the next and represents one of the toughest management challenges a family business will face" (2000:4). Bob had thought that he would sell the business when he retired, but when Tarsha did decide to take over as director of the company, she says that it made him really happy. It wasn't something that he thought would happen, so he didn't have any expectations that either of them would enter the business. So when they did, he was thrilled, and Tarsha believes that this is the reason why it has made it easy to be the successor in the family business.

When asked whether the changeover from the father was difficult, Tarsha said that it wasn't at all, and that everybody said that it would be hard as her father would not want to let go of the reins. She continued saying that from when she started, her father would say, "You're the boss, do what you like." She said that her father would make suggestions but he never interfered. She said that the timing of the changeover was perfect as they had had five years of their father working with them and, even though he retired, he was actually still working. He is doing what he enjoys, that is, building houses, and he does not have the responsibility of running a business.

CHALLENGES AND DIFFICULTIES

The building industry is still very male dominated in New Zealand, as it is in most parts of the world. When asked whether she had encountered any difficulties, Tarsha said she hadn't and that it had taken her a while to learn as she came from a completely different background. Apart from the global recession being a challenge, Tarsha points out that one of the biggest challenges was not so much in taking over the business, but rather in trying to change the direction of the business. She mentioned that 20 years ago people would go to a builder and ask to have a house built, however, nowadays people go to franchise building companies. In a smaller city it certainly is a challenge trying to change the direction of a business.

Tarsha continued by saying that another challenge was building up the company again, but they are lucky because the company had a good reputation. Tarsha's father's reputation for quality work has been an asset for the company. This also represents a challenge for the company, but it is one that Tarsha strives to carry on.

When asked whether she experiences any difficulties as a female director, Tarsha said that now people have accepted that she is the director of the company, but it did take a while. She said that previously most people presumed that she was just doing the books and that she was Cameron's wife. For the first couple of years, she always had to say no, she is his sister and she runs the business. Tarsha said that as a clinical veterinarian, she had more negative gender problems than she does as the director of this building business.

Furthermore, most people Tarsha deals with are men, and when asked how they react to her, she replied jokingly: "I don't know what they say when I'm not around ..." But, on a serious note, she said that it is just a New Zealand thing where it is more acceptable that women are in a variety of jobs. She explained that because of her previous job where she was doing physical farm veterinary work predominantly with men, she was used to talking to and dealing with men.

A SUCCESSFUL ENTREPRENEUR

Tarsha says that she is very proud of the business because it has a good history. This advantage of being proud of "carrying on the family tradition" concurs with Vera and Dean's (2005:333) research findings into female entrepreneurs in family businesses. Tarsha also said that she likes that "we're carrying on something that has been a good thing and that it makes my parents happy." When asked about the radical shift from clinical veterinarian to director of a home building company, Tarsha said that sometimes she misses her previous job, but that it would not suit her current lifestyle. She is happy that she can choose the hours she wants to work, even though they may be very long and she may need to work at night. One of the benefits is that she can take a day off when she needs to in order to go to a school sports event, for example. This is in line with Salganicoff's findings, in that, "Family firms have advantages that have particular relevance for women. In many cases, family businesses can offer flexibility in work schedules to meet the needs of women" (1990:128).

Getz and Carlsen point out that, "Family dynamics are a crucial factor in the family business" (2005:244), and Tarsha believes that the business has worked so well because they get on well as a family and always have. She says that they are a close family and always go on holiday together, they spend Christmas together, and they see each other on the weekends and babysit each others' children. She adds that because they get on so well together, if something should go wrong, they can sit down and discuss the issue or problem and resolve it.

Another success of the company is that "there's just really good communication" and Tarsha believes that this is very important. She says that if, for example, someone is worried about something, then you need to look at those concerns and sort them out. She also pointed out that she does not know how easy it would be working with one's family members if it was just purely business. This concurs with the findings from Vera and Dean's research relating to some of the advantages of working in the family business, namely that "you get to spend a lot of time with your family" and the "feeling that everyone in the business is working toward the same goal" (2005:333). An interesting finding from Nunns' study of New Zealand female family members working in their family's SME business was the description of their family business "being a positive dimension of their family's life, providing family members with focus, cohesiveness and camaraderie" (2001:37).

Tarsha asserted that it would not have mattered what the children decided to do, they knew that their dad was always "a hundred and ten percent" behind them. Tarsha also supposes that it helped that her mother was involved in the business company when her father was running it. The father saw that the mother was managing the business then and he saw that she did well at the job and so there would not have been any negative experiences from Tarsha taking over the business.

CONFLICT

Another difficult aspect of a family business is conflict. Tarsha mentions that a large majority of people ask her how she could work with her family, but she says that they have no problems. She attributes this to the fact that they all work in different areas within the business, and each is responsible for different sections. She says that if she makes a management decision, Cameron doesn't question why she made such a decision. They sit down and discuss everything together but, as far as some of the financial aspects, often she just goes ahead and does what she believes is right for the business.

Conclusion

From the literature and the case study it is clear that "family-business owners no longer can afford to select only the most qualified *men* available to lead their companies because smart businesses know the most qualified "man" for the position may be a *woman*" (Francis, 1999:13). Usry et al. point out that, "Women as successors to the family business are becoming more of an alternative in succession plans than perhaps ever before" (2004:7). Francis also points out that the success of a family business depends on a "complex combination of variables" (1999:77) ranging from timing to hard work, but the most powerful variable between success and failure is "the presence of a strong, healthy family behind the venture" (Ibid.) and this certainly seems to be the case with Tarsha and her family.

From this case study it is clear that Tarsha has successfully embraced her role as director of the residential home building family business. It is also evident that she has adjusted very well with quite a radical career change. A critical and crucial success factor in this business is keeping open channels of communication, and being open and willing to discuss any issues or concerns which arise.

Family dynamics are another important element of a successful family business, and in this case study it is clear that the business works well because they get on so well as a family. Tarsha feels proud of the business and wants to be there rather than feeling that she has been forced to take over the business without any choice. This also attributes to the success of the business. Furthermore, the fact that Bob, the founder of the business, said to Tarsha, "You're the boss, do what you like" when he stepped down, is yet another important factor in the success of a family business. Although a family business successor values what the father did and may ask for suggestions or advice, it is now the successor who runs the business. The successor needs to be able to run the business her way, rather than always have dad look over her shoulder. It is important that the father lets go of the reins.

An interesting observation from this case study is that Tarsha had more negative gender stereotyping as a clinical veterinarian than she does now as a director of a business in a male-dominated industry. Future research could compare gender issues in family businesses versus other professions in general and big corporate companies. The question this raises is whether gender is more or less of an issue in family businesses than is the case in other areas.

References

Battisti, M. 2008. *Succession Perspectives from New Zealand Small Enterprises: A Report based on BusinesSMEasure*, November 2007. Wellington, New Zealand: *New Zealand Centre for SME Research*.

Bollard, A. 1988. *Small Businesses in New Zealand*. Wellington: Allen and Unwin/Port Nicholson Press.

Elections New Zealand. 2010. *Votes for Women*. Available at http://www.elections.org.nz/democracy/history/votes-for-women.html#1 [accessed: 28 April 2010].

Fitzgerald, L.S. 2000. *The Dynamics of the Succession Process Within Ten Small-scale Family Businesses in Christchurch, New Zealand*. Research report presented in partial fulfillment of the requirements for the degree of Masters of Business Studies at Massey University. Palmerston North, New Zealand: Massey University.

Francis, A.E. 1999. *The Daughter Also Rises: How Women Overcome Obstacles and Advance in the Family-owned Business*. San Francisco: Rudi Publishing.

Getz, D. and Carlsen, J. 2005. Family Business in Tourism: State of the Art. *Annals of Tourism Research*, 32(1), 237–258.

Gray, A. 1993. *Women Establishing Businesses: Barriers and Solutions*. Wellington: Ministry of Commerce.

Hausmann, R., Tyson, L.D. and Zahidi, S. 2009. *The Global Gender Gap Report 2009*. World Economic Forum. Available at: http://www.weforum.org/pdf/gendergap/report2009.pdf [accessed: 5 June 2010].

Kirkwood, J. and Mackie, B. 2004. *Working the Nightshift: How do Women Entrepreneurs Balance Work and Family?* Proceedings of Australia and New Zealand Academy of Management Conference, 8–10 December 2004, Dunedin, New Zealand.

Lord, B.R., Shanahan, Y.P. and Robb, A.J. 2003. *Perspectives on Family Businesses in New Zealand and Australia*. Proceedings of the 16th Annual Conference of Small Enterprise Association of Australia and New Zealand, pp.1–20. Ballarat, Australia. Available at: http://www.cric.com.au/seaanz/resources/54LordetalPerspetivesonfamilybusinessfinal.pdf [accessed: 1 June 2010].

Martinez Jimenez, R. 2009. Research on Women in Family Firms: Current Status and Future Directions. *Family Business Review*, 22(1), 53–64.

Massey, C. and Lewis, K. 2003. *New Zealand Women and Micro-finance*. New Zealand Centre for Small & Medium Enterprise Research, Wellington: Massey University.

Massey, C., Lewis, K., Cameron, A., Coetzer, A. and Harris, C. 2006. It's the People that you Know: A Report on NZ SMEs & their Human Resource Practices, in *The Fourth Symposium of the New Zealand Centre for SME Research: The People Behind the Profit* (pp. 15–23), edited by C. Massey. Wellington: NZ Centre for SME Research, Massey University.

McGregor, J. and Tweed, D. 2000. Women in Management and Business Owners in New Zealand, in *Women in Management: Current Research Issues Volume II* (pp. 41–52), edited by M.J. Davidson and R. Burke. London: Sage.

Ministry of Women's Affairs. 1998. *Status of Women in New Zealand: CEDAW Report*. Wellington: Ministry of Women's Affairs.

Ministry of Women's Affairs and Ministry of Economic Development. 2008. *Women in Enterprise: A Report on Women in Small and Medium Enterprises in New Zealand*. Wellington: Ministry of Women's Affairs and Ministry of Economic Development.

Nunns, H. 2001. *An Exploratory Study of the Participation of Female Family Members in Small and Medium-sized Family Businesses in New Zealand*. Research report presented in partial fulfillment of the requirements for the degree of Master of Business Studies at Massey University. Palmerston North, New Zealand: Massey University.

Salganicoff, M. 1990. Women in Family Business: Challenges and Opportunities. *Family Business Review*, 3(2), 125–137.

Smyrnios, K.S. and Dana, L.E. 2007. *The MGI New Zealand Family and Private Business Survey 2007*. Available at: http://www.mgiworld.com/_homepdfs/MGIFamilyBusinessSurvey07_NewZealand.pdf [accessed: 28 April 2010].

Usry, M.L., Wigginton, K.W. and Thomas, D.S. 2004. *Women as Family Business Successors*. Available at: http://www.sbaer.uca.edu/research/ssbia/1992/pdf/18.pdf [accessed: 28 April 2010].

Vera, C.F. and Dean, M.A. 2005. An Examination of the Challenges Daughters Face in Family Business Succession. *Family Business Review*, 18(4), 321–345.

Epilogue: Future Considerations for Cross-Cultural Research in Father–Daughter Succession

DAPHNE HALKIAS

Entrepreneurship is truly a phenomenon which is above all cultural. With this in mind, the successful transmission of a firm involves respecting the national culture in which it is found. The case studies of father–daughter succession in family business presented in this book have presented distinctive links between the internal stakeholders of the family business, the development of the succession process, and the cultural values and precepts faced by the daughter/heiresses in her emerging leadership role.

Yet, in producing profound cultural disparities, these case studies have also brought to the foreground cultural common ground in the patrimonial transfer process. No matter which cultural prism we gazed through to tell the daughter's story, the understanding of emotional ties between father and daughter were paramount to studying the succession process. As well, across cultures we saw the repeated desire to maintain harmonious family relationships. It's as if the daughter was constantly involved in a type of course correction with every new and difficult step in the succession process in order to ensure a state of community with the father and among the various stakeholders of the family business.

For the daughters of our cross-cultural study, the continuity of the family firm depended on the preservation of family emotional and social relationships—and in many cultures this included the extended family as well. These women were emotionally invested in respecting the preceding work of the father to build the business. Even while modernizing the family firm, daughters wished to build on the core values of the father. The succession process for a daughter, cross-culturally, was not a matter of power attainment but of collaboration and inclusion of family and cultural values in the business' growth and development through her leadership.

The cross-cultural study presented in this book provides a basis for continued research in the father–daughter succession process in family business through emerging, innovative methodologies. With respect to the succession process in family firms in general, researchers should be sensitized the cultural context of their investigation. The small number of family business succession studies recognizing culture—including the area of gender differences—as a key element in their investigation, leads us to conclude that best practice research in this area needs further development through both quantitative and qualitative methodologies.

These case studies provide a basis for continuing research in the field of family business dealing with succession issues, in addition to new insights for members of family firms, consultants, academics, and researchers. Finally, we may conclude that best research protocols in family business succession cannot be undertaken as an end to itself. It is essential that family members involved in the succession process identify their own cultural values as well as any departures from the norm for that particular culture. Each family business, within the context of their ethnic culture, is defined by the abiding meanings defining their cultural dialogues.

Index

Page numbers in *italics* refer to figures and tables.

acceptance of successor 28, 170, 199, 299
Africa
  Egypt 93–100
  Nigeria 101–5
Appalachia 235–37
Asia
  China 25–31
  Halkias' study 11–12
  India 35–42, *41*, *42*
  Lebanon 45–53
  Malaysia 55–60
  Pakistan 63–69
  Philippines 73–79
  United Arab Emirates 81–90
Australia
  case study
    conclusions 292
    firm history 288–89
    research limitations 292
    successor as "anchor" 291–92
    successor's history 289–91
    training for succession 291
  cultural values 285–86, *286*
  female entrepreneurship 287–88
  future research 292
  women and minority groups in workforce 286–87

Barbot, M.C. 4, 114
Barrett, M.A. 291, 292
biographical narration 5–6
Brazil
  case study 1
    discussion and conclusion 253
    family versus business 251–52
    father–daughter rivalry 250–51
    firm history 247
    mother's behaviour 251–52
    research limitations 253
    sibling rivalry 250
    succession contenders 247–49
    succession planning 249–50
    successor's history 248–49
  case study 2
    conclusions 260
    firm history 256–57
    founders 257
    founders–successors relationship 259
    gender discrimination 258–59
    research limitations 260
    succession process 257–58
    visibility of female successors 258–59
  family firms 245, 246, 255
  father–daughter succession 246–47
  female entrepreneurship 245–46
  female participation in business 246, 255
  future research 253
  literature review 245–47, 256

Canada
  case study
    discussion and conclusion 214–15
    firm history 207–8
    gender and cultural issues 210–14
    next generation 214
    succession process 208–10
    successor's history 208
  cultural values 205
  female entrepreneurship 206–7
  gender issues 205–6
China
  case study 25–26
    Confucianism, impact of 27–28
    data 27

discussion and conclusion 29–31
gender issues 28–29
literature review 26
planning and training 29
research limitations 31
role of other family members 29
family firms 25
Colombia 263
case study
daughter as successor 266–68
discussion and conclusion 269–70
family history 265–66
firm history 265
present and future of firm 268–69
research limitations 270
son's failure in firm 266
family firms 263–64
succession 264–65
future research 270
women's roles and status 264
Confucianism 27–28
culture's impact on entrepreneurship 3–4, 303

Dean, M.A. 38, 149, 299, 300
D'Iribarne, P. 4
Dumas, C. 150, 151
dysfunction strain 120, 123–24

education, higher
of parents 30, 42, 69, 99, 160
of successors 60, 65, 68, 218, 281
women's access to 36, 46–47, 52, 64, 73, 94
Egypt
case study
discussion and conclusion 99
education 96
the entrepreneur 95–96
father's influence 97–98
firm history 96–97
succession planning 99
Coptic Christian culture 94
cultural context 93–94
future research 99–100
women entrepreneurship 94–95
employees, *see* staff
entrepreneurship, culture's impact on 3–4, 303
ethnic identity issues 129, 137, 227–28
Europe
France 109–14
Germany 117–26, *118*, *119*
Greece 129–38
Italy 141–54, *145*, *146*
Scotland 175–82
Spain 167–74
Sweden 183–90, *186*
Switzerland 193–201, *195*

family firms
Brazil 245, 246, 255
China 25
Colombia 263–64
Germany 117
and global economy 11
India 35
Italy 141
Lebanon 46
Malaysia 56–57
Nigeria 101, 103–4
Pakistan 63
Philippines 73
Russia 158–59
Scotland 175
Spain 167
Switzerland 193
female entrepreneurship
Australia 287–88
Brazil 245–46
Canada 206–7
Greece 130–31
India 36
Italy 142–43
Lebanon 48
Peru 274
Sweden 183–84
United States 218
Fischer, Josephine de Dicourt 15–16
France 109
case study
discussion and conclusion 113–14
family rivalries 112
firm history 110

gender issues 111–12, 113
research limitations 114
succession planning 112
succession process 110–11
successor 111–12
training for succession 111–12
future research 114
literature review 109–10
Francis, A.E. 296, 300
future research 303–4

Gatewood, E. 12–13
gender bias 9, 42, 184, 269
gender discrimination 83, 102–3, 113, 149–50
gender egalitarianism/equality 12, 74–75, 93–94, 130, 184, 206, 264
gender issues 10, 28–29, 205–6, 268, 269
gender roles 102, 120–21, 200, 228
gender stereotyping 9, 113, 168, 239
gender theory 12
Germany 117
case study
discussion and conclusion 125–26
dysfunction strain 123–24
family system/enterprise system paradox 122–23
gender issues 123–24
leadership structure 121
ownership structure 121–22
research limitations 126
trauma strain 125
future research 126
literature review
family firms 117
family system/enterprise system paradox *119*, 119–20
female successors *118*, 118
gender issues 119
gender roles 120–21
succession planning 119
global economy and family firms 11
Graham, Katherine 17–18
Greece
case study
cultural context 136–37
discussion and conclusion 137
father's influence 135–36
firm history 132–33
fourth generation 134–35
management styles 136
spouse's role 134
succession process 133–34
cultural context 129
entrepreneurial business culture 130
family firm culture 131–32
female entrepreneurship 130–31
future research 138
succession issues 132

Halkias, D. 11–12
"handing over"
father's reluctance to 125, 134, 189, 223, 253
importance of letting go 181, 298, 301
d'Hausen, Marguerite 15, *20*
Hofstede's cultural ratings 37, 176, 285–86, *286*
House, R.J. 194, 195, 199
husband, support of 51, 85, 98

India 35
case study
discussion and conclusion 41–42
firm history 39
model of succession in family business *41*
predecessor-successor relationship 40
socio-cultural context 41–42, *42*
succession process 39–40
caste system 38
family firms 35
joint family system 37
literature review 36
culture's influence on family business 37–38
father–daughter succession 38
female entrepreneurship 36
succession planning 37
male preference 37–38
invisibility of women 113, 149, 150, 256
Islamic Law 46, 64–65, 67, 82
Italy
case study 144
discussion and conclusion 152–53

        factors affecting father–daughter succession 148–52
        family tree and successions *145*
        firm history 144, *145*
        organizational chart *146*
        research limitations 153–54
        succession process 147
        successor's character and training 147–48
    cultural context 142–43
    family firms 141
    father–daughter succession 143
    female entrepreneurship 142–43
    future research 154
    literature review 142–43

Kaledgyan, S. 158

Lebanon
    case studies
        discussion and conclusion 51–53
        large business 50–51
        small business 49–50
    cultural impact on working women 46–47
    family firms 46
    father–daughter succession 48–49
    female entrepreneurship 48
    history and demographics 45–46
    literature review 45
    succession process 48
    women's rights, advancement of 47

Malaysia
    case studies
        "Jalur Setia (M) Sdn Bhd" 57–59
        "Seri Optical House (M) Sdn Bhd" 59–60
        training for succession 57–58
    culture and working women 55–56
    family firms 56–57
    planning for succession 56–57
McGregor, J. 295, 296, 297
model of succession in family business 4, *5*, *41*
Moores, K. 291, 292
motivation, "pull" and "push" 12–13

Nelson, Marilyn Carlson 19
New Zealand 295
    case study
        conclusions 300–301
        family relationships 299–300, 301
        firm history 297–98
        succession process 298
        successor's challenges and difficulties 299
        successor's history 298
        successor's success 299–300
    literature review 296–97
Nigeria
    discrimination against women 102–3
    factors affecting father–daughter succession 104–5
    family firms 101, 103–4
    literature review 101–3
    research limitations 105
    theoretical framework 101–3
    unemployment rate by sex 103, *103*
North America
    Canada 205–15
    United States
        South Carolina 217–24
        Washington 227–32
        West Virginia 235–41

Oceania
    Australia 285–92, *286*
    New Zealand 295–301

Pakistan
    case study
        discussion and conclusion 67–69
        family history 65–66
        firm history 65
        limitations of study 69
        succession process 66–67
        training for succession 66
    cultural context 64–65
    family firms 63
    future research 69
    literature review 63–64
    succession process 63–64
Peru 273–74
    case study

age discrimination 279–80
discussion and conclusion 280–81
father–daughter relationship 276, 277
firm history 275
"glass ceiling" issue 280
identity and leadership style 278
non-family members 279
owner's control 276
research limitations 281
sibling relationships 276–77
sibling rivalry 279
succession process 276
successor's history 277
successor's success 279
work–life balance 280
father–daughter succession 274–75
female entrepreneurship 274
future research 281
"Les Petits-Fils de François de Wendel" 15–16
Philippines
case study 75–79
culture 74
family firms 73
father–daughter succession 75
future research 79
literature review 74–75
women in business 73
women, status of 74–75
planning for succession 11, 64, 68, 221, 224
Brazil 249, 257
Canada 214
China 29–30
Egypt 99
France 111, 112
Greece 134, 135
India 37, 40, 41
Lebanon 49, 51
Malaysia 56–57
Scotland 180
Spain 173
United Arab Emirates 83–84
West Virginia 238
Pyromalis, V. 11

relationships
father–daughter 29, 40, 59, 149, 221, 259, 266–68, 276, 277
in Confucianism 28
personal versus professional 240
with siblings 57, 148, 251, 276–77, 279
with staff 28, 31, 49–50, 85, 163, 179, 199, 231
religion 74, 93–94, 104, 129, 228
Islamic Law 46, 64–65, 67, 82
respect
daughter's, for father 52, 259, 266, 268
father's, for daughter 85, 230, 259, 268
Russia 157
case study 159–63
discussion and conclusion 163–64
entrepreneurship 157–58
family firms 158–59
literature review 157–58

Salganicoff, M. 240, 299
Scotland 175
case study
childhood of successor 178–79
discussion and conclusion 181
education of successor 179
firm history 177–78
future of firm 181
succession process 179–81
culture and succession 175–77
family firms 175
future research 182
Sharma, P. 64
Sikhism 228
South America
Brazil 245–47, 255–56
case study 1 247–53
case study 2 256–60
Colombia 263–70
Peru 273–81
Spain
case study 169
discussion and conclusion 172–73
family factors on choice of successor 169–70
family relationships 169–70
succession training 170–72
family firms 167
future research 173–74
literature review 168

socio-cultural context 168
succession process 167
staff
gaining trust of 50, 85, 88, 151, 173, 199, 267
relationship with 28, 31, 49–50, 85, 163, 179, 199, 231
Stider, Annelie Karlsson 16–17
support
of family members 51, 112, 168, 187, 200, 231–32, 269
of father 28, 85, 98, 276
of husband 51, 85
of staff 51, 112, 170
Sweden 183
case study
cultural factors of succession 188–90
discussion and conclusion 190
family history 185–86, *186*
firm history 185
succession of leadership 186–87
succession of ownership 188
succession training 184–85
successor's history 184–85
female entrepreneurship 183–84
Switzerland
case study
discussion and conclusion 199–200
family history 198
firm history 196
GLOBE model evaluation 200–201
research limitations 200–201
succession process 196, 197–98
succession training 199
successor as female CEO 198–99
successor's history 196–97
cultural context 194
GLOBE scores *195*, 195–96
family firms 193
father–daughter succession 194–95
future research 200–201
literature review 194–96

training for succession 239–40, 291
Canada 208, 209
China 29, 30
Colombia 267, 269
France 111–12
Lebanon 49–50, 51
Malaysia 57–58
Pakistan 63–64, 66, 68
Russia 161, 162
Scotland 180
South Carolina 220
Spain 170
Switzerland 199, 200
United Arab Emirates 84
trauma strain 120, 125
trust in successor
of father 52, 60, 66, 76, 269, 270
of staff 50, 51, 88, 199
Tweed, D. 295, 296, 297

United Arab Emirates
case study
family–corporate relationships 87–88
firm history 83
the future 89–90
succession planning 83–84
successor 84–85
transition process 88–89
trust building 88
work–life balance 85–86
cultural context 81–82
United Kingdom, *see* Scotland
United States
ethnic identity issues 227
future research 241
Indian-American cultural values 228–29
literature review
Appalachia culture and economic development 235–37
cultural influences 218–19
father–daughter succession 218
female entrepreneurship 218
Sikhs as cultural group 228
South Carolina case study 217
discussion and conclusion 224
firm history 219
gender and cultural issues 220–23
succession process 220
successor's history 220
successor's success 223–24
work–life balance 223

Washington case study
cultural issues 230–31
firm history 229
succession process 230
vision and strategy 231–32
West Virginia case study
discussion and conclusion 239–40
firm history 237–38
gender issues 239
research limitations 241
succession process 238
successor's history and experiences 238–39

Vera, C.F. 38, 149, 299, 300

de Wendel family 15–16
women
attitudes towards 9, 10–11
"invisibility" of 113, 149, 150, 256
Islamic Law, impact of 46, 64–65, 82
Middle East, status in 82–83, 93
motivation 19–20
opportunities, restriction of 18–19
roles
within business 19–20
traditional 16–18, *17*
work–life balance 85–86, 99, 123–24, 152, 212–13, 223, 259, 280

For Product Safety Concerns and Information please contact our EU representative GPSR@taylorandfrancis.com
Taylor & Francis Verlag GmbH, Kaufingerstraße 24, 80331 München, Germany

www.ingramcontent.com/pod-product-compliance
Ingram Content Group UK Ltd.
Pitfield, Milton Keynes, MK11 3LW, UK
UKHW050053200926
475702UK00019B/2822
9780367605490